LIBELS AND THEATER IN SHAKESPEARE'S ENGLAND

Publics, Politics, Performance

JOSEPH MANSKY
University of Oklahoma

Shaftesbury Road, Cambridge CB2 8EA, United Kingdom

One Liberty Plaza, 20th Floor, New York, NY 10006, USA

477 Williamstown Road, Port Melbourne, VIC 3207, Australia

314–321, 3rd Floor, Plot 3, Splendor Forum, Jasola District Centre, New Delhi – 110025, India

103 Penang Road, #05–06/07, Visioncrest Commercial, Singapore 238467

Cambridge University Press is part of Cambridge University Press & Assessment, a department of the University of Cambridge.

We share the University's mission to contribute to society through the pursuit of education, learning and research at the highest international levels of excellence.

www.cambridge.org
Information on this title: www.cambridge.org/9781009362764
DOI: 10.1017/9781009362795

© Joseph Mansky 2023

This publication is in copyright. Subject to statutory exception and to the provisions of relevant collective licensing agreements, no reproduction of any part may take place without the written permission of Cambridge University Press & Assessment.

First published 2023

A catalogue record for this publication is available from the British Library.

A Cataloging-in-Publication data record for this book is available from the Library of Congress.

ISBN 978-1-009-36276-4 Hardback

Cambridge University Press & Assessment has no responsibility for the persistence or accuracy of URLs for external or third-party internet websites referred to in this publication and does not guarantee that any content on such websites is, or will remain, accurate or appropriate.

For Em

Contents

Acknowledgments	*page* viii
List of Abbreviations	x
Introduction: Seeds of Sedition	1
PART I THE SCENE OF LIBEL	29
1 How to Read a Libel in Early Modern England	31
2 Playing Libel from Cambridge to Kendal	58
PART II LIBELS ON THE ELIZABETHAN STAGE	85
3 Libels Supplicatory: Shakespeare and Peele's *Titus Andronicus*	87
4 Libel, Equity, and Law in *Sir Thomas More*	115
5 Jane Shore's Public: Pity and Politics in Heywood's *Edward IV*	144
6 Turning Plays into Libels: Satire and Sedition in Jonson's *Poetaster*	172
Epilogue: Staging Libel in Early Stuart England	204
Bibliography	214
Index	245

Acknowledgments

This book began its life among the University of California, Berkeley's early modern community. I owe the most to Victoria Kahn, who taught me how to take an argument apart and put it back together again. Oliver Arnold, Déborah Blocker, Jeffrey Knapp, and Shannon Stimson advised my first forays into the world of libels. Jonathan Shelley and Samuel Garrett Zeitlin were exemplary interlocutors.

As the manuscript took shape, it has benefited greatly from the advice and encouragement of many friends and colleagues. I want to thank Stephanie Elsky and Rayna Kalas, Marisa Cull, Jeff Doty and Matt Hunter, Emily Shortslef and Ashley Streeter, and Dan Kapust and Nandini Pandey for the chance to test out ideas at meetings of the Shakespeare Association of America, the Renaissance Society of America, and the (Re)Imagining Empire Workshop at the University of Wisconsin–Madison. Their comments and conversation helped bring the book into focus, as did those of Mark Bayer, Karen Britland, Josh Calhoun, Rob Cioffi, Musa Gurnis, Megan Heffernan, Helen Hull, Ben LaBreche, Bernadette Meyler, and Simone Waller, among others. Emily Mayne and Misha Teramura kindly shared their paleographical expertise. Steve Nadler and Ann Harris made Madison a warm (pun intended) place to spend a year, and Roxanne Mountford has been an unstintingly supportive chair at the University of Oklahoma. At Cambridge University Press, Emily Hockley has generously supported this book through several rounds of revision. Special thanks are due to Andrew Keener, András Kiséry, Victor Lenthe, Justin Sider, and, above all, Jeff Doty and Matt Hunter, who have made this a much better book (all lapses are, of course, entirely my own).

This project received support from the Center for British Studies at the University of California, Berkeley, the Renaissance Society of America, the Folger Shakespeare Library, the Institute for Research in the Humanities at the University of Wisconsin–Madison, the Office of the Vice President for

Acknowledgments ix

Research and Partnerships (VPRP) and the Arts & Humanities Forum at the University of Oklahoma, and the National Endowment for the Humanities. Financial support for publication was provided from the VPRP, the Office of the Provost, and the Dodge Family College of Arts and Sciences, University of Oklahoma. Early versions of Chapters 3 and 5 appeared as, respectively, "'Unlawfully published': Libels and the Public Sphere in *Titus Andronicus*," *Shakespeare Quarterly* 67.3 (2016): 293–318; and "Jane Shore, *Edward IV*, and the Politics of Publicity," *Renaissance Drama* 46.2 (2018): 141–65, © 2018 by Northwestern University. I am grateful to both journals and their publishers for permission to reuse the material here.

My greatest debt of all is to my parents, Art and Shelley. From the day their college freshman told them he was trading physics for Shakespeare, they have gamely come along with me on this academic journey – read every article, Zoomed in to talks – even at its most esoteric. I am thankful beyond words.

I would be remiss not to end with a note of boundless gratitude for Emily Xiao, to whom this book is dedicated with all my love, and for Gabe and Theo, who give daily inspiration and keep us on our toes.

Abbreviations

APC	*Acts of the Privy Council of England*, ed. John Roche Dasent et al., 46 vols. (London, 1890–1964)
BL	British Library; Lansdowne MSS accessed at *State Papers Online, 1590–1714* (Gale Cengage Learning)
Co. Rep.	*The Reports of Sir Edward Coke, Knt. In Thirteen Parts*, ed. John Henry Thomas and John Farquhar Fraser, 6 vols. (London, 1826)
CP	Hatfield House, Hertfordshire, Cecil Papers, accessed at *The Cecil Papers* (ProQuest)
CWBJ	*The Cambridge Edition of the Works of Ben Jonson*, gen. ed. David Bevington, Martin Butler, and Ian Donaldson, 7 vols. (Cambridge: Cambridge University Press, 2012)
REED	Records of Early English Drama
SP	state papers, accessed at *State Papers Online*
STAC	Court of Star Chamber records
TNA	The National Archives of the UK
TRP	*Tudor Royal Proclamations*, ed. Paul L. Hughes and James F. Larkin, 3 vols. (New Haven: Yale University Press, 1964–69)

INTRODUCTION

Seeds of Sedition

"News news I muste you tell." So begins the scrap of paper found in St. Paul's Cathedral on October 10, toward the end of the first decade of the seventeenth century.[1] Despite the opening promise, however, what follows is hardly what we would call news:

> News news I muste you tell
> of a damned kinge and a deuillish Counsaile
> a kinge senseless of any good
> descended linealli of a Whores bloode
>
> . . .
>
> the kinge is poore *th*e Counsell riche
> the Commons beggerd being oppressed muche
> of *th*e Clergie not one honest man
> all must be confounded deni yt *tha*t cann.

This vituperative verse libel continues at length in the same vein. Eight leading councilors are singled out for abuse with epithets such as "misshapen," "pocki," and "papist." In the final lines of the poem, three of those eight – Richard Bancroft, Archbishop of Canterbury; Robert Cecil, Earl of Salisbury and Lord Treasurer; and Edward Coke, Chief Justice of Common Pleas – are subjected to scurrilous mockery, along with the king himself:

> an ars Bisshope to send soules to hell
> a tresorer whose throte is a bottomles well
> a Cuckolly Cooke Iudge fitt for Stygian poole
> a remediles grefe. *th*e kinge is a foole foole
> foole foole foole foole foole foole foole
> whome god of his merci confounde sodaynly
> all *th*e poeple say amen.[2]

---

[1] CP 140/119. The targets of its abuse indicate that the poem was written between 1608, when Robert Cecil was appointed Lord Treasurer, and 1610, when Richard Bancroft died. Throughout this book, I expand abbreviations in early modern sources in italics.

[2] Ibid.

2 Introduction

At several centuries' remove, we may relish the poem's carnivalesque energy and its exuberant orality. We may be drawn in by the crude satire – Archbishop Bancroft becomes an "ars Bisshope," Coke a "Cuckolly Cooke" – or by the poet's obvious delight in railing against England's most powerful men. And we may sympathize with the vigorous defense of the "Commons" from the (real or perceived) oppressions of council, clergy, and king. Certainly it is appealing to find in the archive such a stark and scathing counternarrative to the propaganda disseminated from the pulpit and the press. From the newsmonger's cry at the start, we might discern a public hungry for "underground" media – for rumor, news, and political satire.[3] From the collective amen at the end, we might see a concerted effort to shape the voice of that public. The poem thus comes to resemble "a form of critical political speech" addressed to "an anonymous public," as Alastair Bellany has described the early modern libel.[4] On these grounds, a number of scholars have argued that libels motivated a nascent public sphere.[5]

But the fact remains that "News news I muste you tell" is, as Robert Cecil scribbled on the verso, "[a] filthy and a fals lybell."[6] It is telling that a popular compendium of criminal statutes categorized laws against defamation under the heading of "Newes."[7] For the authorities, there was not much difference between libels and news, or at least between libels and what they called "false news."[8] Scurrilous poems and tracts commonly circulated

---

[3] Thomas Cogswell, "Underground Verse and the Transformation of Early Stuart Political Culture," in *Political Culture and Cultural Politics in Early Modern England: Essays Presented to David Underdown*, ed. Susan D. Amussen and Mark A. Kishlansky (Manchester: Manchester University Press, 1995), 277–300.

[4] Alastair Bellany, "Railing Rhymes Revisited: Libels, Scandals, and Early Stuart Politics," *History Compass* 5.4 (2007): 1154.

[5] In addition to Bellany, "Railing Rhymes," see Cogswell, "Underground Verse"; Pauline Croft, "Libels, Popular Literacy and Public Opinion in Early Modern England," *Historical Research* 68 (1995): 266–85; Andrew McRae, *Literature, Satire and the Early Stuart State* (Cambridge: Cambridge University Press, 2004); David Colclough, *Freedom of Speech in Early Stuart England* (Cambridge: Cambridge University Press, 2005), 196–250; James Loxley, "On Exegetical Duty: Historical Pragmatics and the Grammar of the Libel," *Huntington Library Quarterly* 69.1 (2006): 83–103; Bellany, "The Embarrassment of Libels: Perceptions and Representations of Verse Libelling in Early Stuart England," in *The Politics of the Public Sphere in Early Modern England*, ed. Peter Lake and Steven Pincus (Manchester: Manchester University Press, 2007), 144–67; Peter Lake, *Bad Queen Bess? Libels, Secret Histories, and the Politics of Publicity in the Reign of Queen Elizabeth I* (Oxford: Oxford University Press, 2016); and Lake and Michael Questier, *All Hail to the Archpriest: Confessional Conflict, Toleration, and the Politics of Publicity in Post-Reformation England* (Oxford: Oxford University Press, 2019).

[6] CP 140/119.

[7] Ferdinando Pulton, *An abstract of all the penall Statutes which be generall, in force and vse* (London, 1577), sigs. A8r, II1r–II2r. See Kenneth Gross, *Shakespeare's Noise* (Chicago: University of Chicago Press, 2001), 52.

[8] See, e.g., Francis Bacon, *The Essayes or Counsels, Civill and Morall*, ed. Michael Kiernan, in *The Oxford Francis Bacon*, vol. 15 (Oxford: Clarendon Press, 2000), 43.

Seeds of Sedition 3

alongside reports of current events.[9] At popular gathering places such as St. Paul's Cathedral – where "News news I muste you tell" was found – people came together to partake in all sorts of scandalous talk.[10] Of course, the government was more than ready to condemn popular political talk simply for being popular and political. And polemicists on all sides regularly accused their adversaries of libel not to defend civility but to discredit rival arguments. Still, the essential characteristics of libels – vitriolic satire, anonymous criticism, casual regard for the truth – do not seem conducive to healthy political discourse.

This is a point made forcefully by Debora Shuger in her 2006 monograph, *Censorship and Cultural Sensibility*. Shuger contends that libels, far from cultivating a public sphere, were actually "what we now call hate speech": they purveyed misinformation, conspiracy theories, and incitements to violence.[11] Shuger's remains the minority view. Yet efforts to dismiss her argument have only emphasized its urgency. To recover libels' "artful confusion of the categories of fact and fiction" or to note that their "'scurrilous fantasies' ... were culturally credible ... and politically powerful" does nothing to address – indeed, only exacerbates – the potential harm of the discourse they disseminated.[12] Most recently, Peter Lake has maintained that libels were not "an early modern version of hate speech" but instead "the stuff of early modern political thought." He points out that both the Elizabethan regime and its Catholic critics published libelous "secret histories" – in modern terms, conspiracy theories – and that both sides could plausibly claim some basis in reality. But the resulting picture does little to reassure: "two mutually exclusive and polemically constructed versions of reality were put into play by rival groups, each set on the marginalization, indeed, in an ideal world, on the extinction, of the other."[13] This sounds more like a recipe for bitter polarization if not outright civil war than for a public sphere.[14]

---

[9] Richard Cust, "News and Politics in Early Seventeenth-Century England," *Past and Present* 112 (1986): 66–69; Fritz Levy, "The Decorum of News," in *News, Newspapers, and Society in Early Modern Britain*, ed. Joad Raymond (London: Frank Cass, 1999), 12–38; Alastair Bellany, *The Politics of Court Scandal in Early Modern England: News Culture and the Overbury Affair, 1603–1660* (Cambridge: Cambridge University Press, 2002); McRae, *Literature*, 36–40.

[10] John Earle, *Micro-cosmographie. Or, A Peece of the World Discovered* (London, 1628), sigs. I11v–I12v; Adam Fox, *Oral and Literate Culture in England, 1500–1700* (Oxford: Clarendon Press, 2000), 346–47; Bellany, *Politics*, 80–83.

[11] Debora Shuger, *Censorship and Cultural Sensibility: The Regulation of Language in Tudor-Stuart England* (Philadelphia: University of Pennsylvania Press, 2006), 42–43.

[12] McRae, *Literature*, 35; Bellany, "Railing Rhymes," 1156.   [13] Lake, *Bad Queen Bess*, 468, 474.

[14] See Barbara J. Shapiro, *Political Communication and Political Culture in England, 1558–1688* (Stanford: Stanford University Press, 2012), 283–84.

4   Introduction

Yet I think we need not choose between these possibilities. What libels such as "News news I muste you tell" show is that debate and defamation, free speech and false news, went hand in hand. This is the animating paradox of *Libels and Theater in Shakespeare's England*. I follow scenes of libel through and around the late Elizabethan theater, tracing the contours of a viral (and often virulent) media ecosystem. We will see people taking up, circulating, and recirculating libels – and, in the process, thinking through for themselves the terms of public discourse. The theater is central to this story because of its persistent proximity to libeling. Variously a medium, a metaphor, and a venue for libeling, the theater both dramatized and disseminated libels. Sometimes playgoers encountered libels, sometimes representations of libel, and sometimes – most dizzyingly of all – both at the same time. The book's first part, "The Scene of Libel," examines the reception, publication, and performance of libels. My aim is to sketch from multiple angles the varied publicity tactics that made libels, in the words of one town's disgruntled leaders, "the very seedes, wherof springe seditions, insurrections and Rebellions in Comon weales."[15]

In the book's second part, "Libels on the Elizabethan Stage," I turn to representations of libel in drama. In the 1590s, a series of crises – simmering xenophobia (1592–93), years of dearth and hunger (1595–97), the fall of the Earl of Essex (1599–1601), periodic surges of religious persecution – sparked an unprecedented explosion of libeling. The same years also saw the first documented appearances of libels on the public stage. Libels are launched into the sky (*Titus Andronicus*), cast in a window and affixed to a statue (*Julius Caesar*), recited in court (*Edward IV*), read from the pulpit (*Sir Thomas More*), and seized by informers (*Poetaster*). Slander has long been acknowledged to be a central theme of Renaissance drama, not least of all in Shakespeare.[16] But the libels – furtive, ephemeral, often anonymous – have generally escaped scholarly notice. These scenes, I will argue, share a metadramatic bent that reflects back on the theater's own place in the early modern mediascape.

Libels, Plays, Publics

To describe the interface between media and their audiences, I draw throughout this book from the vocabulary of public sphere theory. The foundational concept is Jürgen Habermas's "bourgeois public sphere,"

---

[15] TNA, SP 12/150, fols. 200v–201r.
[16] See, in recent decades, M. Lindsay Kaplan, *The Culture of Slander in Early Modern England* (Cambridge: Cambridge University Press, 1997); Gross, *Shakespeare's Noise*; and Ina Habermann, *Staging Slander and Gender in Early Modern England* (Aldershot, UK: Ashgate, 2003).

a discursive arena for rational debate that he sees first taking shape in the eighteenth century.[17] Subsequent theorists have revised this normative model to encompass a plurality of publics, "some ephemeral, some enduring, and some shaped by struggle against the dominant organization of others."[18] A public sphere in this sense is as messy and multiple as the society from which it emerges. For many scholars, this post-Habermasian paradigm resonates with the dynamic media landscape of the early modern era. The widening circulation of discourse brought people together in all sorts of public-oriented collectivities, joined by faith, passion, and prejudice as often as by rational interest.[19] The most recent and, for my purposes, most pertinent critical turn has been toward the theater. Public sphere theorists from Habermas to Michael Warner attribute public formation largely if not exclusively to print.[20] Yet as studies by Steven Mullaney and Patricia Fumerton have underscored, early modern publicity was almost always a multimedia practice.[21]

The libel exemplifies this fact. Then as now, the word generally referred to written defamation. Yet few libels remained in writing alone. Their lifecycles took them across the early modern media: speech, manuscript, print, performance. They were multiply mobile, crossing not just media but also class, confessional, and topographical lines.[22] That mobility is encoded in the vocabulary of libeling. Scattered, dispersed, spread, cast,

[17] Jürgen Habermas, *The Structural Transformation of the Public Sphere: An Inquiry into a Category of Bourgeois Society*, trans. Thomas Burger with Frederick Lawrence (Cambridge, MA: MIT Press, 1989), 27.

[18] Craig Calhoun, "Imagining Solidarity: Cosmopolitanism, Constitutional Patriotism, and the Public Sphere," *Public Culture* 14.1 (2002): 162. See also (among others) Nancy Fraser, "Rethinking the Public Sphere: A Contribution to the Critique of Actually Existing Democracy," in *Habermas and the Public Sphere*, ed. Craig Calhoun (Cambridge, MA: MIT Press, 1992), 109–42; and Michael Warner, *Publics and Counterpublics* (New York: Zone Books, 2002).

[19] For surveys of the plural publics of early modernity, see the essays collected in Bronwen Wilson and Paul Yachnin, eds., *Making Publics in Early Modern Europe: People, Things, Forms of Knowledge* (New York: Routledge, 2010); Angela Vanhaelen and Joseph P. Ward, eds., *Making Space Public in Early Modern Europe: Performance, Geography, Privacy* (New York: Routledge, 2013); and Paul Yachnin and Marlene Eberhart, eds., *Forms of Association: Making Publics in Early Modern Europe* (Amherst: University of Massachusetts Press, 2015).

[20] See Jeffrey S. Doty, *Shakespeare, Popularity and the Public Sphere* (Cambridge: Cambridge University Press, 2017), 33–34.

[21] Steven Mullaney, *The Reformation of Emotions in the Age of Shakespeare* (Chicago: University of Chicago Press, 2015); Patricia Fumerton, *The Broadside Ballad in Early Modern England: Moving Media, Tactical Publics* (Philadelphia: University of Pennsylvania Press, 2020). "Publicity" as I use it includes the full range of public-oriented activity, from simply "the quality of being public" to the "public notice or attention given to someone or something" to "the action or process of making someone or something publicly known" ("publicity, n.," *OED Online* [Oxford University Press, 2022]).

[22] I borrow the concept of "multiply moving" media from Fumerton, *Broadside Ballad*, 33–40.

6 Introduction

blown, thrown: libels were understood to be a centrifugal force in early modern society and politics. They were slight objects – etymologically little books, often mere scraps of paper – easily spread and easily concealed. Unmoored from their authors, they circulated like leaves in the wind or projectiles launched into the sky. Any points of origin remain elusive: they seem almost self-propagating in their anonymous, viral diffusion. Libels reached popular audiences not through the efforts of their individual authors but through highly permeable and variously public circuits of communication.

This book locates the theater in that tangled, multimedia web of defamatory discourse. Exploring the contact zones between plays and libels, I at once build on and seek to reorient the recent surge of scholarship on the theater and its publics.[23] I share scholars' vision of the theater as a metropolitan institution that initiated playgoers into new types of communal thinking. Yet the focus on London's commercial theater risks leaving out the host of provincial playmakers who made their own forays onto the literal and metaphorical stages of their communities. And it risks overcorrecting the Habermasian emphasis on print by anchoring theatrical publics too firmly in a single institution.[24] Savvy libelers drew on the resources of performance in all sorts of places and in all sorts of ways. Provincial tenants lampooned their landlords on a makeshift stage. Anonymous poets interlaced their defamatory verses with dramatic allusions and pinned them to walls and posts. Local troublemakers declaimed scurrilous texts with sweeping, theatrical gestures before crowds of commoners. Sectarian polemicists borrowed the rollicking style of the stage. In this book, I argue that theater and theatricality played a central role in making the publics of libel.

Of special importance was the self-reflexive tendency that I identified above. As Warner defines them, publics require both "active uptake" and some degree of "self-understanding."[25] In other words, an association of

---

[23] Recent monographs on the subject include Stephen Wittek, *The Media Players: Shakespeare, Middleton, Jonson, and the Idea of News* (Ann Arbor: University of Michigan Press, 2015); Mullaney, *Reformation*; András Kiséry, *Hamlet's Moment: Drama and Political Knowledge in Early Modern England* (Oxford: Oxford University Press, 2016); Peter Lake, *How Shakespeare Put Politics on the Stage: Power and Succession in the History Plays* (New Haven: Yale University Press, 2016); Doty, *Shakespeare*; Katrin Beushausen, *Theatre and the English Public from Reformation to Revolution* (Cambridge: Cambridge University Press, 2018); Musa Gurnis, *Mixed Faith and Shared Feeling: Theater in Post-Reformation London* (Philadelphia: University of Pennsylvania Press, 2018); Jacqueline Vanhoutte, *Age in Love: Shakespeare and the Elizabethan Court* (Lincoln: University of Nebraska Press, 2019); and Matthew Hunter, *The Pursuit of Style in Early Modern Drama: Forms of Talk on the London Stage* (Cambridge: Cambridge University Press, 2022).
[24] For recent correctives to this tendency, see Beushausen, *Theatre*; and Fumerton, *Broadside Ballad*.
[25] Warner, *Publics*, 88.

strangers becomes a public when its members understand themselves as such – when they take up and recirculate some kind of shared experience, idea, or discourse. The early moderns attributed a similar effect to libels. It is telling that two of the words most often used to describe their dissemination were "scattered" and "dispersed." Magistrates imagine towns, cities, and even the entire country filled with libels "scattered abroade" and "scattered in publique places," "disperste in all places," and "dispersed through this realm."[26] The libels conjure a public coalescing around everyday encounters with scraps of seditious text. Anyone could take up, read, hear, repeat, perform, interpret, or repurpose a libel.

It was this active uptake too that brought theater in contact with libel. Legal accounts of libel, efforts to regulate the stage, and plays themselves all tend to implicate the audience in the act of libel. Antitheatricalists maintained that the theater was a hotbed of libeling in large part due to the activity of its popular playgoers. The law held copyists and, in some cases, even listeners culpable for publishing libels. And plays from the university drama *Club Law* to Jonson's *Poetaster* hinged on their audiences' complicity in the scene of libel. On- and offstage, those scenes tended toward the metadramatic: they staged the kinds of uptake that they asked of their audiences. We see readers talking libelously about libels, libelers sending their texts out to interested parties and indiscriminate publics, spectators laughing or crying or seething at public pitches. These scenes cultivated the self-understanding that separates a public from a crowd or a readership. At stake was not just the content of the speech but also the act of interpretation.

This was true of the early modern libel more broadly. The category was highly elastic, including not only obvious personal attacks but also – depending on the climate – perfectly credible accusations, news, satire, petitions, and polemic. The line between libel and licensed speech could be vanishingly thin, as some playwrights learned to their peril. This is not to say that there were no recognizable markers of libel. Rather, my point is that libels were defined not just by their sedition and scurrility but also by their orientation toward their audience. Or, as Kenneth Gross puts it, "[i]t is . . . not only the truth or lie of the slanderer's word but the mode of its being diffused that counts."[27] The mere fact of public address could be cause for suspicion.

Yet we overlook the seditious cast of that discourse at our peril. In this book, I contend that the metadramatic scenes of libel trained playgoers to

---

[26] TNA, SP 12/179, fol. 92r; J. Alan B. Somerset, ed., *REED: Shropshire*, 2 vols. (Toronto: University of Toronto Press, 1994), 1:123; TNA, SP 12/275, fol. 229r; *TRP*, 3:15.

[27] Gross, *Shakespeare's Noise*, 38.

8 Introduction

navigate the new media landscape springing up around them. My argument here parallels recent studies by Steven Mullaney, András Kiséry, Peter Lake, Jeffrey S. Doty, and Musa Gurnis, who all see the theater equipping its audiences with critical and affective resources for negotiating the faultlines of social, political, and confessional life.[28] This powerful scholarship departs from the new historicist preoccupation with subversion and containment, locating the theater's influence not so much in the ideological positions its practitioners staked out as in the cultural competences it imparted to the tens of thousands who flocked to the playhouses each week.[29] This is a timely correction, attuned to both the material conditions of playgoing and the rich complexity of early modern politics, society, and religion. However, my study calls into question the distinction between critical publicity and partisan positioning. Libels' polemical structure of address practically demanded side-taking. To be sure, some playwrights – not least of all Shakespeare – sharply interrogated that partisan pull. But the manifold theatrical careers of the libel show that publicity and, indeed, theatricality itself remained implicated in sedition, especially if we take sedition in the full range of its early modern senses (faction, fighting words, divisive speech, inciting discord or disaffection or rebellion).[30] It is the generative irony of the early modern public sphere that its critical conversations launched in no small part from the vitriol and violence of libels.

Libel and the Law

The following pages trace the intertwined semantic, cultural, and legal histories of libel from the 1550s to the early 1600s. England experienced an unprecedented volume of libeling between 1580 and

---

[28] Mullaney, *Reformation*; Kiséry, *Hamlet's Moment*; Lake, *How Shakespeare*; Doty, *Shakespeare*; Gurnis, *Mixed Faith*.

[29] For estimates of the playgoing population, see Andrew Gurr, *The Shakespearean Stage, 1574–1642*, 4th ed. (Cambridge: Cambridge University Press, 2009), 260–61. The foundational account of the subversion/containment dialectic comes in Stephen Greenblatt, *Shakespearean Negotiations: The Circulation of Social Energy in Renaissance England* (Berkeley: University of California Press, 1988). Other classic new historicist and cultural materialist studies centrally concerned with the political ideology of Renaissance drama include David Scott Kastan, "Proud Majesty Made a Subject: Shakespeare and the Spectacle of Rule," *Shakespeare Quarterly* 37.4 (1986): 459–75; Jonathan Dollimore, *Radical Tragedy: Religion, Ideology and Power in the Drama of Shakespeare and His Contemporaries*, 2nd ed. (New York: Harvester Wheatsheaf, 1989); Phyllis Rackin, *Stages of History: Shakespeare's English Chronicles* (Ithaca: Cornell University Press, 1990); and Louis Montrose, *The Purpose of Playing: Shakespeare and the Cultural Politics of the Elizabethan Theatre* (Chicago: University of Chicago Press, 1996).

[30] Roger B. Manning, "The Origins of the Doctrine of Sedition," *Albion* 12.2 (1980): 100–1; David Cressy, *Dangerous Talk: Scandalous, Seditious, and Treasonable Speech in Pre-Modern England* (Oxford: Oxford University Press, 2010), 41–43.

1630.[31] Yet the latter half of the period has received the vast majority of the scholarly attention. Only in the past few years have scholars begun to look as closely at the Elizabethan libel.[32] Moreover, the work that has been done treats separately the two most prominent kinds of libel, manuscript verse and printed polemic. The challenge of studying the earlier period is further compounded by the novelty of the word "libel" itself. "Libel" entered common usage only in the mid-sixteenth century, and it would not become a clear legal category for at least several more decades. It remains an open question to what extent the oft-quoted views of Jacobean jurists such as Edward Coke and William Hudson accurately reflect the practices of the previous century. This section looks afresh at the Elizabethan history of libel. In the process, I want to address a misconception repeated in scholarship on drama and defamation: that libel and slander were largely interchangeable.[33] Attending to what the early moderns had to say about libel reveals a particular set of concerns about written defamation and its place in the late Elizabethan public sphere.

There is no space here for a full history of English defamation law.[34] But I want to begin by sketching the situation as it stood by the sixteenth century, when the term "libel" came onto the scene. Defamation, originally defined as the malicious imputation of a crime, had long been the province of the church courts. In the fifteenth century, the scope of ecclesiastical defamation expanded to include insulting and abusive words that did not necessarily allege a specific crime. The same years witnessed an equally consequential development: the rise of the common law action for words. Around 1500, the common law courts assumed jurisdiction over imputations of secular crimes, leaving the church courts with a still formidable caseload of spiritual abuse, most of it sexual slander.

---

[31] Bellany, "Railing Rhymes," 1143.

[32] See Steven W. May and Alan Bryson, eds., *Verse Libel in Renaissance England and Scotland* (Oxford: Oxford University Press, 2016); Lake, *Bad Queen Bess*; and Lake and Questier, *All Hail.*

[33] Kaplan, *Culture*, 12; Gross, *Shakespeare's Noise*, 229–30 n67; Cyndia Susan Clegg, "Truth, Lies, and the Law of Slander in *Much Ado About Nothing*," in *The Law in Shakespeare*, ed. Constance Jordan and Karen Cunningham (Basingstoke, UK: Palgrave Macmillan, 2007), 186 n1.

[34] The definitive history of early modern defamation law is R. H. Helmholz's introduction to *Select Cases on Defamation to 1600*, ed. Helmholz (London: Selden Society, 1985), xiv–cxi. See also S. F. C. Milsom, *Historical Foundations of the Common Law*, 2nd ed. (Toronto: Butterworths, 1981), 379–90; Helmholz, *The Oxford History of the Laws of England*, vol. 1, *The Canon Law and Ecclesiastical Jurisdiction from 597 to the 1640s* (Oxford: Oxford University Press, 2004), 565–98; David Ibbetson, "Edward Coke, Roman Law, and the Law of Libel," in *The Oxford Handbook of English Law and Literature, 1500–1700*, ed. Lorna Hutson (Oxford: Oxford University Press, 2017), 488–92; and John Baker, *An Introduction to English Legal History*, 5th ed. (Oxford: Oxford University Press, 2019), 465–78.

10   Introduction

Such were the remedies for defamation available to private people. For public persons – nobles and highly placed officers – a different but related action was established by the 1275 statute of *scandalum magnatum*, punishing those who "tell or publish any false News or Tales, whereby discord, or occasion of discord or slander may grow between the King and his People, or the Great Men of the Realm."[35] The statute was reenacted in the late fourteenth century and then again, amid a sharp uptick in actions for slander, in 1554 and 1559.[36]

These were crucial years in the semantic history of libel as well. The word itself, derived from the Latin *libellus* (little book), appeared in English as early as the late thirteenth century. But for several hundred years it remained free of any defamatory meaning, denoting simply a short writing or a plaintiff's bill of complaint (*libellus*).[37] Such bills were used in the European system of jurisprudence known as Roman or civil law and, in England, in the church courts and in prerogative courts such as Chancery and Star Chamber. Roman law had another kind of *libellus* too: the *libellus famosus*, a writing, epigram, or poem composed and published to bring someone into infamy.[38] The precise influence of Roman law on the English law of libel remains uncertain.[39] But it was unmistakably through Roman law that the word "libel" acquired its defamatory sense. The earliest usages clearly signal their Roman genealogy, anglicizing *libelli famosi* as "famous lybell*es*" or "infamous libelles."[40] The Roman roots may likewise account for the persistent proximity between bills and libels. The line between a legitimate complaint and a defamatory accusation was slender enough for one alleged libeler to insist punningly that his text "was a true bill, though they called it a libell."[41] In his 1607 law dictionary, John Cowell explicitly

---

[35] 3 Edw. I, c. 34, in *The Statutes of the Realm*, 11 vols. (London, 1810–28; repr. 1963), 1:35.

[36] 2 Ric. II, Stat. 1, c. 5, in *Statutes*, 2:9; 1 & 2 Phil. & Mar., c. 3, in *Statutes*, 4:240–41; 1 Eliz. I, c. 6, in *Statutes*, 4:366–67. On the mid-century rise in actions for words, see Baker, *Introduction*, 470.

[37] "libel, n.," *OED Online* (Oxford University Press, 2022). This paragraph is indebted to Shuger's learned treatment of Roman law in *Censorship and Cultural Sensibility*.

[38] Theodor Mommsen with Paul Krueger, ed., *The Digest of Justinian*, trans. Alan Watson, vol. 4 (Philadelphia: University of Pennsylvania Press, 1985), 47.10.5.9–10, 47.10.15.27. Plays and verse satire too fell within the scope of ancient laws against defamation: see Cicero, *De Re Publica*, in *De Re Publica, De Legibus*, trans. Clinton Walker Keyes (Cambridge, MA: Harvard University Press, 1928), 4.10.10–12; Horace, *Satires*, in *Satires, Epistles, Ars Poetica*, trans. H. Rushton Fairclough (Cambridge, MA: Harvard University Press, 1929), 2.1.

[39] Ibbetson, "Edward Coke"; Joseph Mansky, "Edward Coke, William West, and the Law of Libel," *Journal of Legal History* 42.3 (2021): 328–32.

[40] TNA, SP 1/48, fol. 206v; Thomas Harding, *A Detection of Sundrie Foule Errours, Lies, Sclaunders, Corruptions, and Other false dealings . . . vttered and practized by M. Iewel* (Louvain, 1568), sig. Bb2r.

[41] Samuel Rawson Gardiner, ed., *Reports of Cases in the Courts of Star Chamber and High Commission* (London, 1886), 150. See Shuger, *Censorship*, 303 n6.

Seeds of Sedition

traces the dual meaning of libel to Roman civil law: "it is the originall declaration of any action in the ciuill lawe . . . it signifieth also a criminous report of any man cast abroad, or otherwise vnlawfully published in writing."[42] Bills turn to libels – accusations turn defamatory – when they veer from the legal system and are instead "cast abroad, or otherwise vnlawfully published in writing."

By the end of the sixteenth century, however, there was still no case or statutory law to deal with libel separately from defamation in general. Neither the common law nor the ecclesiastical law distinguished between spoken and written defamation.[43] It is important to note that this does not mean that "libel" and "slander" were used interchangeably. Slander was the broader category, and "[l]ibel (written defamation) was simply a species of slander."[44] But there was a growing sense that writing could be especially dangerous. A 1581 statute made spoken words a felony on the second offense but writing a felony on the first. And in 1583, the subject of a defamatory letter argued in court that "the words were written, not simply spoken, so that they had a more permanently damaging character."[45] At the same time, the government increasingly prosecuted religiously motivated libelers under the statutes against slanderous and seditious speech. Probably the most famous casualty was John Stubbs, who in 1579 lost his right hand for writing *The Discovery of a Gaping Gulf*, a fiery polemic against Elizabeth's prospective marriage to the French Catholic Duke of Anjou.[46] Over the following decades, Puritan and Catholic polemicists continued to face mutilation, branding, and even death for meddling in matters of state. Edmund Spenser allegorized the violent censorship in *The Faerie Queene*'s Malfont, a "Poet bad" whose tongue is "[n]ayld to a post" for slandering Queen Mercilla in speech and verse.[47]

---

[42] John Cowell, *The Interpreter* (Cambridge, 1607), sig. Rr4v. As I have shown elsewhere, earlier English lawyers likewise borrowed their definitions of libel from Roman law (Mansky, "Edward Coke").

[43] Baker, *Introduction*, 475; Helmholz, *Oxford History*, 565.   [44] Baker, *Introduction*, 475.

[45] 23 Eliz. I, c. 2, in *Statutes*, 4:659; Helmholz, *Select Cases*, cii. See Croft, "Libels," 267–68; Kaplan, *Culture*, 65–66; and Shuger, *Censorship*, 173.

[46] For appraisals of this incident in relation to press censorship and to the early modern public sphere, see, respectively, Cyndia Susan Clegg, *Press Censorship in Elizabethan England* (Cambridge: Cambridge University Press, 1997), 123–37; and Natalie Mears, "Counsel, Public Debate, and Queenship: John Stubbs's *The Discoverie of a Gaping Gulf*, 1579," *Historical Journal* 44.3 (2001): 629–50.

[47] Edmund Spenser, *The Faerie Queene*, ed. A. C. Hamilton, text ed. Hiroshi Yamashita and Toshiyuki Suzuki, rev. 2nd ed. (Harlow, UK: Pearson Longman, 2007), 5.9.25. The poet's punishment also revises his name from Bonfont, the source of good, to Malfont, "Eyther for th'euill, which

12 Introduction

But such exemplary punishments fell far short of any kind of universal censorship. Indeed, the late Elizabethan spike in libeling must have made the limitations of the existing system abundantly clear. Both the statute of *scandalum magnatum* and the civil action for words allowed truth as a defense, and, under the statute, spreaders of sedition and slander might get off the hook if they produced the original authors.[48] Moreover, for whatever reason, the vast majority of civil and ecclesiastical defamation actions were brought for spoken words alone.[49] By 1599, the libeling had grown so concerning that one of the queen's privy councilors called for a new statute establishing a "lawe of death" against libelers.[50]

It is likely no coincidence that the crime of libel began to take shape amid flurries of Reformation and post-Reformation polemic. The Marian statute of *scandalum magnatum*, passed in 1554, extended the offense to include not only spoken news and rumors but also those texts that were beginning to be called libels: "sedicious and sclanderous Writinges Rimes Ballades Letters Papers and Bookes."[51] The same year also saw one of the earliest appearances in print of the word "libel" in its defamatory sense. In *An exhortation to all menne to take hede and beware of rebellion* (1554), John Christopherson – Queen Mary's chaplain and later Bishop of Chichester – warns that "malitiouse and sclaunderous wordes" breed "false rumours, and raylynge libelles," and he condemns the "pestilente libelles agaynste certayne of the Quenes most honorable counseyll, yea and agaynst her graces owne person, ... cast in corners to sowe sedition."[52] He clearly has in mind the same seditious and slanderous texts criminalized by the contemporary statute.

It is worth dwelling on Christopherson's *Exhortation* for its remarkably prescient vision of the threat of libels. His anxious rhetoric echoes through Elizabethan and Jacobean proclamations, polemic, statutes, and jurisprudence – through the entire apparatus of what Shuger calls "Tudor-Stuart language regulation."[53] Christopherson locates libels in the arsenal of the religiopolitical dissident. His aim is to reveal how

---

he did therein, / Or that he likened was to a welhed / Of euill words, and wicked sclaunders by him shed" (5.9.26).

[48] Manning, "Origins," 112; Baker, *Introduction*, 474–75.

[49] Helmholz, *Select Cases*, lxii; Helmholz, *Oxford History*, 565.

[50] TNA, SP 12/273, fol. 64r. I examine the context for this remark – the outpouring of libels around the Earl of Essex – at length in Chapter 6.

[51] 1 & 2 Phil. & Mar., c. 3, in *Statutes*, 4:240.

[52] John Christopherson, *An exhortation to all menne to take hede and beware of rebellion* (London, 1554), sigs. B7r–v, Bb1r.

[53] Shuger, *Censorship*, 140.

Seeds of Sedition 13

Protestant polemicists deploy false rumors and defamatory writings (the two media criminalized by the 1554 statute of *scandalum magnatum*) "both to maynteyne their heresye, and also to sowe sedition." Whether they target royal councilors or the queen herself, he argues, these libelers want to stir up sedition and rebellion. Their libels spread at once publicly and surreptitiously, "caste . . . abroad" but also "cast in corners."[54] All these elements would become essential to the paradigm of libel developed in the culture and the courts: the affiliation with sedition and confessional conflict; the symbiotic relationship with false news and gossip; and the language of promiscuous yet covert publication.

There was yet another element that soon became fixed in the popular (although not necessarily in the legal) conception of libel: anonymity.[55] Two decades after Christopherson, the word "libel" remained unfamiliar enough for Protestant controversialists to define it in their pamphlets. And those definitions almost invariably include anonymity: "bookes as rayle against *th*e fame of any person, shewing no name of the author therof," texts "written in verse, or in prose, to *th*e infamy & slander of any man, to *th*e which the author dare not set his name."[56] The actual, still nascent law of libel was more complicated. Writing in 1621, the barrister William Hudson took pains to dispel "two gross errors crept into the world concerning libels: 1. That it is no libel if the party put his hand unto it; and the other, that it is not a libel if it be true."[57] There is some evidence that these two views may have been equally mistaken decades earlier.[58] Yet the practice of the courts was still very much in flux in the 1620s, let alone in the sixteenth century. However the issue stood in the law, we find the belief that libels must conceal their authors' names everywhere from the pseudonymous Marprelate tracts to Elizabethan and Jacobean drama.[59]

---

[54] Christopherson, *Exhortation*, sigs. Dd7v–Dd8r, Dd7v, Bb1r.

[55] See Marcy L. North, *The Anonymous Renaissance: Cultures of Discretion in Tudor-Stuart England* (Chicago: University of Chicago Press, 2003), 117–58.

[56] John Foxe, *The First Volume of the Ecclesiasticall history contaynyng the Actes and Monumentes of thynges passed* (London, 1570), sig. FFf3v; John Whitgift, *The Defense of the Aunswere to the Admonition, against the Replie of T.C.* (London, 1574), sig. Yyy2r. See also the definition in John Bullokar's early dictionary, *An English Expositor* (London, 1616), sigs. K1r–v.

[57] William Hudson, *A Treatise of the Court of Star Chamber*, in *Collectanea Juridica*, ed. Francis Hargrave, vol. 2 (London, 1792), 102.

[58] The early legal definitions of libel say nothing about anonymity, and truth was only a reliable defense in civil (as opposed to criminal) defamation cases (Baker, *Introduction*, 474–76).

[59] Martin Marprelate, *Epistle*, in *The Martin Marprelate Tracts: A Modernized and Annotated Edition*, ed. Joseph L. Black (Cambridge: Cambridge University Press, 2008), 35; Ben Jonson, *Poetaster*, ed. Gabriele Bernhard Jackson, in *CWBJ*, 2:5.3.43–44; Thomas Dekker, *Satiromastix*, in *The Dramatic Works of Thomas Dekker*, ed. Fredson Bowers, vol. 1 (Cambridge: Cambridge University Press, 1953), 3.1.67; David L. Hay, ed., *Nobody and Somebody: An Introduction and Critical Edition* (New York:

14   Introduction

Mischievous libelers played with the power of anonymity. "[T]he man or the woman shall never be knowne / yat caused this rime in the towne to be blowne," rhymed one verse libel spread through the town of Tenterden in 1607. The author was, in fact, discovered: the only reason the libel survives is because it was entered as evidence in court.[60] But the anonymity of most libels remained impenetrable.

The essence of libel, then, was the fearful fusion of anonymous accusation with promiscuous publicity (with, of course, a healthy dose of railing, invective, and scurrility).[61] This paradigm comes clearly into focus in the enduring trope of the libeler's corners. Polemicists on all sides conjured a literary underground shot through with anonymous, dangerously public allegations. So argued the Catholic exile Thomas Harding in his 1565 response to Bishop John Jewel's anonymous *Apologie, or aunswer in defence of the Church of England* (1562). According to Harding, Jewel's tract is really "a famous libell, . . . as that which semeth to haue ben made in a corner." He maintains that Jewel has unlawfully taken his invective from the corners to the streets, having it "cast abrode for any body to take vp" and "offering [his] cause to be examined and iudged by the temeritie of the common multitude."[62] In the language of public sphere theory, this is a reasonably accurate account of how an audience becomes a public: through universal access, open-ended address, and appeal to the judgment of any and all.

But Harding's accusation of libel is more than a little disingenuous. Jewel may not have signed his name to the *Apologie*, but his pamphlet was nonetheless the authorized defense of the Elizabethan religious settlement. By contrast, Harding's own book was printed abroad and smuggled into England.[63] Moreover, Harding and Jewel alike pitched their polemic to what Harding himself calls "the indifferent reader" – an ideal member of the same judging public that he condemns.[64] Jewel soon responded to Harding's attack by turning the allegation of libel back against his

---

Garland, 1980), 1968–71; John Webster, *The Duchess of Malfi*, ed. Brian Gibbons, 5th ed. (London: Methuen Drama, 2014), 2.3.42–43.

[60] James M. Gibson, ed., *REED: Kent: Diocese of Canterbury*, 3 vols. (Toronto: University of Toronto Press, 2002), 2:884. But the author, one Herbert Whitfield, came off relatively unscathed, having secured a royal pardon on the grounds that his libel "did not touche or concerne his maiesties Royall person or any of his Nobles Peeres or Bishopps" (2:885; see 3:1378).

[61] One late Elizabethan commentator neatly summed up this paradigm in a marginal note: "publik sclander / secret aucthor" (BL, Harley MS 6849, fol. 330r).

[62] Thomas Harding, *A Confutation of a Booke Intituled An Apologie of the Church of England* (Antwerp, 1565), sigs. D1r, F2v, K1v.

[63] See Peter Milward, "The Jewel-Harding Controversy," *Albion* 6.4 (1974): 320–41.

[64] Harding, *Confutation*, sig. C3r.

Seeds of Sedition   15

accuser: "Whereas it liked you to terme our Apologie a Sclaunderous Libel, I doubt not, but who so euer shal indifferently consider your Booke, shal thinke M. Hardinges tonge wanteth no sclaunder."[65] But Jewel, like Harding, can only retort by mounting his own open-ended appeal to "who so euer shal indifferently consider" the matter. The multiplying allegations of libel suggest that the category had as much to do with one's confessional stance as with the content of the polemic. This is not to deny that there was real slander in Harding's (or, indeed, in Jewel's) writings. Shuger is surely right to argue that post-Reformation polemic regularly adopted "defamatory smear-tactics."[66] Yet "libel" quickly became a catch-all to denigrate the controversial writings of the other side, whether Catholic or Protestant or Puritan.[67] It was not only a defamatory genre but also a metadiscursive category: it gave polemicists a culturally legible way to talk openly about the terms of public debate.

A fairly explicit example of this strategy comes amid the intra-Catholic dispute known as the Archpriest Controversy. In a 1603 pamphlet, the English priest Robert Charnock contends that his opponent, the prolific Jesuit Robert Persons, "calleth [certain priests' books] *libels*, to shift them off by one meanes or other." Charnock rejects the label and instead, like Harding and Jewel before him, appeals to the judgment of his own ideal audience: "But the indifferent reader will weigh his reasons, and not his foule words; and iudge of matters, not as they are said to be, but as they are prooued."[68] It is revealing that this argument for rational reading comes only in response to "foule words" and only amid a furious and largely anonymous spate of polemic. Not only were Charnock's and Persons's pamphlets both published anonymously, but Charnock even deploys the very strategy that he condemns: he attacks Persons's book as "a notorious libell."[69] Anonymous accusations beget anonymous accusations. Faced with these proliferating libels, judgment indeed rests with the reader, indifferent or otherwise. Charnock's rhetoric of rationality offers as compelling an account as any of how libels might elicit a critical public, a public tasked with sifting through the reasons behind foul words.

It is against this background of confessional conflict that Sir Edward Coke came to define the crime of libel in his 1605 report *De libellis famosis*.

---

[65] John Jewel, *A Defence of the Apologie of the Churche of Englande* (London, 1567), sig. C3r.

[66] Shuger, *Censorship*, 20.   [67] See Lake and Questier, *All Hail*, 182.

[68] Robert Charnock, *A Reply to a notorious Libell Intituled A Briefe Apologie or defence of the Ecclesiastical Hierarchie* ([London], 1603), sigs. Kk4r, Kk4v. For the context of this argument, see Lake and Questier, *All Hail*, 180–82.

[69] Charnock, *Reply to a notorious Libell*.

16 Introduction

From around 1600, libel increasingly attracted the attention of the Court of Star Chamber, the conciliar court principally concerned with public disorder.[70] The seminal case (at least in retrospect) was *Attorney General v. Pickering* (1605), prosecuted by Coke and subsequently reported in print under the title *De libellis famosis*.[71] The offending object in this case was a mock epitaph pinned to the hearse of John Whitgift, Archbishop of Canterbury, at his funeral in March 1604. Titled "The Lamentation of Dickie for the Death of his Brother Jockie," the verse libel colorfully rehearses Puritan grievances against the ecclesiastical policy of the late archbishop ("Jockie") – "Reformers hinderer, trew pastors slanderer, / The papists broker, the Atheists Cloker" – and of his successor, Richard Bancroft ("Dickie").[72] The alleged author and publisher of the libel, Lewis Pickering, was eventually found guilty in Star Chamber, and fined, imprisoned, and sentenced to the pillory.[73]

Coke's report on the case has long been taken to be "the formal starting point of the English law of libel."[74] Yet in their efforts to trace its roots to Roman, common, or statute law, legal historians have largely overlooked its debt to post-Reformation controversy.[75] *De libellis famosis* synthesizes tropes repeated from Christopherson to Charnock. Like the earlier polemicists – including Whitgift himself – Coke contrasts lawful complaint with extrajudicial accusation.[76] He maintains that "in a settled state of government the party grieved ought to complain for every injury done him in an ordinary course of law, and not by any means to revenge himself, either by the odious course of libelling, or otherwise." And he too stresses the danger of anonymity. Coke compares the libeler to the poisoner, who works "so secretly that none can defend himself against it; *for which cause the offence is the more dangerous, because the offender cannot easily be known.*"[77] Coke does not say that a signed accusation cannot be

---

[70] Hudson, *Treatise*, 100; Ibbetson, "Edward Coke," 493–94.
[71] Edward Coke, *Quinta Pars Relationum / The Fift Part of the Reports* (London, 1605), sigs. Y5r–Y6r.
[72] Alastair Bellany, "A Poem on the Archbishop's Hearse: Puritanism, Libel, and Sedition after the Hampton Court Conference," *Journal of British Studies* 34.2 (1995): 137, 138.
[73] John Hawarde, *Les Reportes del Cases in Camera Stellata, 1593 to 1609*, ed. William Paley Baildon (London, 1894), 230. See Bellany, "Poem," 160.
[74] Van Vechten Veeder, "The History of the Law of Defamation," in *Select Essays in Anglo-American Legal History*, vol. 3 (Boston: Little, Brown, 1909), 467.
[75] See, e.g., ibid., 464–67; W. S. Holdsworth, *A History of English Law*, 17 vols. (London: Methuen, 1903–72), 5:208; Manning, "Origins," 113–21; Shuger, *Censorship*, 80–102; and Ibbetson, "Edward Coke."
[76] Writing in the 1570s, Whitgift challenged his accuser: "if you haue any thing to say against me, do it orderly, do it lawfully, not in corners, not in libels" (*Defense*, sig. B5r).
[77] 5 Co. Rep. 125b. Riffing on Coke a few years later, Ferdinando Pulton tellingly elaborates this account with the trope of the libeler's corners (*De Pace Regis et Regni* [London, 1609], sig. B1v).

a libel. Yet he sketches the same paradigm: anonymous allegations litigated not in the courts but in public.

It is only after he has explained the dangers of libeling that Coke defines the object itself. Here too the roots of his report are to be found in the later sixteenth century. Closely following the second part of William West's popular lawbook *Symboleography* (1594), Coke divides libels into the written (*in scriptis*) and the unwritten (*sine scriptis*):

> a scandalous libel *in scriptis* is, when an epigram, rhime, or other writing is composed or published to the scandal or contumely of another, by which his fame and dignity may be prejudiced. And such libel may be published, 1. *Verbis aut cantilenis:* as where it is maliciously repeated or sung in the presence of others. 2. *Traditione*, when the libel or any copy of it is delivered over to scandalize the party. *Famosus libellus sine scriptis* may be, 1. *Picturis*, as to paint the party in any shameful and ignominious manner. 2. *Signis*, as to fix a gallows, or other reproachful and ignominious signs at the party's door or elsewhere.[78]

Coke's taxonomy reflects two key features of the early modern libel: its materiality and its mobility. Libels are tangible objects, most often writings – and poetic writings ("epigram, rhime") at that – but also defamatory pictures and symbols. And these were not mutually exclusive media. The traces of libels reveal that they moved readily across writing, speech, image, and performance. Coke evokes that dangerous mobility when he enumerates how libels may be published: "repeated or sung in the presence of others" or copied and "delivered over." To these means of publication we should add performance. Years later, Hudson would note that libels may take the form of "the personating [someone], thereby to make him ridiculous."[79] These accounts match one of the premises of this book: that libeling, generally studied as a scribal practice, is best understood as a multimedia phenomenon.[80]

The law of libel continued to evolve in the decades after Coke's report. But the cultural paradigm of anonymous, extralegal accusation remained firmly in place. I take that accusatory structure of address to evoke the constitutive tensions of early modern publicity that I outlined above. If libels were avatars of sedition, they also carved out spaces for ordinary

---

[78] 5 Co. Rep. 125b. On Coke's use of West – who himself borrowed from the German civilian Hermann Vulteius – see Mansky, "Edward Coke."

[79] Hudson, *Treatise*, 100.

[80] Clare Egan has recently made a similar case in "Performing Early Modern Libel: Expanding the Boundaries of Performance," *Early Theatre* 23.2 (2020): 155–68. See also Fox, *Oral and Literate Culture*, 299–405; and Chapter 2.

18   Introduction

people to pass judgment on the most controversial issues and persons of
the day. To be sure, it is a peculiar kind of publicity indeed that turns on
anonymous defamation. This was neither an Arendtian "space of appearance" nor an ideal Habermasian sphere of rational-critical debate.[81] Yet
libelers and libeled alike were convinced that what went on in the corners
decisively shaped public discourse. And the evidence examined in this book
suggests that they were not mistaken.

Open Ears and Free Judgments

The word "libel" had not long since entered the vernacular before it began to
be linked to playing. In the 1560 visitation articles of Matthew Parker,
Archbishop of Canterbury, we find an inquiry about "common slaunderars
of theyr neighbours, raylers or scolders, sowers of discord betwene neighbours, by plaies, rymes, famous libels, or otherwise."[82] Parker's concerns are
much the same as Coke's would be half a century later. Both see defamation
as a grave threat to public order, and both implicate popular poetry and
performance in the crime of libel. These concerns soon became a refrain of
the antitheatricalists. As early as 1574, Geoffrey Fenton translated from
a French moralist the telling question, "If Libels of diffamation bee punished
with rigorous paine, why should publike sclanders on scaffoldes escape the
sentence, where euery eare is open, & free liberty of iudgement?"[83] Like
libels, plays submit their "publike sclanders" to an indiscriminate audience.
And perhaps most worryingly, all that it takes to join the slanderous playgoing public is an open ear and liberty of judgment.

   From Stephen Gosson to John Melton, antitheatrical writers continued
to assimilate the theater to the paradigm of libel surveyed above. Their
central complaint was that drama subjected persons and issues to popular,
extrajudicial scrutiny. Gosson sees the stage as a demotic perversion of the
courts. "At Stage Plaies it is ridiculous, for the parties accused to replye," he
contends, "beecause the worste sorte of people haue the hearing of it." And
for Gosson, the judgment of the worst (that is, common) sort amounts to
little more than libeling: "If the common people which resorte to Theaters
being but an assemblie of Tailers, Tinkers, Cordwayners, Saylers, olde

---

[81] Hannah Arendt, *The Human Condition*, 2nd ed. (Chicago: University of Chicago Press, 1998), 198.
    On Arendt's concept – founded in self-disclosure and intersubjective experience – see Paul Yachnin,
    "Performing Publicity," *Shakespeare Bulletin* 28.2 (2010): 203–4.
[82] Matthew Parker, *Articles for to be inquired of, in the Metropolitical visitation of the moste Reuerende
    father in God Matthew . . . Archebyshop of Canterbury* (London, 1560), sig. A4r.
[83] Jean Talpin, *A forme of Christian pollicie*, trans. Geoffrey Fenton (London, 1574), sig. T1v.

Seeds of Sedition

Men, yong Men, Women, Boyes, Girles, and such like, be the iudges of faultes there painted out, the rebuking of manners in that place, is neyther lawfull nor conuenient, but to be held for a kinde of libelling, and defaming."[84] Decades later, Melton advanced a similar argument in response to the early seventeenth-century vogue for political satire. His premise is the same one that governed early modern writings on libel: that it is "necessarie for the safetie of any state" for the rulers' authority to be kept free of "any manner of spot or touch of derogation, either publique spred, or closly insinuated." He accordingly urges that "some seuere law might be enacted, for the punishing of such scandalous libelling as is, or may be at any time coloured vnder the name of poetising, and play-making."[85]

Gosson's and Melton's arguments may have been extreme. Certainly plays and playgoing were not generally illegal, nor were they universally held to be a kind of libeling. Yet the antitheatricalist views echo the principal concerns of Elizabethan and Jacobean dramatic censorship. The tone was set by a 1559 proclamation prohibiting plays "wherein either matters of religion or of the governance of the estate of the commonweal shall be handled or treated."[86] Most of the subsequent crackdowns accordingly targeted libel and sedition: plays that not only mocked identifiable individuals but that also exposed religion and politics to public scrutiny. In 1589, the Privy Council devised a new censorship committee in response to plays that handled "certen matters of Divinytie and of State unfitt to be suffred."[87] In 1597, Thomas Nashe and Ben Jonson's *The Isle of Dogs*, allegedly "a lewd plaie ... contanynge very seditious and sclanderous matter," landed Jonson in prison and may even have provoked the royal order that the playhouses "shalbe plucked downe."[88] And in 1605, Samuel Calvert reported that players continued to represent "the whole Course of this present Time, not sparing either King, State or Religion."[89]

Yet for all the complaints there were few serious repercussions. Some decades ago, Philip J. Finkelpearl went so far as to contend that "not one prominent poet or playwright was punished for libel."[90] The truth of this

---

[84] Stephen Gosson, *Playes Confuted in fiue Actions* (London, 1582), sigs. C8v, D1r.

[85] John Melton, *A Sixe-folde Politician* (London, 1609), sigs. D5r, D5v.   [86] *TRP*, 2:115.

[87] *APC*, 18:215, reproduced in E. K. Chambers, *The Elizabethan Stage*, 4 vols. (Oxford: Clarendon Press, 1923), 4:306.

[88] *APC*, 27:338, 314, reproduced in Chambers, *Elizabethan Stage*, 4:323, 322.

[89] Samuel Calvert to Ralph Winwood, March 28, 1605, in *Memorials of Affairs of State in the Reigns of Q. Elizabeth and K. James I*, ed. Edmund Sawyer, 3 vols. (London, 1725), 2:54.

[90] Philip J. Finkelpearl, "'The Comedians' Liberty': Censorship of the Jacobean Stage Reconsidered," *English Literary Renaissance* 16.1 (1986): 124.

20   Introduction

proposition turns on how one construes both prominence and punishment. To take the example of one rather prominent playwright, Ben Jonson landed in prison several times, was called before the Privy Council, and even, at least in his own telling, faced charges as grave as treason and punishment as severe as mutilation.[91] But subsequent theater historians, above all Richard Dutton, have sustained the core of Finkelpearl's insight: that theatrical censorship was intermittent and inconsistent, concerned not so much with ideological heterodoxy as with "the over-specific shadowing of particular people and current events."[92] The fragmentary evidence reveals a sporadic series of crackdowns that went largely unenforced. Jonson got off each time he was accused, little worse for the wear; no special censorship committee was formed in 1589, despite the Privy Council's order; and, of course, the theaters were not torn down in 1597. Theatrical censorship was not a totalitarian system but a patchwork of responses, each emerging from a highly specific matrix of reputational and political concerns.[93]

I will shortly discuss possible explanations for this relative latitude. First, though, I want to stress that we ought not to exaggerate the extent of the players' liberty. Numerous traces of censorship and reprisal survive, not to mention the surely pervasive yet elusive phenomenon of self-censorship. In the late Elizabethan era alone, clear attempts were made to censor or to suppress outright the Marprelate plays (1589), *Sir Thomas More* (1590–1610), Shakespeare's *Henry IV* plays (1596–97), *The Isle of Dogs* (1597), Jonson's *Every Man Out of His Humour* (1599) and *Poetaster* (1601), and George Chapman's *The Old Joiner of Aldgate* (1603).[94] But even a cursory glance at these cases substantiates Dutton's contention that dramatic censorship was neither monolithic nor uniformly repressive. Behind the official responses we find a variety of agents sometimes working at cross-purposes, including

---

[91] Ben Jonson, *Discoveries*, ed. Lorna Hutson, in *CWBJ*, 7:545, ll. 952–53n; Jonson, *Informations to William Drummond of Hawthornden*, ed. Ian Donaldson, in *CWBJ*, 5:373, ll. 207–10; 375, ll. 251–52.

[92] Richard Dutton, *Mastering the Revels: The Regulation and Censorship of English Renaissance Drama* (Basingstoke, UK: Macmillan, 1991), 85. See also Dutton, *Licensing, Censorship and Authorship in Early Modern England: Buggeswords* (Basingstoke, UK: Palgrave, 2000). For a contrasting view, see Janet Clare, *'Art made tongue-tied by authority': Elizabethan and Jacobean Dramatic Censorship*, 2nd ed. (Manchester: Manchester University Press, 1999).

[93] A similar picture has emerged of early modern press censorship: see Clegg, *Press Censorship in Elizabethan England*; and Clegg, *Press Censorship in Jacobean England* (Cambridge: Cambridge University Press, 2001).

[94] See Dutton, *Mastering*, 74–141; and Clare, *Art*, 48–118. From more uncertain bibliographical evidence, Clare identifies several other possible instances of late Elizabethan dramatic censorship, including Marlowe's *Doctor Faustus*, Shakespeare's *2 Henry VI*, *3 Henry VI*, and *Richard II*, and the anonymous history *Jack Straw*.

Seeds of Sedition 21

the Master of the Revels, assorted privy councilors and patrons, London's mayor and aldermen, and the Court of Star Chamber. The responses were as various as the interested parties, ranging from relatively slight revisions (*Henry IV* plays, *Every Man Out*) to total suppression accompanied by broader restraints on playing (Marprelate plays, *Isle of Dogs*). Even in the most serious cases, however, none of the playwrights or players involved is known to have suffered any fate worse than a short stay in prison.

So what accounts for the players' liberty in a state that was quite capable of concerted, violent campaigns of repression (see: the Catholic or radical Puritan experience)?[95] The answer is certainly not that the stage largely avoided topical commentary. In fact, Dutton argues that "politically-charged analogical reading was ... the *usual* condition of writing and reading in the period," practiced by playwrights, playgoers, and censors alike.[96] This would seem to make the theater precisely the den of libeling that antitheatricalists so feared. Scholars have taken two complementary approaches to explain the situation, the first grounded in theater history and the second in cultural history. The first answer, advanced by Dutton and now widely (but not universally) accepted, looks to the commercial theater's ties to the court. Even the 1559 proclamation against staging matters of religion and state made an exception for courtly or learned audiences "of grave and discreet persons."[97] Those grave and discreet audiences, Dutton argues, were what the Master of the Revels had in mind when plays came before him for licensing. In this view, the notion that commercial performance was a rehearsal for performance at court was not merely a convenient fiction deployed to shield acting companies from civic displeasure but also the operative principle of dramatic censorship.[98]

The second approach situates the regulation of drama within a broader "culture of slander," as M. Lindsay Kaplan calls it. Kaplan sees defamation as just too slippery to be contained (or appropriated) by any regime of censorship, dramatic or otherwise.[99] Shuger takes a very different view, and one more in line with Dutton's. She argues that dramatists and censors shared a "charitable hermeneutic" informed by the principle of defamation law known as *mitior sensus* ("the milder sense").[100] From the 1560s on, the courts held that potentially defamatory words ought to be construed as leniently as possible – that "in general or doubtful words the milder sense is

---

[95] See Lake, *How Shakespeare*, 53–55.   [96] Dutton, *Licensing*, xi.   [97] *TRP*, 2:115.
[98] Dutton, *Mastering*; Dutton, *Licensing*. See also Dutton, *Shakespeare, Court Dramatist* (Oxford: Oxford University Press, 2016); and W. R. Streitberger, *The Masters of the Revels and Elizabeth I's Court Theatre* (Oxford: Oxford University Press, 2016), 219–38.
[99] Kaplan, *Culture*.   [100] Shuger, *Censorship*, 195.

22 Introduction

to be preferred."[101] Shakespeare's Olivia in *Twelfth Night* neatly sums up
how such charitable interpretation might defang defamation: "To be
generous, guiltless and of free disposition is to take those things for bird-
bolts that you deem cannon bullets. There is no slander in an allowed fool
though he do nothing but rail."[102] Shuger's and Dutton's accounts put all
professional players in the position of the allowed or licensed fool, given
scope to rail and mock so long as the veil of fiction was just thick enough to
allow for a charitable construction, however strained it might be.[103]

There is much to recommend Dutton's and Shuger's views. Together,
they outline the institutional and cultural frameworks within which the
commercial theater could thrive despite – or, perhaps, because of – its
proclivity for news, scandal, and controversy. Yet their emphasis on shared
incentives and values is only half of the picture. While those arguments
make good sense of the relationship among the theater industry, its
censors, and the court, they tell us much less about the theater's orientation
toward the broader public. Shuger's "charitable hermeneutic" in particular
does not fit especially well with what we know about the reception of plays
and libels. Responding to Martin Marprelate's libeling in 1593, Richard
Hooker explicitly exempts questions of public policy from the dictates of
charity: "That *things doubtful are to be construed in the better part*, is
a principle not safe to be followed in matters concerning the public state
of a commonweal."[104] The few traces of politically engaged playgoing
likewise reveal interpretive practices more suspicious and cynical than
charitable.[105] And while Shuger sees charitable principles behind

[101] *Stanhope* v. *Blythe* (1585), in John Baker, *Baker and Milsom Sources of English Legal History: Private Law to 1750*, 2nd ed. (Oxford: Oxford University Press, 2010), 702 n28. This rule produced some fairly amusing interpretive contortions. In one case, the King's Bench determined that the words "He is a Blood-sucker, and seeketh others blood" were not actionable because they "may be taken in some good sence": that the plaintiff, a justice of the peace, thirsted for blood merely "in executing his office" (*Hilliard* v. *Constable* [1595], in *The First Part of the Reports of Sr George Croke* [London, 1661], 433). For more examples, see John March, *Actions for Slaunder* (London, 1647), 26–34; Milsom, *Historical Foundations*, 386–88; and Baker, *Introduction*, 471–72.
[102] Shakespeare, *Twelfth Night*, ed. Keir Elam (London: Arden Shakespeare, 2008), 1.5.87–90.
[103] Shuger, *Censorship*, 183–202; Dutton, *Licensing*, 16–40. For a similar view, see Annabel Patterson, *Censorship and Interpretation: The Conditions of Writing and Reading in Early Modern England* (Madison: University of Wisconsin Press, 1984).
[104] Richard Hooker, *Of the Laws of Ecclesiastical Polity: A Critical Edition with Modern Spelling*, ed. Arthur Stephen McGrade, 3 vols. (Oxford: Oxford University Press, 2013), 1:38. See Jesse M. Lander, *Inventing Polemic: Religion, Print, and Literary Culture in Early Modern England* (Cambridge: Cambridge University Press, 2006), 105.
[105] Doty, *Shakespeare*, 29–31; Charles Whitney, *Early Responses to Renaissance Drama* (Cambridge: Cambridge University Press, 2006), 154–60; Thomas Cogswell and Peter Lake, "Buckingham Does the Globe: *Henry VIII* and the Politics of Popularity in the 1620s," *Shakespeare Quarterly* 60.3 (2009): 277–78.

Seeds of Sedition 23

Shakespeare's history plays, Lake just as convincingly locates them within the "paranoid hermeneutic style" of late Elizabethan politics.[106]

I believe these divergent accounts help explain the theater's proximity to libeling. At issue was not just the substance of the plays but also the way they were interpreted. Or, I should say, ways: no single hermeneutic can account for the diversity of audience response. Playgoers and patrons and magistrates continuously drew and redrew the line between topical allusion and libel. Of special concern was the judgment of the popular elements. Above, I followed this view from Gosson and his fellow antitheatricalists through the proclamations and proscriptions of the queen and her council. As the 1559 exception for audiences of "grave and discreet persons" suggests, the danger was not topical drama per se but rather the indiscreet, popular playgoers. This concern with unruly response likewise lay behind the drive to hold audiences culpable for the crime of libel. Libels' listeners are said to be "maynteyners and favourers of the same," their laughter or "merriment" taken as "a publication in law."[107] Publication here is not a unilateral transmission but a social scene, implicating speakers and merry audiences alike.[108] It is a scene where, to return to Fenton's apt translation, "euery eare is open, & free liberty of iudgement." For modern scholars, those attentive ears and free judgments were what made the theater "the leading arena of public-making practices."[109] For the early moderns, they again and again brought theater – amateur and professional, urban and provincial alike – into the ambit of libel.

***

From the 1590s on, libels regularly appear in early modern drama. The following is a nonexhaustive list of plays up to 1630 that bring libels or libelers onstage: Shakespeare and George Peele's *Titus Andronicus* (1591–94), Christopher Marlowe's *Edward II* (1592), Shakespeare's *Richard III* (1593), Anthony Munday and others' *Sir Thomas More* (1590–1610), Shakespeare's *Julius Caesar* (1599), Thomas Heywood's *Edward IV* (1599), Jonson's *Poetaster* (1601), *Nobody and Somebody* (1605), Barnabe Barnes's *The Devil's Charter* (1606), John Marston, William Barksted, and Lewis Machin's *The Insatiate Countess* (1610), *Thomas of Woodstock* (1610–16), Thomas Dekker's *Match Me in London* (1621) and *The Noble Spanish Soldier* (1622), Philip

---

[106] Shuger, *Censorship*, 202; Lake, *How Shakespeare*, 574.

[107] TNA, SP 12/273, fol. 61r; Hudson, *Treatise*, 102. A similar logic seems to underlie the stipulation in the statute of *scandalum magnatum* that any who spread false and defamatory tales will be punished if they cannot produce the author.

[108] On publication in this sense, see Warner, *Publics*, 90–91; and Mullaney, *Reformation*, 167–69.

[109] Yachnin, "Performing Publicity," 201.

24   Introduction

Massinger's *The Roman Actor* (1626), and William Davenant's *The Cruel Brother* (1627). Some form of the word "libel" appears in all of these save for *Julius Caesar* and *Sir Thomas More*. Passing mentions of libels or libeling appear in a number of other plays too, including Thomas Lodge and Robert Greene's *A Looking Glass for London and England* (1589), Dekker's *Satiromastix* (1601), Jonson's *Sejanus* (1603), John Day's *The Isle of Gulls* (1606), Dekker's *The Whore of Babylon* (1606), Dekker and Thomas Middleton's *The Roaring Girl* (1611), and John Fletcher and Massinger's *Thierry and Theodoret* (1617).[110]

The uncertainty of dating and the limited archive make it difficult to draw many firm conclusions. But the evidence strongly suggests that libels first emerged on the stage in the long 1590s (1588–1603) and then continued to appear through the 1620s and beyond. It is perhaps no coincidence that historians have identified precisely those decades – the 1590s and the 1620s – as periods of especially intense libeling on a national scale.[111] These were years of turmoil, marked by crises domestic and foreign, murky successions, and rising factionalism.[112] For many, the pervasive libels were both a cause and a symptom of the darkening picture, "the Epidemicall disease of those dayes" and the "suntomes [symptoms] of ill government."[113] Paranoid and violent talk spread through the country and the theater alike. From *Titus* to *The Cruel Brother*, early modern drama locates libels in a world of propaganda, faction, and political unrest.

The acting companies had their own parts to play in the polemical climate. Over the past few decades, theater historians have argued that the leading troupes of the 1570s and 1580s, namely the Earl of Leicester's Men and the Queen's Men, were at least in part formed to spread Protestant propaganda and to extend their patrons' influence across England.[114]

---

[110] Dates (often conjectural) come from Martin Wiggins with Catherine Richardson, *British Drama 1533–1642: A Catalogue*, 10 vols. (Oxford: Oxford University Press, 2012–), with the exception of *Titus*, where I think we can be more precise about the possible limits (see Chapter 3).

[111] Croft, "Libels"; Bellany, "Railing Rhymes."

[112] John Guy, ed., *The Reign of Elizabeth I: Court and Culture in the Last Decade* (Cambridge: Cambridge University Press, 1995); Alastair Bellany and Thomas Cogswell, *The Murder of King James I* (New Haven: Yale University Press, 2015).

[113] BL, Lansdowne MS 620, fol. 50r, quoted in Alastair Bellany, "Singing Libel in Early Stuart England: The Case of the Staines Fiddlers, 1627," *Huntington Library Quarterly* 69.1 (2006): 182; John Holles to Thomas Wentworth, November 15, 1628, in *Wentworth Papers, 1597–1628*, ed. J. P. Cooper (London: Royal Historical Society, 1973), 309, quoted in James Doelman, *The Epigram in England, 1590–1640* (Manchester: Manchester University Press, 2016), 289.

[114] Paul Whitfield White, *Theatre and Reformation: Protestantism, Patronage, and Playing in Tudor England* (Cambridge: Cambridge University Press, 1993), 62–66; Scott McMillin and Sally-Beth MacLean, *The Queen's Men and their Plays* (Cambridge: Cambridge University Press, 1998). These arguments remain largely speculative and have received some pushback: see, e.g., W. R. Streitberger,

Seeds of Sedition 25

Lawrence Manley and Sally-Beth MacLean have recently developed a similar if more nuanced account of the repertory of Lord Strange's Men, the company patronized by Ferdinando Stanley, Lord Strange and later fifth Earl of Derby. They contend that Strange's Men, "as the preeminent London company of the early 1590s, were positioned to play a leading role in the theatrical dimensions of this public-making process." But Manley and MacLean find that the plays, like their patron, were rather more heterodox than their theatrical forebears: they espoused a "politique manner" that joined skeptical critique of religious and political controversy with fundamental loyalty to the crown.[115]

It is thus highly suggestive that several of the late Elizabethan plays about or implicated in libel have been linked to Strange's Men (or to their successor, the Earl of Derby's Servants), including *Titus Andronicus*, *Richard III*, *Edward IV*, *Sir Thomas More*, and the lost Marprelate plays.[116] Yet many company attributions from the early 1590s remain speculative. *Titus* and *Richard III* can just as plausibly be linked to Pembroke's Men, who also performed *Edward II* and *The Isle of Dogs*.[117] *Sir Thomas More* may well postdate Strange's Men entirely. Several other companies were involved in the Marprelate controversy too.[118] And by 1600, it was the recently revived boy companies that were making their name for edgy political satire. Even when we are relatively sure of the company attribution, it is impossible (as Manley and MacLean themselves point out) to disentangle the complex assortment of motives – aesthetic, commercial, confessional, factional – behind a given play.[119] The difficulty is only compounded by the scarcity of evidence for patrons' involvement in the activities of their companies.[120] The heterodox leanings of Lord Strange and his company may well have contributed to the initial interest in libel. But so too did popular tastes, creative sensibilities, and scandalous events. Whatever the confluence of factors, one thing is clear: there was an unprecedented turn toward the politics of libel on the late Elizabethan stage.

"Adult Playing Companies to 1583," in *The Oxford Handbook of Early Modern Theatre*, ed. Richard Dutton (Oxford: Oxford University Press, 2009), 25–26.

[115] Lawrence Manley and Sally-Beth MacLean, *Lord Strange's Men and Their Plays* (New Haven: Yale University Press, 2014), 217, 246.

[116] Ibid., 37–43, 106–110, 113–22, 313–20; Richard Rowland, introduction to Thomas Heywood, *The First and Second Parts of King Edward IV*, ed. Rowland (Manchester: Manchester University Press, 2005), 1–2.

[117] Andrew Gurr, *The Shakespearian Playing Companies* (Oxford: Clarendon Press, 1996), 269–73, 276.

[118] McMillin and MacLean, *Queen's Men*, 53–54.

[119] Manley and MacLean, *Lord Strange's Men*, 217.

[120] Gurr, *Shakespearian Playing Companies*, 32–33.

This Book

As I mentioned at the outset, I have divided this book into two parts, "The Scene of Libel" and "Libels on the Elizabethan Stage." The first part tracks the circulation of libels across manuscript, print, and performance. Where the archive allows I focus on the late Elizabethan era, but otherwise my sources range from the 1580s to the 1620s. The first chapter studies scenes of reading. I consider not only scribal annotations and semi-official responses to libels but also representations of reading in printed polemic and Shakespearean drama. These eclectic sources, I argue, outline the publics of libel: the physical and virtual associations of strangers joined in seditious talk and defamatory judgment.

In Chapter 2, I turn to the first of two primary contact zones between libels and theater: the dramatic performance of libel. To be sure, entire monographs could be – and have been – written about plays that fell afoul of the authorities for their topical content.[121] Yet this invaluable work, like the scholarship on plays and their publics, has been dominated by the institution of the commercial theater. One of the aims of this book is to put the drama of the metropolitan center in dialogue with the performance of libel in the provinces. The tireless efforts of the Records of Early English Drama (REED) editors have made readily available an extensive archive of Star Chamber cases documenting the performance and publication of libel. Together with other sources, those records give us what is largely lacking for the London stage: a granular view of ordinary people reading, watching, and performing libels.

The second contact zone is at the core of this book: representations of libel in late Elizabethan drama. While such scenes appear in every chapter, they are the primary focus of the book's second part. Chapters 3–6 examine the four Elizabethan plays most concerned with libel: Shakespeare and Peele's *Titus Andronicus*, the collaborative *Sir Thomas More*, Heywood's *Edward IV*, and Jonson's *Poetaster*. Some of these, namely *Sir Thomas More* and *Poetaster*, were themselves libelous, or at least came close enough to contemporary controversies as to face censorship. But the others were not, or at least not in any obvious way. The four plays stage not merely generalized defamation but the specific crime of libel: subversive texts declaimed, scattered, seized, or otherwise made public. Here I depart from previous scholarship on drama and defamation, which either focuses on the orality of slander or treats libel and slander interchangeably. As

---

[121] See, e.g., Dutton, *Mastering*; Clare, *Art*.

Seeds of Sedition

I argued above, both the law and the culture at large understood libel to be a distinct type of slander. This distinction matters because dramatists, like jurists and polemicists, were keenly aware of the power and perils of written allegations.

Each chapter in the second part reflects a particular historical moment and a particular strain of libel. *Titus* dramatizes the sectarian libeling of the late 1580s and early 1590s (Chapter 3). *Sir Thomas More* stages the xenophobic libeling that peaked in 1593 but continued throughout the decade (Chapter 4). *Edward IV* riffs on a historical libel against the tyrannical Richard III while evoking the economic strain of the later 1590s (Chapter 5). And *Poetaster* allegorizes the crackdown on libel and sedition in the wake of the Essex Rising of 1601 (Chapter 6). These are four distinct yet overlapping visions of libel: as confessional complaint, as citizen grievance, as commoner resistance, as satirical critique. Together, the plays probe the politics of the early modern libel. They explore a host of questions about the place of faction, violence, xenophobia, and populism in the public sphere. And they orient the theater toward the seditious speech that swirled around and through it.

PART I

The Scene of Libel

CHAPTER I

How to Read a Libel in Early Modern England

How did early modern people read libels? This is no simple question given their remarkable spatial and interpretive mobility. Even a single text could mean different things to different people at different moments. Popular libels like the "Parliament Fart" and *Leicester's Commonwealth* remained current for decades, their meanings evolving along with their copyists' agendas and the temper of the times.[1] The scholarly focus, however, has naturally remained on the scribal archive in which most libels survive. Primarily from the study of manuscript miscellanies, scholars have found that libels were read for their aesthetic qualities, for their wit, for their newsworthiness, for their scandalous content, and for their political counsel.[2] Yet this archive has its limits. As Alastair Bellany points out, scribal sources such as newsletters, commonplace books, and miscellanies provide "better evidence of the circulation of these materials among the social elite than among the middling and lower sorts."[3] We need to take a wider view to understand how libels interfaced with the English public.

This chapter accordingly examines how reading – and sharing and discussing and debating – libels brought early modern people together as publics. I begin with a small but representative slice of the scribal archive to

---

[1] On the circulation of the "Parliament Fart," see Arthur F. Marotti, *Manuscript, Print, and the English Renaissance Lyric* (Ithaca: Cornell University Press, 1995), 113–15; and Michelle O'Callaghan, "Performing Politics: The Circulation of the 'Parliament Fart,'" *Huntington Library Quarterly* 69.1 (2006): 121–38. I discuss the case of *Leicester's Commonwealth* below.

[2] See Andrew McRae, *Literature, Satire and the Early Stuart State* (Cambridge: Cambridge University Press, 2004), 23–50; David Colclough, *Freedom of Speech in Early Stuart England* (Cambridge: Cambridge University Press, 2005), 196–250; Andrew McRae, ed., "'Railing Rhymes': Politics and Poetry in Early Stuart England," special issue, *Huntington Library Quarterly* 69.1 (2006); Alastair Bellany, "The Embarrassment of Libels: Perceptions and Representations of Verse Libelling in Early Stuart England," in *The Politics of the Public Sphere in Early Modern England*, ed. Peter Lake and Steven Pincus (Manchester: Manchester University Press, 2007), 144–67; and Joshua Eckhardt, *Manuscript Verse Collectors and the Politics of Anti-Courtly Love Poetry* (Oxford: Oxford University Press, 2009).

[3] Alastair Bellany, "Railing Rhymes Revisited: Libels, Scandals, and Early Stuart Politics," *History Compass* 5.4 (2007): 1147.

explore how libels spread and were read. My sources include Francis Bacon's government white papers, a poem by King James, and two libels bearing annotations – the first in the hand of Robert Cecil, the second by an anonymous copyist – that have received virtually no attention. In the final two sections of the chapter, I turn to a different kind of evidence: fictional representations of reading. I consider successively *Leicester's Commonwealth* – an anonymous Catholic prose tract printed in 1584 – and Shakespeare's *Julius Caesar*. Both the pamphlet and the play show readers encountering libels. These scenes not only indicate how such texts circulated but also train their audiences in the art of interpreting libels.

As I discussed in the Introduction, this "reflexive circulation of discourse" is what distinguishes a public from a readership or a crowd.[4] Public discourse in this sense directs audiences' attention not just to the topic at hand but also to their own critical activity. This is how strangers come to understand themselves as part of larger social entities: in this case, publics of libel readers come together to exercise their own (libelous) judgment. To delineate the contours of those publics, I follow the conjoined careers of libels and talk about libels. The sources that I examine adopt a range of stances toward libels and their audiences, from concern to complicity. But all foreground the dynamics of public address. Together, they sketch the interpretive practices that characterized the circulation of libels across manuscript, print, and performance.

That trajectory – from manuscript to print to performance – roughly tracks the multimedia circuits that brought libels to large, heterogeneous audiences of mixed literacy. Print and performance helped the middling and lower sorts join in conversations otherwise reserved for the elites. Yet this was not a matter of superseding the handwritten word. Scholars have amply demonstrated that manuscript remained a vibrant and, in the case of libels, a dominant medium for publication throughout the period.[5] My point is rather the one I made at the start: that libels were eminently mobile. The texts I study in this chapter were reportedly dropped in a performance venue (or government building), thrown in at a window, shared with friends, and talked about at tables. They eluded suppression and circulated widely enough

---

[4] Michael Warner, *Publics and Counterpublics* (New York: Zone Books, 2002), 90.
[5] See, e.g., Mary Hobbs, *Early Seventeenth-Century Verse Miscellany Manuscripts* (Aldershot, UK: Scolar Press, 1992); Harold Love, *Scribal Publication in Seventeenth-Century England* (Oxford: Clarendon Press, 1993); Marotti, *Manuscript*; H. R. Woudhuysen, *Sir Philip Sidney and the Circulation of Manuscripts, 1558–1640* (Oxford: Clarendon Press, 1996); Eckhardt, *Manuscript Verse Collectors*; and Noah Millstone, *Manuscript Circulation and the Invention of Politics in Early Stuart England* (Cambridge: Cambridge University Press, 2016).

How to Read a Libel in Early Modern England   33

to force responses from the center of the regime, including the monarch. They crossed class and confessional lines to reach gentlemen and commoners, Catholics and Protestants alike. Reading was not primarily a solitary endeavor but rather a social, even dialogic process – a multidirectional conversation that quickly exceeded the initial terms of address. To be sure, these conversations were halting and defamatory. Yet, I will argue, their promiscuous circulation maps the networks of physical and discursive spaces that made up the early modern public sphere.

Bacon's Advertisements

Around 1589, Francis Bacon was reading libels. We know this because he wrote and circulated in manuscript two "advertisements" (essentially white papers) on the proliferating polemic. In October 1588, the first tract by the pseudonymous Martin Marprelate emerged from Robert Waldegrave's Puritan press.[6] Its rollicking prose and scurrilous satire of church leaders immediately seized the attention of a regime that had already begun to crack down hard on Presbyterianism. As further Marprelate pamphlets followed through late 1589, ecclesiastical authorities commissioned several writers – including John Lyly and Thomas Nashe – to respond in kind. These anti-Martinist pamphlets consciously adopted Martin's own scandalous style "to giue them a whisk with their owne wand," as Lyly put it.[7] The campaign soon spilled over onto the stage. The Queen's Men, the Lord Admiral's Men, Lord Strange's Men, and Paul's Boys were all implicated in the mockery of Martin Marprelate.[8] But if the government condoned the printed satire, the performances apparently went too far. On November 6, 1589, the Lord Mayor of London reported that he had required the Lord Admiral's and Lord Strange's Men to cease playing and then jailed several members of the latter company when they refused to comply. Less than a week later, the Privy Council prepared orders to censor all "partes and matters . . . unfytt and undecent to be handled in playes, bothe for Divinitie and State."[9]

---

[6] Martin Marprelate, *Epistle*, in *The Martin Marprelate Tracts: A Modernized and Annotated Edition*, ed. Joseph L. Black (Cambridge: Cambridge University Press, 2008), 3–45. For a detailed account of the controversy, see Black, introduction to *Martin Marprelate Tracts*, xv–cxii.

[7] John Lyly, *Pappe with an Hatchet*, in *The Complete Works of John Lyly*, ed. R. Warwick Bond, vol. 3 (Oxford: Clarendon Press, 1902), 396. See Joseph Black, "The Rhetoric of Reaction: The Martin Marprelate Tracts (1588–89), Anti-Martinism, and the Uses of Print in Early Modern England," *Sixteenth Century Journal* 28.3 (1997): 714.

[8] Black, introduction to *Martin Marprelate Tracts*, lxv.

[9] *APC*, 18:215. See Lawrence Manley and Sally-Beth MacLean, *Lord Strange's Men and Their Plays* (New Haven: Yale University Press, 2014), 41–42.

34 The Scene of Libel

Bacon was not much impressed with either side. In *An advertisement touching the controuersyes of the Church of England* (1589), he urges Puritan and Anglican polemicists alike to hold their fire. "And first of all," he writes, "it is more then tyme there were an end and surceance made of this vnmodest and deformed manner of writing lately entertayned whereby matters of religion are handled in the stile of the stage."[10] Bacon is alert to the dangers of a mocking, scurrilous, performative style – the style of libel which, for him, is also the style of the stage. Evidently the two styles were close for the pamphleteers too. The anti-Martinist authors claimed that Martin had borrowed his "tinkers termes, and barbers iestes" from the Queen's Men's famous clown, Richard Tarlton, and that he had learned his "*twittle twattles* . . . at the Theater of Lanam [John Laneham, also of the Queen's Men] and his fellowes."[11] Controversial satire moved readily between stage and page. The upshot of all this mockery, Bacon feared, would be "to turne religion into a comedy or Satyre."[12]

For Bacon, the style of the stage was not just "vnmodest and deformed" but also dangerously public. He chides the polemicists for "search[ing] and ripp[ing] vpp woundes with a laughing countenance," exposing ecclesiastical controversy to public scrutiny (and derision). At the end of the *Advertisement,* he makes clear why this publicity is such a problem. "Lastly," he concludes, "what soeuer be pretended the people is no meet iudg or arbitratour but rather the quiet modest & private assemblies and conferences of the learned."[13] We saw the same premise in the Jewel-Harding controversy and in the other spates of religious polemic surveyed in the Introduction: that appealing to the people is itself a sign of libeling. Remarkably, though, Bacon does not distinguish between the appeals of the church and those of its critics. Both inappropriately, even libelously, take sensitive religiopolitical questions from "private assemblies" to a judging public.

Bacon elaborates this dynamic in another, roughly contemporary advertisement, this one "touching seditious writing." He does not name these seditious writings – they may well include the Marprelate tracts or other Puritan pamphlets – but his description of their "calling in question the

---

[10] Bacon, *An advertisement touching the controuersyes of the Church of England*, in *The Oxford Francis Bacon*, vol. 1, ed. Alan Stewart with Harriet Knight (Oxford: Clarendon Press, 2012), 163. On the style of the stage in post-Reformation performance and polemic, see Katrin Beushausen, *Theatre and the English Public from Reformation to Revolution* (Cambridge: Cambridge University Press, 2018), 27–79.

[11] *Mar-Martine* ([London, 1589]), sig. A4v; *Martins Months minde* ([London], 1589), sig. F2r. See Manley and MacLean, *Lord Strange's Men*, 38.

[12] Bacon, *Advertisement touching the controuersyes*, 164. [13] Ibid., 164, 194.

How to Read a Libel in Early Modern England   35

most cleere and vndoubted right of our naturall souueraigne" suggests that they are primarily Catholic libels.[14] Before sketching their contents, he opens with an account of their place in the public sphere:

> As it hath allwayes been an honorable and wise Custome with Princes & superiors in regarde of their owne good name & the contentmente of all sortes to publish advertisementes and declaracions, whereby to iustify their proceedinges, and to direct the fame which attendeth vpon all great accions, & easily declyneth to obloquy if it be not forestalled. So in contrary manner hath it ever been a corrupt and perverse practise of evill subiectes to sowe abroade libells and invectiues of purpose to deface their gouvernors, & by imbasing their estimacion to supplante the allegeaunce and dutyes of the people, & the quyet of their cowntryes.[15]

On the one side, there are all the rulers' "advertisementes and declaracions" that together amount to a kind of public relations machine. In Bacon's telling, England's governors have long disseminated such writings to manage public opinion, "to direct the fame which attendeth vpon all great accions." On the other, there are the "libells and invectiues" dispersed by "evill subiectes . . . to deface their gouvernors." Bacon's "as . . . so" structure sets up a parallel between the two sides. Governors and libelers alike churn out writings for public consumption. The difference, of course, comes in the desired effect on popular opinion: to defend or to defame members of the ruling classes.

But advertisements and declarations alone were not enough to counter seditious libels. In Bacon's view, the problem was not just the texts themselves but also the people's own perverse judgments. He continues:

> And yet neverthelesse in the creditt and allowaunce which is given to these writinges of so severall natures the iudgemente of men swarveth greatly and offereth very harde condicion where it least appertayneth. For the Iustifycacions, and Apologyes of personages in authority are for the most parte taken & deemed to be but colours and pretenses, . . . whereas on the other side these malitious Pamphlettes are thought to be the flying sparkes of trewthe forcibly kept downe and choked by those which are possessed of the state.[16]

Bacon imagines a remarkably skeptical and even paranoid reading public, a public suspicious of the authorities' apologies and drawn to seditious pamphlets. While the former are taken to be mere "colours and pretenses," the latter seem more credible precisely because they are suppressed. Censorship only justifies the popular conviction that seditious writings are

---

[14] Bacon, *An aduertisement touching seditious writing*, in *Oxford Francis Bacon*, 1:311; see 1:305.
[15] Ibid., 309.   [16] Ibid.

36   The Scene of Libel

"the flying sparkes of trewthe forcibly kept downe and choked by those which are possessed of the state." This leaves the state in a difficult position indeed. Neither answering nor suppressing libels can tame the uncooperative judgment of "the most parte" of the people.

Bacon's account closely matches the "post-Reformation public sphere" sketched by Peter Lake and Steven Pincus. They trace its origins to the "public pitch making ... conducted both by members of the regime, its supporters, loyal opposition and overt critics and opponents."[17] Periodic appeals to the people came not only from England's governors but also from Catholics, nonconformists, and others whom Bacon would consider "evill subiectes." For Lake and Pincus, the result was "an adjudicating public or publics able to judge or determine the truth of the matter in hand on the basis of the information and argument placed before them."[18] But Bacon was rather less sanguine about the critical capacities of the people. The central proposition of his *Aduertisement touching seditious writing* was precisely to help the reading public make better judgments. Because some libels will always elude suppression, Bacon concludes, "therefore is it very meete that all good subiectes, & every other indifferent or reasonable person be faith-fully & fully advertised towching these writinges" so that "by the Circumstances men may iudge of the matter." His hope is that revealing the libels' nefarious origins and aims – their "manyfest vntrewthes" and "odious ... discourses" – will counter the credulity of the people.[19] But the problem with the style of the stage was that audiences could and did render judgment in whatever way they pleased.

Royal Reading

Several decades later, King James rehearsed similar complaints about libelers' style of the stage in what is probably the best-known response to a libel. The topic of the day was the king's unpopular foreign policy, and in particular the prospect of a Spanish bride for Prince Charles.[20] In 1620 and then again in 1621, the king issued proclamations "against excesse of Lavish and Licentious Speech of matters of State."[21] But royal decrees did little to

---

[17] Peter Lake and Steven Pincus, "Rethinking the Public Sphere in Early Modern England," in *Politics of the Public Sphere*, ed. Lake and Pincus, 6.

[18] Ibid., 6.   [19] Bacon, *Aduertisement touching seditious writing*, 312.

[20] See Thomas Cogswell, *The Blessed Revolution: English Politics and the Coming of War, 1621–1624* (Cambridge: Cambridge University Press, 1989), 20–53.

[21] James F. Larkin and Paul L. Hughes, eds., *Stuart Royal Proclamations*, 2 vols. (Oxford: Clarendon Press, 1973–83), 1:495, 519.

stem the tide of libels, news, and gossip. "State meddlers," as one observer termed them, wrote and talked incessantly about the Spanish Match; "daylie moor and moore libels weere dispersed," Sir Simonds D'Ewes recorded in his diary.[22] So, in late 1622 or early 1623, James entered the fray himself with a poem "made upon a Libell lett fall in Court."[23] The king's poem vigorously defends his foreign policy, religious politics, and choice of favorites from the "railing rymes and vaunting verse" of the meddlesome libelers (23).

The poem's central concern echoes one of Bacon's objections in *An advertisement touching the controuersyes of the Church of England*: that libels supplant the closed-door deliberations of the elite with the faulty judgment of the people. James begins by mocking the people's critical capacities:

> O stay your teares yow who complaine
> Cry not as Babes doe all in vaine
> Purblinde people why doe yow prate
> Too shallowe for the deepe of state
> You cannot judge what's truely myne. (1–5)

The king infantilizes his subjects. Their talk is mere "cry[ing]" and "prat[ing]" that cannot hope to plumb "the deepe of state." Or, as Bacon wrote, "the people is no meet iudg." James likewise argues that popular judgment is not only vain but dangerous. "What counsells would be overthrowne / If all weere to the people knowne?" he asks, and then does not hesitate to give an unequivocal answer: "Then to noe use were councell tables / If state affaires were publique bables" (77–80). The scene of private, conciliar deliberation gives way to the people's incoherent clamor. For James, libels conjure a world where affairs of state are discussed and debated by the babbling public.

Again like Bacon, James describes the result of this public chatter in theatrical terms. He laments,

> O what a calling weere a King
> If hee might give, or take no thing
> But such as yow should to him bring
> Such were a king but in a play. (41–44)

---

[22] Joseph Mead to Martin Stuteville, January 18, 1623, in *The Court and Times of James the First*, comp. Thomas Birch, ed. Robert Folkestone Williams, 2 vols. (London, 1848), 2:355; *The Diary of Sir Simonds D'Ewes (1622–1624)*, ed. Elisabeth Bourcier (Paris: Didier, 1974), 135, quoted in Cogswell, *Blessed Revolution*, 46.

[23] "O stay your teares yow who complaine," in *Early Stuart Libels: An Edition of Poetry from Manuscript Sources*, ed. Alastair Bellany and Andrew McRae, Early Modern Literary Studies Text Series 1 (2005), Nvi1, http://purl.oclc.org/emls/texts/libels/; subsequently cited parenthetically by line number.

38   The Scene of Libel

If libelers had their way, James claims, he would be reduced to a mere stage king, his every act scripted by their prating, babbling, and railing. But the king may, or at least should, have seen this coming. In *Basilikon Doron*, written in the final years of Elizabeth's reign, James warns his son that kings "are as it were set ... vpon a publike stage, in the sight of all the people; where all the beholders eyes are attentiuely bent to looke and pry in the least circumstance of their secretest drifts."[24] "You cannot judge what's truely myne," he would write decades later – but in the theater of state, even the "secretest drifts" of kings are subject to the people's judgment.

And, ironically, James's poem appeals to the very judgment that it decries. With its rhymed doggerel and topical satire, the poem looks much like a verse libel itself. Contemporaries evidently picked up on the generic continuity, copying the king's poem in manuscript miscellanies alongside examples of the "railing rymes and vaunting verse" that he attacks. "[B]y responding to the libel in kind," Jane Rickard argues, "James inadvertently helps to legitimise manuscript verse as a forum for political commentary and invites further response."[25] That response was not slow in coming. One answer poem preserved in several copies rejects the king's premise that the people's complaints are vain and infantile. "Contemne not Gracious King our plaints and teares," the anonymous libel begins, "Wee are no babes the tymes us witnesse beares."[26] This is a remarkably explicit defense of the judgment of the people (or at least of the political observers among them). Whatever his intent, James found himself in dialogue with the libelous commentary that his poem purported to silence. He may not have wanted the libelers to talk back, but it comes as no surprise that they did.

The fate of James's poem suggests how libels could sustain conversations between rulers and ruled – if conversations that were uneven, anonymous, and more than a little vituperative. Clearly the king did not care to hear what the libelers had to say. At least in private, however, England's rulers

[24] James VI and I, *Basilicon Doron*, in *King James VI and I: Political Writings*, ed. Johann P. Sommerville (Cambridge: Cambridge University Press, 1994), 4.
[25] Jane Rickard, *Writing the Monarch in Jacobean England: Jonson, Donne, Shakespeare and the Works of King James* (Cambridge: Cambridge University Press, 2015), 118. See also Kevin Sharpe, "The King's Writ: Royal Authors and Royal Authority in Early Modern England," in *Culture and Politics in Early Stuart England*, ed. Sharpe and Peter Lake (Stanford: Stanford University Press, 1993), 130; Curtis Perry, "'If Proclamations Will Not Serve': The Late Manuscript Poetry of James I and the Culture of Libel," in *Royal Subjects: Essays on the Writings of James VI and I*, ed. Daniel Fischlin and Mark Fortier (Detroit: Wayne State University Press, 2002), 217; and McRae, *Literature*, 34.
[26] "Contemne not Gracious king our plaints and teares," in *Early Stuart Libels*, ed. Bellany and McRae, Nvi2, ll. 1–2.

How to Read a Libel in Early Modern England 39

were not always so hostile to personal criticism. Evidence of this appears in a libel that made its way into the hands of Robert Cecil, Earl of Salisbury and the king's principal secretary, likely toward the end of 1610. The anonymous manuscript was a scathing response to the recent collapse of Cecil's negotiations with parliament for raising royal revenues.[27] It lambasts those evil counselors "who doeth studye noething but insatiable glory and power to themselues" and, in a gibe at Cecil's short stature, laments that the king's "greatest offices [are] placed in one litle person." While professing loyalty to the king, the libeler issues a naked threat to resist any unjustified impositions: "I must confess wee are soe vnwillinge to parte with the least parte of our fortunes vnder collor of his highnes vse, to fill the purses of such abusers both of Kynge and Contrey that wee will first parte with our Liues … [I]f any rebellion euer shall happen theyre insolent actions wilbe the Cause." Cecil evidently read this libel with care. Someone, perhaps Cecil himself, underlined the most seditious lines, including the mockery of his "litle person" and the threat of rebellion. Most revealing is the single marginal note, in Cecil's hand. Next to a sentence blaming him for the breakdown of negotiations, he wrote, "This is part of my fawlt."[28] This private admission of guilt shows Robert Cecil, probably the most powerful person in England next to King James, taking seriously an anonymous ad hominem criticism of royal policy.

Discreet Friends

To be sure, any dialogue between Cecil and his critics takes place only in the margins of the manuscript. Reading the libel remains a largely private activity, confined to the councilor's chambers. The same held true for readers outside of the government too. When Joseph Mead of Cambridge sent a verse libel to his friend Sir Martin Stuteville in 1627, he cautioned, "I know you will not think it fitt to be showen, though I send it you. If you do, at your owne perill. Ile deny it: if it prove naught." Even as he warns his friend against sharing the text, however, Mead marks himself as the nexus

---

[27] On the failed negotiations for the so-called Great Contract between king and parliament, see Theodore K. Rabb, *Jacobean Gentleman: Sir Edwin Sandys, 1561–1629* (Princeton: Princeton University Press, 1998), 140–73. Cecil was a popular target for libelers before and after his death: see Pauline Croft, "The Reputation of Robert Cecil: Libels, Political Opinion and Popular Awareness in the Early Seventeenth Century," *Transactions of the Royal Historical Society* 1 (1991): 43–69; and James Knowles, *Politics and Political Culture in the Court Masque* (Basingstoke, UK: Palgrave Macmillan, 2015), 29–41.

[28] CP 140/121. See also CP 128/78.

40   The Scene of Libel

of an epistolary network. "[I]t came from London in the same manner I send it you," he informs Stuteville.[29] And though he presumes his addressee will have the discretion to keep the poem private, Mead is prepared to deny any responsibility if Stuteville does dare to share it. Libels and news regularly spread through this kind of social contact: letters to friends, table talk, and other semi-private exchanges.[30] But Mead's caution suggests just how porous the boundaries of those social networks could be.

A libel held at the Folger Shakespeare Library, shelfmark X.d.634, evokes that porousness with unusual clarity. The manuscript is a single leaf containing an early Stuart verse libel on Elizabethan corruption followed by two notes in the same hand describing its circulation. Under the title "The state of the lande as it was in the latter end of our Late Quenes gouernement," the poem begins,

> The Lordes craved all
> The Quene gave all
> The parlament passed all
> The Keper sealed all.

The targets include not only the queen, her lords, and parliament but also ladies of honor, unscrupulous judges, and the "crafty intelligencer." "And except your majestie mend all," the poem concludes, "without the mercy of god the devell will have all."[31]

This libel began its life in French with a very different topic: the "great broyles" racking late sixteenth-century France. The original version was translated into English around 1585 and spread through scribal circles.[32] Sometime after Elizabeth's death in 1603, libelers repurposed the epistrophic structure – each short line ending with "all" – to comment on the domestic situation. The poem's satire of the French king, the Queen Mother, the Guises, and other alleged malefactors morphed into an equally

---

[29] Mead to Stuteville, January 13, 1627, in "A Critical Edition of the Letters of the Reverend Joseph Mead, 1626–1627, Contained in British Library Harleian MS 390," ed. David Anthony John Cockburn, unpublished PhD thesis, University of Cambridge (1994), 615. See McRae, *Literature*, 36–37.

[30] Alastair Bellany, *The Politics of Court Scandal in Early Modern England: News Culture and the Overbury Affair, 1603–1660* (Cambridge: Cambridge University Press, 2002), 85–111; Adam Fox, "Rumour, News and Popular Political Opinion in Elizabethan and Early Stuart England," *Historical Journal* 40.3 (1997): 597–620; James Daybell, "The Scribal Circulation of Early Modern Letters," *Huntington Library Quarterly* 79.3 (2016): 365–85.

[31] Folger Shakespeare Library, MS X.d.634.

[32] "The Lords do now Crave all, *c.* 1585," in *Verse Libel in Renaissance England and Scotland*, ed. Steven W. May and Alan Bryson (Oxford: Oxford University Press, 2016), 111, l. 4.

How to Read a Libel in Early Modern England 41

blunt criticism of the Elizabethan court. The Stuart rendition also added a final appeal to the new king, "*your majestie*," to save the state from perdition.

This petitionary stance was typical of the early modern libel. In fact, David Colclough goes so far as to argue that "[r]ather than being primarily attacks on persons, libels acted as an unofficial means of counsel."[33] Colclough rightly draws attention to the political sophistication of many libels. But his effort to separate the personal from the political seems to me anachronistic.[34] To attack public persons was to give counsel, if of an unwanted and seditious sort. Sir Edward Coke makes just this point in his 1605 report *De libellis famosis*. He argues that libels against magistrates are especially damaging, "for what greater scandal of government can there be than to have corrupt or wicked magistrates to be appointed and constituted by the King to govern his subjects under him?" Even if the target has died, Coke adds, the libeler still "traduces and slanders the state and government, which dies not."[35] For Coke, attacks on individual magistrates are inseparable from criticism of the state itself. This is certainly the case for the poem in X.d.634. From its very title – "The state of the lande as it was in the latter end of *our* Late Quenes gou*er*nement" – the libel purports to anatomize a government riddled with corruption.

According to the first of the two notes following the poem, the libel's seditious counsel was delivered directly to its addressee: the king himself. The note reads, "as is reported lett fall to the Kinge in the cocke pitt."[36] Steven W. May and Alan Bryson conclude from the handwriting that this "Kinge" is either James or Charles, and they suggest that the "cocke pitt" is not the London playhouse of that name (which neither king is known to have attended) but instead "the Cockpit-in-Court at Whitehall Palace, which housed government offices."[37] Given the libel's petition for a post-Elizabethan purge, I think that the king in question is far more likely to be James than Charles. And while the cockpit could refer to a cluster of royal properties at Whitehall, there was among those structures an actual cockpit that gave them their name.[38] This royal cockpit hosted not only cockfighting (of which James was a fan) but also other types of shows, including, by

---

[33] Colclough, *Freedom*, 205.

[34] See McRae, *Literature*, 51–52; and Debora Shuger, *Censorship and Cultural Sensibility: The Regulation of Language in Tudor-Stuart England* (Philadelphia: University of Pennsylvania Press, 2006), 67–68.

[35] 5 Co. Rep. 125a.   [36] Folger MS X.d.634.   [37] May and Bryson, *Verse Libel*, 114.

[38] See Frances Teague, "The Phoenix and the Cockpit-in-Court Playhouses," in *The Oxford Handbook of Early Modern Theatre*, ed. Richard Dutton (Oxford: Oxford University Press, 2009), 242.

The Scene of Libel

1607 and perhaps earlier, plays.[39] Any kind of spectacle would have provided a suitable distraction for an anonymous troublemaker to "lett fall to the Kinge" a scrap of seditious verse.

Whatever the libel's origins, the copyist of X.d.634 was just as worried as Mead that the text would circulate too widely. Yet also like Mead, this scribe shared the poem nonetheless. Below the libel and the note on its royal delivery, the copyist wrote to the manuscript's recipient, "Sir I pray you lett not this or the other be shewed but to discrete frendes for that it is not knowne by whome they wer made or howe they will bee taken."[40] Such caution is unsurprising. For Coke, "it is great evidence that he published it, when he, knowing it to be a libel, writes a copy of it" – let alone when the copyist shares the libel with a friend or acquaintance.[41] In one Star Chamber case, "the Cheife publishers & delyuerers of Copies" of a libel were sentenced to be fined, imprisoned, whipped, and pilloried. "[I]t seemethe to be a perylouse thinge to keepe a lybelle," the court warned, "especiallye yf it touche the state."[42] Reading libels could be a risky business.

But libels still circulated widely. The transmission of "The state of the lande," from a scrap of writing reportedly "lett fall to the Kinge in the cocke pitt" to a scribal copy shared among "discrete frendes," is entirely typical. Contemporary accounts suggest that libels pervaded the city of London: they turned up everywhere, from the steps of the Royal Exchange to the boards of Old Fish Street to the gates of St. Paul's Cathedral to the pulpit of the royal chapel.[43] Through word of mouth and written copies, they spread through variously public networks of readers and listeners.[44] Because the

---

[39] Glynne Wickham, *Early English Stages, 1300 to 1660,* vol. 2, *1576 to 1660,* pt. 2 (London: Routledge and Kegan Paul, 1972), 79–80.

[40] Folger MS X.d.634. "The other" libel referred to here has apparently not survived.

[41] *John Lamb's Case* (1610), 9 Co. Rep. 59b. See also *De libellis famosis* (1605), 5 Co. Rep. 125b, where Coke describes one of the two means of publishing a written libel: "*Traditione,* when the libel or any copy of it is delivered over to scandalize the party."

[42] John Hawarde, *Les Reportes del Cases in Camera Stellata, 1593 to 1609,* ed. William Paley Baildon (London, 1894), 373. See McRae, *Literature,* 36–37.

[43] CP 181/127, 180/21; *The Works of the Most Reverend Father in God, William Laud,* ed. William Scott and James Bliss, 7 vols. (Oxford, 1847–60), 3:229; Mead to Stuteville, January 18, 1623, in *Court and Times,* 2:355. On these and other libels found in the city, see Pauline Croft, "Libels, Popular Literacy and Public Opinion in Early Modern England," *Historical Research* 68 (1995): 266–85; and Andrew Gordon, "The Act of Libel: Conscripting Civic Space in Early Modern England," *Journal of Medieval and Early Modern Studies* 32.2 (2002): 375–97.

[44] See Love, *Scribal Publication,* 82–83; James Knowles, "To 'scourge the arse / Jove's marrow so had wasted': Scurrility and the Subversion of Sodomy," in *Subversion and Scurrility: Popular Discourse in Europe from 1500 to the Present,* ed. Dermot Cavanagh and Tim Kirk (Aldershot, UK: Ashgate, 2000), 79–80; and Bellany, *Politics,* 107–11.

How to Read a Libel in Early Modern England 43

identities of both the copyist and the recipient of X.d.634 remain unknown, we cannot fully reconstruct its trajectory. Yet the warning that the libel should be shown only to "discrete frendes" is highly suggestive. While the copyist wanted the libel to stay within a limited social network, the cautionary note betrays a measure of anxiety that it might end up in the hands of decidedly indiscreet readers. Neither the authorities nor even their disseminators could control the circulation of libels. All that it took for a libel to spread from a private community of discreet friends to a heterogeneous public was an indiscreet acquaintance, or an errant copy, or a fresh rumor.

Libeling Leicester

Such a moment of apparent indiscretion transpires at the end of the anonymous pamphlet known as *Leicester's Commonwealth*. The book, printed in 1584 under the title *The Copy of a Letter Written by a Master of Art of Cambridge to his Friend in London*, consists of a fictional – and highly scurrilous – conversation between the scholar who supposedly wrote the letter, a gentleman, and a lawyer about Elizabeth's favorite, Robert Dudley, Earl of Leicester. As their discussion wraps up, the lawyer is particularly anxious to keep their defamatory gossip private. "[I]f ever I hear at other hands of these matters hereafter," he confesses, "I shall surely be quake-britch and think every bush a thief."[45] Actual readers and sharers of libels, from the X.d.634 scribe to Joseph Mead, expressed a similar fear that the texts they transcribed would escape their control. At least in *Leicester's Commonwealth*, this fear at first seems justified. The three men go to dine in a larger company, where "a gentleman or two began again to speak of my Lord [of Leicester], and that so conformable to some of our former speech (as indeed it is the common talk at tables everywhere) that the old lawyer began to shrink and be appalled, and to cast dry looks upon the gentleman our friend, doubting lest something had been discovered of our conference" (195). The lawyer's paranoia reflects the real perils that could attend seditious speech.

Yet the final sentence of *Leicester's Commonwealth* reveals that the lawyer's fear of the gentleman's indiscretion was unfounded: "But indeed, it was not so" (195). It turns out that the rumors about Leicester have

---

[45] D. C. Peck, ed., *Leicester's Commonwealth: The Copy of a Letter Written by a Master of Art of Cambridge (1584) and Related Documents* (Athens: Ohio University Press, 1985), 195; hereafter cited parenthetically in the text.

44 The Scene of Libel

simply grown so pervasive as to have become a staple of dinner-table talk. This conclusion might tend to reassure any readers who turned a little quakebritch themselves at the pamphlet's seditious conversation. But it also normalizes that defamatory discourse. Far from remaining at the Catholic fringe, the gossip about Leicester is "the common talk at tables everywhere." Libeling Leicester brings together a virtual association of strangers talking about matters of public concern.

But this vision of a spontaneous anti-Leicestrian public obscures the designs of the tract itself. Although no author has ever been conclusively identified, scholars largely agree that the pamphlet emerged from a circle of English Catholic exiles based in France.[46] Dwight C. Peck attributes to the authors three primary aims: to attack Leicester; to defend Mary, Queen of Scots, and the Stuart claim to the throne; and to assuage religious strife, above all for persecuted Catholics.[47] Unsurprisingly, the book is tonally incongruous. Meticulous consideration of the succession and high-minded pleas for toleration appear alongside a host of insinuations, allegations, and outright fabrications marshaled against the Earl of Leicester. From one perspective – which may well have been shared by the authors themselves – this all amounts to a loyalist effort to save England and Elizabeth from the supposedly Machiavellian Leicester. For the regime, however, the result was a treatise brimming with "slaunderous and hatefull matter."[48] There is some truth on both sides. Many of the allegations against Leicester are slanderous and hateful, not to mention false. Yet Leicester did patronize Puritan and anti-Catholic campaigns, and the persecution Catholics suffered at the hands of the state was all too real.[49]

My interest here is less in the confessional politics of the moment – recently explicated with admirable clarity by Peter Lake[50] – than in the book's discursive strategies. Its dialogic framing devices have received little attention. Yet I believe that these metafictional moments are central to the tract's

---

[46] For varying views, see Peter Holmes, "The Authorship of 'Leicester's Commonwealth,'" *Journal of Ecclesiastical History* 33.3 (1982): 424–30; Peck, introduction to *Leicester's Commonwealth*, 25–32; and Victor Houliston, "Persons' Displeasure: Collaboration and Design in *Leicester's Commonwealth*," in *Publishing Subversive Texts in Elizabethan England and the Polish-Lithuanian Commonwealth*, ed. Teresa Bela, Clarinda Calma, and Jolanta Rzegocka (Leiden: Brill, 2016), 155–66.

[47] Peck, introduction to *Leicester's Commonwealth*, 4.

[48] TNA, SP 12/179, fol. 92r. For a modernized transcription of this document, see Peck, *Leicester's Commonwealth*, 283–84.

[49] Eleanor Rosenberg, *Leicester, Patron of Letters* (New York: Columbia University Press, 1955), 184–277; Geoffrey F. Nuttall, "The English Martyrs 1535–1680: A Statistical Review," *Journal of Ecclesiastical History* 22.3 (1971): 191–97.

[50] Peter Lake, *Bad Queen Bess? Libels, Secret Histories, and the Politics of Publicity in the Reign of Queen Elizabeth I* (Oxford: Oxford University Press, 2016), 97–152.

How to Read a Libel in Early Modern England

purpose. As its characters read, share, and discuss libels, we see the authors trying self-consciously to cultivate an anti-Leicestrian public.[51] *Leicester's Commonwealth* is an especially important case because it found such a wide audience. After its 1584 printing (likely in Rouen, after which copies were smuggled into England), the book was not printed again until 1641.[52] However, over ninety full or partial manuscript copies survive, making the libel, in H. R. Woudhuysen's words, "one of the most widely circulated prose tracts of the late sixteenth and early seventeenth centuries."[53] *Leicester's Commonwealth* prophetically represents the very circuits of communication that would bring it to a mass readership.

Through its epistolary frame, the tract pretends to let readers eavesdrop on a private conversation among friends. The title page announces it as *The Copy of a Letter Written by a Master of Art of Cambridge to his friend in London, concerning some talk passed of late between two worshipful and grave men about the present state and some proceedings of the Earl of Leicester and his friends in England*. The main personae are all fabricated, of course. But even if most readers saw through the fiction, it nonetheless lends a certain verisimilitude to the conversation. The pamphlet suggests that this was the kind of talk that might well pass in private between subjects concerned about the future of their country. In the "Epistle Directory" addressed to a certain "Mr. G. M. in Gracious Street in London," the Cambridge scholar emphasizes the secrecy of their proceedings. It is only with the "assurance of secrecy" that the gentleman and lawyer have agreed to have their dialogue published, and only then "with this PROVISO, that they will know nothing nor yet yield consent to the publishing hereof" (64). This was Mead's proviso too in his letter to Stuteville: "If you do, at your owne perill. Ile deny it." Printed and (as the title page proclaims) "made common to many," *Leicester's Commonwealth* purports to bring the English public into a covert, anonymous network of libelers and libel readers (63).

After the epistle directory, the scholar begins by setting the scene. "Not long before the last Christmas," he received an invitation to spend the holiday at the house of "a very worshipful and grave gentleman," the father

---

[51] Jacqueline Vanhoutte has recently sketched the contours of this public from a different angle, focusing on Shakespeare's theater and the trope of the aging lover: see *Age in Love: Shakespeare and the Elizabethan Court* (Lincoln: University of Nebraska Press, 2019).

[52] See Peck, introduction to *Leicester's Commonwealth*, 5–13.

[53] Woudhuysen, *Sir Philip Sidney*, 149. The count of extant manuscript copies comes from Peter Beal, *Catalogue of English Literary Manuscripts 1450–1700*, www.celm-ms.org.uk/introductions/AnonLei cestersCommonwealth.html.

46   The Scene of Libel

of one of his pupils (65). There, the gentleman and the scholar (both Protestants) are joined by an old lawyer, who is a moderate Catholic and the gentleman's trusted confidant. As the three men retire for an after-dinner chat,

> this lawyer by chance had in his hand a little book then newly set forth, containing *A Defense of the Public Justice Done of Late in England upon Divers Priests and Other Papists for Treason*, which book the lawyer had read to himself a little before and was now putting it up into his pocket. But the gentleman my friend, who had read over the same once or twice in my company before, would needs take the same into his hand again and asked the lawyer his judgment upon the book. (66)

The "little book" that the lawyer – supposedly "by chance" – has in his hand is William Cecil's *Execution of Justice in England* (1583), a defense of the recent executions of Catholic priests.[54] All three of the interlocutors have read this book, whether alone ("read to himself") or together ("read . . . in my company"). When the lawyer makes a show of "putting it up into his pocket," the gentleman eagerly solicits "his judgment upon the book." It is this question that launches the meandering, defamatory dialogue of *Leicester's Commonwealth*. The catalyst for the conversation is a scene of communal reading.

At least for some, the text at the center of that community was itself a libel. In his *Defence of English Catholiques* (1584), William Allen argues that *The Execution of Justice* has all the marks of "an infamous Libel": anonymity ("passing forth without priuilege and name ether of writer or printer"), meddling in matters of state ("mouing indiscret, odious, and dangerous disputes of estate"), and defamatory lies ("manifest vntruthes, open slaunders of innocent persons").[55] In the Introduction, I examined similar accusations of libel leveled by all sides in post-Reformation controversy. The difference between Catholic and Anglican polemic, of course, was that the latter in many cases had the backing of the government. But Allen turns this fact to his advantage. He acknowledges that the unrestrained publication of Cecil's *Execution* at home and abroad means that it is "like to proceed (though in close sort) from authoritie." Yet the imprint of authority does not make the book any less libelous. Rulers "haue a thousand pretences, excuses, and coulors, of their iniust actions," he explains, and "they may print or publish what they like, suppresse what

---

[54] William Cecil, *The Execution of Iustice in England for maintenaunce of publique and Christian peace* (London, 1583).

[55] William Allen, *A True Sincere and Modest Defence of English Catholiques* ([Rouen, 1584]), sig. *2r.

How to Read a Libel in Early Modern England 47

they list."[56] Allen's skepticism of state propaganda is certainly slanted by his own polemical stance. Yet Lake has shown that he was more or less right. The Elizabethan government indeed practiced the same anonymous, defamatory publicity tactics that it condemned.[57]

If far more subtly, *Leicester's Commonwealth* offers a similar assessment of Cecil's *Execution of Justice*. The tract calls it "a little book," a meaning of libel (from the Latin *libellus*) still current in the sixteenth century. But the defamatory sense was surely the more pertinent one amid the vituperative religious polemic of 1584. While the Catholic polemicists labeled Cecil's *Execution* a libel, the publication of their pamphlets prompted a royal proclamation in October against "false, slanderous, wicked, seditious, and traitorous books and libels."[58] Cecil's book may have looked like a libel, especially to persecuted Catholics. But *Leicester's Commonwealth* equally fits the criteria for libel laid out by Allen (anonymity; disputing matters of state; lies and slanders). Indeed, the Catholic pamphlet is itself a little book, printed as it was in octavo format. The tract's initial scene of reading, then, is self-reflexive. Even as *Leicester's Commonwealth* suggests that Cecil's *Execution* is a libel, it presents itself too as a small book easily stowed in a pocket to be brought out among sympathetic friends.

As I noted above, the appearance of the little book in *Leicester's Commonwealth* sparks the conversation that takes up the rest of the pamphlet. That conversation begins with an appeal to readerly judgment. When the gentleman asks the lawyer "his judgment upon the book," the lawyer immediately starts to interrogate Cecil's account of Catholic "treason" (66). He maintains that "hot Puritans" no less than "busy Papists ... may be called all traitors" (67). Before long, the scholar too is wondering whether most Catholics are guilty of so grave a crime. Even if "the most part of Papists in general might be said to deal against the state of England," he concedes, "yet (perhaps) not so far forth nor in so deep a degree of proper treason as in this book is presumed or enforced" (70). Just as the men turn to the subject of the recently executed priests, the gentleman pauses and appears to defer to the orthodox line: "howsoever this be, which indeed appertaineth not to us to judge or discuss, but rather to persuade ourselves that the state hath reason to do as it doth" (70). Far from ceding judgment to the state, however, the gentleman continues by offering his own opinion. "[Y]et for my own part," he says, "I must confess unto you that upon some considerations which use to come unto my mind, I take no small grief of these differences among us

---

[56] Ibid., sigs. *2r, *4r.   [57] Lake, *Bad Queen Bess*, 136.   [58] *TRP*, 2:506.

48 The Scene of Libel

(which you term of divers and different religions), for which we are driven of necessity to use discipline towards divers who possibly otherwise would be no great malefactors" (71). He bemoans the confessional divisions that force the state to turn religious dissidents into political criminals. The gentleman's posture of deference is short-lived indeed.

This skeptical discussion of state violence and confessional politics soon turns to the man allegedly responsible for all England's ills: the Earl of Leicester. By the end of the dialogue, he has been found guilty of a stunning array of crimes: "more theft oftentimes in one day than all the waykeepers, cutpurses, cozeners, pirates, burglars, or other of that art in a whole year within the realm"; "more blood lying upon his head . . . than ever had private man in our country before"; "intolerable licentiousness in all filthy kind and manner of carnality, with all sort of wives, friends, and kinswomen"; "treasons, treacheries, and conspiracies about the crown"; "rapes and most violent extortions upon the poor"; and a good deal more (191). The gentleman, who has just rehearsed all these accusations, wants to bring them against Leicester at trial. He declares, "[I]f, I say, we should lay together all these enormities before her Majesty, and thousands more in particular which might and would be gathered if his day of trial were but in hope to be granted, I do not see in equity and reason how her Highness . . . could deny her subjects this most lawful request" (191–92). *Leicester's Commonwealth* similarly claims to lay bare Leicester's "enormities" for the good of queen and country.

The call for a trial is especially telling. As I explained in the Introduction, the early moderns consistently defined the libel in terms of its extrajudicial accusations. The danger of libels was that they put their victims on trial not in the courts of law but in the court of public opinion. Yet for libelers and, at least in one letter, for John Donne, that was also their promise. Reflecting on the "multitude of libells" unleashed upon the death of Robert Cecil in 1612, Donne posits that, while it is "unexcusable" to libel the dead, "there may be cases, where one may do his Countrey good service, by libelling against a live man. For, where a man is either too great, or his Vices too generall, to be brought under a judiciary accusation, there is no way, but this extraordinary accusing, which we call Libelling."[59] Donne frankly acknowledges the limits of the legal system. When the offender is too powerful or his vices "too generall" (perhaps shared even by those who would be doing the judging), libeling offers an "extraordinary" path to civic justice.

---

[59] John Donne, *Letters to Severall Persons of Honour* (London, 1651), sigs. N1r, N1v–N2r.

How to Read a Libel in Early Modern England   49

This is certainly the case in the world imagined by *Leicester's Commonwealth.* "But what would you have her Majesty to do?" the scholar asks in response to the gentleman's catalogue of Leicester's crimes (192). As he points out, the gentleman has shown the earl to be "a great man, strongly furnished and fortified for all events" (192). In Donne's terms, the earl is far "too great . . . to be brought under a judiciary accusation." The Catholic polemicists behind the pamphlet, if not its characters, have no reason to expect that Leicester will get his day in court anytime soon. The recourse that remains is what Donne calls "extraordinary accusing": to bring Leicester's alleged crimes before the reading public. Early in the dialogue, the gentleman urges "that this man's actions might be called publicly to trial, and liberty given to good subjects to say what they knew against the same" (75). *Leicester's Commonwealth* is just such a public reckoning of the earl's supposed sins. Defaming Leicester promises to bring together readers, "good subjects" or otherwise, in a national discussion about matters of state.

If they were not already, then, the pamphlet aims to make the libels against Leicester "common talk at tables everywhere" (195). No longer confined to the gentleman's gallery, the defamatory talk circulates through an indiscriminate public. At times, the subject matter even comes surprisingly close to the Habermasian paradigm of "rational-critical" discourse.[60] Of course, vitriol flows freely. The characters never run out of vituperative epithets for Leicester ("insolent, cruel, vindicative, expert, potent, subtile, fine, and fox-like," runs one representative list [75]). Yet within the pamphlet's fiction, demonizing Leicester is what makes possible a cross-confessional conversation. Leicester, described as an enemy to Puritans, Protestants, and Papists alike, becomes the only thing standing in the way of that "qualification, tolerance, and moderation in our realm" which would quell sectarian strife (185). In this "politique" worldview, the real problem is not religious difference but the sway of evil counselors and tyrannical favorites.[61] The language of libel provides a common idiom for political critique in a mixed-faith society.[62]

---

[60] Jürgen Habermas, *The Structural Transformation of the Public Sphere: An Inquiry into a Category of Bourgeois Society*, trans. Thomas Burger with Frederick Lawrence (Cambridge, MA: MIT Press, 1989), 28.

[61] On this "politique" view, see Peck, introduction to *Leicester's Commonwealth*, 36; and Lake, *Bad Queen Bess*, 129–32.

[62] For a parallel argument about the London theater itself, see Musa Gurnis, *Mixed Faith and Shared Feeling: Theater in Post-Reformation London* (Philadelphia: University of Pennsylvania Press, 2018).

The Scene of Libel

But this utopian vision is only one side of the early modern libel. If *Leicester's Commonwealth* advocates free conversation and religious toleration, it also fits the mold anatomized by Bacon in his *Aduertisement touching seditious writing*:

> pretendinge in goodly & entycing manner Relligion, defence of Innocency, and protestacion of troth, and bearinge before them deceiueable titles, and feyned occasions of their sendinge forthe; but indeede making evident digressions and excursions into matters of state, Debatinge titles, and Iurisdictions, . . . & euery way presuming to moue question of the proceedinges both abroade and at home, aswell in the Churche as in the civill estate; and not onely soe but farther entringe into vndutyfull & dispitefull defamacion of their superiors, depravinge their accions publike and private, and contriving and Imagenyng odious brutes, and vntrewthes against them.[63]

Leicester's Commonwealth makes a show of religious moderation and of defending the innocent. Its epistolary frame is indeed feigned. Its entire substance digresses into matters of state, and it examines the title to the throne at length. It sharply questions the proceedings of Church and state. And, of course, it is packed with "odious brutes, and vntrewthes" against Leicester. To try to separate the "excursions into matters of state" from the slander and lies is fruitless if not anachronistic. Defamation and critical conversation go hand in hand.

This is true not only of the libel's fictional dialogue but also of the anti-Leicestrian public that quickly took shape around it. Beyond the sheer number of extant manuscripts, evidence of the tract's influence abounds. It circulated at court, at the universities, and in the Tower, and it was sold by at least one member of the Stationers' Company.[64] It spawned several spin-offs and sequels, including a French addition, a pornographic narrative of the earl's descent into hell, a ghostly complaint in the style of the *Mirror for Magistrates*, and a "Letter of Estate" imitating its epistolary frame.[65] Its scandalous anecdotes filtered onto the public stage, inspiring scenes of court corruption in Thomas Kyd's *The Spanish Tragedy* and John Webster's *The White Devil*, and perhaps even informing the dramatic

---

[63] Bacon, *Aduertisement touching seditious writing*, 309–10.

[64] Peck, introduction to *Leicester's Commonwealth*, 8; Woudhuysen, *Sir Philip Sidney*, 148–49; Joseph Mansky, "The Case of Eleazar Edgar: *Leicester's Commonwealth* and the Book Trade in 1604," *Papers of the Bibliographical Society of America* 115.2 (2021): 233–41.

[65] Peck, *Leicester's Commonwealth*, 228–48; Peck, "'News from Heaven and Hell': A Defamatory Narrative of the Earl of Leicester," *English Literary Renaissance* 8.2 (1978): 141–58; Thomas Rogers, *Leicester's Ghost*, ed. Franklin B. Williams, Jr. (Chicago: University of Chicago Press, 1972); Peck, "'The Letter of Estate': An Elizabethan Libel," *Notes and Queries* 28.1 (1981): 21–35.

How to Read a Libel in Early Modern England   51

vogue for lecherous old courtiers, Shakespeare's Falstaff above all.[66] For its readers, the pamphlet's truth or falsity was almost incidental to the stories it purveyed and the lessons it taught. In the words of one poem inscribed on a copy of the text, "Truths or untruths, whats'ere they be / Which here you read, yet not in vain."[67] Read in vain they did not. *Leicester's Commonwealth* provided its readers with a rich set of representational resources for imagining the late Elizabethan court.

There would not be another such flood of libels around a single figure until the fall of the Earl of Essex in the late 1590s, roughly a decade after Leicester's death. Each man exercised in his time nearly unmatched cultural and political sway. Leicester and Essex shared too a proclivity for what Lake calls "the dark arts of popularity," courting public audiences to promote themselves and their interests.[68] But their proto-celebrity also made them especially vulnerable to criticism. Whether motivated by enmity or enterprise, less-than-flattering talk about Leicester and Essex circulated widely in print, manuscript, and performance. These courtiers cultivated a new media landscape that ultimately eluded their control.

Leicester's Commonwealth and its reception history illustrate this process more clearly than perhaps any other text. Life soon imitated art: the anti-Leicestrian discourse spread just as widely as the tract had imagined. As early as February 1585, Sylvanus Scory testified that the book had already become the common table talk that it purports to be in the dialogue's closing scene. Scory, the profligate son of the Bishop of Hereford and a crypto-Catholic affiliated with Leicester, maintained in an examination that he had never seen *Leicester's Commonwealth* but had "herd moch talke of yt." Pressed for details, he claimed that "he can name none specially, but hath herd yt comenly at tables."[69] *Leicester's Commonwealth* may have failed in its specific pro-Catholic aims, but its long, multimedia career suggests that it was eminently successful in catalyzing a cross-confessional public organized by scurrilous political satire.

---

[66] Curtis Perry, *Literature and Favoritism in Early Modern England* (Cambridge: Cambridge University Press, 2006), 34–36; Vanhoutte, *Age in Love*.

[67] Peck, *Leicester's Commonwealth*, 294.

[68] Peter Lake, *How Shakespeare Put Politics on the Stage: Power and Succession in the History Plays* (New Haven: Yale University Press, 2016), 286. See Vanhoutte, *Age in Love*; Paul Hammer, "The Smiling Crocodile: The Earl of Essex and Late Elizabethan 'Popularity,'" in *Politics of the Public Sphere*, ed. Lake and Pincus, 95–115; and Jeffrey S. Doty, *Shakespeare, Popularity and the Public Sphere* (Cambridge: Cambridge University Press, 2017).

[69] TNA, SP 12/176, fol. 172r. On Scory, see Peck, *Leicester's Commonwealth*, 245–46 n9; and Simon Adams, *Leicester and the Court: Essays on Elizabethan Politics* (Manchester: Manchester University Press, 2002), 190.

52 The Scene of Libel

Brutus the Reader

The final scene of reading that I want to examine is at once the most private and the most public. Alone in his orchard but certainly not alone in the playhouse, Shakespeare's Brutus in *Julius Caesar* struggles to "piece ... out" an anonymous letter found in the window of his "closet" (2.1.51, 35).[70] For Brutus, interpreting this letter (clearly marked as a libel, as I'll explain shortly) is an eminently private task.[71] No friends, discreet or otherwise, are anywhere nearby. The site of the letter's discovery underscores his solitude: the closet was "the most private, inward room of the early modern house."[72] When Brutus reads the letter and takes it to be a "petition" from the Roman people (2.1.58), it is up to him alone to decide a matter of the greatest public interest: what to do about Julius Caesar.

In the theater – a venue for public judgment – Shakespeare stages a scene of private judgment. And, as many scholars have shown, there are plenty of reasons to be skeptical of Brutus' judgment. Before receiving the anonymous letter, he explains his decision to join the conspiracy in a soliloquy that critics have long found unconvincing.[73] "It must be by his death," Brutus begins, starting with what we might expect to come at the end (2.1.10). His reasoning in the rest of the speech is equally muddled. Self-defeating concessions punctuate the soliloquy: "I know no personal cause to spurn at him"; "I have not known when his affections swayed / More than his reason"; "the quarrel / Will bear no colour for the thing he is" (2.1.11, 20–21, 28–29). At the outset, Brutus denies any "personal" animus against Caesar and appeals instead to "the general" interest (2.1.12). But "the general" rests on shaky grounds. Brutus marshals commonplaces – "It is the bright day that brings forth the adder"; "lowliness is young ambition's ladder" (2.1.14, 22) – to explain why crowning Caesar would make him dangerous. Yet he admits that he has no evidence that Caesar would prove tyrannical, that

---

[70] All quotations of the play are from Shakespeare, *Julius Caesar*, ed. David Daniell (Walton-on-Thames: Thomas Nelson, 1998), cited parenthetically in the text.

[71] Several recent scholars have likewise taken the letter to be a libel: see Alan Stewart, *Shakespeare's Letters* (Oxford: Oxford University Press, 2008), 86–87; David Colclough, "Talking to the Animals: Persuasion, Counsel and their Discontents in *Julius Caesar*," in *Shakespeare and Early Modern Political Thought*, ed. David Armitage, Conal Condren, and Andrew Fitzmaurice (Cambridge: Cambridge University Press, 2009), 225–27; James Loxley and Mark Robson, *Shakespeare, Jonson, and the Claims of the Performative* (New York: Routledge, 2013), 57–60; and Lake, *How Shakespeare*, 468.

[72] Stewart, *Shakespeare's Letters*, 86.

[73] See, e.g., Ronald Knowles, *Shakespeare's Arguments with History* (Basingstoke, UK: Palgrave, 2002), 104–7; Andrew Hadfield, *Shakespeare and Republicanism* (Cambridge: Cambridge University Press, 2005), 179–81; Warren Chernaik, *The Myth of Rome in Shakespeare and His Contemporaries* (Cambridge: Cambridge University Press, 2011), 98–99; and Doty, *Shakespeare*, 122.

Caesar's "affections" would overpower his "reason." By the end of the soliloquy, Brutus frankly concedes that Caesar's past and present behavior cannot justify the assassination – "the quarrel / Will bear no colour for the thing he is" – and so the murder can only be explained as a preemptive act, a morally dubious proposition at best. "Fashion it thus," Brutus decides: "that what he is, augmented, / Would run to these and these extremities" (2.1.30–31). As scholars have observed, this political "fashion[ing]" looks less like logical or moral reasoning than the beginnings of a "public relations campaign" or "spin control."[74] Brutus is grasping for a justification with which he might persuade both the people and himself.

It is in this state of mind that Brutus reads the letter thrown in at his window. From just two lines of text, he extracts a clear call to action on behalf of Rome:

> "Brutus, thou sleep'st; awake and see thyself.
> Shall Rome, et cetera. Speak, strike, redress."
> "Brutus, thou sleep'st; awake."
> Such instigations have been often dropped
> Where I have took them up.
> "Shall Rome, et cetera." Thus must I piece it out:
> Shall Rome stand under one man's awe? What Rome?
> My ancestors did from the streets of Rome
> The Tarquin drive, when he was called a king.
> "Speak, strike, redress." Am I entreated
> To speak and strike? O Rome, I make thee promise,
> If the redress will follow, thou receivest
> Thy full petition at the hand of Brutus. (2.1.46–58)

Brutus interprets the letter methodically, clause by clause, yet he makes several crucial (and, we will see, not wholly warranted) assumptions along the way. First, he immediately categorizes it as one of the anonymous "instigations" that he has found throughout the city. In the late 1590s, Londoners likewise encountered scraps of seditious writing dropped in public spaces and stuck to civic surfaces. Libels, like Shakespeare's letter, penetrated private spaces too: in 1601 a servant was making his nighttime rounds when he found a libel "cast into the entrie" of the house.[75] Such scenes of discovery closely resemble the one in *Julius Caesar*, in which Brutus' servant Lucius finds the letter while "[s]earching the window for

---

[74] Anthony B. Dawson, "The Arithmetic of Memory: Shakespeare's Theatre and the National Past," *Shakespeare Survey* 52 (1999): 61; Oliver Arnold, *The Third Citizen: Shakespeare's Theater and the Early Modern House of Commons* (Baltimore: Johns Hopkins University Press, 2007), 155.

[75] CP 77/25, quoted in Gordon, "Act," 388.

54 The Scene of Libel

a flint" late at night (2.1.36). One Elizabethan libel similarly took the form of a letter "without any name and so sealed up and left . . . in a window."[76] The epistolary format was evidently quite common. By the early 1620s, the barrister William Hudson could remark that "for scandalous letters, the precedents are infinite."[77]

The letter is marked as a libel not only by its seditious content and anonymous delivery but also by the protocols of interpretation that Brutus applies. As he unpacks the final string of imperatives – "Speak, strike, redress" – Brutus directs his response to the city of Rome itself. "O Rome, I make thee promise," he declares, "If the redress will follow, thou receivest / Thy full petition at the hand of Brutus." Understanding the letter as a libel explains why Brutus so readily assumes that it is the voice of Rome. Whether they took the form of letters, poems, or petitions, libels often claimed to ventriloquize the popular voice. One Elizabethan libel against corrupt grain hoarders and enclosers was signed, "The Quenes true subiectes the poore," and a libel cast into the choir of a church in Lincolnshire in 1607 excoriated local landlords in the voice of "we yor tenants."[78] This claim to articulate collective grievances meant that the line between libeling and petitioning was often quite tenuous – a fact, as I discuss at length in Chapter 3, of which Shakespeare was very much aware. Brutus takes the libelous letter to be a "petition" from the Roman people, and one that only "the hand of Brutus" can resolve.

As Brutus himself acknowledges, this interpretation of the letter hinges on a critical lacuna in its text. "Shall Rome, et cetera," he reads, determining that he alone "must . . . piece it out" and fill in the "et cetera." In *Julius Caesar*, however, interpretation is always fraught.[79] The play's Cicero provides what critics have called the "emblematic" or "key" statement of this problem when he says, "men may construe things after their fashion /

---

[76] K. J. Kesselring, ed., *Star Chamber Reports: BL Harley MS 2143* (Kew: List and Index Society, 2018), 63.

[77] William Hudson, *A Treatise of the Court of Star Chamber*, in *Collectanea Juridica*, ed. Francis Hargrave, vol. 2 (London, 1792), 101. For reports of libels sent "in the forme and likenes of letters," see James Stokes and Robert J. Alexander, eds., *REED: Somerset, including Bath*, 2 vols. (Toronto: University of Toronto Press, 1996), 1:37; and Rosalind Conklin Hays et al., eds., *REED: Dorset, Cornwall* (Toronto: University of Toronto Press, 1999), 221. On the genre, see Gary Schneider, "Libelous Letters in Elizabethan and Early Stuart England," *Modern Philology* 105.3 (2008): 475–509; and Daybell, "Scribal Circulation," 372–75.

[78] CP 185/129; John Walter, "'The Pooremans Joy and the Gentlemans Plague': A Lincolnshire Libel and the Politics of Sedition in Early Modern England," *Past and Present* 203 (2009): 66.

[79] Many critics have pointed this out: see, e.g., Ian Donaldson, "'Misconstruing Everything': *Julius Caesar* and *Sejanus*," in *Shakespeare Performed: Essays in Honor of R. A. Foakes*, ed. Grace Ioppolo (Newark: University of Delaware Press, 2000), 88–107; Colclough, "Talking to the Animals," 227; and Doty, *Shakespeare*, 98–130.

How to Read a Libel in Early Modern England 55

Clean from the purpose of the things themselves" (1.3.34–35).[80] "Misconstru[ing] everything," as another character later puts it, seems to be the lot of nearly everyone in the play, Brutus included (5.3.84). In fact, we have already learned that the letter comes not from the city of Rome but from Cassius, the chief conspirator. In his only soliloquy in the play, Cassius schemes,

> I will this night
> In several hands in at his windows throw,
> As if they came from several citizens,
> Writings all tending to the great opinion
> That Rome holds of his name – wherein obscurely
> Caesar's ambition shall be glanced at.   (1.2.314–19)

Cassius co-opts the popular politics of libel. His forged letters, purportedly from "several citizens," are just another ploy to get Brutus to join the conspiracy. What Brutus takes to be the voice of Rome is a patrician construction rather than a plebeian reality.

As Brutus pieces out the forged libel, he too is complicit in the eclipse of the popular voice.[81] He fills in the "et cetera" not with genuine popular grievances but with his own storied ancestry: "Shall Rome stand under one man's awe? What Rome? / My ancestors did from the streets of Rome / The Tarquin drive, when he was called a king." Whether we punctuate "What Rome?" or "What, Rome?" Brutus' question is telling. He displays none of Robert Cecil's humility in the face of a libel. For Brutus, the letter's "Rome" is the Rome of his ancestors, the Rome of the famed founder of the Republic, Lucius Junius Brutus. This is a republican Rome, but one with a Brutus at the center of things. If in his earlier soliloquy he "fashion[ed]" Caesar into a would-be tyrant, now he fashions himself as the savior of the Republic. Political fashioning, like libeling, seems to be an exercise reserved for the patrician class. Interpretations are hashed out behind closed doors and only then foisted upon the citizens.

Yet the citizens soon burst into the play and insist on making their own judgments. "We will be satisfied: let us be satisfied," they cry in the wake of Caesar's assassination (3.2.1). At first, they act like a model deliberative body. "I will hear Brutus speak," one citizen announces; "I will hear Cassius, and compare their reasons / When severally we hear them rendered," responds another (3.2.8–10). This is a metatheatrical moment: like these ordinary

---

[80] Naomi Conn Liebler, *Shakespeare's Festive Tragedy: The Ritual Foundations of Genre* (London: Routledge, 1995), 98; Doty, *Shakespeare*, 122.

[81] See Arnold, *Third Citizen*, 153–56; and Doty, *Shakespeare*, 121–22.

56 The Scene of Libel

Romans, Shakespeare's audience will soon find themselves comparing "reasons" as they watch the dueling speeches (Brutus' and Antony's) that follow. If only in passing, the play shows its spectators how they might exercise their own critical faculties in the theater.

Before long, of course, any prospect of measured deliberation vanishes as the plebeians devolve into an angry mob, out for blood. "Revenge! About! Seek! Burn! Fire! Kill! Slay!" is certainly not the sound of citizens comparing reasons (3.2.199). But the patricians, as discussed above, show little better judgment. In *Julius Caesar*, libels merely lend a populist gloss to the self-interested (or at least self-absorbed) machinations of the nobility. Brutus' solitary reading and the citizens' collective clamor seem like opposite poles of political judgment. Yet both end in bloodshed. The conspirators stab Caesar to death in the Capitol; the mob tears Cinna the poet to pieces in the street. Brutus maintains that he has "reasons . . . full of good regard" while the citizens kill Cinna only for his name and his "bad verses," but by this point the play has taught us to be skeptical of both parties (3.1.224, 3.3.30). *Julius Caesar* makes misjudgment a matter of life and death for plebeians, for patricians, and for the Republic itself.

But if the play's characters remain mired in their interpretive failures, Shakespeare's audiences need not have. Jeffrey S. Doty convincingly argues that *Julius Caesar* "opens a space of critical distance" in the theater, "[t]reating interpretation itself as a matter of shared, public inquiry." For Doty, however, this public inquiry stands in sharp contrast to the culture of libel. He argues that "Shakespeare shears off the overheated ad hominem rhetoric and protocols of secrecy that defined politics, creating opportunities instead for cool analysis of how princes gain, legitimate, and secure their authority. This poses a corrective to a public sphere that was dominated by slander and personal attacks."[82] Yet I have argued that ad hominem attack and cool analysis were practically inseparable. Libels such as *Leicester's Commonwealth* opened up spaces for public political judgment precisely by purporting to pierce the veil of secrecy around the court. The early modern public sphere was not just dominated but in no small measure constituted by defamatory discourse. Even if Shakespeare tried to shear off the slander – and I am not sure that he did – it remained an essential mode of political analysis, not least of all in the theater.

In any case, Shakespeare's scene of libel shares a reflexive style of address with the other representations of reading I've examined in this chapter. Each in its own way calls attention to the interpretive agency of the

---

[82] Doty, *Shakespeare*, 118, 130, 129.

How to Read a Libel in Early Modern England 57

audience. Or, to borrow Bacon's language, each "advertise[s]" its audience so that "by the Circumstances men may iudge of the matter."[83] What exactly that judgment should look like is another matter altogether. Bacon hopes his exposé of seditious writing will help the English people – or at least the good, indifferent, and reasonable among them – to see through the libelers' false pretenses. The authors of *Leicester's Commonwealth* want readers to believe or at least to recirculate its seditious talk. And Shakespeare shows playgoers the perils of misreading libels. Whatever their particular ends, however, all three works turn on the judgment of the people. Having considered the circumstances, the readers or listeners or spectators would judge however they saw fit. So it went with libels' style of the stage – a theatrical analogy that will continue to reverberate through the rest of this book.

---

[83] Bacon, *Aduertisement touching seditious writing*, 312.

CHAPTER 2

Playing Libel from Cambridge to Kendal

I now want to turn from the reception of libels to their publication – and, in particular, to their performance. In his pioneering monograph *Lost Plays of Shakespeare's Age* (1936), C. J. Sisson mined the Star Chamber records to recover rich traces of libelous performance. He concluded from his research "that of the various ways of publishing a libel, none was so effective as presentation in dramatic form."[1] This is something of an oversimplification. Adam Fox has shown that even illiterate libelers went to great lengths to get their doggerel written down and posted throughout their communities.[2] Writing was central to both the culture and the crime of libel. Yet Sisson's insight into the theatricality of libel has since been largely overlooked. Following the scribal archive in which most libels survive – miscellanies, newsletters, commonplace books – scholars generally approach the libel as a textual form. Studies of libel in performance remain scattered and, with a few exceptions, confined to several pages in essays on other topics.[3] In a recent series of articles, however, Clare Egan has convincingly located libels on "a spectrum of performance," from fully realized stage plays to festive rituals to dramatic recitations and parodies.[4]

This chapter ranges across that spectrum, bringing together varieties of libelous performance that remain underexplored: festive games, pageants,

---

[1] C. J. Sisson, *Lost Plays of Shakespeare's Age* (Cambridge: Cambridge University Press, 1936), 9.

[2] Adam Fox, *Oral and Literate Culture in England, 1500–1700* (Oxford: Clarendon Press, 2000), 43.

[3] More substantial studies include Martin Ingram, "Ridings, Rough Music and Mocking Rhymes in Early Modern England," in *Popular Culture in Seventeenth-Century England*, ed. Barry Reay (London: Croom Helm, 1985), 166–97; Fox, *Oral and Literate Culture*, 299–334; and Alastair Bellany, "Singing Libel in Early Stuart England: The Case of the Staines Fiddlers, 1627," *Huntington Library Quarterly* 69.1 (2006): 177–93.

[4] Clare Egan, "Performing Early Modern Libel: Expanding the Boundaries of Performance," *Early Theatre* 23.2 (2020): 156. See also Egan, "'Now fearing neither friend nor foe, to the worldes viewe these verses goe': Mapping Libel Performance in Early-Modern Devon," *Medieval English Theatre* 36 (2014): 70–103; and Egan, "Jacobean Star Chamber Records and the Performance of Provincial Libel," in *Star Chamber Matters: An Early Modern Court and Its Records*, ed. K. J. Kesselring and Natalie Mears (London: University of London Press, 2021), 135–53.

songs, and shows; amateur theater; university drama; and professional performance. Like Sisson's, Fox's, and Egan's, my primary archive is the records of the Court of Star Chamber, particularly those cases excerpted and transcribed by the Records of Early English Drama (REED) project. The complaints, interrogatories, depositions, and other documents paint a vivid picture of multimedia libeling across England. Beyond the restrictions inherent in REED's editorial scope, however, this archive necessarily has its limitations. The legal records that survive give only a partial view of each case, and one often seen through the plaintiff's eyes. We do not always know how the court ruled, even on matters of fact. Moreover, the records largely date to the Jacobean era, when the Star Chamber began to hear a rapidly growing number of libel cases (although I will foreground several late Elizabethan examples). This archive shows the court trying to delineate the crime of libel in the wake of Sir Edward Coke's *De libellis famosis* (1605). Yet the law remained fluid for decades.[5] Given this book's focus on the long 1590s, I examine Jacobean cases not to track the evolving contours of criminal libel but to sketch a set of cultural practices that continued across the early modern period.

The Star Chamber records are especially useful because of the court's preoccupation with sedition. As Coke explains, libels against private and public persons alike were held to foster disorder and violence, and to interfere with the course of justice.[6] To be sure, many libelers had no designs against the government at any level of its administration. In more than a few cases, the offenders were trying to defend communal norms themselves through the time-tested tactic of public shaming. The immediate cause of provincial libeling was generally neighborhood rivalry rather than public policy. Yet in an age of extensive local officeholding – an age in which the governors' "reputation was the very essence of their ability to govern" – bad publicity was itself a political problem.[7] Reputational anxiety intersected with a variety of social, economic, religious, and political concerns, from enclosure to ecclesiastical reform. The evidence tends to justify the fear of many magistrates that libels indeed were the seeds of sedition (at least if we construe sedition as expansively as did the early moderns).

---

[5] David Ibbetson, "Edward Coke, Roman Law, and the Law of Libel," in *The Oxford Handbook of English Law and Literature, 1500–1700*, ed. Lorna Hutson (Oxford: Oxford University Press, 2017), 501–3.

[6] *De libellis famosis* (1605), 5 Co. Rep. 125a–b.

[7] A. J. Fletcher, "Honour, Reputation and Local Officeholding in Elizabethan and Stuart England," in *Order and Disorder in Early Modern England*, ed. Fletcher and John Stevenson (Cambridge: Cambridge University Press, 1985), 115. See Mark Goldie, "The Unacknowledged Republic: Officeholding in Early Modern England," in *The Politics of the Excluded, c. 1500–1850*, ed. Tim Harris (Basingstoke, UK: Palgrave, 2001), 153–94.

60   The Scene of Libel

That is the case, at any rate, for each of my two major case studies: the Kendal Stage Play of 1621 and the university play *Club Law* (1599–1600). I argue that these performances are prime examples of activist theater: they aimed not just to entertain their audiences but also to mobilize them, defame them, or otherwise incite them to action. *Club Law* was a scathing satire of Cambridge's leading citizens put on by the students of the university, while the Kendal play was part of the local tenants' struggle to defend their rights from encroaching landlords. These two instances are unusual only in the extent of the documentary evidence that has survived. Aggrieved amateur playmakers across England made canny use of costume, props, meter, and other theatrical technologies to disseminate libels. I am especially interested in what the records of their activities and audiences can tell us that the playscripts produced for the commercial theater cannot. As Erika T. Lin has recently suggested, the traces of communal performance traditions point to "a whole host of ephemeral embodied experiences" that might otherwise be overlooked.[8] So it is with the libel. This chapter charts the repertoire of performance practices that make the libel so central to the history of early modern publicity.

Bad Publicity

I begin in London, at the more familiar end of the spectrum of performance: professional theater. A number of commercial plays sparked accusations of libel. But in few cases do we know as much about the local context as we do for George Chapman's *The Old Joiner of Aldgate* (1603). The play, now lost, dramatized the convoluted marriage negotiations of the young Agnes Howe, caught between several unpleasant suitors and an avaricious father. Its colorful cast of characters included Snipper Snapper the barber (for John Howe, Agnes's father), his daughter Ursula (Agnes), a bevy of suitors with names such as Tresacres (Thomas Field) and Touchbox (John Flaskett), and a French doctor (Agnes's eventual husband, the preacher Dr. John Milward).[9] Several parties quickly took offense. Flaskett, for instance, testified that "he was at the first offended with the said Play." But he claimed that after he saw it, he understood it "to be but a iest" and "a merrie Toye."[10]

---

[8] Erika T. Lin, "Festive Friars: Embodied Performance and Audience Affect," *Journal of Medieval and Early Modern Studies* 51.3 (2021): 488.

[9] Mary C. Erler, ed., *REED: Ecclesiastical London* (Toronto: University of Toronto Press, 2008), 203, 191; Sisson, *Lost Plays*, 67. For a detailed account of the scandal, see Sisson, 12–79.

[10] *REED: Ecclesiastical London*, 191.

Playing Libel from Cambridge to Kendal

Flaskett's equanimity may have been more than a little disingenuous, however. After Agnes and Milward were married in an irregular ceremony in 1601, Flaskett and the other suitors took their own claims of precontract to court. The tangle of suits and countersuits dragged on until Milward turned to Star Chamber for relief.[11] In the bill of complaint, Attorney General Coke pinned *The Old Joiner* on none other than Flaskett himself. Flaskett and his accomplices (including Anges's own father) allegedly arranged for Chapman to write the play "vpon a plott giuen vnto him," after which it was sold to Thomas Woodford and Edward Pearce, the managers of Paul's Boys, for twenty marks. Flaskett's motive was simple: blackmail. He reportedly sought to "publish the dealing of [Agnes's] father towards her concerning his practize with seuerall sutors to bestow her in Marriage with one that might forgoe her portion" so that Agnes "might shutt vp & conclude a match with the said fflaskett rather then to suffer her name to be so traduced in euery play house."[12] If this account is to be believed, Flaskett put the theater to his own mercenary use. Agnes evidently faced an unpalatable choice: marry Flaskett or suffer the defamatory play. Flaskett's hope was that the threat of bad publicity would win him Agnes and, especially, her substantial "portion."

If blackmail – with an eye to Agnes's inheritance – was Flaskett's motive, it is not hard to guess Chapman's. The playwright maintained that he was not part of "anie confederacy or combinacion" and that *The Old Joiner* was not intended "to shame & disgrace the said Agnes How, her ffather & others her sutors."[13] Yet he (not to mention Woodford and Pearce) must have seen the commercial appeal of a local marriage scandal. From their revival in 1599 through their dissolution less than a decade later, the Children of Paul's – as well as the other boy companies – were known for sharp satire that sometimes came dangerously close to libel.[14] The 1603 premiere of *The Old Joiner* was one of those times. Revealingly, the Star Chamber suit alleged that the company's poets or players had threatened to publish a further libel against anyone who tried to suppress their play, warning "[t]hat yf they hindred the playinge therof there woulde be and was a prologue made to the Spectatours in excuse of the nott playing ytt that woulde disgrace them muche more."[15] True or not, this accusation suggests how readily the whole theatrical apparatus, prologue included, could be turned to public shaming.

---

[11] Sisson, *Lost Plays*, 38–44. [12] *REED: Ecclesiastical London*, 183. [13] Ibid., 195.
[14] For a short history of Paul's Boys and their repertory, see Andrew Gurr, *The Shakespearian Playing Companies* (Oxford: Clarendon Press, 1996), 337–46.
[15] *REED: Ecclesiastical London*, 196.

62   The Scene of Libel

There is a fair distance between *The Old Joiner of Aldgate* and the dramatic recitation of someone such as William Williams of Wells, who in 1607 recited a libelous ballad "with the action of his foote and hand, much like a player."[16] But the two incidents share the visual language of the theater. Surveying the Star Chamber archive, Egan finds that "there was a certain accepted way to read a text like this": "as a performance on a stage."[17] Provincial libelers no less than professional players found that the actor's craft might best generate publicity (or, as it were, notoriety). Whether mocking Puritans or resisting enclosure or merely defaming neighbors, libels consistently tended toward the performative. Matthew Chubb, bailiff of Dorchester, allegedly stood at the town's market cross in August 1606 and "with a lowde voyce in the presence and hearing of many persons" read a libel beginning, "Yow Puritans all wheresoeuer yow dwell / ymitateing your master the dyvell of hell." In his defense, Chubb maintained that he had actually read the libel "in privat . . . with a loe voyce," suggesting just how central publication and performance were to the crime of libel.[18] The emerging legal standards for criminal libel likely have something to do with the plaintiffs' consistent emphasis on the size of the audiences and the publicity of the performances. But that publicity also reflects the substantial overlap between libeling and the cultures of performance.

This lesson was not lost on William Tyxall of Lees Hill, Staffordshire and his confederates. By 1615, Tyxall had been mired for several years in a land dispute with his neighbor Anthony Kynnersley, a justice of the peace and quorum. Kynnersley evidently took his civic role seriously, cracking down on "the vnreasonable number of Alehowses, and Alehowse keepers" in the county. Tyxall and his coconspirators allegedly seized on this move to attack Kynnersley's overzealous administration in a mocking libel that began, "The Iustice vniust and Iacob his man, oppresse the poore alewives with an vnreasonable Can."[19] According to Kynnersley's complaint, the libelers took to the nearby market town of Uttoxeter to scatter written copies of their verse both in the streets and, fittingly, in

---

[16] James Stokes and Robert J. Alexander, eds., *REED: Somerset, including Bath*, 2 vols. (Toronto: University of Toronto Press, 1996), 1:354. The ballad was inspired by the 1607 Wells Shows, discussed below.

[17] Egan, "Now fearing," 76.

[18] Rosalind Conklin Hays et al., eds., *REED: Dorset, Cornwall* (Toronto: University of Toronto Press, 1999), 175, 180, 188. See David Underdown, *Fire from Heaven: Life in an English Town in the Seventeenth Century* (New Haven: Yale University Press, 1992), 27–30.

[19] The "vnreasonable Can" is probably a can of ale, although it may also refer to Kynnersley's "power, ability" ("can, n.2," *OED Online* [Oxford University Press, 2021]).

Playing Libel from Cambridge to Kendal

alehouses. But Tyxall went further still. In December, he (allegedly) had the libel sung "by Players att a publique stage playe or Comedie" performed in Uttoxeter. It's not clear whether these players were traveling actors, local amateurs, or – as Kynnersley insinuates – "disordered persons" masquerading as players.[20] Whatever the case, the libelous poem and the comedy were symbiotic dramatic events, and the platform for both was a public stage.

Libel and performance come together still more vividly in the more elaborate amateur productions. In 1611, a band of conspirators in Somerset seized William Swarfe's prized mare, fastened horns to her head, tied a libelous verse to her tail, and paraded the symbol of cuckoldry before a crowd of a hundred rowdy spectators.[21] In 1621, when Humphrey Elliotts of Claverley failed to win the hand of Elizabeth Ridge, the wealthy parson's daughter, he and his accomplices allegedly accused her of adultery through a libelous play written "dyaloggwise wherin it was devysed that one of the actors should bee apparelled in womens apparell & bolstered & sett forth as though shee were great with Child & should apparsonatt the said Elizabeth vnder the name of Ienney."[22] And in the summer of 1607, a band of traditionalist citizens in the town of Wells put on a series of festive shows defaming their reformist rivals. Hundreds or even (by some accounts) thousands came out to see the alleged conspirators ride through the town while impersonating several leading citizens. A week later, the libelers returned to the streets to play a game of nineholes featuring painted caricatures of the inopportunely named John Hole and Anne Yarde accompanied by sexually suggestive chants punning on their surnames.[23] These three examples alone involve a lengthy catalogue of props: the horns and the horse, the bolster (cushion) and the women's apparel, and the host of items used in the Wells processions (including a brush, old hats, a spinning wheel, a hammer, scales, and painted boards).[24] Such resourcefulness reveals a considerable degree of theatrical literacy among provincial libelers and their audiences.

---

[20] "Kynnersley v. Tyxall et al," in J. Alan B. Somerset, ed., *REED: Staffordshire*, *REED Online*, https://ereed.library.utoronto.ca/collections/staff/.

[21] *REED: Somerset*, 1:36.

[22] J. Alan B. Somerset, ed., *REED: Shropshire*, 2 vols. (Toronto: University of Toronto Press, 1994), 1:26. On this play, see Sisson, *Lost Plays*, 140–56.

[23] *REED: Somerset*, 1:263–66, 2:725–27. On the Wells Shows, see Sisson, *Lost Plays*, 162–77; James Stokes, "The Wells Shows of 1607," in *Festive Drama*, ed. Meg Twycross (Cambridge: D. S. Brewer, 1996), 145–56; and David Underdown, "'But the Shows of Their Street': Civic Pageantry and Charivari in a Somerset Town, 1607," *Journal of British Studies* 50.1 (2011): 4–23.

[24] *REED: Somerset*, 1:263–65.

64   The Scene of Libel

Indeed, provincial libeling was informed by a range of popular performance genres. The fate of Swarfe's mare is a variety of the skimmington or charivari, a cacophonous procession to shame those, especially women, who violated community norms.[25] Elliotts's contrivance looks more like a stage play, if a rather vulgar one. And the Wells Shows joined public shaming rituals with festive traditions of play and performance. In fact, one supporter claimed that the entertainments "were the shewes of their streete," locating them in a tradition of neighborhood festivity.[26] Street theater, professional playing, and everything in between provided both inspiration and occasion for libeling.

Shakespeare himself evokes the varied roots of defamatory performance in *The Merry Wives of Windsor*. At the play's end, Falstaff finds himself the unwitting star of a mocking show. The titular merry wives, Mistress Page and Mistress Ford, get him to dress as the legendary spirit of Herne the Hunter – complete with a pair of horns – and meet them in the woods in expectation of the sexual encounter that he has spent the play pursuing. Falstaff, however, is met with something else altogether. The two women have arranged an elaborate pageant featuring children dressed as "urchins, oafs and fairies, green and white, / With rounds of waxen tapers on their heads / And rattles in their hands." Outfitted with these theatrical "properties," as Mistress Page calls them, the children pinch and burn Falstaff while singing "a scornful rhyme" mocking his lust.[27] As Natasha Korda points out, this show has all the trappings "commonly found in public shaming rituals: the 'rough music' or cacophony produced by beating pots and pans, the 'mocking rhymes, songs or lampoons,' and the 'display of animals' horns or horned heads.'"[28] It is a folk ritual, but one rehearsed in the language of the professional theater in which it is being performed. By putting Falstaff's shaming on the public stage, Shakespeare alludes to the carnivalesque continuity between traditional festivity and comic theater.[29]

---

[25] See Martin Ingram, "Ridings, Rough Music and the 'Reform of Popular Culture' in Early Modern England," *Past and Present* 105 (1984): 79–113.

[26] *REED: Somerset*, 2:946.

[27] Shakespeare, *The Merry Wives of Windsor*, ed. Giorgio Melchiori (Walton-on-Thames: Thomas Nelson, 2000), 4.4.48–50, 76, 5.5.91.

[28] Natasha Korda, *Shakespeare's Domestic Economies: Gender and Property in Early Modern England* (Philadelphia: University of Pennsylvania Press, 2002), 96, quoting Ingram, "Ridings, Rough Music and the 'Reform of Popular Culture,'" 86.

[29] On that continuity, see C. L. Barber, *Shakespeare's Festive Comedy: A Study of Dramatic Form and its Relation to Social Custom* (Princeton: Princeton University Press, 1959); Michael D. Bristol, *Carnival and Theater: Plebeian Culture and the Structure of Authority in Renaissance England* (New York: Methuen, 1985); and Erika T. Lin, "Festivity," in *Early Modern Theatricality*, ed. Henry S. Turner (Oxford: Oxford University Press, 2013), 212–29.

Playing Libel from Cambridge to Kendal

The case of "The Death of the Lord of Kyme" in August 1601 well illustrates the characteristic hybridity of libelous performance. On a maypole green hard by the house of Sir Edward Dymoke, Edward's brother Tailboys put on a play that, he claimed, was meant to mark "an ende of the Sommer Lord game in South kyme for that yeare."[30] But his intention was apparently not so innocent as festive celebration. The Dymokes were embroiled in a long-running feud with their deeply unpopular uncle, Henry Clinton, second Earl of Lincoln. At least in the earl's telling, the play was one more salvo in that dispute. Lincoln alleged that Tailboys himself, "being the then principall actour therein," impersonated the earl by name "in scornefull manner" and portrayed him being carried away by the devil. As many as 400 spectators were said to have been in attendance.[31]

Assuming that Lincoln's allegations are more or less accurate – and there is good reason to think they are, given Tailboys's personal history of libeling, the ongoing feud, and the fact that the court eventually found in Lincoln's favor – they reveal a play at the intersection of several traditions of popular performance.[32] The most obvious is festive misrule. The public mockery licensed by holiday shows easily crossed over into ad hominem abuse.[33] Tailboys could thus claim in his defense that he was merely playing the part of "Lord Pleasure her & did Calle the Lord of North kyme (being another Sommer Lord that yeare) my vncle Prince."[34] What Lincoln interpreted as defamatory allusion, Tailboys argues, was actually a traditional festive role. But festival and libel were not so easily separated. Despite his protestations, Tailboys was in all likelihood trying to exploit that very ambiguity by mocking his uncle under cover of a holiday tradition.

Behind the mockery also lay another dramatic tradition: the morality play. Lincoln alleged that one Roger Bayard played not only the part of the devil who carried him off to hell but also

> the parte of the ffoole and the parte of the vyce . . . and then & there in the hearing of all the persons assembled to see and heare the said playe did

---

[30] James Stokes, ed., *REED: Lincolnshire*, 2 vols. (Toronto: University of Toronto Press, 2009), 1:277. On "The Death of the Lord of Kyme," see Norreys Jephson O'Conor, *Godes Peace and the Queenes: Vicissitudes of a House, 1539–1615* (Cambridge, MA: Harvard University Press, 1934), 108–26; and Barber, *Shakespeare's Festive Comedy*, 36–50.

[31] *REED: Lincolnshire*, 1:271, 302.

[32] Lincoln several times accused Tailboys of composing and publishing libels, and in 1599 Tailboys's pseudonymously published *Caltha Poetarum* was included among the verse satires prohibited by the Bishops' Ban. See CP 37/3; and Leslie Hotson, "Marigold of the Poets," *Essays by Divers Hands: Being the Transactions of the Royal Society of Literature of the United Kingdom*, n.s., 17 (1938): 47–68.

[33] See Barber, *Shakespeare's Festive Comedy*, 36.   [34] *REED: Lincolnshire*, 1:278.

> bequeathe his woodden dagger to your said Subiecte by the name of the Earle of lincolne and his Cockscombe & bable vnto all those that would not goe to Hornecastle with the said Sir Edward Dymocke against him.[35]

Many of these elements echo the fifteenth-century *Mankind* and other medieval morality plays, including the unflattering allusion to a local grandee, the roles of the devil and vice, the symbolic props, and the direct appeal to the audience.[36] The Dymokes were far from the first to turn the genre toward personal or political satire. In January 1531, Thomas Boleyn, Earl of Wiltshire, and Thomas Howard, Duke of Norfolk, put on for the French ambassador "a farce ... of the Cardinal (Wolsey) going down to Hell."[37] Greg Walker sees this as a savvy diplomatic maneuver, designed to remind the ambassador of the "new dispensation" at the English court: Wolsey and the Roman Church were out, and Wiltshire and Norfolk themselves were in.[38] The ambassador reportedly took offense, but that may well have been the point. Norfolk was pleased enough with the play that he sought to circulate it more widely, "ordering the said farce to be printed."[39]

The Dymokes' play had a parallel aim, if one much more local in its ambitions. When the fool or vice urged the audience to go to Horncastle with Sir Edward, he brought them into the feud between the Dymokes and Lincoln. The town of Horncastle was the site of a bitter property dispute between the two parties. Just a month before the play's performance, Sir Edward and his followers broke into the Horncastle parsonage house "and Claymed divers duties of right" that, Lincoln alleged, really belonged to him. The earl suggested that the play threatened to incite a reprise of that riot on a larger scale. According to his complaint, Sir Edward had sent his servants out to spread the word and invite all his neighbors – "the whole hundred and wapentage adioyning" – to come feast on venison and see the play.[40] "The Death of the Lord of Kyme" brought the community together to defend the Dymokes' property rights and to mock the Earl of Lincoln, their rival claimant.

---

[35] Ibid., 1:271.

[36] Clare Egan, "Reading *Mankind* in a Culture of Defamation," *Medieval English Theatre* 40 (2018): 151–54.

[37] Pascual de Gayangos, ed., *Calendar of Letters, Despatches, and State Papers, Relating to the Negotiations between England and Spain, Preserved in the Archives at Simancas and Elsewhere*, vol. 4, pt. 2 (London, 1882), 40.

[38] Greg Walker, *Plays of Persuasion: Drama and Politics at the Court of Henry VIII* (Cambridge: Cambridge University Press, 1991), 20.

[39] Gayangos, *Calendar*, 41. [40] *REED: Lincolnshire*, 1:271, 270.

Playing Libel from Cambridge to Kendal

For many in the audience, it would not have taken much to turn them against Lincoln, especially in matters of land rights. The earl was by all accounts a highly unpleasant character and, more to the point, a "notorious encloser" who earned a well-deserved reputation as "an oppressor of your Majesties inferior subjectes."[41] His administration of Lincolnshire was marked by land grabs, lawsuits, and violence. Even if the Dymokes had only their own grievances in mind, the success of their show would have turned on Lincoln's notoriety. Their personal animus spoke to the broader socioeconomic issues afflicting the community. The same was true in many other instances of libelous performance. The Wells Shows, for example, erupted from a simmering conflict between (to use the two sides' own terms of abuse) "professional puritans" and the "popishlie affected." James Stokes convincingly argues that the shows were in fact "a concerted attempt to re-establish traditional festive summer entertainments" that the Puritan-leaning reformists wanted to keep suppressed.[42] When libelers went public, they necessarily navigated – and often aggravated – the fissures running through their communities.

So far, I have focused on scenes of performance. But it is important to note that virtually all of the cases discussed above also involved writing. Admittedly, it is not entirely clear whether writing was a necessary component of criminal libel in the seventeenth-century Star Chamber. By 1631, Chief Justice Thomas Richardson could hold that "a libell may be in word as well as in writing."[43] Yet Richardson's phrasing ("word *as well as . . .* writing") – not to mention the fact that he needed to make the remark at all – implies that the category of libel in writing preceded that of libel in word. When Coke defined criminal libel in 1605, he included only writing on the one hand and pictures and signs on the other. Words (*verba*) in his account were merely a medium in which written libels might be published.[44] If by the 1630s Star Chamber dealt with all kinds of defamation under the rubric of libel, the evidence suggests that writing remained a constitutive element of libel in the earlier years of the seventeenth century and, certainly, in the later sixteenth century.

---

[41] John Walter, *Crowds and Popular Politics in Early Modern England* (Manchester: Manchester University Press, 2006), 23; Walter, "'The Pooremans Joy and the Gentlemans Plague': A Lincolnshire Libel and the Politics of Sedition in Early Modern England," *Past and Present* 203 (2009): 49. For complaints about the earl's oppressions, see BL, Lansdowne MS 77, fol. 144r; CP 141/173; and O'Conor, *Godes Peace*, 45–126.

[42] Stokes, "Wells Shows," 146, 145.

[43] Samuel Rawson Gardiner, ed., *Reports of Cases in the Courts of Star Chamber and High Commission* (London, 1886), 71.

[44] *De libellis famosis* (1605), 5 Co. Rep. 125b.

68 The Scene of Libel

Whatever the legal picture, the records show that libeling was most often a multimedia project. Libelers devised all sorts of ingenious ways to combine text and performance. Often, as in the case of William Tyxall's pro-alehouse poem, the written copy served as a script for performance. The libel pinned to William Swarfe's mare exemplifies another function: text as prop. In the case of "The Death of the Lord of Kyme," the Dymokes posted a libel as a kind of epilogue. The play ended with one of the actors fixing "a slaunderous Ryme concerninge the Earle on the Mayepole and the Earles Coate of Armes over yt," leaving behind a public, textual trace of the performance.[45] Finally, a libelous ballad written and widely circulated in the wake of the Wells Shows illustrates a fourth function: text as eyewitness history. This poem gleefully recounts "the sportes of Welles May men" that transpired a month earlier, including the libelous "holinge game" and pageant.[46] Script, prop, epilogue, history: these four functions by no means exhaust the possible relationships between text and performance, but they do suggest how integral multimedia publication was to libelers' efforts. Joining manuscript verse to a range of performance genres, people across England tried to saturate their communities with libels.

Few libelers, then, were content to disseminate their message from a single stage. The libels that I've discussed were posted and performed at markets and maypoles, highways and shops, churches and alehouses, theaters and streets. Public spaces were the libelers' stages, civic structures their bulletin boards. As locals gathered for work or for play, they found themselves called upon to take a position in a dispute, if only through their derisory laughter. And at least for one legal authority, that laughter was itself a sign of complicity. William Hudson reports that "to hear [a libel] sung or read, and to laugh at it, and to make merriment with it, hath ever been held a publication in law."[47] The law (in Hudson's account) implicates merry audiences in the act of libel.

Taken together, the Star Chamber records locate provincial libeling in a culture of popular performance. Bands of commoners took to the public spaces of their communities and performed libels before audiences numbering in the hundreds or even, in a few cases, in the thousands. A rough statistical breakdown supports this picture of plebeian politics. From 1603 to 1625, around 80 percent of plaintiffs in Star Chamber defamation cases

---

[45] REED: Lincolnshire, 1:302. [46] REED: Somerset, 1:267.
[47] William Hudson, A Treatise of the Court of Star Chamber, in Collectanea Juridica, ed. Francis Hargrave, vol. 2 (London, 1792), 102.

were above the rank of yeoman, while the defendants were typically of lower status.[48] Yet these figures are somewhat misleading. Plaintiffs from the upper classes were more likely to have the financial resources needed to bring a suit to Star Chamber. And, as Andrew McRae points out, plenty of cases "frustrate attempts to identify coherent subordinate groups" or involve libelers of higher status putting popular culture to their own use.[49] We saw this social complexity in the case of "The Death of the Lord of Kyme." The play was contrived and produced by the brothers Dymoke, members of one of Lincolnshire's most powerful families; it mocked their uncle, the Earl of Lincoln, by exploiting the popular resentment against his tyrannical administration in the county; and its actors and accomplices included yeomen and servants linked to the Dymokes.[50] If we include the merry (or offended) spectators and the prospective marchers on Horncastle, then virtually the whole community had parts to play. What is clear is that such performances sought to enlist as wide a swath of the local population as possible in the scene of libel.

Protest Theater in Kendal

By 1621, Kendal had seen plenty of theater. Traveling players visited at least forty times between 1585 and 1637, and the town was known for its own "yearely stageplayes," as Thomas Heywood noted in his 1612 *Apology for Actors*.[51] Kendal was a logical choice of venue for both local and itinerant players. Located in the northern county of Westmorland, the town was a modest market center and commercial hub, and the seat of the barony of Kendal.[52] Actors and civic officials alike evidently saw Kendal as a regional center for theater too. The contrivers of the libelous play of 1621 had some trouble getting it approved until they reminded the town's alderman that the play "woulde bringe a great Concourse of people to the

---

[48] Fox, *Oral and Literate Culture*, 309; Laura Gowing, "Women, Status and the Popular Culture of Dishonour," *Transactions of the Royal Historical Society* 6 (1996): 226.

[49] Andrew McRae, "The Verse Libel: Popular Satire in Early Modern England," in *Subversion and Scurrility: Popular Discourse in Europe from 1500 to the Present*, ed. Dermot Cavanagh and Tim Kirk (Aldershot, UK: Ashgate, 2000), 66.

[50] *REED: Lincolnshire*, 1:269–71.

[51] Audrey Douglas and Peter Greenfield, eds., *REED: Cumberland, Westmorland, Gloucestershire* (Toronto: University of Toronto Press, 1986), 27; Thomas Heywood, *An Apology for Actors* (London, 1612), sig. G3r. The yearly play seems to have been Kendal's Corpus Christi play, a longstanding tradition until it was suppressed in 1605 (*REED: Cumberland*, 18).

[52] See C. B. Phillips, "Town and Country: Economic Change in Kendal, c. 1550–1700," in *The Transformation of English Provincial Towns 1600–1800*, ed. Peter Clark (London: Hutchinson, 1984), 99–100.

70   The Scene of Libel

towne & woulde cause much money to be spent there."[53] This was
apparently a persuasive argument in 1621. Kendal was the perfect place
to gather the local population for commerce, for entertainment, or – as
the alderman discovered too late – for libeling.

The Kendal Stage Play was performed in July on the grounds of Kendal
Castle, a medieval ruin just across the river from the town.[54] In the Star
Chamber records, we find several different accounts of the play. All,
however, describe a pointed critique of agrarian exploitation. The bill of
complaint alleges that the actors portrayed the Kendal landlords themselves "to bee in hell."[55] The play's author, a onetime schoolmaster named
Jasper Garnett, insisted that he had written it some years before and that
none of the lords were themselves "represented or personated." Instead, he
claimed that the play's satire was a generalized allegory rather than
a personal libel: a "representacion of ravens feedinge of poore sheepe in
Hell which ravens were compared to greedy landlordes & the sheepe to
their poore tennantes."[56] One spectator filled in some more details about
the scene in question. A boy gazes into hell; two clowns accost the boy and
ask "who he did see there." "Land lordes & puritanes & Sheriffe Bailiffes,"
he replies. According to this witness, the clowns helpfully explained to the
audience that the landlords were in hell because "they did seeke to make
their tennantes, tennantes at will."[57]

If landlords were indeed "personated," there is some evidence that the
personation was libelous. Garnett admitted that the actors had borrowed
"the best & the greatest parte of their apparrell & playing Clothes" from
their supporters among the Kendal gentry.[58] Any actor playing a landlord,
then, may very well have been wearing the costume of a local landlord. On
and off the professional stage, clothing remained a key marker of social
rank even after the repeal of the sumptuary laws in 1604.[59] The Kendal
players conscripted this theatrical technology into the service of their
public protest.

The sole surviving snatch of verse comes from an examination of one of the
players, Richard Helme. Helme relates that the play had some twenty
actors.[60] Many of these, including Helme and the two clowns, appear to

---

[53] TNA, STAC 8/34/4, fol. 18r. See *REED: Cumberland*, 196.   [54] *REED: Cumberland*, 236.
[55] STAC 8/34/4, fol. 55. See *REED: Cumberland*, 188.
[56] STAC 8/34/4, fol. 18v. See *REED: Cumberland*, 196, 197.
[57] STAC 8/34/4, fol. 35v. See *REED: Cumberland*, 193.
[58] STAC 8/34/4, fol. 18v. See *REED: Cumberland*, 197.
[59] Robert I. Lublin, *Costuming the Shakespearean Stage: Visual Codes of Representation in Early Modern Theatre and Culture* (Burlington, VT: Ashgate, 2011), 45.
[60] STAC 8/34/4, fol. 54v. See *REED: Cumberland*, 190.

Playing Libel from Cambridge to Kendal

have been tenants themselves.[61] In Helme's recollection, one of the clowns glossed the representation of ravens feeding on the carcasses of sheep with the following lines:

> Rauens quotha no, thou art farr byth square,
> it*es* false landlord*es* makes all that Croakinge there,
> & those sheepe wee poore men, whose right these by their skill,
> would take awaie, & make vs tenn*antes* at will,
> & when *our* ancient liberties are gone,
> theile picke & poole & peele vs to the bare bone.[62]

In rhyming couplets and a (very rough) iambic pentameter, these lines conjure an allegorical vision of rapacious landlords devouring their poor tenants. The "false landlord*es*" are greedy ravens, croaking gleefully as they peck away at the customary rights, the "ancient liberties," of their impoverished tenants. This blunt allegory culminates in a viscerally alliterative description of the landlords' predatory violence: "theile picke & poole & peele vs to the bare bone."

Despite Garnett's protestations, there is little doubt that the Kendal landlords were the prime target. When the clown spoke of tenants' "right," of efforts to reduce them to "tenn*antes* at will," and of "*our* ancient liberties," he was taking a clear stance in the ongoing dispute over tenant right in the barony of Kendal. Many tenants in the northern counties, including in Westmorland, held their lands by a set of customs collectively known as tenant right. In return for military service on the Scottish border, these tenants enjoyed low rents and fines and, crucially, the right to inherit and sell their lands.[63] Unlike tenants at will – who held their lands at the will of their lords – tenant-right tenants could not easily be evicted.[64]

---

[61] Anthony Duckett, whose family was among the play's backers, deposed that Helme and Henry Ward (who played one of the clowns) were his father's tenants (STAC 8/34/4, fol. 35v; see *REED: Cumberland*, 194). See also *REED: Cumberland*, 235.

[62] STAC 8/34/4, fol. 54v; lineation mine. See *REED: Cumberland*, 191. The REED editors read "puke" instead of "picke."

[63] S. J. Watts, "Tenant-Right in Early Seventeenth-Century Northumberland," *Northern History* 6 (1971): 64–66. For another useful overview of tenant right, see R. W. Hoyle, "Lords, Tenants, and Tenant Right in the Sixteenth Century: Four Studies," *Northern History* 20 (1984): 39. The most detailed study of the struggle over tenant right in Kendal is Joe Scott, "The Kendal Tenant Right Dispute 1619–26," *Transactions of the Cumberland and Westmorland Antiquarian and Archaeological Society* 98 (1998): 169–82; other accounts of the dispute include Mildred Campbell, *The English Yeoman Under Elizabeth and the Early Stuarts* (New Haven: Yale University Press, 1942), 149–52; Watts, "Tenant-Right," 74–78; and Andrew B. Appleby, *Famine in Tudor and Stuart England* (Stanford: Stanford University Press, 1978), 77–79.

[64] Edward Coke, in *The Compleate Copy-Holder* (London, 1641), describes "meere Tenants at will" as those tenants who, "though they keepe the Customes inviolated, yet the Lord might, sans controll, eject them" (sig. K2r).

72 The Scene of Libel

As recently as 1619, the Court of Chancery had confirmed to certain Kendal tenants the "good and lawfull customary [estate] of inheritance ... commonly called tenant right by and according to *th*e Custome of *th*e barony of Kendall."[65]

But tenant right in Kendal was already under siege. The accession of King James and the union of the crowns of England and Scotland in 1603 brought border service to an end – and a decidedly less sympathetic monarch to the throne. Pressed for cash, northern landlords tried to raise rents and fines on the grounds that the end of border service meant the end of tenant right. Lawsuits quickly multiplied. The crown's 1619 confirmation of tenant right in Kendal came at the cost of a £2,700 settlement paid by the tenants of Prince Charles, the barony's largest landlord.[66] After the prince's settlement, the tenants of the barony's other landlords soon began to agitate for a similar confirmation of their rights.[67] Kendal's supposedly "good and lawfull" custom of tenant right looked increasingly precarious.

The assault on tenant right reached a climax in July 1620, one year before the Kendal play. Frustrated by the tide of litigation, James issued a proclamation "against Tenant-rights." He declared it settled law that

> Tenant-rights, since the most happy Union of these two renowmed Kingdomes of England and Scotland in Our person, are utterly by the ancient and fundamentall rule of Law of this Our Kingdome of England extinguished and abolished ... And yet neverthelesse divers Suits are continually raised and prosecuted in Our Courts of Justice here in England, grounded upon the said claime of Tenant-right, or Customarie estate of Inheritance, under that pretence, whereby ... the memory of the said Tenant-right is continued, which ought to be damned to a perpetuall oblivion.[68]

To extirpate tenant right once and for all, James attacks its cultural and legal foundation: memory. Memory had a privileged place in England's common law culture. Lawyers described the common law itself as, in the words of John Davies, "the *Common custome* of the Realme ... recorded and registred no where, but in the memory of the people."[69] Arguments

---

[65] TNA, SP 14/203, fol. 54v.
[66] Campbell, *English Yeoman*, 149–50; Watts, "Tenant-Right"; Appleby, *Famine*, 76–77; Scott, "Kendal," 170–71.
[67] STAC 8/34/4, fols. 14r–v, 42r, 42v, 43r, 49.
[68] James F. Larkin and Paul L. Hughes, eds., *Stuart Royal Proclamations*, 2 vols. (Oxford: Clarendon Press, 1973–83), 1:488–89.
[69] John Davies, *Le primer report des cases & matters en ley resolues & adiudges en les courts del Roy en Ireland* (Dublin, 1615), sig. *2r. See J. G. A. Pocock, *The Ancient Constitution and the Feudal Law: A Study of English Historical Thought in the Seventeenth Century*, 2nd ed. (Cambridge: Cambridge University Press, 1987).

Playing Libel from Cambridge to Kendal

from popular memory could prevail in the courts. The standard legal test was whether it could be shown that a given custom "hath been used from time whereof the memory of men runneth not to the contrary."[70] The fight over tenant right, however, shows that custom was not an immutable fact but an "ideological battleground," as Andy Wood puts it.[71] In just one year, the crown went from confirming that the prince's tenants in Kendal had enjoyed tenant right since "tyme whereof *th*e memory of man was not to *th*e contrary" (the language of the 1619 Chancery decree) to "damn[ing]" that same memory to "a perpetuall oblivion" (the language of the 1620 proclamation).[72]

The tenants of Kendal, however, kept that memory alive. In the surviving lines of the play, they defend their "right" from those "false landlord*es*" – including the crown – who would make them mere "tenn*antes* at will." It would take far more than a royal proclamation to eradicate the memory of tenant right. Indeed, the tenants even rebut James's invocation of "the ancient ... rule of Law" with their own claim to "*our* ancient liberties." These dueling appeals to antiquity played out not only in the law courts but also in the court of public opinion. It is fitting that the tenants should have countered the royal proclamation with a libelous play. In the previous chapter, I discussed how writers such as Francis Bacon understood libels as the seditious double of authorized decrees – as "proclamations and Trumpettes of sedition," to quote one government official.[73] Both the proclamation and the play addressed the inhabitants of Kendal. James, however, imagined an audience of docile "loving Subjects," while the libelous play appealed to a collective of aggrieved tenants.[74]

Even as the lawsuits dragged on, then, the tenants met the crown on the terrain of the early modern public sphere. The play is as good an example as any of how theater lent commoners a public platform otherwise reserved for their governors. But theater was less an instrument of rational argument than it was an "affective technology," to use Steven Mullaney's term.[75]

---

[70] Thomas Littleton, *Littleton's Tenures*, ed. Eugene Wambaugh (Washington, D.C.: John Byrne, 1903), 82. See Charles Calthorpe, *The Relation betweene the Lord of a Mannor and the Coppy-holder His Tenant* (London, 1635), sig. D1v; and Andy Wood, *The Memory of the People: Custom and Popular Senses of the Past in Early Modern England* (Cambridge: Cambridge University Press, 2013), 94–96.

[71] Wood, *Memory*, 31.   [72] TNA, SP 14/203, fol. 54v.

[73] BL, Harley MS 6849, fol. 325r. Libelers were just as attuned to the subversive kinship between libels and proclamations: see Andrew McRae, *Literature, Satire and the Early Stuart State* (Cambridge: Cambridge University Press, 2004), 38–39; and Egan, "Performing Early Modern Libel," 161–62.

[74] *Stuart Royal Proclamations*, 1:489.

[75] Steven Mullaney, *The Reformation of Emotions in the Age of Shakespeare* (Chicago: University of Chicago Press, 2015), 23.

74   The Scene of Libel

On that July day at Kendal Castle, tenants played tenants before an audience that included tenants. The few surviving lines imagine the agrarian community coming together to contest the royal and, in their view, exploitative stance on tenant right. The clown's first-person plural pronouns – "vs," "our," "wee" – assert a collective voice that will not be silenced. It's easy to imagine the raucous feelings that would have shot through the assembly and, as the landlords complained, made them "the more odious to the people."[76] From costume to couplets, the tenants exploited the resources of the theater to subject the landlords to popular odium.

We don't know whether the play really did sway public opinion, but the history of the tenant right dispute suggests that it did. The Kendal play was part of a protest movement that had begun months before. In January 1621, in the wake of the king's draconian proclamation against tenant right, groups of tenants – just how many is unclear – met at a local chapel and bridge to organize their protests.[77] Pooling their resources, they raised money to get a petition to the king and a bill before the House of Commons in defense of tenant right.[78] They were also said to have drafted a remarkable statement of solidarity, resolving that an injury done to any one of them "shall be reputed as done unto all of us."[79]

The tenants' threat of collective action quickly spread through Kendal. There was allegedly talk of an "insurreccion" if the king's proclamation should stand; several tenants reportedly declared "that they would loose theire lives before theire lyvinges And that theire Lordes were but a handfull or a Breakfaste, And that first they wold endevour by Lawe, but if that would not doe then they would fighte for it."[80] Words that might previously have been spoken only behind closed doors began to find wider audiences. Other than the play, the item that most caught the landlords' attention was a document titled "Reasons of all the Commons of

---

[76] STAC 8/34/4, fol. 55. See *REED: Cumberland*, 188. This was a common complaint of the libeled. The enclosing landlord Andrew Abington expressed a similar fear of "publicke disgrace and infamye," and the Earl of Lincoln complained that "The Death of the Lord of Kyme" would "bring him into the scorne and Contempte of the vulgar people" (*REED: Dorset*, 235; *REED: Lincolnshire*, 1:269).

[77] The Attorney General alleged that the largest gathering numbered "One hundred persons att the leaste," while some witnesses testified that there could not have been many more than twenty people present (STAC 8/34/4, fol. 55; see fols. 42r, 42v, 43r, 50r).

[78] STAC 8/34/4, fols. 31v, 42r, 42v, 44r. See Scott, "Kendal," 172–73; Campbell, *English Yeoman*, 150–51; and Watts, "Tenant-Right," 75–76.

[79] Joseph Nicolson and Richard Burn, *The History and Antiquities of the Counties of Westmorland and Cumberland*, 2 vols. (London, 1777), 1:53.

[80] STAC 8/34/4, fol. 55; see also fols. 43v, 45v, 46r; and Andy Wood, "'Poore men woll speke one daye': Plebeian Languages of Deference and Defiance in England, *c.* 1520–1640," in *Politics of the Excluded*, ed. Harris, 89–90.

Playing Libel from Cambridge to Kendal

Westmerland to vphold theire Custome of Tennantright." Parts of this "most dangerous and seditious libell," as the Star Chamber complaint termed it, were supposedly read by a protest leader at the January 1621 meeting at Staveley Chapel. The "Reasons" marshaled selections from scripture and chronicle histories in support of tenant right, including a pointed adaptation of Ezekiel 46:18: "The kinge shall not take of the peoples inheritance by oppression nor thrust them out of theire posses-sions, but shall cause his sonne to inheritt of his owne."[81] In a provocative departure from the texts of the Geneva and King James Bibles, the "Reasons" replaces "prince" with "kinge" and "sons" with "sonne."[82] Thus altered, the verse directly admonishes King James and his son Charles, who, as mentioned above, was Kendal's foremost landlord. By repurposing scriptural authority, the tenants suggested that God was on their side.

This was a common strategy for the poor and disenfranchised. John Walter has shown that commoners often justified their protests by appro-priating their rulers' own legitimizing rhetoric, which "ground[ed] legit-imacy in the use of power to protect ... the subsistence of subordinate groups."[83] The "Reasons" and the stage play both exploited this populist tradition. Indeed, the scene of landlord-ravens devouring tenant-sheep could have come straight from a contemporary sermon. Brodie Waddell notes that "the most common representation of wealthy oppressors in Elizabethan and Jacobean preaching was probably the image of the raven-ous bird," and the oppressed were often figured as poor sheep.[84] The Kendal tenants took that imagery from the pulpit to the stage.

By September 1621, two months after the play, the landlords felt belea-guered enough to take their case to Star Chamber. The Attorney General's

---

[81] STAC 8/34/4, fol. 55; see also fols. 42r, 45v.

[82] The Authorized Version reads: "the prince shall not take of the people's inheritance by oppression, to thrust them out of their possession; *but* he shall give his sons inheritance out of his own possession" (Robert Carroll and Stephen Prickett, eds., *The Bible: Authorized King James Version* [Oxford: Oxford University Press, 1997], Ezekiel 46:18).

[83] John Walter, "Public Transcripts, Popular Agency and the Politics of Subsistence in Early Modern England," in *Negotiating Power in Early Modern Society: Order, Hierarchy and Subordination in Britain and Ireland*, ed. Michael J. Braddick and Walter (Cambridge: Cambridge University Press, 2001), 128.

[84] Brodie Waddell, "Economic Immorality and Social Reformation in English Popular Preaching, 1585–1625," *Cultural and Social History* 5.2 (2008): 172. For images of the oppressed – tenants in particular – as poor sheep preyed upon by wolves, see CP 76/97; *The True Narration of the Entertainment of his Royall Maiestie* (London, 1603), sig. F2r; Robert Sanderson, *Ten Sermons Preached* (London, 1627), sig. Q4v; and Peter Corbin and Douglas Sedge, eds., *Thomas of Woodstock, or Richard the Second, Part One* (Manchester: Manchester University Press, 2002), 4.2.31–36.

76 The Scene of Libel

bill of complaint accuses the tenants' ringleaders of publishing libels and disseminating seditious talk "to incite and stirre vp the poorer sort of people to raise a daungerous and Riotous assemblie ... and thereby to enforce the Lord*es* of the Mannors to suffer theire Tennant*es* to Contynue in theire Tenem*entes* by the pretended Custome of Tennantright."[85] But the tenants remained firm. Indeed, they evidently succeeded in doing exactly what the Attorney General and the aggrieved landlords worried they would: rally the community to compel their lords to allow them their customary tenure. In brazen defiance of the king's proclamation, the tenants put enough pressure on the local and national authorities to win a favorable judgment. The case took several years to wend its way through the court, but in 1626 Star Chamber ultimately reaffirmed the tenants' "customary estates of inheritance" – essentially what the Court of Chancery had decreed for Prince Charles's tenants back in 1619.[86] The protests, and the protest theater, worked.

To sum up the strain of seditious discourse that the play fostered, I want to return to a piece of menacing talk that allegedly circulated through Kendal at the time. According to "com*m*on Report," one of the protesters declared that "the Landslord*es* were but a breakfast for theire tenant*es*" (or "but a handfull or a Breakfaste" in the version quoted above), and that "rather then the tenant*es* wold loose theire lyveing*es* they wold all ioyne togeather and loose theire lyves."[87] This rumored speech in many ways resembles the surviving scene of the play. Both disseminate a libelous cocktail of mocking comedy, violent threat, and tenant solidarity. Judging by the landlords' suit and the protest's success, this libelous talk briefly shifted the parameters of public discourse in Kendal. Tenants reimagined themselves as political agents and their landlords as "but a breakfast"; at least for a moment, the eaten became the eaters.

Club Law in Cambridge

My final case study examines the play known as *Club Law*, one of those rare instances in which both an account of the performance and a largely intact script survive. In *The History of the University of Cambridge* (1655), Thomas

---

[85] STAC 8/34/4, fol. 55.

[86] Nicolson and Burn, *History*, 1:59. However, this was a victory for the tenants of Kendal but not for tenant right itself. To reconcile the king's proclamation with the tenants' claims, the court held that their privileged tenure was, by the local customs of Kendal, independent of border service and thus was not actually tenant right at all (Watts, "Tenant-Right," 78).

[87] STAC 8/34/4, fol. 43v.

Playing Libel from Cambridge to Kendal 77

Fuller reports a curious incident of libelous theater at the university. It was the winter of 1599–1600, and the young scholars of Cambridge, "conceiving themselves somewhat wronged by the *Townsmen*," decided to prosecute their revenge through a libelous play.[88] Having discovered "some *Town privacies*," the scholars

> composed a merry (but abusive) *Comedy*, (which they call'd *CLUB-LAW*) in *English*, as calculated for the capacities of such, whom they intended *spectatours* thereof. *Clare-Hall* was the place wherein it was acted, and the Major [mayor], with his Brethren, and their Wives, were invited to behold it, or rather themselves abused therein. A convenient place was assigned to the *Townsfolk*, (riveted in with *Schollars* on all sides) where they might see and be seen. Here they did behold themselves in their own best cloathes (which the Schollars had borrowed) so livelily personated, their *habits*, *gestures*, *language*, *lieger-jests*, and *expressions*, that it was hard to decide, which was the *true Townsman*, whether he that *sat by*, or he who *acted on the Stage*. *Sit still* they could not for *chafing*, *go out* they could not for *crowding*, but impatiently patient were fain to attend till dismissed at the end of the *Comedy*.[89]

This was a canny use of theatrical space. Evidently exploiting the townsfolk's own desire to "see and be seen," the scholars scripted them into the performance. The "chafing" spectators became the spectacle themselves, surrounded by merry scholars eager to watch their rage and humiliation at the sight of their caricatures strutting across the stage. The citizens must have quickly discovered the perils of publicity: they certainly were seen, but not at all to their advantage. Far from cutting a stately figure, the assembled dignitaries suffered the same ignominious fate as their dramatic counterparts did in the play.

In Fuller's telling, the mayor and his brethren quickly complained to the Privy Council, and the Council "sent some *slight* and *private check* to the *principall Actors*." But this apparently left the citizens unsatisfied. Fuller relates "a *tradition*, many earnestly engaging for the *truth* thereof," that the citizens demanded "*some more severe and publick punishment*" for the culprits. According to this bit of Cambridge folklore, the lords of the Privy Council mischievously replied with an offer to come to Cambridge and see for themselves "the same *Comedy*, with all the *properties* thereof, *acted over*

---

[88] Thomas Fuller, *The History of the University of Cambridge*, printed with *The Church-History of Britain* (London, 1655), sig. Vuuu2v. The dating of the play comes from a note by G. C. Moore Smith, printed in W. W. Greg, Review of *Club Law*, ed. Smith, *Modern Language Review* 4.2 (1909): 268–69.

[89] Fuller, *History*, sig. Vuuu2v.

78   The Scene of Libel

again, (the *Townsmen* as formerly, being enjoyned to be *present thereat*) that
so they might the better proportion the *punishment* to the *fault.*"[90] Reluctant
to suffer further humiliation, the townsmen dropped the matter.

Scholars disagree about the credibility of Fuller's account.[91] After all,
Fuller, a clergyman and historian who spent over a decade at Cambridge in
the 1620s and 1630s, was given to embellishment.[92] He liberally sprinkles
his histories with entertaining (and likely apocryphal) anecdotes, derided
by one contemporary critic as "*Merry Tales,* and scraps of *Trencher-jests,*
frequently interlaced in all parts of the History."[93] And he himself admits
that the story of the Privy Council's response is just a "tradition," albeit one
with many supporters. G. C. Moore Smith, *Club Law*'s early twentieth-
century editor, finds it "very improbable that the actors should have been
able to borrow the clothes of the townspeople whom they were caricatur-
ing; and a little unlikely that they should have induced them to come to
Clare Hall to see the play."[94] The anecdote certainly sounds exaggerated, to
say the least.

But several pieces of evidence argue for the plausibility of the general
scene if not of all its particulars. First, a 1601 complaint by the town of
Cambridge includes an allegation that "[t]he Schollers of the
Vniuersitie . . . doe greevouslie, and very disorderlye misvse in generall all
free burgesses, and in particuler the Magestrates of the towne" through,
among other means, "their playes in Colledges."[95] There is only one
Cambridge play abusing the town magistrates that we know was performed
around 1600: *Club Law.* The citizens' complaint suggests that they knew of
the play, if not necessarily that they attended its premiere.

The other evidence has to do with the techniques of libelous theater.
Mocking members of a group to their face in their own clothes might
sound improbable, but that is what the tenants of Kendal did two

---

[90] Ibid.

[91] For partial endorsements, see Alan H. Nelson, ed., *REED: Cambridge,* 2 vols. (Toronto: University
      of Toronto Press, 1989), 2:709; and Paul Whitfield White, *Drama and Religion in English Provincial
      Society, 1485–1660* (Cambridge: Cambridge University Press, 2008), 127. For more skeptical views,
      see Andrew Gurr, "Professional Playing in London and Superior Cambridge Responses,"
      Shakespeare Studies 37 (2009): 48; and Christopher Marlow, *Performing Masculinity in English
      University Drama, 1598–1636* (Farnham, UK: Ashgate, 2013), 50–53.

[92] On Fuller's time at Cambridge, see W. B. Patterson, *Thomas Fuller: Discovering England's Religious
      Past* (Oxford: Oxford University Press, 2018), 18–41.

[93] Peter Heylyn, *Examen Historicum: Or A Discovery and Examination of the Mistakes, Falsities, and
      Defects in some Modern Histories* (London, 1659), sig. b2r.

[94] G. C. Moore Smith, introduction to *Club Law: A Comedy Acted in Clare Hall, Cambridge, about
      1599–1600,* ed. Smith (Cambridge: Cambridge University Press, 1907), liv.

[95] TNA, SP 12/279, fol. 117v.

decades later: they borrowed their costumes from the landlord class, and the lords whom they mocked may well have been in attendance.[96] Provincial libelers went to great lengths to entice local audiences to watch their performances. Finally, there is the text of *Club Law* itself. The play was lost (aside from a passing mention in the eighteenth century) until Smith discovered a manuscript copy in 1906 and published an edition a year later.[97] Fuller's anecdote bears a remarkable resemblance to the climax of the play, a scene in which a band of citizens come to a show expecting to see one thing but instead come away publicly humiliated. None of this evidence can prove the truth of Fuller's account. Perhaps he fabricated it entirely, perhaps he wove it from the threads of the play, or perhaps some version really did take place on that day in Clare Hall. But what we can say for sure is that his account is grounded in the same tropes of libelous performance that the script of *Club Law* both exploits and dramatizes.

The play's performance came at a decisive moment in the history of town–gown relations in Cambridge. By the late sixteenth century, the balance of power had tilted in favor of the university even as the town vigorously contested its authority.[98] The rhetoric on both sides grew increasingly heated. In 1601, university leaders wrote several letters to Secretary Robert Cecil complaining of "our Towne adversaries" and "our insolent and malitious Townesmen."[99] Among the broadsides from the scholars were, as the citizens alleged, at least a few satirical plays. In February 1583, Thomas Mudd of Pembroke Hall was briefly imprisoned for lampooning the mayor in a comedy. Mudd spent three days in the Tolbooth and was forced to apologize, but drama remained an outlet for student disorder.[100] University records document crowds clamoring at the college gates, stones thrown and clubs swung, broken and bloodied heads,

---

[96] The Star Chamber bill of complaint claims that the Kendal play's representation of landlords in hell nearly "prouoked [the lords] to haue fallen into outrage and to haue broken your Majesties peace and haue sought private Revenge of suche disgracefull iniuries" (STAC 8/34/4, fol. 55; see *REED: Cumberland*, 188).

[97] Smith, introduction to *Club Law*, ix–xi.

[98] *REED: Cambridge*, 2:708–9; Smith, introduction to *Club Law*, xv–xxxi.

[99] TNA, SP 12/279, fols. 113r, 195r. Victor Morgan with Christopher Brooke, in *A History of the University of Cambridge*, vol. 2, *1546–1750* (Cambridge: Cambridge University Press, 2004), speaks of the "exceptionally intense antagonism between university and town" (242). For a different view, emphasizing cooperation as well as conflict, see Alexandra Shepard, "Contesting Communities? 'Town' and 'Gown' in Cambridge, *c.* 1560–1640," in *Communities in Early Modern England: Networks, Place, Rhetoric*, ed. Shepard and Phil Withington (Manchester: Manchester University Press, 2000), 216–34.

[100] *REED: Cambridge*, 1:308, 2:1150–51.

80   The Scene of Libel

and considerable property damage.[101] Above, I traced such misrule and mockery to their roots in England's traditional festive culture. Fuller himself calls *Club Law* a "festiuissima" play.[102]

Fittingly, *Club Law* is itself about bad publicity. Set in an Athens that clearly stands for Cambridge, the play dramatizes the contemporary town–gown conflict. On one side are the newly elected burgomaster (mayor) of Athens, Niphle, and his fellow townsmen. On the other are the "gentle Athenians," the students and scholars of the Academy.[103] The play's satire is harsh and, as Smith shows in his edition of the play, transparent. The lecherous, arrogant townsmen of Athens are crude caricatures of Cambridge's mayor and civic officials – the very citizens who, Fuller claimed, attended the performance.[104] In the play, both sides are constantly scheming to humiliate each other in public. Their favored method for shaming, and clobbering, their opponents is "Clubb lawe," a term that makes its first known appearance in the play (28 n). Niphle rallies the townsfolk to "rout out the whole generacion" of scholars, while the scholars Philenius and Musonius resolve to "renewe the ancient Club-lawe" and "curbe [the townsmen's] foming mouthes" (520–21, 206–7, 207–8). A century later, Joseph Addison would describe the "Club-Law" of the universities of Renaissance Europe: "When they were not able to confute their Antagonist, they knock'd him down."[105] In the play's Athens, might (with a healthy dose of wit) makes right.

The scholars in *Club Law* aim not only to beat down the townsfolk but also, like their Cambridge counterparts, to publicize their misdeeds. "[P]lay[ing] the Eivesdroper," the young student Cricket discovers the illicit plots and transgressions of the citizens (1001–2). He overhears Niphle arranging a nighttime tryst with a "good holsome wench," and, in one of many metadramatic moments, he outlines his own plan to render the encounter in libelous verse (1089–90). Cricket gleefully crows, "how I triumph in this, that wee may cry out of this lecherous villaine, and tell him of his holesome girle and of his burnings. If we can doe nothing els, wele fill all the Towne full of Rimes of him. wele paint all the Boggards [privies] with papers and so disgrace him, that wele make him hange him

---

[101] Ibid., 1:309, 360–61, 385–90, 407–9, 411–12, 424–86, 583. See Alexandra Shepard, *Meanings of Manhood in Early Modern England* (Oxford: Oxford University Press, 2003), 106–8.

[102] *REED: Cambridge*, 1:377. On festive misrule at Cambridge, see Shepard, *Meanings*, 99–100.

[103] *Club Law*, ll. 99–100. Subsequent quotations of the play will be cited parenthetically by line number.

[104] Smith, introduction to *Club Law*, xli–xlix.

[105] Joseph Addison, *Spectator* 239, December 4, 1711, in *The Spectator*, ed. Donald F. Bond, vol. 2 (Oxford: Clarendon Press, 1965), 429.

Playing Libel from Cambridge to Kendal

selfe" (1122–27). Of course, this moment is designed to "disgrace" the actual mayor of Cambridge too. Speaking for the real and staged students alike, Cricket revels in the damage that these libels will inflict on the burgomaster's reputation. He imagines scraps of scurrilous verse filling the town and, in an especially vicious turn, even driving Niphle to suicide.

"Papers" and "rimes" are not the only means of public shaming that appear in the comedy. As the conflict between town and gown comes to a head, Musonius and Philenius learn that the townsmen plan to humiliate the students at a holiday game. The town magistrates' own wives betray their husbands' plot. "I heard all the men in our towne crying out against Clublawe," Mistress Colby (one of the wives) informs the scholars, "and in the end determined to beate you with your owne weapons, and make you feele Clublawe" (940–41, 943–44). The venue for their revenge, she adds, will be tomorrow's "Cudgill play" (946). Violent sports such as cudgel playing (a kind of stick fighting), wrestling, and football were popular entertainments and tests of manhood across England.[106] In *Hesperides* (1648), Robert Herrick elegizes the festive sports – "Morris-danc[ing]," "Pagentrie," "*Cudgell*-Play" – of "Happy Rusticks."[107] These were the types of "lewed games" that, much to the chagrin of the university's leaders, regularly drew its students to the nearby town of Chesterton and to the Gog Magog Hills, a few miles southeast of Cambridge.[108] By 1620, the games and shows performed at the hills included running, jumping, wrestling, horseracing, and bear- and bull-baiting.[109] We don't know the precise occasion for *Club Law*'s performance, but Fuller's description of it as a "festiuissima" comedy puts it in the same category of holiday entertainment. It is a festive show featuring a festive show.

The play thus becomes a metatheatrical contest. Whichever side proves to be better at staging club law – and consequently *Club Law* – will triumph. Musonius and Philenius suggest as much when, after learning about the planned cudgel play, they resolve to "see the performance of Clublawe" (985). "Clublawe" here points both to the beating that the townsmen will soon receive and to the university play in which the characters all appear. Cricket sustains the metatheatrical language. "I play my part" and "Ile make a shewe," he says at different moments in the play (1281–82, 1394). Meanwhile, the townsmen try to take the "holy daye" show

---

[106] Paul Griffiths, *Youth and Authority: Formative Experiences in England, 1560–1640* (Oxford: Clarendon Press, 1996), 136–40.

[107] *The Complete Poetry of Robert Herrick*, ed. Tom Cain and Ruth Connolly, 2 vols. (Oxford: Oxford University Press, 2013), 1:242.

[108] *REED: Cambridge*, 1:270; see 2:723–27.   [109] Ibid., 1:571–72.

82 The Scene of Libel

in a very different direction (1840). They stockpile "staves" and gather "all the ladds in the towne" – their weapons/props and their soldiers/actors – to turn the holiday game into a public cudgeling of the students (1846).

This scheme was not without precedent. On Shrove Tuesday 1579, the scholars of Cambridge came to the neighboring village of Chesterton to partake in that "bloody and murthering practise" consisting of "nothinge but beastly furie and exstreme violence": football.[110] Shrove Tuesday, the day before the beginning of Lent, was notorious for violent games and popular disorder.[111] On this particular holiday, the moralistic attacks on the sport proved justified. The scholars reportedly came to play "peaceably, withowte anye weapons," but the townsmen of Chesterton were not so virtuous: they "had layd divers staves secretly in the Church porch." The Vice-Chancellor of Cambridge recalled that the townsmen "in playing did pike quarrells agenst the schollers," while a witness from Chesterton related that as the two sides "were hotte in playe sodenlye one cryed staves."[112] Either way, the townsmen promptly brought out their weapons and beat the scholars bloody.

The Athenian townsmen plot to restage this scene of football hooliganism at a different kind of festival game: a cudgel play. But this time the scholars come out on top. The townsmen's wives again betray their husbands and reveal the hoard of hidden staves to the scholars. The scholars steal the weapons; when the townsmen "begin to picke the quarrell" at the cudgel play, Cricket cries, "Clubs for theis Clounes here, Clubs" (2125–26, 2192–93). The students immediately arm themselves and soundly thrash the weaponless townsmen. Unsurprisingly, the scholars turn out to be the more resourceful actors and playmakers.

The echoes of Shrove Tuesday 1579 – townsfolk secretly gathering staves and picking a quarrel with students at a holiday game, a surprise beating at the cry of "Clubs"/"staves" – seem too close to be merely coincidental. Two decades elapsed between the football match at Chesterton and the performance of *Club Law* at Cambridge. But their similarities suggest that the events of 1579 were ingrained in the cultural memory of the university. Perhaps by 1600 the football game had become, like the Privy Council's

---

[110] Phillip Stubbes, *The Anatomie of Abuses* (London, 1583), sig. P6r; Thomas Elyot, *The boke named the Gouernour* (London, 1531), sig. N1v. Ronald Hutton describes the sport as follows: "The game in its traditional form had no clearly defined teams and effectively no rules; and goals, if they existed at all, were of secondary importance to the thrill of fighting for possession of the ball" (*The Stations of the Sun: A History of the Ritual Year in Britain* [Oxford: Oxford University Press, 1996], 154).

[111] See Griffiths, *Youth*, 147–51; Hutton, *Stations*, 151–56; and François Laroque, *Shakespeare's Festive World: Elizabethan Seasonal Entertainment and the Professional Stage*, trans. Janet Lloyd (Cambridge: Cambridge University Press, 1991), 96–103.

[112] BL, Lansdowne MS 33, fols. 67r, 69r.

Playing Libel from Cambridge to Kendal

supposed offer to see *Club Law* restaged with the citizens once more in attendance, "a *tradition*, many earnestly engaging for the *truth* thereof." Such a tale would have fit well in Cambridge lore alongside the other incidents of town–gown violence. Between 1579 and 1599, there were plenty of scuffles between students and townsmen, and clubs were often the weapon of choice.[113]

In addition to this local history, the echoes of 1579 also point to a common cultural script of festive abuse. At South Kyme, at Wells, at Kendal, and elsewhere, communities gathered to see dramatic shows that turned out to defame some person or group among them. And as Shakespeare demonstrates in *The Merry Wives of Windsor*, that public mockery could easily turn violent. The merry wives' pageant leaves Falstaff pinched, burned, and, in Mistress Ford's words, "publicly shamed."[114] *Club Law* and *The Merry Wives* alike join festive, violent shows with public shaming rituals – a familiar recipe for provincial libel.

If the tenants of Kendal turned the eaters into the eaten, *Club Law*'s cudgel play turns the would-be beaters into the beaten: the Athenian townsmen suffer the violent humiliation they had hoped to inflict on the scholars. The students make their town adversaries play a highly unflattering part in the festival show – exactly what Fuller claimed happened at the play's performance in Clare Hall, when the student spectators encircled the citizens and prevented them from leaving. At the cudgel play, there is even a stage direction for "Spectators" to come in (2112). If there is any truth to Fuller's account, this would have been a dizzyingly metatheatrical moment: townsfolk surrounded by spectators watching townsfolk surrounded by spectators. Both the real and the staged citizens would have been chafing, to say the least.

Other than Fuller's anecdote and the possible allusion to the play in the town's contemporary complaint, we know nothing about the reception of *Club Law*. Certainly it would only have inflamed the conflict between town and gown. In 1601, the university flatly denied the allegation that the scholars were performing abusive plays in their colleges (along with many other grievances brought by the citizens).[115] Robert Cecil, recently elected chancellor of the university, found fault on both sides in the "over growing quarrells,"

---

[113] See, e.g., BL, Lansdowne MS 54, fol. 12r, transcribed in Charles Henry Cooper, *Annals of Cambridge*, 5 vols. (Cambridge, 1842–1908), 2:440–41; and BL, Lansdowne MS 87, fols. 50, 58, transcribed in Cooper, *Annals*, 2:499–501. In 1575, the former Cambridge professor William Soone wrote that the scholars, who "are perpetually quarrelling and fighting" with the townsmen, "go out in the night to shew their valour, armed with monstrous great clubs furnished with a cross piece of iron to keep off the blows, and frequently beat the watch" (Cooper, *Annals*, 2:329).
[114] Shakespeare, *Merry Wives*, 4.2.209–10.   [115] TNA, SP 12/279, fol. 118r.

84 The Scene of Libel

blaming "bussie persons" in the town and "Rash headed Schollers" alike.[116] *Club Law* restaged that drama of division. The probably young and certainly rash scholars responsible for the play drew on local memory, festive traditions, and theatrical techniques to defame the townsfolk. And in Fuller's telling, they successfully scripted town–gown relations not only on the stage but also, at least within the doors of Clare Hall, in reality.

***

For all their differences, the performances that I've examined above share not only a repertoire of theatrical techniques but also an activist style of public address. When the tenants of Kendal saw their landlords in hell, when (or rather, if) the citizens of Cambridge saw themselves satirized onstage, they found themselves playing roles of their own in a real-life drama. The situation was somewhat different on the London stage, where profit was usually the greater consideration. But the example of Chapman's *The Old Joiner of Aldgate* shows that professional playmakers could stage an equally defamatory vision of neighborhood politics, if to capitalize on local scandals rather than from more personal motives. Whether on the stage or in the streets, these performances turned audiences into (sometimes unwilling) accomplices. The cumulative evidence explains why William Hudson and other authorities were so quick to implicate listeners and spectators in the act of libel. It was the public merriment or shame or anger – the circulation of communal feelings – that made libelous performance such a potent medium for bad publicity.

Of course, most plays performed in London's playhouses were not so obviously defamatory. And while some of those that did veer toward libel were local allegories such as Chapman's *Old Joiner*, others – from the lost Marprelate plays in the 1580s to Middleton's *A Game at Chess* in 1624 – took aim at figures and events on a national (or even international) scale. I examine two such plays in the following chapters, *Sir Thomas More* and Jonson's *Poetaster*. Both came close enough to politically sensitive events as to face some form of censorship. The other two plays that I discuss, Shakespeare and Peele's *Titus Andronicus* and Heywood's *Edward IV*, are not as nakedly topical, although both (especially *Titus*) evoke contemporary controversies. Yet my premise is that the ways of thinking and feeling activated by the provincial performance of libel were equally at play in the commercial theater. In London, repeated performances before large, diverse assemblies of strangers brought the scene of libel to a playgoing public.

---

[116] TNA, SP 12/281, fol. 21r.

PART II

Libels on the Elizabethan Stage

CHAPTER 3

Libels Supplicatory: Shakespeare and Peele's Titus Andronicus

For several months in 1591, three Puritan extremists bent on ecclesiastical revolution carried on an indefatigable campaign of letters. They wrote to prominent Presbyterians, to several gentlemen and lords, and even to the queen herself. The biggest push came in mid-July, just days before they took to the streets themselves. "[F]or preparing ... of the mindes of the people, and to stirre them vp to be in readines," the conspirators scattered "certaine seditious letters" – two hundred copies, the Attorney General would allege at trial – "in many of the streetes of *London*."[1] This was not the first time London was blanketed with sectarian libels, nor would it be the last. Writing in 1593, Francis Bacon reflected on the "plentifull yeald of libell*es*" emanating from confessional strife.[2] The most prominent libels of the 1580s and early 1590s – *Leicester's Commonwealth* (1584), the Marprelate tracts (1588–89), the Cecil's commonwealth pamphlets (1592–93) – came from the Catholic and Puritan extremes.[3] The same years also witnessed savage waves of religious persecution. One Catholic polemicist wrote of a "new *Cecillian Inquisition*" – named for Elizabeth's chief secretary, William Cecil – and at the same time Anglican leaders were persecuting Presbyterians with considerable zeal.[4] Among the casualties were scores of

---

[1] Richard Cosin, *Conspiracie, for Pretended Reformation: viz. Presbyteriall Discipline* (London, 1592), sigs. F2r–v; Historical Manuscripts Commission (HMC), *Fourteenth Report, Appendix, Part IV: The Manuscripts of Lord Kenyon* (London, 1894), 608. For lucid histories of the affair and its relationship to Elizabethan Puritanism, see Alexandra Walsham, "'Frantick Hacket': Prophecy, Sorcery, Insanity, and the Elizabethan Puritan Movement," *Historical Journal* 41.1 (1998): 27–66; and Michael P. Winship, "Puritans, Politics, and Lunacy: The Copinger-Hacket Conspiracy as the Apotheosis of Elizabethan Presbyterianism," *Sixteenth Century Journal* 38.2 (2007): 345–69.

[2] Francis Bacon, *Certaine obseruations vppon a libell*, in *The Oxford Francis Bacon*, vol. 1, ed. Alan Stewart with Harriet Knight (Oxford: Clarendon Press, 2012), 346.

[3] Peter Lake has exhaustively examined the printed Catholic libels in *Bad Queen Bess? Libels, Secret Histories, and the Politics of Publicity in the Reign of Queen Elizabeth I* (Oxford: Oxford University Press, 2016).

[4] Richard Verstegan, *A Declaration of the True Causes of the Great Troubles, Presupposed to Be Intended against the realme of England* ([Antwerp], 1592), sig. E5r; Patrick Collinson, *The Elizabethan Puritan Movement* (Berkeley: University of California Press, 1967), 403–31. For an overview of later

87

88   Libels on the Elizabethan Stage

Catholics and a handful of Puritans, including William Hacket, the figure at the center of the 1591 affair.[5]

Shakespeare and Peele's *Titus Andronicus*, probably written between 1591 and 1594, stages both the proliferating texts and the religious violence of the early 1590s.[6] Each aspect has received ample attention on its own.[7] But rarely have the play's echoes of Elizabethan confessional conflict and its obsession with writing been considered together. The recent exception is Joseph Sterrett, who perceptively describes the petitionary texts that fly through the second half of the play as oppositional prayers directed not just to higher powers but also to a wider audience.[8] Yet Sterrett's focus on Catholic petitions and prayers misses the broader cross-confessional category evoked by *Titus*' texts: the libel. The play is filled with ephemeral scraps of writing disseminated at a distance, texts that join appeals for redress with violent threats. In my Introduction, I traced this paradigm of libel through post-Reformation controversy. Libels and accusations of libel came from all sides, Catholic, Protestant, and Puritan alike. In this chapter, I will argue that the writings in *Titus Andronicus* clearly evoke the sectarian libels of the day and, indeed, seem to allude directly to the seditious letters scattered in the streets by Hacket and his coconspirators in 1591.

Elizabethan religious persecution, see John Coffey, *Persecution and Toleration in Protestant England, 1558–1689* (Harlow, UK: Longman, 2000), 86–98.

[5] Geoffrey F. Nuttall, "The English Martyrs 1535–1680: A Statistical Review," *Journal of Ecclesiastical History* 22.3 (1971): 193; Cosin, *Conspiracie*, sigs. L2v–L3r.

[6] The most comprehensive case for Peele's co-authorship is Brian Vickers, *Shakespeare, Co-Author: A Historical Study of Five Collaborative Plays* (Oxford: Oxford University Press, 2002), 148–243. The current consensus holds that Peele wrote the first scene and perhaps the second while Shakespeare was primarily responsible for the rest (Gary Taylor and Rory Loughnane, "The Canon and Chronology of Shakespeare's Works," in *The New Oxford Shakespeare: Authorship Companion*, ed. Taylor and Gabriel Egan [Oxford: Oxford University Press, 2017], 491).

[7] On writing in the play, see, e.g., Mary Laughlin Fawcett, "Arms/Words/Tears: Language and the Body in *Titus Andronicus*," *ELH* 50.2 (1983): 261–77; and Gillian Murray Kendall, "'Lend me thy hand': Metaphor and Mayhem in *Titus Andronicus*," *Shakespeare Quarterly* 40.3 (1989): 299–316. On its confessional politics – a more recent topic of attention – see Lukas Erne, "'Popish Tricks' and 'a Ruinous Monastery': *Titus Andronicus* and the Question of Shakespeare's Catholicism," *SPELL: Swiss Papers in English Language and Literature* 13 (2000): 135–55; Nicholas R. Moschovakis, "'Irreligious Piety' and Christian History: Persecution as Pagan Anachronism in *Titus Andronicus*," *Shakespeare Quarterly* 53.4 (2002): 460–86; John Klause, *Shakespeare, the Earl, and the Jesuit* (Madison, NJ: Fairleigh Dickinson University Press, 2008), 131–43; Jennifer R. Rust, *The Body in Mystery: The Political Theology of the Corpus Mysticum in the Literature of Reformation England* (Evanston: Northwestern University Press, 2014), 67–102; Paulina Kewes, "'I Ask Your Voices and Your Suffrages': The Bogus Rome of Peele and Shakespeare's *Titus Andronicus*," *Review of Politics* 78.4 (2016): 551–70; Stephanie M. Bahr, "*Titus Andronicus* and the Interpretive Violence of the Reformation," *Shakespeare Quarterly* 68.3 (2017): 241–70; and Peter Lake, *Hamlet's Choice: Religion and Resistance in Shakespeare's Revenge Tragedies* (New Haven: Yale University Press, 2020), 17–70.

[8] Joseph Sterrett, *The Unheard Prayer: Religious Toleration in Shakespeare's Drama* (Leiden: Brill, 2012), 1–33. Kewes makes a similar connection in passing ("I Ask," 561).

Shakespeare and Peele's Titus Andronicus

I do not want to limit the play's interest in these matters to late Elizabethan allegory, however. The same questions of popularity and public address run through the long history of rhetoric. Cicero, the foremost Roman rhetorician, calls the public meeting (*contio*) the orator's greatest stage, adding that "the effect produced by numbers is of such a kind that a speaker can no more be eloquent without a large audience than a flute-player can perform without a flute."[9] But the fall of the Roman Republic marked the decline of the *contio*, the assembly where the people gathered to hear and judge political orations. For the speaker Maternus in Tacitus' *Dialogus de Oratoribus*, this may have been a good thing. His central argument – likely leavened with bitter irony – is that the rise of the emperors has made the art of rhetoric not just obsolete but positively dangerous. "What is the use of one harangue after another on public platforms [*multis apud populum contionibus*]," he asks, "when it is not the ignorant multitude that decides a political issue, but a monarch who is the incarnation of wisdom?"[10] A millennium and a half later, humanists such as Juan Luis Vives retold this story of oratorical decay and extended it to their own Renaissance monarchies.[11]

Titus Andronicus initially stages the Tacitean-humanist history of rhetorical decline under monarchy. But when the emperor Saturninus silences public speech, he and his family are met with a flurry of texts: letters, petitions, even an allusion to printing. This turn to writing reflects the fate of rhetoric in the Renaissance. As Cicero and Tacitus indicate, classical rhetoric was above all an art of speaking designed for public delivery. In early modern England, rhetoric remained the backbone of the grammar school curriculum. Yet an aspiring orator was at least as likely to find a mass audience in writing as in speech. The rhetorical culture accordingly shaped not only the spoken word in plays, preaching, and parliament but also all sorts of written media, from newsletters to pamphlets to libels.[12] In *Titus* as

---

[9] Cicero, *De Oratore*, trans. E. W. Sutton and H. Rackham, 2 vols. (Cambridge, MA: Harvard University Press, 1948), 2.338.

[10] Tacitus, *Dialogus de Oratoribus*, trans. W. Peterson, rev. M. Winterbottom, in *Agricola, Germania, Dialogus* (Cambridge, MA: Harvard University Press, 1970), 41.4.

[11] Juan Luis Vives, "From *On the Causes of the Corruption of the Arts*," in *Renaissance Debates on Rhetoric*, ed. and trans. Wayne A. Rebhorn (Ithaca: Cornell University Press, 2000), 87–91.

[12] See Peter Mack, *Elizabethan Rhetoric: Theory and Practice* (Cambridge: Cambridge University Press, 2002); David Colclough, *Freedom of Speech in Early Stuart England* (Cambridge: Cambridge University Press, 2005); Colclough, "Verse Libels and the Epideictic Tradition in Early Stuart England," *Huntington Library Quarterly* 69.1 (2006): 15–30; and Markku Peltonen, *Rhetoric, Politics and Popularity in Pre-Revolutionary England* (Cambridge: Cambridge University Press, 2013).

90 Libels on the Elizabethan Stage

in Elizabethan England, textual technologies offer to reconstitute the public meeting or *contio* in virtual form.

But this republican vision remains unrealized, not least of all because the people themselves are practically absent from the play. Titus and his family may air injustice, but they do so in the interest of factional grievance and bloody revenge. They are as much demagogues as dissidents, as much politicking aristocrats as fugitive nonconformists – indeed, as much Stanleys as Hackets. Ferdinando Stanley, Lord Strange and later fifth Earl of Derby, patronized one of England's most controversial acting companies until his untimely death in April 1594. Suspicions of Catholic sympathy, some more justified than others, swirled around the Stanley family for decades. Ferdinando himself was reputedly of "doubtful" religion, "so as some do thinke him to be of al three religions [Protestant, Catholic, Puritan], and others of none."[13] Given that the 1594 title page of *Titus Andronicus* attributes it to Strange's Men, it is tempting to link the play to the enigmatic, heterodox reputation of its possible patron. Yet two other troupes, Pembroke's and Sussex's, are also listed on the title page, and scholars remain divided about the play's theatrical provenance.[14] Whatever its original company, *Titus'* scenes of sectarian libeling bring the theater into the religious controversies of the early 1590s.

Yet Shakespeare is not much interested in side-taking.[15] To borrow William Hudson's terms, his chief concern is the "manner" rather than the "matter" of confessional dispute. Hudson explains that truth may be a defense for spoken but not for written defamation, "for then the manner is examinable and not the matter."[16] Behind this terse rationale lurks the specter of promiscuous publication, of unsigned accusations flying through the town, city, or even state – just as they do in *Titus*. A playgoer circa 1591–94 would have found echoes of both Puritan and Catholic campaigns – and very recent or still ongoing ones at that – in the Andronici's texts. And the allusions are by no means wholly flattering.

---

[13] Robert Persons, *A Conference about the Next Succession to the Crowne of Ingland* ([Antwerp], 1594/5), sig. Ii4r. On Lord Strange's Men, their patron, and their plays, see Lawrence Manley and Sally-Beth MacLean, *Lord Strange's Men and Their Plays* (New Haven: Yale University Press, 2014).

[14] The two most likely scenarios have the play: 1) written for Strange's Men by early 1592; or 2) originating with a consortium of actors from Derby's (as the company was known after Ferdinando Stanley inherited his father's earldom), Pembroke's, and Sussex's Men in 1593–94. See Manley and MacLean, *Lord Strange's Men*, 106–110; and Jonathan Bate, introduction to Shakespeare, *Titus Andronicus*, ed. Bate (London: Routledge, 1995), 69–79.

[15] Several critics have noted the play's confessional ambivalence or ambiguity: see, e.g., Moschovakis, "Irreligious Piety"; Kewes, "I Ask," 557; and Bahr, "*Titus Andronicus*."

[16] William Hudson, *A Treatise of the Court of Star Chamber*, in *Collectanea Juridica*, ed. Francis Hargrave, vol. 2 (London, 1792), 104.

Shakespeare and Peele's Titus Andronicus 91

By yoking libels not just to the pursuit of justice but also to factionalism and violence, *Titus* takes a hard look at the viral and virulent media of the late Elizabethan public sphere.

Libels Supplicatory

On July 16, 1591, Edmund Coppinger and Henry Arthington, self-proclaimed prophets of mercy and judgment, climbed atop an empty cart near Cheapside Cross and declared to the crowd that Jesus Christ had come to earth in the person of the illiterate maltmaker William Hacket. Their "newes from heauen" quickly shot through the city. Needless to say, the authorities were not convinced that Hacket was the messiah. All three men were promptly arrested. By the end of the month, Coppinger had starved himself to death in prison and Hacket had been publicly executed, cursing and raving of revenge until the very end. Only Arthington escaped alive by "acknowledging his dangerous error, and diuelish seduction."[17] Almost immediately, the conspiracy found an afterlife in Anglican propaganda. The first and most detailed account came in Richard Cosin's 1592 *Conspiracie, for Pretended Reformation*, followed by several more narratives over the ensuing years.[18]

For some time now, scholars have found the spirit of Hacket in Shakespeare's *2 Henry VI*, particularly in the character of Jack Cade.[19] More recently, Nicholas R. Moschovakis has argued that *Titus* too alludes to the affair. He focuses on the clown scene, finding parallels that include a verbal echo ("news, from heaven" [4.3.77]), references to hanging, mad or "distract" protagonists (4.3.26), calls for revenge and violent justice, a letter and knife meant for a monarch, and a sense of the carnivalesque.[20] Moschovakis's evidence is fairly convincing. Yet I believe that the play's debt to the Hacket conspiracy goes deeper still. At least in Cosin's telling, Coppinger and Arthington were compulsive writers. They produced and disseminated a barrage of texts, including "letters," "writings," "petitions," "a supplication," "a treatise," "pamphlets," and "libels."[21] The Andronici

---

[17] Cosin, *Conspiracie*, sigs. I2v, L3v.   [18] Walsham, "Frantick Hacket," 30.

[19] Brents Stirling, "Shakespeare's Mob Scenes: A Reinterpretation," *Huntington Library Quarterly* 8.3 (1945): 214–21; Randall Martin, "Elizabethan Civic Pageantry in *Henry VI*," *University of Toronto Quarterly* 60.2 (1990–91): 255–56; Chris Fitter, *Radical Shakespeare: Politics and Stagecraft in the Early Career* (New York: Routledge, 2012), 46–75.

[20] Nicholas R. Moschovakis, "Topicality and Conceptual Blending: *Titus Andronicus* and the Case of William Hacket," *College Literature* 33.1 (2006): 130–37. All quotations from *Titus* follow Bate's Arden edition, cited parenthetically.

[21] Cosin, *Conspiracie*, sigs. B2v, E4v, F1v, K2v, F2v, B4v.

92   Libels on the Elizabethan Stage

likewise prosecute their plot through a literal hail of texts that are equal parts petition and threat. Later in this chapter, I will discuss several echoes in the play of the writings spread by Hacket's allies in 1591.

But I do not want to suggest that the Andronici, sometimes seen as a Catholic faction, are really crypto-Puritans.[22] Emptied of their religious content, the play's sectarian texts stand for a particular kind of confessional polemic that circulated widely in the 1580s and 1590s: the public petition or supplication. From *A lamentable complaint of the commonalty, by way of supplication to the high court of parliament, for a learned ministery* (1585) to *A petition directed to her most excellent Maiestie* (1591), a series of printed Puritan petitions took their case for ecclesiastical reform not just to queen and parliament but also to a wider public.[23] Catholic petitions were circulating (although largely in manuscript) in these years too, most notably Robert Southwell's *An Humble Supplication to Her Maiestie* (1591).[24] Petitioning had long been recognized as a legitimate way to communicate collective complaints.[25] But these Puritan and Catholic tracts "broke with the norms that supposedly governed petitioning by addressing a large audience beyond the authority they were supposedly supplicating."[26] Publication was a conscious strategy – and one that brought the petitions perilously near if not fully into the territory of libel.

The authors of the petitions were well aware that their heterodox complaints might not be safely delivered directly to the queen or parliament. And they knew too that publication, especially when anonymous, left them vulnerable to charges of libel and sedition. So, they repeatedly

---

[22] For Catholicizing readings, see Erne, "Popish Tricks"; and Klause, *Shakespeare*, 131–43.

[23] *A Lamentable Complaint of the Commonalty* ([London], 1585); *A petition directed to her most excellent Maiestie* ([1591]). The others include *The humble petition of the communaltie* ([1587]; rept. 1588 with *A Lamentable Complaint*); John Penry, *A Treatise Containing the Aequity of an Humble Supplication* (Oxford, 1587); and Penry, *A viewe of some part of such publike wants & disorders as are in the seruice of God* ([Coventry, 1589]), known by its running title as "A Supplication unto the High Court of Parliament" (William Pierce, *John Penry: His Life, Times and Writings* [London: Hodder and Stoughton, 1923], 217). See David Coast, "Speaking for the People in Early Modern England," *Past and Present* 244 (2019): 60–61.

[24] Robert Southwell, *An Humble Supplication to Her Maiestie*, ed. R. C. Bald (Cambridge: Cambridge University Press, 1953). Another Catholic petition was given directly to the Queen in 1585: see Roger B. Manning, "Richard Shelley of Warminghurst and the English Catholic Petition for Toleration of 1585," *Recusant History* 6.6 (1961–62): 265–74.

[25] Annabel Patterson, "A Petitioning Society," in *Reading between the Lines* (Madison: University of Wisconsin Press, 1993), 57–79; David Zaret, *Origins of Democratic Culture: Printing, Petitions, and the Public Sphere in Early-Modern England* (Princeton: Princeton University Press, 2000), 81–99; R. W. Hoyle, "Petitioning as Popular Politics in Early Sixteenth-Century England," *Historical Research* 75 (2002): 365–89.

[26] Coast, "Speaking," 66.

Shakespeare and Peele's Titus Andronicus 93

characterize publication as the last resort of the persecuted minority. As the authors of the *Lamentable Complaint* put it, "Because our desire was, that this our complaint should be communicated to euery one of the honorable of parliament, and finding no other waies to perfourme the same: we desired that it might be done by the way of printing."[27] John Penry's "Supplication unto the High Court of Parliament" similarly explains that "it is published to the ende, that the parliament may bee acquainted with the suite, which could not be done by priuate writing." Of course, print had the added benefit of reaching a broader audience too. Penry insists on the "necessitie of the publishing" not just to reach parliament but also so that "the worlde may see."[28] And the authors of the *Lamentable Complaint* imagine their appeal not just as an agent of reformation but also as an affective invasion: "we vncouer the tiles of your house of Parliament, & let the*m* downe with cordes before you, to stirre vp your bowels of compassion towards them."[29] Reaching even into the house of parliament, the supplication offers to "stirre vp" the compassion and, presumably, the reformist zeal of any lukewarm readers.

Similar rhetoric appears in contemporary Catholic petitions, including Southwell's *Humble Supplication*. Like the Puritan polemicists, Southwell describes publication as a last resort. He writes,

> We are forced to divulge our Petitions, and by many mouthes to open vnto your Highnes our humble suites. For neither daring our selues to present them in person, being terrified with the president of his Imprisonment that last attempted it, nor having the favour of any such Patron, as would be willing to make himself Mediator to your Maiestie, we are forced to committ it to the multitude, hoping that among soe many as shall peruse this short and true Relation of our troubles, god will touch some mercifull heart to let your Highnes vnderstand th'extremity of them.[30]

When presenting such a petition in person means risking imprisonment or worse, publication ("divulg[ing]") is a matter of self-preservation. But it also expands the audience from the nominal addressee, the queen, to "the multitude." Silenced by religious persecution, the "many mouthes" of English Catholics can speak only through the people – or at least through those "mercifull heart[s]" who, Southwell hopes, will take up their cause and propagate their petitions.

---

[27] *Lamentable Complaint*, sig. A1v.　　[28] Penry, *Viewe*, sigs. H1r, H1v.

[29] *Lamentable Complaint*, sig. A3v. See Oliver Arnold, *The Third Citizen: Shakespeare's Theater and the Early Modern House of Commons* (Baltimore: Johns Hopkins University Press, 2007), 38.

[30] Southwell, *Humble Supplication*, 45.

94　　　　　　　　　　Libels on the Elizabethan Stage

The Puritan petitioners, at least, found some sympathizers in parliament.[31] Yet that did not protect them from the crackdown led by Archbishop John Whitgift. The *Lamentable Complaint* and several other "seditious books" apparently landed their printer, Robert Waldegrave, in prison for twenty weeks.[32] Whitgift likewise imprisoned Penry in 1587 for publishing a reformist petition and delivering it to parliament, and in May 1593 Penry's vigorous campaign for reform ended with his execution.[33] On the other side of the confessional spectrum, Southwell met no better fate. The fugitive priest was arrested, tortured, and, after two and a half years in the Tower, hanged, drawn, and quartered.[34] And the Catholic layman Richard Shelley was imprisoned in 1585 merely for delivering a petition into the hands of the queen (this was the terrifying "Imprisonment" that Southwell cites).[35] For religious minorities, the dangers of public petitioning were all too real.

Of course, some of these "petitions" and "supplications," not least of all the ones disseminated by Hacket, Coppinger, and Arthington, were thinly disguised assaults on the ecclesiastical polity. Beyond their seditious content, however, publication itself was cause for suspicion. Matthew Sutcliffe, dean of Exeter and a prominent Anglican polemicist, makes this very point in a 1592 rejoinder to a printed Puritan petition. The text at issue purported to be *A petition directed to her most excellent Maiestie*. But if it really is "directed to her Maiestie," Sutcliffe asks, then "to what ende is the same put in print?" He has an answer ready: "belike the mans purpose is, that so much as the Queene by wisedome shall denie, the people by force, and furie shall establish. which in deede is his drift. for the same was neuer presented to her Maiestie, but onely to the people."[36] Sutcliffe pierces the pretense of humble petitioning to uncover a seditious appeal to the people. His title page recasts the Puritan petition as a "libel

---

[31] Collinson, *Elizabethan Puritan Movement*, 273–88, 303–16.

[32] Martin Marprelate, *Hay Any Work for Cooper*, in *The Martin Marprelate Tracts: A Modernized and Annotated Edition*, ed. Joseph L. Black (Cambridge: Cambridge University Press, 2008), 135. See Collinson, *Elizabethan Puritan Movement*, 273–74.

[33] Pierce, *John Penry*, 173–77, 472–81.

[34] Nancy Pollard Brown, "Southwell, Robert [St Robert Southwell] (1561–1595)," *Oxford Dictionary of National Biography*, online ed. (Oxford University Press, 2008).

[35] Manning, "Richard Shelley."

[36] Matthew Sutcliffe, *An Answere to a Certaine Libel Supplicatorie, or Rather Diffamatory . . . put forth vnder the name and title of a Petition directed to her Maiestie* (London, 1592), sig. B3r. See Patterson, "Petitioning Society," 72–75. Over a decade later, Sutcliffe would level the same accusation against a printed Catholic supplication in his informatively titled *The Supplication of Certaine Masse-Priests falsely called Catholikes. Directed to the Kings most excellent Maiestie, now this time of Parliament, but scattered in corners, to mooue mal-contents to mutinie. Published with a Marginall glosse, and an answer to the Libellers reasons* (London, 1604), sig. B2r.

Shakespeare and Peele's Titus Andronicus 95

supplicatorie, or rather diffamatory" merely masquerading "vnder the name and title of a Petition."

Talk of sectarian libels disguised as petitions persisted through the following decades. The spy Robert Poley reported in 1600 on the Jesuits' "infamous lybels, (howsoever disgvisde vnder forme of Petitions and other Tytles) printed, and disperste in all places," and a few years later Lord Chancellor Thomas Egerton singled out the two most dangerous sorts of "meinteiners & moouers of sedition": libelers and "petitioners that either Come in multitudes, or presume of multitudes of subscriptions of handes, as papistes & sectaryes or puritans."[37] Like Sutcliffe, Poley and Egerton are quick to put public petitioning under the sign of sedition. Publication and religious heterodoxy together turn a supplication into a libel supplicatory.

It was around the height of the late Elizabethan surge in persecution and petitioning that Shakespeare and Peele wrote *Titus Andronicus*. The first known performance of the play was in January 1594, just months after Penry and the separatists Henry Barrow and John Greenwood were executed for publishing seditious and slanderous books against church and state.[38] Earlier datings put the play's composition closer to the Hacket affair and Southwell's *Humble Supplication* (both 1591), as well as to the series of Puritan petitions printed between 1585 and 1592. Either way, the first audiences would have readily recognized the sectarian supplications brought onstage. Indeed, scholars have discerned allusions in *Titus* to several of these texts and events: not only the Hacket affair but also Southwell's *Humble Supplication*, Richard Shelley's petition and imprisonment, and the hangings of Barrow and Greenwood.[39] Yet the confessional diversity of the potential parallels suggests that we should not press too hard on any one of them. Rather, the play shares the broader early modern concern with the "manner" of religiopolitical speech.[40] The slew of libels supplicatory spreading through ancient Rome take the Tacitean-humanist history of political communication into its Elizabethan future.

---

[37] TNA, SP 12/275, fol. 229r; John Hawarde, *Les Reportes del Cases in Camera Stellata, 1593 to 1609*, ed. William Paley Baildon (London, 1894), 188. Poley's letter was a response to the posthumous printing of Southwell's *Humble Supplication*: see Bald, introduction to Southwell, *Humble Supplication*, xiii–xiv.

[38] Pierce, *John Penry*, 465; *The Writings of John Greenwood and Henry Barrow, 1591–1593*, ed. Leland H. Carlson, Elizabethan Nonconformist Texts 6 (London: George Allen and Unwin, 1970), 272–78.

[39] Klause, *Shakespeare*, 132–36; Sterrett, *Unheard Prayer*, 23–28; Jina Politi, "'The Gibbet-Maker,'" *Notes and Queries* 38.1 (1991): 54–55.

[40] The sectarian petitioners themselves use the same word to characterize their public "manner of deliuery" (Penry, *Viewe*, sig. H1r).

96 Libels on the Elizabethan Stage

From the vantage of the theater, that future also meant a return to the past. Vives himself identifies the *contio*, the long-defunct assembly of the Roman Republic, with the theater. Recounting the imperial decay of oratory, he explains that the emperor "did not allow the people to gather together very often or in very great numbers, nor did he let anyone speak freely in public ... Thus, eloquence was excluded from public meetings [*concionibus*], that is, from the theater [*theatro*], its nurse."[41] Motivating the analogy between *contio* and *theatrum* are the crowds who gathered to hear and pass judgment. Yet Vives soon makes the theater stand for a very different kind of audience activity. Under the emperor, he continues, the people gathered "not, as before, in order to consider what was transpiring and whether it was credible or not, ... but as if they were going to be entertained in the theater [*theatrum*]."[42] For Vives, the theater figures the public assembly in both its republican vigor and its imperial impotence.

This paradox suggests a metatheatrical reading of *Titus*' synoptic media history. In the second half of the play, the turn to writing marks a turn to a wider audience – a virtual or, in the playhouse, a physical *contio*. This is not to say that Shakespeare or any other dramatist set out to recreate the space of republican rhetoric. Yet I think a play as preoccupied with political communication as *Titus* is cannot but reflect back on its own medium. Just as the Andronici find new media for public address, so too does the London theater represent a (relatively) new platform for mass entertainment. The theater, moreover, blurred the line between considering credibility and being entertained. Playgoing was, to borrow Paul Yachnin's phrase, an "affective-critical" experience: feelings at least as much as thoughts structured the deliberation that took place in the playhouse.[43] One of the prime pleasures was the chance to render judgment oneself. As Thomas Dekker memorably put it, at plays "your Car-man and Tinker claime as strong a voice in their suffrage, and sit to giue iudgement on the plaies life and death, as well as the prowdest *Momus* among the tribe of *Critick*."[44] At stake is whose voice counts when the time comes to pass judgment – precisely the question that *Titus* insistently poses to its audiences. And while I think the play's answer is fairly pessimistic, in the

---

[41] Vives, "From *On the Causes*," 88; Vives, *De disciplinis libri XX* (Antwerp, 1531), sig. O4v.

[42] Vives, "From *On the Causes*," 89; Vives, *De disciplinis*, sig. P1r.

[43] Paul Yachnin, "Performing Publicity," *Shakespeare Bulletin* 28.2 (2010): 216. See also Steven Mullaney, *The Reformation of Emotions in the Age of Shakespeare* (Chicago: University of Chicago Press, 2015); Jeffrey S. Doty, *Shakespeare, Popularity and the Public Sphere* (Cambridge: Cambridge University Press, 2017); and Musa Gurnis, *Mixed Faith and Shared Feeling: Theater in Post-Reformation London* (Philadelphia: University of Pennsylvania Press, 2018).

[44] Thomas Dekker, *The Guls Horne-booke* (London, 1609), sig. E2v.

Shakespeare and Peele's Titus Andronicus 97

playhouse it was up to the car-man and tinker as well as the proudest critic to decide.

"Play[ing] the Scribe": From Speech to Text

Titus Andronicus fittingly begins with a glimmer of republican rhetoric. Saturninus and Bassianus, the two sons of the late Roman emperor, each appeal for support in their contest for the throne. From the play's first words, however, Saturninus makes clear who he is really talking to: "Noble patricians, patrons of my right" (1.1.1). He issues a blunt call for violence, urging his aristocratic followers to "[p]lead" his cause not with words but "with your swords" (1.1.4). Saturninus stakes his play for the throne on three not so auspicious pillars: elite support, force, and primogeniture (he is the "first-born son" [1.1.5]). In stark contrast, Bassianus appeals to a very different audience, and to a very different measure of legitimacy. His first word is not patricians but "Romans," addressing (at least in theory) the citizenry at large (1.1.9). And unlike his brother, Bassianus asks Rome to judge him by merit instead of birth: "let desert in pure election shine" (1.1.16). In the dueling speeches that open the play, the sons of the deceased emperor invoke competing constitutional principles: hereditary succession versus popular election.[45]

The unsettled succession thus opens up, if only for a moment, a Ciceronian scene of public pleading before a large audience. Yet already the state is riven by "faction," a word that appears four times in the first act (1.1.18, 218, 409, 456). The tribune Marcus Andronicus seemingly quells the strife by reporting the results of an election. "Princes, that strive by factions and by friends / Ambitiously for rule and empery," he addresses the brothers,

> Know that the people of Rome, for whom we stand
> A special party, have by common voice
> In election for the Roman empery
> Chosen Andronicus, surnamed Pius [that is, Titus].   (1.1.18–23)

But Marcus' own faction and friends quickly corrupt the electoral process.[46] Back from his wars against the Goths, Titus has little appetite for rule – and little respect for the common voice. "I will restore to thee / The people's hearts," he tells Saturninus, "and wean them from themselves" (1.1.214–15).

---

[45] See Andrew Hadfield, *Shakespeare and Republicanism* (Cambridge: Cambridge University Press, 2005), 156–58.
[46] See Arnold, *Third Citizen*, 105–12; and Kewes, "I Ask," 564.

98   Libels on the Elizabethan Stage

Because we never hear from the people themselves, there's no way to know whether Titus makes good on this promise to redirect their favor. The Andronici instead continue to speak for the people of Rome: Titus crowns Saturninus, "our emperor's eldest son," and Marcus immediately confirms his brother's choice "[w]ith voices and applause of every sort, / Patricians and plebeians" (1.1.228, 234–35). Yet in a scene filled with speechifying patricians, the voices of the plebeians are conspicuously absent. Titus and Marcus collude to turn the election into a hereditary succession.

At the same time, the Andronici precipitate the play's devastating vendetta with an act of religious violence that carries fairly clear Catholic overtones. Titus' son Lucius requests "the proudest prisoner of the Goths, / That we may hew his limbs and on a pile / *Ad manes fratrum* [to our brothers' spirits] sacrifice his flesh" (1.1.99–101). Tamora, conquered Queen of the Goths, pleads for mercy for her family already groaning under the "Roman yoke" (1.1.114). But Titus insists that his slain sons "[r]eligiously ... ask a sacrifice" (1.1.127). Lucius and his brothers duly perform "[o]ur Roman rites," butchering Tamora's son Alarbus, and incinerating his limbs and entrails on "the sacrificing fire, / Whose smoke like incense doth perfume the sky" (1.1.146, 147–48). Several critics have interpreted the ritual violence as a grotesque parody of the Catholic mass, from the Latin tag to the liturgical incense to the repeated emphasis on the Romanness of these bloody rites.[47] This view chimes with the well-documented anti-Catholicism of Peele, to whom the first act is generally attributed.[48]

But the rest of the play, generally held to be Shakespeare's work, is more confessionally elusive. The "ruinous monastery," "popish tricks," and "martyred signs" signal not sectarian allegiance but the trauma of Reformation and post-Reformation violence (5.1.21, 76, 3.2.36).[49] All sides are implicated in the cycle of vengeance launched by the Andronici's human sacrifice. Lavinia is "martyred" by Tamora's sons, Chiron and Demetrius, and Titus in turn "martyr[s]" them (3.1.82, 5.2.180). Especially amid the executions of the early 1590s, audiences would have recalled the reciprocal martyr-making that, for some groups, had not yet ended.

---

[47] Barbara L. Parker, *Plato's "Republic" and Shakespeare's Rome: A Political Study of the Roman Works* (Newark: University of Delaware Press, 2004), 117–18; Moschovakis, "Irreligious Piety," 464–45; Helga L. Duncan, "'Sumptuously Re-edified': The Reformation of Sacred Space in *Titus Andronicus*," *Comparative Drama* 43.4 (2009): 436–37; Ryan J. Croft, "Embodying the Catholic *Ruines of Rome* in *Titus Andronicus*: du Bellay, Spenser, Peele, and Shakespeare," *Spenser Studies* 31/32 (2018): 328–29.

[48] Kewes, "I Ask," 556–57; Croft, "Embodying," 324–29.

[49] Moschovakis, "Irreligious Piety"; Rust, *Body*, 67–102; Bahr, "*Titus Andronicus*."

Confessional lines are further blurred in the precipitous political realignment that follows the sacrifice of Alarbus. The hitherto ascendant Andronici fall from favor when Titus' sons side with Bassianus against Saturninus in a fight over which of the two will get to marry their sister, Lavinia. Although Titus remains loyal to the emperor, even killing his son Mutius in the struggle, Saturninus disowns the entire "stock" and "faction" of the Andronici (1.1.305, 409). He instead elevates Tamora to empress, redrawing alliances at the new imperial court. With Saturninus' tacit license, Tamora vows revenge against the Andronici for the slaughter of her son: "I'll find a day to massacre them all, / And raze their faction and their family" (1.1.455–56). The relatively new English word "massacre" evokes the infamous St. Bartholomew's Day Massacre of French Protestants in 1572, dramatized in Marlowe's *Massacre at Paris* (1593).[50] Religious violence morphs into factional enmity without ever fully losing its confessional overtones.

All these machinations and murders take the play from its vaguely republican opening to a Tacitean (or, by some accounts, late Elizabethan) world of silenced speech, secret plots, and state-sanctioned persecution. Tamora soon makes good on her vow of vengeance. She and her allies – Aaron the Moor (her lover) and her two surviving sons – take advantage of a hunt to perpetrate "rape and villainy" in the secrecy of the woods (1.1.616). Chiron and Demetrius kill Bassianus and rape and mutilate Lavinia, cutting off her hands and tongue; Aaron and Tamora frame two of Titus' sons, Quintus and Martius, for the murder. Presented with forged proof of Quintus and Martius' guilt, Saturninus summarily condemns them to "[s]ome never-heard-of torturing pain" (2.2.285). Titus' religious and political misjudgments – from brutally sacrificing Alarbus to crowning Saturninus – have devastated the most vulnerable members of his family.

As the Andronici suffer under the imperial regime, speech repeatedly fails them. Titus, for instance, pleads fruitlessly for a fair trial for his framed sons:

> High emperor, upon my feeble knee
> I beg this boon with tears not lightly shed:
> That this fell fault of my accursed sons,
> Accursed if the fault be proved in them – .   (2.2.288–91)

---

[50] Lisa Hopkins, *The Cultural Uses of the Caesars on the English Renaissance Stage* (Aldershot, UK: Ashgate, 2008), 20–21; Bahr, "*Titus Andronicus*," 249 n26.

The rise of the new emperor and his Gothic allies has transformed the conditions of public speech, at least for the now out-of-favor Andronici. Instead of drawing authority (however speciously) from the "common voice," Titus the victorious general and kingmaker must now beg for mercy from the monarch. Yet Titus still assumes that there remains some vestige of an independent legal system. He pleads not only for sympathy – drawing attention to his "tears not lightly shed" – but also for judicial procedure. His sons are "accursed," he says, only if "the fault be proved in them." But Saturninus indignantly interrupts Titus, dismissing his appeal for due process: "If it be proved? You see it is apparent" (2.2.292). Even after Saturninus denies a trial, Titus asks to "be [his sons'] bail," but the emperor rejects this plea too and commands that the alleged "murderers" be taken away at once (2.2.295, 300). As Lorna Hutson argues, Rome's imperial law (or, as the case may be, imperial fiat) displaces "an open, participatory justice system."[51] Saturninus crushes the fleeting prospect of participatory justice precisely by refusing to hear Titus' plea. He silences Titus' sons too, preventing them from speaking in their own defense: "Let them not speak a word: the guilt is plain" (2.2.301). Under a ruler who has no time for due process, oral rhetoric not only fails to persuade but cannot even find an audience.

This predicament is characteristic of revenge tragedy. The aggrieved revengers take matters into their own hands only after corrupt nobles or arbitrary rulers thwart their attempts to plead publicly for justice.[52] In *The Spanish Tragedy* – one of the earliest examples of the genre and an important influence on *Titus* – Hieronimo resolves to "go plain me to my lord the King, / And cry aloud for justice through the court" for his murdered son. But one of the perpetrators, the king's nephew Lorenzo, "intercepts [his] suits."[53] His pleas prevented, Hieronimo plots his famously theatrical revenge: a multilingual play-within-the-play that leaves many prominent members of the state dead. *Titus* follows the same pattern. After Titus' speech is silenced, the play culminates in a bloody, elaborately staged scene of slaughter that decimates the royal family.

---

[51] Lorna Hutson, *The Invention of Suspicion: Law and Mimesis in Shakespeare and Renaissance Drama* (Oxford: Oxford University Press, 2007), 92.

[52] See Fredson Thayer Bowers, *Elizabethan Revenge Tragedy, 1587–1642* (Princeton: Princeton University Press, 1940); and Linda Woodbridge, *English Revenge Drama: Money, Resistance, Equality* (Cambridge: Cambridge University Press, 2010), 167–88.

[53] Thomas Kyd, *The Spanish Tragedy*, in *English Renaissance Drama: A Norton Anthology*, ed. David Bevington et al. (New York: W. W. Norton, 2002), 3.7.69–70, 3.14.133.

Shakespeare and Peele's Titus Andronicus

Yet oral pleading is not the only way to seek redress. The Andronici perform their revenge only after repeatedly demanding justice in writing.[54] Even as Titus mounts a second unsuccessful plea for his sons' lives, the language of writing already begins to infiltrate his rhetoric. "Hear me, grave fathers; noble tribunes, stay!" he cries before the supposed arbiters of justice, once more begging tearfully for "pity" for his sons and for himself (3.1.1, 2). But the tribunes process silently across the stage and ignore his cries. While they "*pass by him*," however, Titus turns for the first time from speech to writing: "For these two, tribunes, in the dust I write / My heart's deep languor and my soul's sad tears" (3.1.11 sd, 12–13). Of course, this is a rhetorical gesture, and one that remains illegible to the tribunes. Writing with tears is no more effective than pleading with them. But although Titus fails to win mercy by writing in the dust, his family does get closer to revenge by writing in the sand and, especially, on epistolary scrolls. Their complaints register only when they give up public speech in favor of written media delivered at a distance.

Lavinia's trajectory – from enforced silence to inscribing the names of her rapists in the sand – both embodies and motivates the shift from speech to writing. Dragged offstage about a hundred lines before Titus' first plea for his sons' lives, Lavinia is brutalized by the empress's sons at the same time as her father's speech is silenced by the emperor. In between Titus' two failed appeals for mercy, Chiron and Demetrius bring Lavinia back onstage, "*her hands cut off and her tongue cut out, and ravished*" (2.3 sd). Lavinia, who used to read "Tully's *Orator*" to her nephew (4.1.14), "comes almost to represent a violated Lady Rhetorica."[55] The empress's sons viciously mock her inability to communicate in speech or in writing:

DEMETRIUS So, now go tell, and if thy tongue can speak,
 Who 'twas that cut thy tongue and ravished thee.
CHIRON Write down thy mind, bewray thy meaning so,
 And if thy stumps will let thee, play the scribe. (2.3.1–4)

Chiron and Demetrius have inflicted the imperial censorship directly on Lavinia's body. By cutting off both tongue and hands, they make her the limit case of the crackdown on the Andronici's speech.

It is precisely by "play[ing] the scribe," however, that Lavinia leads the Andronici to their revolutionary revenge. Her interactions with the written

---

[54] Shakespeare may well be taking inspiration from *The Spanish Tragedy* here too. Although we never see Hieronimo writing to king or court (despite a passing mention of his "supplications"), he does himself receive several texts, one termed a "humble supplication," from a group of "poor petitioners" (3.14.78, 3.13.78, 46).

[55] J. L. Simmons, "The Tongue and Its Office in *The Revenger's Tragedy*," *PMLA* 92.1 (1977): 57.

102 Libels on the Elizabethan Stage

word launch her family's multimedia campaign against the imperial government. Lavinia first sifts through her nephew Lucius' schoolbooks, a pile of markedly Elizabethan codices.[56] These books are not privileged cultural objects but tools of communication in desperate times. The boy "throw[s]" them to the ground for fear of his aunt, and then Lavinia "tosseth" one in particular: Ovid's *Metamorphoses*, the Renaissance textbook that patterned Chiron and Demetrius' horrific violence (4.1.25, 41). "[T]urn[ing] the leaves" to the "tragic tale of Philomel," Lavinia starts to tell her story through Ovid's popular myth (4.1.45, 47). Her recourse to Ovid parodies the humanist imperative to imitate the classics.[57] Yet here the text also gives her a voice, if one tragically scripted by the Ovidian role she has been forced to assume.[58] Having identified the tale of Philomela as the pattern for her plight, Lavinia uses a staff to write three revelatory words in the sand: "*Stuprum – Chiron – Demetrius*" (4.1.78). Her inscription takes the classical text ("stuprum" is Latin for rape) from the study or schoolroom to the highly visible yet ephemeral medium beneath her feet.

To describe this act of writing, Marcus uses a decidedly post-classical vocabulary. It is he who invents a way to write in the sand "[w]ithout the help of any hand at all," guiding his staff with just his mouth and feet (4.1.71). "Heaven guide thy pen to print thy sorrows plain," he tells his niece, and she follows his example: "*She takes the staff in her mouth, and guides it with her stumps, and writes*" (4.1.75, 76 sd). Scholars have noticed the mixed media at play here: even as Lavinia employs the "scribal process," Marcus anachronistically borrows "terms from print culture" when he characterizes her writing as hands-free "print[ing]."[59] The allusions to scribal and print technologies punctuate the Andronici's turn from oral to written communication. As Mary Laughlin Fawcett argues in her astute reading of this scene, "In Lavinia we see the possibility for communication moving from the tongue to the pen/staff. ... Speech may be silenced, but as long as the

---

[56] Alan Stewart, *Shakespeare's Letters* (Oxford: Oxford University Press, 2008), 82. Commenting on the play's other anachronistic texts, Stewart notes that its letters take the form of scrolls, which "might suggest letters from antiquity to early modern audiences" (83). Intriguingly, scrolls might also evoke libels: John Bullokar's dictionary defines "Libell" as "a defamatorie scroll, or slanderous writing ... without any knowne name of the Author" (*An English Expositor* [London, 1616], sigs. K1r–v).

[57] See Vernon Guy Dickson, "'A pattern, precedent, and lively warrant': Emulation, Rhetoric, and Cruel Propriety in *Titus Andronicus*," *Renaissance Quarterly* 62.2 (2009): 376–409.

[58] See Bethany Packard, "Lavinia as Coauthor of Shakespeare's *Titus Andronicus*," *Studies in English Literature 1500–1900* 50.2 (2010): 281–300.

[59] Liz Oakley-Brown, "*Titus Andronicus* and the Cultural Politics of Translation in Early Modern England," *Renaissance Studies* 19.3 (2005): 346; Patrick Cheney, *Shakespeare's Literary Authorship* (Cambridge: Cambridge University Press, 2008), 71.

Shakespeare and Peele's Titus Andronicus   103

body can move at all, writing will out."[60] Violently silenced, the Andronici can still write – and write they do. Writing and (if only metaphorically) printing open up new avenues of communication in the wake of the imperial suppression of public speech.

Lavinia's writing in the sand soon catalyzes the Andronici's revenge. "There is enough written upon this earth / To stir a mutiny in the mildest thoughts," Marcus says (4.1.84–85). Taking his cue from her text, he leads the Andronici in swearing "[m]ortal revenge upon these traitorous Goths" (4.1.93). Marcus, like so many characters in the play, looks to the classics for both precedent and inspiration. "[S]wear with me," he urges, "as, with the woeful fere / And father of that chaste dishonoured dame, / Lord Junius Brutus swore for Lucrece' rape" (4.1.89–91). Lucretia's rape and suicide precipitated the expulsion of the Tarquins and the founding of the Roman Republic. In Shakespeare's own *Rape of Lucrece*, published the same year as *Titus*, Junius Brutus rallies Lucrece's bereft family to "revenge the death of this true wife." That personal vengeance soon becomes political. In the final lines of the poem, "The ROMANS plausibly did give consent / To TARQUINS' everlasting banishment." The prefatory Argument describes this republican moment in greater detail: "the Tarquins were all exiled, and the state government changed from kings to consuls."[61] In *Titus*, Lavinia likewise embodies both the trauma of monarchical violence and the possibility of republican revenge.

Titus, though, is not quite so ready for an open revolt. His brother Marcus wants to plunge ahead and "see [the Goths'] blood, or die with this reproach" (4.1.94). But Titus advises caution. He warns, "if you hunt these bear-whelps, then beware: / The dam will wake, and if she wind ye once / She's with the lion deeply still in league" (4.1.96–98). Wary of Tamora's sway, Titus searches for other ways to answer the call of Lavinia's inscription. He first proposes to monumentalize her writing, to "get a leaf of brass / And with a gad of steel ... write these words, / And lay it by" (4.1.102–4). While the "angry northern wind" will easily efface Lavinia's writing in the sand, brass promises to preserve her message (4.1.104).

For Titus, however, the brass leaf is to be laid by; it is a medium fit for private commemoration, not public communication. Eschewing (for the moment) both brass and bloodshed, Titus instead follows his daughter's lead and turns to more ephemeral kinds of writing. He leads his grandson

---

[60] Fawcett, "Arms/Words/Tears," 266.

[61] Shakespeare, *The Rape of Lucrece*, in *Shakespeare's Poems*, ed. Katherine Duncan-Jones and H. R. Woudhuysen (London: Arden Shakespeare, 2007), ll. 1841, 1854–55; Argument, ll. 40–41.

104 Libels on the Elizabethan Stage

Lucius into his armory to give him a "message" for Tamora's sons (4.1.117). The boy assumes that the message will be violent retribution, eagerly agreeing to deliver it "with my dagger in their bosoms" (4.1.118). "No, boy," Titus responds, "not so; I'll teach thee another course" (4.1.119). In the next scene, we see that other course: Titus sends Chiron and Demetrius weapons wrapped in a scroll. Turning from the Andronici's private community to the seat of power, he tells Marcus, "Lucius and I'll go brave it at the court" (4.1.121). Lavinia's writing sparks neither memorial inscription nor outright rebellion but instead a profusion of letters that soon spread throughout the city.

Yet even as the Andronici turn outward, the "common voice" that Marcus channeled in the first scene remains silent. To be sure, the Andronici repeatedly claim to stand and speak for the people.[62] And perhaps they have some warrant to do so: Marcus is the people's tribune, Titus their conquering hero, and the Andronici evidently the preeminent Roman family (Saturninus and Bassianus don't even get a family name).[63] Titus accordingly identifies his own plight with Rome's even as he recalls how he disenfranchised the people. "Ah, Rome!" he exclaims, "I made thee miserable / What time I threw the people's suffrages / On him that thus doth tyrannize o'er me" (4.3.18–20). Titus takes responsibility for the tyrannical regime that he installed. But he still can't (or won't) distinguish between Rome's misery and his own. We never hear from the citizens whose votes Titus and Marcus manipulated, nor do we learn the fate of any plebeian characters (aside from the nameless nurse and clown who meet their own bloody ends). But as patricians plot and letters fly in the final acts, Rome's rulers grow increasingly concerned with popular opinion. The move from speech to writing threatens to bring a broader audience into the bitter struggle between the Andronici and the imperial family.

Titus' Libels

Titus' campaign begins in earnest soon after he sends the scroll-wrapped weapons to Chiron and Demetrius. At the beginning of the following scene, the Andronici take the stage "*with bows; and Titus bears the arrows with letters on the ends of them*" (4.3 sd). We never find out exactly what these letters say, but their theme is clear: "justice," a word that Titus repeats seven times in under a hundred lines of dialogue (4.3.9–103). Or rather, the lack thereof. "*Terras Astraea reliquit,*" Titus tells his brother Marcus; in

---

[62] See Arnold, *Third Citizen*, 101–39.   [63] Kewes, "I Ask," 567.

Shakespeare and Peele's Titus Andronicus

English, "Astraea [goddess of Justice] has left the earth" (4.3.4, 4 n). This Latin tag comes from Ovid's *Metamorphoses*, the text that Lavinia had used to translate her trauma into language that her father and uncle could understand. Ovid relates how the earth degenerated from the golden age to the iron – and it was only in this final age that "Astraea, last of the immortals, abandoned the blood-soaked earth."[64] In Elizabethan iconography, Astraea represented the queen as Protestant reformer and ruler, heralding the dawn of a new golden age.[65] Astraea's absence may well evoke the plight of religious minorities in the early 1590s.[66] But the absent goddess also figures the central problem of the play: how to seek justice from an impossibly distant or, worse yet, deeply hostile audience.

Titus leads his kinsmen on a frantic search for Astraea, for justice personified. "Happily you may catch her in the sea," he tells some; "you must dig with mattock and with spade," he instructs others, and "when you come to Pluto's region, / I pray you deliver him this petition" (4.3.8, 11, 13–14). Marcus thinks this is mere madness, lamenting that his brother is "thus distract" (4.3.26). But Titus is simply facing the same problem as did Southwell, Penry, Coppinger and Arthington, and the other sectarian petitioners of the early 1590s. Violently persecuted, he and his family are desperately searching for an audience that might hear their complaints. Yet Astraea is nowhere to be found – and to solicit Saturninus for redress, as Titus bitterly observes, "were as good to shoot against the wind" (4.3.58). So, because "there's no justice in earth nor hell," Titus turns to "heaven" (4.3.50, 51). He gives his kinsmen the arrows bearing letters to the gods – "*ad Jovem*," "*ad Apollinem*," "*ad Martem*" – but before they fire into the skies, Marcus adds a further instruction: "Kinsmen, shoot all your shafts into the court; / We will afflict the emperor in his pride" (4.3.54–55, 62–63). Late Elizabethan libelers were accused of similar assaults on city and court, reportedly scattering their texts "in many *partes* of the Cittie of London, yea and in her M*aiesties* Court it self."[67] Their speech thwarted, the Andronici launch their petitionary texts at once into the sky and into the court – much like the Puritan and Catholic writers who claimed they could only reach queen or parliament by publishing their petitions.

---

[64] Ovid, *Metamorphoses*, trans. Frank Justus Miller, rev. G. P. Goold, 2 vols. (Cambridge, MA: Harvard University Press, 1977–84), 1.149–50.

[65] Frances A. Yates, *Astraea: The Imperial Theme in the Sixteenth Century* (London: Routledge and Kegan Paul, 1975), 29–87.

[66] Klause, *Shakespeare*, 133–34; Sterrett, *Unheard Prayer*, 1–2; Lake, *Hamlet's Choice*, 33–34.

[67] TNA, SP 12/273, fol. 61r.

106   Libels on the Elizabethan Stage

While Titus' letters evidently solicit justice for his persecuted family, their method of delivery issues a naked threat. Classical and Renaissance rhetoricians often described words as weapons: Cicero compares speech to "a weapon either employed for use, to threaten and to attack, or simply brandished for show," and Henry Peacham calls figures of speech "martiall instruments both of defence & inuasion."[68] The Andronici literalize this verbal violence in the hail of arrow-texts fired abroad. Arrows are an especially apt vehicle for this message given their association with slanderous speech. From their biblical origins in the Psalms, the "arrowes of slaunder" shot through early modern preaching and polemic.[69] As George Webbe explains, slander is an arrow because it "woundeth a farre off."[70] The Andronici's arrows are at once violent projectiles and defamatory petitions – libels supplicatory, as it were – shot from afar.

In the next scene, we learn that the arrows have hit their targets. Saturninus storms onstage clutching the arrows and ranting,

> Why, lords, what wrongs are these! Was ever seen
> An emperor in Rome thus overborne,
> Troubled, confronted thus, and for the extent
> Of equal justice used in such contempt?
> My lords, you know, as know the mightful gods,
> However these disturbers of our peace
> Buzz in the people's ears, there nought hath passed
> But even with law against the wilful sons
> Of old Andronicus.   (4.4.1–9)

Although Titus supposedly "writes to heaven for his redress," Saturninus reveals that the letters have reached an earthly audience (4.4.13). The emperor complains that the Andronici "buzz in the people's ears," publicly challenging the emperor's claim to have proceeded "with law" against Titus' sons. And he shares the early modern fear of libels propagating without limit. "Sweet scrolls to fly about the streets of Rome!" Saturninus exclaims, "What's this but libelling against the senate / And blazoning our injustice everywhere?" (4.4.16–18). The scrolls take on a life of their own as they fly about the streets and spread their message of imperial injustice.

---

[68] Cicero, *De Oratore*, 3.206; Henry Peacham, *The Garden of Eloquence* (London, 1593), sig. AB4r. See Wayne A. Rebhorn, *The Emperor of Men's Minds: Literature and the Renaissance Discourse of Rhetoric* (Ithaca: Cornell University Press, 1995), 34–35, 41–42.

[69] Henry Smith, *The Sermons of Master Henrie Smith, gathered into one volume* (London, 1592), sig. XIV. In Psalms 64:3, we hear of backbiters who have "shot *for* their arrowes bitter wordes," with "arrowes" glossed in the Geneva Bible as "Fals reportes & slanders" (*The Bible and Holy Scriptures Conteined in the Olde and Newe Testament* [London, 1576], sig. Qq3v).

[70] George Webbe, *The Araignement of an vnruly Tongue* (London, 1619), sig. D5r.

These texts evoke not only the sectarian libels of the early 1590s but also the broader paradigm of promiscuously published accusation. Several early modern observers record libels flying through the city and even infiltrating the theaters. In late 1599, libels reportedly "did fly about in London streets and theatres," and several decades later, Archbishop Laud remarked on the "libels which fly abroad in all places."[71] Saturninus' screed against "blazoning ... injustice" likewise reflects the tropes of libel. One Elizabethan verse libel against Edward Bashe, an upwardly mobile bureaucrat, sets out "[t]o blaze his name in riding rime."[72] And in 1596, the mayor of London complained about libelers who "desire nothing more then to have [their writings] blased & scattered abroad."[73] Blazoning alleged injustices was the prime threat of the early modern libel.

Titus' libels thus offer a stark counternarrative to the emperor's line about the due administration of justice. Saturninus repeatedly and implausibly insists that he adhered strictly to the law in condemning Titus' sons: they received "equal justice," "nought hath passed / But even with law" against them, they "died by law" (4.4.4, 7–8, 53). But the flying scrolls make the opposite claim. They blazon the emperor's injustice, asserting that Quintus and Martius "[h]ave by [his] means been butchered wrongfully" (4.4.54). Since the emperor has failed to provide the redress they so desperately seek, the Andronici, under the guise of petitioning the gods, come to litigate their grievances in public.

Unsurprisingly, Saturninus is entirely unsympathetic to the Andronici's criticism. He sees the letters to the gods for what they are: libels. "A goodly humour, is it not, my lords? / As who would say, in Rome no justice were," he says, helpfully explaining their message (4.4.19–20). Not at all fooled by Titus' antic disposition, Saturninus rails against his "feigned ecstasies" and brands him a "conspirator" (4.4.21, 26). Just as the emperor is ready to "drag the villain hither by the hair," however, a messenger brings word that Titus' son Lucius has raised an army of Goths and is marching on Rome (4.4.55). Saturninus suddenly deflates. "'Tis he the common people love so much," he frets, stricken with anxiety that "the citizens favour Lucius / And will revolt from me to succour him" (4.4.72, 78–79). It is no coincidence that the emperor's fear of a popular revolt comes right on the heels of the

---

[71] *The Letters and the Life of Francis Bacon*, ed. James Spedding, 7 vols. (London, 1861–74), 2:177; *The Works of the Most Reverend Father in God, William Laud*, ed. William Scott and James Bliss, 7 vols. (Oxford, 1847–60), 7:348.

[72] "The Bashe Libel (*c.* 1575–83)," in *Verse Libel in Renaissance England and Scotland*, ed. Steven W. May and Alan Bryson (Oxford: Oxford University Press, 2016), 77, l. 34.

[73] BL, Lansdowne MS 81, fol. 72r.

108   Libels on the Elizabethan Stage

Andronici's libeling. Indeed, Saturninus worries much more about Lucius' popularity among the Roman plebeians than he does about his army of Goths. The threat of violence issued by Titus' weapon-writings shifts into the prospect of a citizen rebellion. At least according to Saturninus, the Andronici have successfully spoken to the people – and he fears that the people will answer with a vengeance.

As the Andronici disseminate their petitionary texts, they increasingly resemble a marginalized Catholic or radical Protestant faction trying to mobilize support for their cause. I have suggested above that there is material in the play to support confessionalized readings at both extremes. To begin with the Catholic side: it is tendentious but not entirely implausible to take the play as a seditious allegory of the "new *Cecillian Inquisition*" allegedly launched by William Cecil, Lord Burghley, in the early 1590s. Cecil himself was known, at least in one 1591 letter, by the epithet "olde Saturnus."[74] And a central theme of the Catholic libels, including the 1592 broadside against the Cecilian inquisition, was "the marginalization of the 'auncient nobilitie of the Realme' by the upstart Protestant favorites and leading ministers of the queen."[75] So it goes in *Titus*. Saturninus elevates a band of (proto-Protestant?) Goths to the heights of power, casting aside a now violently persecuted Roman (Catholic?) family, the Andronici. This would be a daring story to tell indeed, even through the veil of ancient Rome.

Yet the closest parallel from the early 1590s may well be a Puritan conspiracy: the Hacket affair. The Andronici roughly reprise the trajectory of Hacket and his accomplices. Just as the Andronici shoot letters "about the streets of Rome," Hacket, Coppinger, and Arthington scattered "seditious letters . . . in many of the streetes of *London*" to stir up the people. And where the Andronici "buzz in the people's ears," the exploits of the three Puritan fanatics quickly spread through the city and set "all . . . in a buzze," reaching even the queen herself.[76] Then there is the question of madness. Although Hacket was reputed to be mad – "distracted of his wits," "franticke" – the state insisted that such a nefarious plot could not have been concocted "by men possessed with frency or lunacies."[77] Titus is likewise thought to be "distract," "frantic," and suffering from "frenzy," yet Saturninus sees the seditious intent behind his "feigned ecstasies" (4.3.26, 4.4.58, 12, 21). Titus' talk of gods and divine justice would only have reinforced the echoes of confessional conspiracy.

---

[74] HMC, *Report on the Manuscripts of Lord de L'Isle and Dudley Preserved at Penshurst Place*, vol. 2, ed. C. L. Kingsford (London: His Majesty's Stationery Office, 1934), 123.
[75] Manley and MacLean, *Lord Strange's Men*, 223, quoting Verstegan, *Declaration*, sig. A7v.
[76] Cosin, *Conspiracie*, sigs. F2v, I4v.   [77] Ibid., sig. M3v; HMC, *Fourteenth Report*, 608, 609.

Shakespeare and Peele's Titus Andronicus 109

Moreover, the libel-arrows are not the only Hacketian texts that spread in the fourth act. After Titus and his family fire their messages abroad, a Clown ambles onto the stage on his way to settle an imperial legal dispute of his own ("a matter of brawl betwixt my uncle and one of the emperal's men" [4.3.92–93]). Titus or, in the first quarto, the Clown himself cries, "News, news, from heaven," perhaps echoing the "newes from heauen" declaimed by Coppinger and Arthington to the Cheapside crowd in July 1591 (4.3.77).[78] Titus takes the Clown to be Jupiter's postman, prompting a bit of macabre wordplay when the Clown mishears Jupiter as gibbet-maker: "Ho, the gibbet-maker? He says that he hath taken them down again, for the man must not be hanged till the next week" (4.3.80–82). These lines may likewise refer to recent Puritan tribulations, namely the April 1593 hangings of Barrow and Greenwood a week after they received a last-minute reprieve and were taken down from the gallows.[79] Titus then gives the Clown an "oration" or "supplication" with a knife enclosed to deliver to the emperor "like an humble suppliant" (4.3.97, 106, 116). John Klause suggests that this language alludes to Southwell's *Humble Supplication to Her Maiestie*.[80] But the "supplication" and "humble suppliant" equally evoke the Puritan petitions of the early 1590s, with titles such as *The humble petition of the communaltie* and "A Supplication unto the High Court of Parliament." In fact, much like Titus, Coppinger and Arthington themselves solicited an intermediary to send "certaine petitions" and "a supplication" to the queen, including a menacing missive that "lewdely, and falsely accuseth and reuileth" two privy councilors and threatens Elizabeth herself with "the iudgementes of God."[81]

All these echoes of Puritan libeling fit Robert Hornback's account of the stage clown as a vehicle for topical religious satire. In the wake of the Marprelate controversy, a new stock character emerged on the stage: the comic Puritan caricature.[82] The role was developed in the early 1590s by, among others, Shakespeare and Will Kemp (the latter may well have originated the Clown's part in *Titus*).[83] At the same time, Anglican propagandists were eager to cast real-life Puritans in the same clownish mold.[84] This is precisely what happened to Hacket. In the chamber of the

---

[78] Cosin, *Conspiracie*, sig. I2v. See Moschovakis, "Topicality," 131.   [79] Politi, "Gibbet-Maker."

[80] Klause, *Shakespeare*, 133.   [81] Cosin, *Conspiracie*, sigs. E4v, F4r, F2r.

[82] Robert Hornback, *The English Clown Tradition from the Middle Ages to Shakespeare* (Cambridge: D. S. Brewer, 2009); Patrick Collinson, "Ecclesiastical Vitriol: Religious Satire in the 1590s and the Invention of Puritanism," in *The Reign of Elizabeth I: Court and Culture in the Last Decade*, ed. John Guy (Cambridge: Cambridge University Press, 1995), 150–70.

[83] David Wiles, *Shakespeare's Clown: Actor and Text in the Elizabethan Playhouse* (Cambridge: Cambridge University Press, 1987), 34.

[84] Hornback, *English Clown*, 102–42.

110   Libels on the Elizabethan Stage

Puritan preacher Giles Wigginton, the authorities allegedly found a broadsheet titled *The Fooles bolte* on one side and bearing a "halting ryme" on the other. This incriminating rhyme suggested that not even the monarch could deny the instruction of a poor Christian clown like Hacket: "A Christian true although he be a clowne, / May teach a king to weare scepter and crowne."[85] At least according to the anti-Puritan polemic churned out in the wake of his execution, Hacket was a seditious, illiterate clown rightly sent to the gallows.

The same fate befalls *Titus'* own illiterate, Puritan-adjacent clown.[86] He delivers the seditious supplication to Saturninus, and the emperor immediately sends him away to be hanged. Of course, the difference between Hacket and the Clown is that the latter is manifestly innocent. Titus conscripted him into the campaign of libeling by promising, "By me thou shalt have justice at [the emperor's] hands" (4.3.103). Yet as Titus remarked earlier in the same scene, soliciting Saturninus for justice "were as good to shoot against the wind" (4.3.58). He knows full well there's no justice to be had from the emperor or his court. In the context of the play, then, the Clown is less Puritan conspirator than hapless bystander tricked into playing a bit part – and a fatal one at that – in Rome's political drama. Together with his homely English prose, this role puts him in the clown's characteristically liminal position between actors and audience.[87] He is a humble Londoner, an ordinary playgoer, a Will Kemp stumbling into an outlandishly violent factional struggle. His death belies the Andronici's pretense to popularity, implicating them in the very injustice that they publicly decry.

Pitiless Politics

Vexed by the Andronici's libels and terrified by Lucius' putative popularity, Saturninus readily agrees to Tamora's final plot: to thwart Titus by indulging his apparent madness. But Titus proves to be sane if insatiably bloodthirsty. In a dizzying chain of violence, he seizes the empress's sons, bakes them into a pie, feeds them to the emperor and their mother, kills

---

[85] Cosin, *Conspiracie*, sig. F2v. Compare Sutcliffe, *Answere*, sig. Ee1v and Richard Bancroft, *Daungerous Positions and Proceedings, published and practised within this Iland of Brytaine, vnder pretence of Reformation, and for the Presbiteriall Discipline* (London, 1593), sig. Y1v.

[86] On the Clown's evident illiteracy, see Arnold, *Third Citizen*, 133–39.

[87] Scholars have long remarked on the clown's liminality: see, e.g., Robert Weimann, *Shakespeare and the Popular Tradition in the Theater: Studies in the Social Dimension of Dramatic Form and Function*, ed. Robert Schwartz (Baltimore: Johns Hopkins University Press, 1978); Edward Berry, *Shakespeare's Comic Rites* (Cambridge: Cambridge University Press, 1984); Wiles, *Shakespeare's Clown*; and Richard Preiss, *Clowning and Authorship in Early Modern Theatre* (Cambridge: Cambridge University Press, 2014).

Shakespeare and Peele's Titus Andronicus

Lavinia, kills Tamora, and finally is killed by Saturninus who is in turn killed by Lucius.

Lest the body politic remain in tatters, Marcus once more takes center stage. The play ends, as it began, with a series of formal orations moderated by the tribune. "O let me teach you how to knit again / This scattered corn into one mutual sheaf, / These broken limbs again into one body," he declaims (5.3.69–71). Yet he (or, in the quartos, a Roman lord) worries that his intense grief will interrupt his tale of woe, that

> floods of tears will drown my oratory
> And break my utterance even in the time
> When it should move ye to attend me most,
> And force you to commiseration. (5.3.89–92)

Now that the imperial family has been eradicated, tears begin to regain their persuasive power – to become "prevailing orators," as Titus called them while he wept fruitlessly for his sons' lives (3.1.26). Far from "drown-[ing] . . . oratory" and "break[ing] . . . utterance," "floods of tears" finally win over their audience. Lucius recounts for the assembled Romans a brief history of his family's tears: "Our father's tears despised," he himself "turned weeping out / To beg relief among Rome's enemies, / Who drowned their enmity in my true tears" (5.3.100, 104–6). The sympathy even of Rome's enemies marks the return of pity to political life.

Marcus ends the Andronici's series of speeches by staking their very lives on the success of their rhetoric. He asks his audience,

> what say you, Romans?
> Have we done aught amiss, show us wherein,
> And from the place where you behold us pleading,
> The poor remainder of Andronici
> Will hand in hand all headlong hurl ourselves
> And on the ragged stones beat forth our souls
> And make a mutual closure of our house. (5.3.127–33)

This is the kind of public, pitiful "pleading" that had failed so miserably through the play's first four acts. As in the opening scene, it is (supposedly) up to the Romans themselves to determine the fate of their city. At least one Roman, the imperial envoy Emillius, needs no more convincing. "Come, come, thou reverend man of Rome," he enthusiastically responds, "And bring our emperor gently in thy hand, / Lucius, our emperor, for well I know / The common voice do cry it shall be so" (5.3.136–39). If we are to believe Emillius, the "common voice" – the same voice that elected Titus in

112   Libels on the Elizabethan Stage

the play's first scene – has again sided with the Andronici. The two elections that frame the play join public oratory with republican politics.

Yet this scene is shot through with irony. As in the first act, it's by no means clear whether the "common voice" really does speak, or whether it is once more usurped by the patricians. After Emillius claims that the "common voice" has elected Lucius, Marcus, presumably acting in his capacity as the people's tribune, hails Lucius as "Rome's royal emperor" (5.3.140). A subsequent line assigned by most modern editors to "Romans" or "All Romans" seemingly confirms the people's will: "Lucius, all hail, Rome's gracious governor!" (5.3.145).[88] The early quartos and the folio, however, give this line to Marcus, suggesting that the Andronici may again silence, or at least unilaterally speak for, the people.[89] Even more bitterly ironic are the Andronici's key means of persuasion: their tears and appeals for pity. These are the same Andronici who, in the first scene, pitilessly rejected Tamora's tears as she pled for the life of her son Alarbus. "Victorious Titus, rue the tears I shed, / A mother's tears in passion for her son!" Tamora had cried (1.1.108–9). But she begged in vain, just as Titus later would for his own sons' lives. Lucius led the sons of Titus off to "hew [Alarbus'] limbs" and incinerate his corpse on the sacrificial pyre, thereby launching the play's all-consuming vendetta (1.1.132).

It thus comes as little surprise when pity is among the first casualties of the new imperial regime. After the Andronici tearfully pay their respects to the corpse of their patriarch, Lucius issues his first decree as emperor: summarily sentencing Aaron to a lingering death. Of course, Aaron, unlike Titus' sons Martius and Quintus, really is guilty. But he too is condemned without any semblance of a trial. "Set him breast-deep in earth and famish him," Lucius commands, adding a stern warning for anyone who might feel a twinge of compassion: "If anyone relieves or pities him, / For the offence he dies" (5.3.178, 180–81). Unrepentant to the last, Aaron angrily wishes only that he had done more ill. "If one good deed in all my life I did," he cries, "I do repent it from my very soul" (5.3.188–89). In the play's final lines, Lucius continues to institute a pitiless polity. He orders that Tamora's corpse be left "to beasts and birds to prey: / Her life was beastly and devoid of pity, / And being dead,

---

[88] In addition to Bate's Arden edition, see *Titus Andronicus*, ed. Eugene M. Waith (Oxford: Clarendon Press, 1984), 5.3.145; and *Titus Andronicus*, in *The New Oxford Shakespeare: The Complete Works: Critical Reference Edition*, gen. ed. Gary Taylor et al., vol. 1 (Oxford: Oxford University Press, 2017), 5.3.145.

[89] See Hadfield, *Republicanism*, 165; and Arnold, *Third Citizen*, 132–33.

Shakespeare and Peele's Titus Andronicus

let birds on her take pity" (5.3.197–99). The repetition of "pity" in the last two lines decisively exorcises it from the state. Aaron, Tamora, even anyone who "relieves or pities" the condemned – all are denied pity. Once Lucius takes the throne, the only public pleading to be heard is Aaron's "rav[ing]" (5.3.179) – and his cries and curses promise to continue long after the play ends with the new emperor's official rejection of pity.

This is not a very auspicious end to the play's brutal cycle of violence. Nor do the final lines hold out much hope for a Ciceronian future of public oratory. *Titus* remains a Tacitean play, its Rome mired in faction, corruption, and violence. Indeed, it is perhaps no coincidence that the first English translation of Tacitus was published in 1591. The translation's pseudonymous preface invites the reader to behold a litany of Roman ruin that could equally stand as an advertisement for *Titus*: "thou shalt see all the miseries of a torne and declining state: The Empire vsurped; the Princes murthered; the people wauering; the souldiers tumultuous; nothing vnlawfull to him that hath power, and nothing so vnsafe as to bee securely innocent." The writer, sometimes thought to be the Earl of Essex, goes on to insist that England is much the opposite, blessed with a "wise, iust, and excelent Prince."[90] But for some Elizabethan malcontents, including many religious dissidents, the worlds of Tacitus and *Titus* were all too familiar.

The Andronici's libels supplicatory are at once a solution and a symptom in that Tacitean or, indeed, Elizabethan political world. In their pursuit of justice, the Andronici shoot beyond the claustrophobic confines of the court to address a broader public. Yet their letters usher in not toleration but a further frenzy of violence and revolution. Then again, early modern confessional libels were little different. Many came (in Peter Lake's words) from "rival groups, each set on the marginalization, indeed, in an ideal world, on the extinction, of the other."[91] Publicly petitioning for

[90] Tacitus, *The Ende of Nero and Beginning of Galba. Fower Bookes of the Histories of Cornelius Tacitus. The Life of Agricola*, trans. Henry Savile (Oxford, 1591), sigs. ¶3r, ¶3v. According to William Drummond, Ben Jonson attributed the preface to Essex (*Informations to William Drummond of Hawthornden*, ed. Ian Donaldson, in *CWBJ*, 5:377, ll. 285–86). For varying views on Savile's Tacitus, the identity of the preface's author, and Elizabethan Tacitism more broadly, see David Womersley, "Sir Henry Savile's Translation of Tacitus and the Political Interpretation of Elizabethan Texts," *Review of English Studies* 42 (1991): 313–42; Paulina Kewes, "Henry Savile's Tacitus and the Politics of Roman History in Late Elizabethan England," *Huntington Library Quarterly* 74.4 (2011): 515–51; Mordechai Feingold, "Scholarship and Politics: Henry Savile's Tacitus and the Essex Connection," *Review of English Studies* 67 (2016): 855–74; and R. Malcolm Smuts, "Varieties of Tacitism," *Huntington Library Quarterly* 83.3 (2020): 441–65.

[91] Lake, *Bad Queen Bess*, 474.

justice and inciting sectarian violence were two sides of the same rhetorical strategy. It is thus fitting that the Andronici repeatedly attach their writings to weapons: the letters launched on the tips of arrows, the supplication wrapped around a knife. There could hardly be better figures for the ambivalent impulses of the early modern libel.

CHAPTER 4

Libel, Equity, and Law in Sir Thomas More

Perhaps the most explosive – and certainly the most famous – encounter between libels and the theater world occurred in the anxious spring of 1593. After months of plague, economic stress, and urban unrest, resentment against "strangers" burst out in a spate of viciously xenophobic libels posted throughout London.[1] Few of those libels survive, but a copy of one – discovered in 1971 – has entered the annals of the Elizabethan stage. Posted on the wall of the Dutch churchyard in Broadstreet Ward on May 5, 1593, the so-called Dutch Church libel repeatedly alludes to the plays of Christopher Marlowe, including *The Jew of Malta* ("like the Jewes, you eate us vp as bread"), *The Massacre at Paris* ("Not paris massacre so much blood did spill"), and *Tamburlaine the Great* (the poem is signed "*per.* Tamberlaine").[2] The official response was swift and severe. Among the first to be arrested (and likely tortured) was Marlowe's fellow dramatist and sometime roommate, Thomas Kyd. Marlowe himself soon came before the Privy Council, and ten days later, at a fatal gathering that has spawned more than a few conspiracy theories, he was killed at the age of twenty-nine.[3]

Quite possibly around the same time, although perhaps several years later, Anthony Munday and others put together a playscript titled *Sir*

---

[1] *APC*, 24:187, 200–1, 222; John Strype, *Annals of the Reformation and Establishment of Religion . . . during Queen Elizabeth's Happy Reign*, 4 vols. (Oxford, 1824), 4:234–36. See Ian W. Archer, *The Pursuit of Stability: Social Relations in Elizabethan London* (Cambridge: Cambridge University Press, 1991), 5–10.

[2] Dutch Church Libel, ll. 8, 40, 53–54, transcribed in Arthur Freeman, "Marlowe, Kyd, and the Dutch Church Libel," *English Literary Renaissance* 3.1 (1973): 50–51. Subsequent quotations from the libel are cited parenthetically by line number. On the allusions to Marlowe's plays, see Charles Nicholl, *The Reckoning: The Murder of Christopher Marlowe* (New York: Harcourt Brace, 1992), 285–86; and David Riggs, *The World of Christopher Marlowe* (New York: Henry Holt, 2004), 319.

[3] The events leading up to Marlowe's death have been probed at length by his biographers, who have come to divergent (and sometimes conspiratorial) conclusions: see Nicholl, *Reckoning*; Riggs, *World*; and Constance Brown Kuriyama, *Christopher Marlowe: A Renaissance Life* (Ithaca: Cornell University Press, 2002).

116   Libels on the Elizabethan Stage

Thomas More and submitted it to the Master of the Revels, Edmund Tilney.[4] The play survives only in this manuscript, a patchwork of pages written, censored, and revised in seven hands.[5] Tilney's marks of censorship reveal that he found much to object to. He deleted most of the climactic moment, in which Thomas More resigns his office rather than sign certain articles from King Henry VIII, and wrote in the margin, "All alter" (10.88).[6] But, perhaps surprisingly for a play about a Catholic martyr, Tilney's main concern was not its religious politics but rather its depiction of xenophobic unrest. The opening scenes dramatize the anti-immigrant Evil May Day riot of 1517 with an eye to the 1590s, showing the strangers' crimes and the determined resistance of English citizens. Among other excisions, Tilney crossed out the highly inflammatory first scene in its entirety and warned the playwrights in the margin to "[l]eave out the insurrection wholly and the cause thereof" and instead narrate its outcome "by a short report, and not otherwise, at your own perils" (Tilney.1–2, 5–6). At some point, several playwrights – probably including Shakespeare – were brought in to assist in revising the play. We do not know whether the play, in any form, was ever licensed or staged.

Sir Thomas More reprises the incendiary confluence of xenophobia, libel, and drama that took place in 1593. Scholars have long noted the parallels between the play's rising and the anti-alien unrest of the 1590s.[7] But what has not been appreciated is that the document at the core of the rising, the citizen John Lincoln's "<bill> of our wrongs and the strangers' insolencies," is itself a libel (1.99–100).[8] I argue that the play identifies the bill with the now-familiar

---

[4] Until recently, most scholars dated the original version of the play to 1592–93. John Jowett, in his Arden edition of the play, has made the case for *c*.1600 (Anthony Munday et al., *Sir Thomas More*, ed. Jowett [London: Arden Shakespeare, 2011], 424–32), a date also supported by MacDonald P. Jackson, "Deciphering a Date and Determining a Date: Anthony Munday's *John a Kent and John a Cumber* and the Original Version of *Sir Thomas More*," *Early Modern Literary Studies* 15.3 (2011), http://purl.org/emls/15-3/jackdate.htm; and Hugh Craig, "The Date of *Sir Thomas More*," *Shakespeare Survey* 66 (2013): 38–54. Lawrence Manley and Sally-Beth MacLean have in turn interrogated Jowett's case and argued once more for the 1592–93 date (*Lord Strange's Men and Their Plays* [New Haven: Yale University Press, 2014], 114–19).

[5] For a detailed account of the manuscript and its history, see *Sir Thomas More*, ed. Jowett, 344–94.

[6] All quotations from the play come from Jowett's Arden edition and are cited parenthetically in the text by scene and line number, including the replaced passages from the original text (OT) reproduced in Appendix 1, 327–43.

[7] See, e.g., Alfred W. Pollard, introduction to *Shakespeare's Hand in the Play of Sir Thomas More*, ed. Pollard (Cambridge: Cambridge University Press, 1923), 22–27, 33–40; and Scott McMillin, *The Elizabethan Theatre and "The Book of Sir Thomas More"* (Ithaca: Cornell University Press, 1987), 67–73.

[8] The one partial exception is Nina Levine, *Practicing the City: Early Modern London on Stage* (New York: Fordham University Press, 2016), 58–64. The angle brackets denote a gap in the manuscript.

Libel, Equity, and Law in Sir Thomas More 117

paradigm of extrajudicial complaint. Lincoln and his coconspirators take their grievances public – suborning a preacher to read their text from the pulpit – once all legal avenues for redress have failed. At issue here are the parameters of publicity: who gets a platform for public address, what does it look like, and how do they use it. But it was not just unlawful publication that made libels so menacing. Theirs was an idiom of vitriol and violence, sedition and scurrility – channeled, in 1593 and in *Sir Thomas More* alike, against religious refugees. Like the Dutch Church libeler, the play's citizens couch their complaints in a viciously xenophobic register. *Sir Thomas More* realizes the specter of populist violence conjured by the libels of 1593.

Yet libel is not the only extralegal recourse in the play. As its title indicates, the xenophobic scenes are just one part (if a central one) of the story of *Sir Thomas More*. The latter two-thirds of the play track the rise and fall of the titular character. In the process, they throw into sharp relief the issue at the root of the citizens' rebellion: the limits of the law. Like his historical counterpart, the theatrical Thomas More moves through the justice system. He enters the play as sheriff of London, quickly ascends to Lord Chancellor – an office that puts him at the head of the Court of Chancery, England's highest court of equity – and finally finds himself on the other side of the law when he is executed for refusing to subscribe to the king's articles on the grounds of conscience. His career extends the initial dramatization of libel into an extended meditation on the remedies available to any subject afflicted by unjust law, from bills and libels to riot, the vexed administration of equity, and the vagaries of conscience. Given the gaps and sutures in the surviving playscript, it is no surprise that *Sir Thomas More* declines to offer any easy resolution. But the play insistently stages the causes and consequences of extralegal action. And those actions, I will argue, repeatedly bring subjects onto the stage of state to publish their own complaints, critiques, and (in the end) metatheatrical meditations.

The Dutch Church Libel and the Stranger Crisis of 1593

Assessments of early modern attitudes toward immigrants vary, from rising xenophobia to relative tolerance.[9] But on at least two points historians agree: immigrants were easy scapegoats in times of economic stress; and the

---

[9] See, e.g., Laura Hunt Yungblut, *Strangers Settled Here Amongst Us: Policies, Perceptions and the Presence of Aliens in Elizabethan England* (London: Routledge, 1996); Lien Bich Luu, "'Taking the Bread Out of Our Mouths': Xenophobia in Early Modern London," *Immigrants and Minorities* 19.2 (2000): 1–22; Nigel Goose, "'Xenophobia' in Elizabethan and Early Stuart England: An Epithet Too Far?" in *Immigrants in Tudor and Early Stuart England*, ed. Goose and Lien Luu (Brighton,

118   Libels on the Elizabethan Stage

late 1580s and the 1590s were a time of stress par excellence.[10] The Dutch and the French, many of them religious refugees, were the largest and most visible populations as well as the primary targets of abuse.[11] From 1586 to 1595, the resentment approached levels not seen since the infamous May Day rising of 1517. The main grievances had to do with immigrants' commercial activities. Throughout the later sixteenth century, English artisans and shopkeepers brought a steady stream of petitions and complaints against foreign craftsmen and merchants.[12] The most common refrain was that the immigrants were taking business from English workers. But there were other (and uglier) grievances too. Immigrants were blamed for a host of social and economic ills, including – in one representative list from 1583 – "*the* encrease of *the* pryses of vyctualles, rayesinge *the* Rentes of tenementes, and encreasinge of syckenesse by theyere ou*er*pesteringe of smalle roomes w*ith* manye of them."[13] In addition to driving up rents and spreading disease, immigrants were accused of hoarding commodities, exporting English wealth, usury, religious nonconformity (or even atheism), and espionage.[14]

The crisis year – and the year Marlowe and Kyd were caught up in the furor – was 1593. Apprentice riots in the summer of 1592 had already led the Privy Council to ban plays and sparked fears of violence against Dutch craftsmen living in London.[15] Over the following months, a severe

---

 UK: Sussex Academic Press, 2005), 110–35; and Brodie Waddell, "The Evil May Day Riot of 1517 and the Popular Politics of Anti-Immigrant Hostility in Early Modern London," *Historical Research* 94 (2021): 716–35. I borrow the apt term "stranger crisis" in the section title from Eric Griffin, "Shakespeare, Marlowe, and the Stranger Crisis of the Early 1590s," in *Shakespeare and Immigration*, ed. Ruben Espinosa and David Ruiter (Farnham, UK: Ashgate, 2014), 13–36.

[10] Andrew Pettegree, *Foreign Protestant Communities in Sixteenth-Century London* (Oxford: Clarendon Press, 1986), 291; Archer, *Pursuit*, 1–14; Yungblut, *Strangers*, 31–33; Luu, "Taking the Bread"; Goose, "Xenophobia," 119–21.

[11] Pettegree, *Foreign Protestant Communities*; Lien Bich Luu, "Migration and Change: Religious Refugees and the London Economy, 1550–1600," *Critical Survey* 8.1 (1996): 98–99. For data on the make-up of London's immigrant population, see Luu, *Immigrants and the Industries of London, 1500–1700* (Aldershot, UK: Ashgate, 2005), 87–140.

[12] Andrew Pettegree, "'Thirty years on': Progress Towards Integration amongst the Immigrant Population of Elizabethan London," in *English Rural Society, 1500–1800: Essays in Honour of Joan Thirsk*, ed. John Chartres and David Hey (Cambridge: Cambridge University Press, 1990), 298. On these suits, see Ronald Pollitt, "'Refuge of the distressed Nations': Perceptions of Aliens in Elizabethan England," *Journal of Modern History* 52.1, on demand supplement (1980): D1001–19; Irene Scouloudi, *Returns of Strangers in the Metropolis 1593, 1627, 1635, 1639: A Study of an Active Minority* (London: Huguenot Society of London, 1985), 59–63; and Jacob Selwood, *Diversity and Difference in Early Modern London* (Farnham, UK: Ashgate, 2010), 51–86.

[13] BL, Lansdowne MS 39, fol. 144r.

[14] TNA, SP 12/81, fols. 83v–84r, 97r–100r; BL, Lansdowne MS 13, fols. 120r–122r; Lansdowne MS 66, fols. 157r–158r.

[15] *APC*, 22:549–51; BL, Lansdowne MS 71, fol. 32r.

Libel, Equity, and Law in Sir Thomas More

outbreak of plague devastated the economy, kept the theaters closed, and felled roughly 8 percent of London's population in a single year.[16] Tensions continued to rise through the spring of 1593. In March, the House of Commons took up a bill that would restrict strangers from retailing foreign wares. Vigorous debate ensued. Proponents of the bill advanced the by-then familiar arguments: immigrants drove up prices, put English artisans out of work, and took English wealth abroad. If economic nationalism was the driving force behind the bill, some speakers also registered more insidious stereotypes. Sir Walter Ralegh, for instance, declared, "The nature of this Dutchman is to fly to no man but for his profit, and to none they will obey longe; . . . The Dutchman by his policy hath gott the trade of all the world into his hand." But the strangers found plenty of defenders too. The most eloquent of these – and one echoed in the Shakespearean lines of *Sir Thomas More* – was Henry Finch. Finch reminded his fellow MPs that they had once been religious refugees themselves: "in Quene Marye's tyme when our case was as theirs now, those contryes did allow us all those liberties which now we seeke to deny them. They are strangers now. We may be strangers hereafter, therefore let us doe as we would be done to."[17] Finch's Protestant cosmopolitanism did not carry the day in the Commons – where the bill passed by a comfortable margin – but it prevailed in the House of Lords, where the bill was subsequently rejected.[18]

Reports of anti-alien libels began to surface less than a week after the parliament was dissolved.[19] The timing seems to have been no coincidence. A few scholars have suggested that the bill's backers, thwarted in parliament, may have stirred up or inspired the libelers.[20] An equally plausible scenario is that the dissolution of parliament unleashed a surge of pent-up rage. Whatever their immediate cause, the libels quickly multiplied. Fearing a rising on the scale of 1517 – "an other yll May day," as it were – the Privy Council authorized its commissioners to round up suspects and "put them

---

[16] Archer, *Pursuit*, 9; Andrew Gurr, *The Shakespearian Playing Companies* (Oxford: Clarendon Press, 1996), 91; Paul Slack, *The Impact of Plague in Tudor and Stuart England* (Oxford: Clarendon Press, 1990), 151.

[17] T. E. Hartley, ed., *Proceedings in the Parliaments of Elizabeth I*, 3 vols. (London: Leicester University Press, 1981–95), 3:143, 138–39.

[18] Ibid., 3:148; *Journals of the House of Lords*, vol. 2, 1578–1614 (London, n.d.), 184.

[19] *APC*, 24:187.

[20] Margaret Tudeau-Clayton, "Shakespeare and Immigration," *SPELL: Swiss Papers in English Language and Literature* 27 (2012): 85–86; Siobhán Higgins, "'Let us Not Grieve the Soul of the Stranger': Images and Imaginings of the Dutch and Flemish in Late Elizabethan London," *Dutch Crossing* 37.1 (2013): 23–25.

120   Libels on the Elizabethan Stage

to the torture."[21] This was the dragnet that ensnared Kyd and Marlowe. And the two dramatists were only the most famous of the suspected libelers. For "writinge a libell in thretinge of strangars, and setinge the same on a strangars dore," a scrivener named Shore or Short was fined a hefty sum, sentenced to three days in the pillory and four years in prison, and (according to one report) banished.[22]

But as was so often the case, the libels' anonymity remained largely impenetrable. The scrivener is the only known convicted libeler from the crisis of 1593. Marlowe himself may have escaped more or less unscathed, his death ten days after his appearance before the Privy Council a terrible coincidence. Kyd was eventually released from prison, although perhaps left a broken man.[23] "Some of thease libellers are found oute and tortured," an English informant reported in late May, "but the residew hold on still."[24] Libels materialized not only on the wall of the Dutch Churchyard but also on the mayor's and sheriff's gates, and in other places "in and about the cittie."[25] Their message was twofold: a clear and targeted threat (against the congregants of the Dutch Church, the mayor, and the sheriff), but also a broader effort to rally public opinion against immigrants and to put pressure on London's leaders. Sites of authority became sites of notoriety in what amounted to a xenophobic revision of London's civic topography.[26]

Among the most virulent of the libels – the one that "doth excead the rest in lewdnes" – was the Dutch Church libel.[27] Scholars have traced its anti-alien rhetoric to a range of sources, from Ralegh's 1593 speech in parliament to plays and ballads from the 1580s and 1590s.[28] But the closest

---

[21] BL, Harley MS 6849, fol. 326r; *APC*, 24:222.

[22] BL, Harley MS 247, fol. 217, transcribed in Ethel Seaton, "Marlowe, Robert Poley, and the Tippings," *Review of English Studies* 5 (1929): 274. This report names the scrivener Shore. A different account, calendared in K. J. Kesselring, ed., *Star Chamber Reports: BL Harley MS 2143* (Kew: List and Index Society, 2018), gives his name as Short and records the sentence of banishment (63). Based on this report, Shore/Short may well have been the author of the only anti-alien libel other than the Dutch Church libel known to have survived from 1593: compare Kesselring, *Star Chamber*, 63 to Strype, *Annals*, 4:234–35.

[23] Kuriyama, *Christopher Marlowe*, 120–41; Arthur Freeman, *Thomas Kyd: Facts and Problems* (Oxford: Clarendon Press, 1967), 28.

[24] *The Letters and Despatches of Richard Verstegan (c. 1550–1640)*, ed. Anthony G. Petti, Catholic Record Society 52 (London, 1959), 164.

[25] Ibid., 155; *APC*, 24:200.

[26] On libels and civic space, see Andrew Gordon, "The Act of Libel: Conscripting Civic Space in Early Modern England," *Journal of Medieval and Early Modern Studies* 32.2 (2002): 375–97.

[27] *APC*, 24:222.

[28] Nicholl, *Reckoning*, 285–86, 291–93; Higgins, "Let us Not Grieve," 23–26; Lloyd Edward Kermode, *Aliens and Englishness in Elizabethan Drama* (Cambridge: Cambridge University Press, 2009), 72–73, 78; Mathew Dimmock, "Tamburlaine's Curse: An Answer to a Great Marlowe Mystery," *Times*

Libel, Equity, and Law in Sir Thomas More 121

echoes I have found are, tellingly, not in speeches or drama but in the Elizabethan petitions against strangers. I suggested the scope of their allegations above: market manipulation, greed, usury, spreading disease, espionage, and the like. Sir Thomas Mildmay gathered all these grievances together in a 1591 proposal for a yearly register of strangers. Unchecked, he argues, immigrants threaten to "Engrosse *our* commodities into theire handes, and transporte the same" abroad, causing English "Artisans & mechanicall *persons* to be empoverished." With a register in hand, the queen could send the "serviceable men" off to the wars. The surveillance would help the state crack down on a range of supposed undesirables: those who "make Religion the culler of theire com*m*inge," who practice usury, who "gredelie" amass "grete Riches" and then "suddeyenelie dep*arte* the Reallme," who are really "Spyes and Intelligencer*es*." And it would help the state discover whether the strangers are the cause of "the extreme prices of victuells, or the grete Inhauncinge the Rent*es* of howses."[29]

The Dutch Church libel repeats Mildmay's accusations, some nearly verbatim:[30]

> Your Machiavellian Marchant spoyles the state,
> Your vsery doth leave vs all for deade
> Your Artifex, & craftesman works our fate,
> And like the Jewes, you eate us vp as bread
> The Marchant doth ingross all kinde of wares
>
> . . .
>
> You are intelligencers to the state & crowne
> And in your hart*es* doe wish an alteracion,
> You transport goods, & bring vs gawds good store
> Our Leade, our Vittaile, our Ordenance & what nott
>
> . . .
>
> Our pore artificers doe starve & dye
> For y^t they cannot now be sett on worke
> And for your worke more curious to the ey[.]
> In Chambers, twenty in one house will lurke,
> Raysing of rents, was never knowne before
> Living farre better then at native home

Literary Supplement (November 19, 2010), 16–17. Dimmock makes a suggestive yet highly speculative case for Thomas Deloney's authorship of the libel.

[29] BL, Lansdowne MS 66, fols. 157r–158r. John Strype prints a modernized text of a 1594 version of this suit in *Annals*, 4:296–301.

[30] To my knowledge, only Jonathan Gil Harris, in *Sick Economies: Drama, Mercantilism, and Disease in Shakespeare's England* (Philadelphia: University of Pennsylvania Press, 2004), has noticed the striking echoes of Mildmay's suit (67–68). But he (based on Strype's transcript) assumes that the suit postdates the libel and, in any event, only draws attention to a few of the many parallels.

Libels on the Elizabethan Stage

> And our pore soules, are cleane thrust out of dore
> And to the warres are sent abroade to rome,
> . . .
> . . . we will doe iust vengeance on you all
> In counterfeitinge religion for your flight.
>
> (5–9, 15–18, 25–32, 41–42)

The merchant's depredations, the usury, the engrossing and transportation of goods, the intelligencers, the out-of-work English artificers, the immigrants crowded in chambers and driving up rents, the feigned religion, the foreign wars – all these grievances recur throughout the anti-immigrant petitions. This is not to implicate any of the petitioners, least of all Mildmay, in the libeling. Rather, these parallels underscore that petitions and libels inhabited adjacent and sometimes overlapping spheres. An allowed suit or bill could easily veer toward libel through intemperate rhetoric and, especially, through illicit publication.

The latter is precisely what happened in the case of a weavers' petition printed in 1595. In a lengthy letter to the minister and elders of the French Church in London, a group of English journeymen complained of the alleged abuses of immigrant weavers, including their bypassing apprenticeships and undercutting prices. Along with these accusations, the petitioners issued a warning:

> [B]efore we will any longer beare the great wronges we have done, wee intend to proceede further, Nothing doubtinge but soe longe as we have such a gracyous and mercyfull a Queene, soe honorable and prudent a Councell, and such carefull and upright Judges and Majestrates, that we shall finde speedy helpe and redresse of our long sorrow.[31]

The not-so-subtle implication is that if England's governors really are as good and gracious as they claim to be, then they will have no choice but to come to the petitioners' aid. But redress was not forthcoming. Lord Mayor John Spencer tracked down all those "privye to the printing thereof" and committed the principal culprits, along with the printer, to Newgate.[32] Spencer's primary concern, shared by Elizabeth's chief secretary, William Cecil, was not merely the accusations but their dissemination in print. Responding to Cecil's request "to be farther advertised toutching the printinge of the pamphlet," Spencer reported the identity of the printer (Gabriel Simson), how many copies were printed (twenty-two), and to

---

[31] Frances Consitt, *The London Weavers' Company*, vol. 1 (Oxford: Clarendon Press, 1933), 316.

[32] Ibid., 318. With the support of Lord Chief Justice Popham, though, the weavers were soon freed, and they secured new ordinances in their favor the next year (ibid., 152).

whom they were supposed to be delivered (the stranger churches and London's civic leaders). Spencer does not use the word "libel" to describe what he calls the culprits' "foul practice."[33] But the prime fear seems to be that the petition's incendiary charges might go public.[34]

The same was true in the case of the Dutch Church libel. Its anonymous posting on the wall of the Dutch churchyard recast a place of refuge as a den of economic predation. But it was not just illicit publication that distinguished the libel from a petition like Mildmay's. The poem turns the tropes of libel to chilling effect. Violent threats sit uneasily alongside protestations of loyalty to the crown:

> Weele cutt your throtes, in your temples praying
> Not paris massacre so much blood did spill
> As we will doe iust vengeance on you all
> . . .
> With Spanish gold, you all are infected
> And with y^r gould our Nobles wink at feats
> Nobles said I? nay men to be reiected,
> Upstarts y^t enioy the noblest seat*es*
> That wound their Countries brest, for lucres sake
> And wrong our gracious Queene & Subiects good
> By letting strangers make our harts to ake
> For which our swords are whet, to shedd their blood.
>
> (39–41, 45–52)

The threat is stark and brutal: "Fly, Flye, & never returne," or else the anonymous collective of Londoners will rise up and slaughter the strangers (53). At the same time, the author sets the "gracious Queene & Subiects good" against the corrupt nobility. This peculiarly seditious loyalism reflects the rhetoric of popular protest in early modern England. Especially in times of hardship, commoners joined violent threats with appeals to royal beneficence in their efforts to pressure local leaders to take action. One Lincolnshire libeler in 1607 insisted that the commons meant "no harme to o[u]^r gracious King Quene Prince or any of those" immediately after reporting their resolution to prosecute "a bloody enterprise" against enclosing landlords.[35] This rhetorical strategy could prove highly effective. John Walter has documented several cases in which populist policymaking followed closely on the heels of

---

[33] Ibid., 318.

[34] See Roger A. Ladd, "Thomas Deloney and the London Weavers' Company," *Sixteenth Century Journal* 32.4 (2001): 984.

[35] John Walter, "'The Pooremans Joy and the Gentlemans Plague': A Lincolnshire Libel and the Politics of Sedition in Early Modern England," *Past and Present* 203 (2009): 66.

124 Libels on the Elizabethan Stage

anonymous threats.[36] The rhetoric of violence got results by playing on real fears of sedition and rebellion.

The tropes of libel in no way mitigate the vicious xenophobia of the poem. But they do explain its communicative strategies. The Dutch Church libel was an extralegal complaint – a bill of wrongs, as it were – leavened with violent threats, crude stereotypes, and populist rage. And its impact was remarkable. It brought the crisis of 1593 to a head; it got Kyd and Marlowe in some trouble, not to mention the fate of the humble scrivener; and it remained in circulation years later.[37] The poem shows how xenophobic grievance, published in the language of libel, could seize the attention of the public and the state alike – precisely what John Lincoln's bill of wrongs does in *Sir Thomas More*'s Henrician England and, the censor evidently feared, would do were it to be staged in late Elizabethan London.

Lincoln's Libel

Sir Thomas More makes Lincoln's bill even more central to the Evil May Day riot than it is in the play's source, Holinshed's *Chronicles*. Holinshed is a little hazy about the immediate cause of the rising. To be sure, he calls Lincoln "the author of ill Maie daie" and reports that he was charged as its "principall procurer" on the grounds that he had solicited Doctor Standish and Doctor Beal to read his "bill of complaint" in their Spital sermons (held the week after Easter).[38] But Holinshed also stresses that the rising was more spontaneous eruption than premeditated plot. In his telling, the plan that "on Maie daie next the citie would rebell and slea all the aliens" was "a secret rumour, and no man could tell how it began." And the actual outbreak of violence begins with an alderman's attempt to enforce curfew on a crowd of unruly youths. Holinshed sums up the official determination that, while Lincoln may have been the author of the rising, there was no larger conspiracy: "it could neuer be prooued of anie meeting, gathering, talking, or conuenticle, at anie daie or time before that daie; but that the chance so happened without anie matter prepensed of anie creature sauing Lincolne, and neuer an honest person in maner was taken but onelie he."[39] Lincoln's bill certainly

---

[36] John Walter, "Public Transcripts, Popular Agency and the Politics of Subsistence in Early Modern England," in *Negotiating Power in Early Modern Society: Order, Hierarchy and Subordination in Britain and Ireland*, ed. Michael J. Braddick and Walter (Cambridge: Cambridge University Press, 2001), 123–48; Walter, "Pooremans Joy."

[37] The only known text of the poem was transcribed around 1600 (Freeman, "Marlowe," 48).

[38] Raphael Holinshed, *The Third volume of Chronicles* (London, 1587), sigs. Llll6r, Llll5r.

[39] Ibid., sigs. Llll5r, Llll5v.

Libel, Equity, and Law in Sir Thomas More

plays some role in stirring up popular anger. But it is neither part of a broader plot nor the inciting event. And, in any case, the "honest" Lincoln is one of few upstanding citizens to take part in a riot driven by apprentices, servants, and other lowly Londoners.

The picture looks very different in the opening scene of *Sir Thomas More*.[40] The disgruntled Londoners are all honest citizens (plus one citizen's wife): Lincoln the broker, Doll Williamson and her carpenter husband, Sherwin the goldsmith, and the Betts brothers of unknown occupations. After witnessing the strangers' outrages, Lincoln steps forward to induct the citizens into his plot. He slips into the conversation with an easy camaraderie. Just as Sherwin is lamenting that "how to redress" their wrongs "is a matter beyond all our abilities," Lincoln interjects: "Not so, not so, my good friends" (1.86–88, 89). He lays out his plan with the help of George Betts:

> LINCOLN You know the Spital sermons begin the next week. I have drawn a \<bill\> of our wrongs and the strangers' insolencies.
> GEORGE BETTS Which he means the preachers shall there openly publish in the pulpit. (1.98–102)

Lincoln then produces a "copy" of the bill (1.115) – suggesting other copies may be in circulation – and reads it aloud:

> To you all the worshipful lords and masters of this city that will take compassion over the poor people your neighbours, and also of the great importable hurts, losses and hindrances whereof proceedeth extreme poverty to all the King's subjects that inhabit within this city and suburbs of the same. For so it is that aliens and strangers eat the bread from the fatherless children, and take the living from all the artificers, and the intercourse from all merchants, whereby poverty is so much increased that every man bewaileth the misery of other; for craftsmen be brought to beggary, and merchants to neediness. Wherefore, the premises considered, the redress must be of the commons knit and united to one part. And as the hurt and damage grieveth all men, so must all men set to their willing power for remedy, and not suffer the said aliens in their wealth, and the natural-born men of this region to come to confusion. (1.118–34)

The text, lifted directly from Holinshed, resonates with the anti-alien complaints that circulated widely in late Elizabethan bills and libels.[41] And so too does the material object, a short writing to be "publish[ed] in the pulpit." On the stage, the bill surely would have called to mind the

---

[40] See Levine, *Practicing*, 61–63.   [41] See Holinshed, *Third volume*, sig. Lllll5r.

126 Libels on the Elizabethan Stage

other xenophobic bills stuck to gates, posts, and walls in the final decades of the sixteenth century.

Unlike Holinshed, *Sir Thomas More* puts the bill at the center of a citizen conspiracy. Doll enthusiastically endorses its contents, and then George Betts explains the plot: "No doubt but this will store us with friends enough, whose names we will closely keep in writing, and on May Day next in the morning we'll go forth a-Maying, but make it the worst May Day for the strangers that ever they saw" (1.139–44). This is a far cry from Holinshed's account of a "secret rumour" that the city would rise on the first of May. If any such rumor spread, the play suggests, it would have emerged from this band of citizens. And those citizens quickly take up the bill's call for class solidarity, for "the commons knit and united to one part." Doll is the first to "subscribe" to the secret list of names, and her husband urges them all to "swear true secrecy upon our lives" (1.144, 150–51).

A seditious bill composed, copied, and published by a band of conspirators: Lincoln's text is clearly marked as a libel. Indeed, a bill of wrongs was quite literally a libel – although not necessarily a defamatory one. Even after "libel" acquired its slanderous sense in the sixteenth century, it remained the technical term for a bill of complaint. The two meanings were closely related, not least of all because the courts held malicious accusation to be the essence of defamation. Unlawful publication was all that it took to turn a legitimate *libellus* or bill of wrongs into a *libellus famosus*, a defamatory libel. This explains the play's emphasis on the publication of Lincoln's bill. Copied and delivered from the Spital pulpit, it is not a private, legitimate complaint but – like the libels of 1593 and the weavers' petition of 1595 – an unlawfully published text.

Lincoln's bill has precisely the effect that the Privy Council feared from the libels of 1593: that "soche lewde beginninges" would beget "further mischeife."[42] In *Sir Thomas More*, rebels and rulers alike take the publication of the bill to be the direct cause of the rising. As I discussed above, Lincoln and Betts explain that "openly publish[ing]" it will help them rally Londoners to their cause. And that is exactly what happens. When the violence breaks out, we learn that "[t]his follows on the doctor's publishing / The bill of wrongs in public at the Spital" (3.79–80). This assessment, generally attributed to Sir Roger Cholmley (damage to the manuscript leaves the speaker uncertain), redundantly but emphatically blames the rising on the public publication of Lincoln's bill. In the play as in late

---

[42] *APC*, 24:187.

Libel, Equity, and Law in Sir Thomas More

Elizabethan London, libel joins popular complaint with the threat of xenophobic violence.

Following Holinshed, *Sir Thomas More* also implicates the pulpit in the dissemination of populist grievance. This move reflects not only earlier Tudor history but also the contested politics of the pulpit in Elizabethan England. By the 1590s if not in 1517, the city's two major outdoor pulpits – Paul's Cross and St. Mary's Spital – were sites of both communication and controversy. Mary Morrissey accordingly describes Paul's Cross, which drew the largest and most frequent crowds, as a "constitutive element" of the post-Reformation public sphere.[43] Neither pulpit was merely an instrument of state propaganda. Court, church, and city all tried to control the sermons, and their interests were not always aligned.[44] In fact, Arnold Hunt has argued that "the Paul's Cross preacher seems to have been popularly regarded as 'the poor man's lawyer,' that is, an advocate on behalf of the poorer inhabitants of London, and a spokesman for the redress of grievances."[45] The same is true of Doctor Beal, who reads Lincoln's bill of wrongs from the Spital pulpit.

The Easter sermons delivered at St. Mary's Hospital (known as the "Spital") were an especially apt venue for airing the grievances of poor citizens. Sponsored by London's mayor and aldermen, the Elizabethan Spital sermons typically joined exhortations to charity with sharp satire of the rich and powerful.[46] This message resonates with the opening scenes of *Sir Thomas More*, which pit impoverished London artisans against wealthy, domineering strangers. A proverb cited in a 1588 Spital sermon is particularly relevant to the play: "The *Lawes* are like *Cobwebbs:* that they hold fast the seely *flies*, but the great *Hornetts* breake through them, as oft as they list."[47] The inequities of the law, as I will discuss shortly, are a central theme of *Sir Thomas More*. Interestingly, though, the same sermon also commends "the exiled Churches of *Strangers*" for their exemplary charity.[48] Economic populism and xenophobia did not necessarily go hand in hand.

---

[43] Mary Morrissey, *Politics and the Paul's Cross Sermons, 1558–1642* (Oxford: Oxford University Press, 2011), 69.

[44] Ibid., 68–101.

[45] Arnold Hunt, *The Art of Hearing: English Preachers and Their Audiences, 1590–1640* (Cambridge: Cambridge University Press, 2010), 330. Hunt cites the example of Thomas Millington (a grocer), who, much like Lincoln, presented "a libell to the preacher at Paules Crosse againste the magistrates of the Cyttye" (330; see also Morrissey, *Politics*, 104).

[46] *Lancelot Andrewes: Selected Sermons and Lectures*, ed. Peter McCullough (Oxford: Oxford University Press, 2005), 304–5. On the Spital sermons, see also Sonia Suman, "'A Most Notable Spectacle': Early Modern Easter Spital Sermons," in *Spoken Word and Social Practice: Orality in Europe (1400–1700)*, ed. Thomas V. Cohen and Lesley K. Twomey (Leiden: Brill, 2015), 228–50.

[47] Andrewes, *Selected Sermons*, 43.   [48] Ibid., 72.

128   Libels on the Elizabethan Stage

But they do in *Sir Thomas More*, and they did in the anti-alien libels spread in late Elizabethan London. Evidently that incendiary blend of popular grievance and topical xenophobia was Tilney's main concern when the play came before him for licensing. "Leave out the insurrection wholly and the cause thereof," he warned (Tilney.1–2). The "cause" that Tilney had in mind is surely in part the outrageous behavior of the strangers. Not only did he mark the entire first scene and much of the other citizen scenes for deletion, but he also replaced "stranger" and "Frenchmen" with "Lombard," presumably to redirect the animus toward what was in the 1590s a much less prominent immigrant group (3.49, 53). But it is also revealing that, as I noted above, the play explicitly blames the insurrection on Doctor Beal's "publishing / The bill of wrongs in public at the Spital." The "cause" that Tilney insisted be left out may very well have been the bill itself. In the tense climate of the 1590s, an anti-alien libel inciting a popular rising would have been a disturbing sight indeed.

Whatever Tilney's thinking, the logic of libel – at root a form of extrajudicial complaint – structures the play's opening scenes. From the start, it is clear that the strangers have the law on their side. De Barde the Lombard seizes Doll Williamson and declares, in a brusque and dehumanizing parody of a legal plea, "Thou art my prize, and I plead purchase of thee" (1.2–3). Doll's spirited resistance sends the strangers off to "complain to my Lord Ambassador," revealing the court's complicity in the plight of the citizens (1.77–78). And the citizens themselves repeatedly lament that the law and its administrators favor the strangers: the Londoners are "curbed by duty and obedience" and bound to "strict obedience" (1.57–58, 85). No option seemingly remains but to take matters into their own hands. As Doll warns, "If our husbands must be bridled by law, and forced to bear your wrongs, their wives will be a little lawless, and soundly beat ye" (1.74–76).

There is something of the carnivalesque in the image of the bridled husband and the lawless wife. But Doll's threat and, indeed, her character also develop a hint in the chronicles about the place of women's speech in the May Day rising. In the wake of the rebellion, "proclamations were made, that no women should come togither to babble and talke, but all men should keepe their wiues in their houses."[49] *Sir Thomas More* to

---

[49] Holinshed, *Third volume*, sig. Llll5v. See also Rawdon Brown et al., eds., *Calendar of State Papers and Manuscripts, Relating to English Affairs, Existing in the Archives and Collections of Venice*, 38 vols. (London, 1864–1947), 2:383.

Libel, Equity, and Law in Sir Thomas More   129

some extent shares this view of the rising in terms of the breakdown of patriarchal order. But the lawless Doll also paves the way for Lincoln's extralegal bill. When she and the other citizens learn of Lincoln's plot, Doll is the first and most enthusiastic conspirator. "Ay, and if you men durst not undertake it," she declares, "before God, we women <will>" (1.105–6). It is not entirely clear whether "it" refers to procuring the preachers to publish the bill or publishing it oneself. Either way, Doll imagines herself as an agent of publication.

As the citizens look to take their complaint public, they disingenuously insist that it is entirely legitimate. Lincoln asserts that "there's no hurt in the bill," and Doll "maintain[s] the suit to be honest" (1.114–15, 135–36). Yet even if these claims were true, publication makes all the difference. Read from the pulpit, the bill spurs not legal reform but an outbreak of vigilante justice increasingly consumed by the xenophobia at its core. The rebels' only law is club law. "Since justice keeps not them in greater awe, / We'll be ourselves rough ministers at law," Lincoln urges his compatriots as they set out to burn the strangers' houses (4.31–32, OT1a.14–15). So too did the libelers of 1593 threaten to "trie theire cause lege manuum, by the lawe of theire owne private handes and armes."[50] In *Sir Thomas More*, Lincoln's libel conjures the same vision of extralegal violence.

But the bill also issues a clear call for "redress," a term repeated across the play's opening scenes. In Holinshed, Lincoln tells Doctor Beal that his grievances, and perhaps the bill itself, "hath beene shewed to the councell, and cannot be heard."[51] Taking the accusations public is the last resort. It is only after king and council have failed to help that the libeler turns to a wider audience. So it goes in *Sir Thomas More*. The injunction to obey, as Sherwin says, puts "redress ... beyond all our abilities" (1.87–88). So, the citizens all grow a little (or a lot) lawless and join Lincoln's plot to publish the bill. Their purpose is clear from the bill's appeal for collective action: "the redress must be of the commons knit and united to one part" (1.129–30). Redress may be beyond the individual abilities of the citizens, but together – united by a populist, xenophobic text – they might achieve what each alone could not.

Significantly, the play introduces a scene (with no precedent in Holinshed) in which the nobles endorse the citizens' view. In one of the

---

[50] BL, Harley MS 6849, fol. 325v.   [51] Holinshed, *Third volume*, sig. Llll4v.

130   Libels on the Elizabethan Stage

play's many puns on "strange" and "stranger," the Earl of Surrey wonders how the king's merciful policies should have led to such abuses:[52]

> 'Tis strange, that from his princely clemency
> So well a tempered mercy and a grace
> To all the aliens in this fruitful land,
> That this high-crested insolence should spring
> From them that breathe from his majestic bounty,
> That, fattened with the traffic of our country,
> Already leap into his subjects' face.   (3.9–15)

While reiterating the citizens' complaints – "insolence" echoes the strangers' "insolencies" enumerated in Lincoln's bill (1.100) – Surrey also does what they had not: bring the king into it. His point is to contrast Henry's abundant virtues – "princely clemency," "mercy" and "grace," "majestic bounty" – with the aliens' abuses. But the question lingers: is it not strange that such an (allegedly) merciful king should not hear his subjects' complaints? Later in the scene, Sir Roger Cholmley provides a cutting explanation for this strange predicament in lines tellingly marked for deletion by Tilney. He turns to Surrey and the Earl of Shrewsbury, and pins the blame directly on them, saying,

> Now afore God, your honours, pardon me.
> Men of your place and greatness are to blame –
> I tell ye true, my lords – in that his majesty
> Is not informed of this base abuse,
> And daily wrongs are offered to his subjects;
> For if he were, I know his gracious wisdom
> Would soon redress it.   (3.64–70)

Cholmley's prefatory plea for pardon and his parenthetical "I tell ye true, my lords" suggest that the earls might be bristling at his accusation that they and their peers have failed to inform the king of the strangers' abuses. But we never get to hear their response. A messenger enters with news of the rising, and after that Cholmley practically vanishes from the play. Still, his account raises two uncomfortable possibilities: either the nobility is complicit in the strangers' crimes, or the king is.

Both scenarios pit the working classes not merely against the strangers but also against their powerful English allies. This was a long-standing trope of Tudor anti-immigrant discourse, and one with a modicum of

---

[52] On the play's discourse of strangeness, see Gillian Woods, "'Strange Discourse': The Controversial Subject of *Sir Thomas More*," *Renaissance Drama* 39 (2011): 3–35.

Libel, Equity, and Law in Sir Thomas More

truth to it. Whether or not the foreign craftsmen and merchants really did disadvantage their English competitors, their business provided an economic stimulus welcomed by many parties, including company elites, privy councilors, and English monarchs.[53] These class tensions underlie the Dutch Church libel's attack on those "Nobles" who "wound their Countries brest, for lucres sake / And wrong our gracious Queene & Subiects good / By letting strangers make our harts to ake" (46, 49–51). Cholmley's sharp criticism of the earls and other "men of your place and greatness" expresses the same sentiment, if rather more diplomatically. The trope of the "gracious" monarch, invoked by Cholmely and the Dutch Church libeler alike, appears too in the 1595 weavers' petition, whose authors appeal to the "gracyous and mercyfull" queen for "redresse."[54] Figuring the monarch as gracious puts pressure on England's rulers to "redress" (a word used by the weavers and by Cholmley, Lincoln, and Sherwin) the artisans' grievances.

Of course, the orthodox view held that redress could only come from the monarch, peers, or magistrates. Lincoln himself ultimately takes this line in his gallows speech. After Thomas More defuses the riot with his famous plea for empathy (discussed below), the rebellious citizens yield on the condition that More procure them pardon. But the pardon comes too late for Lincoln. Under pressure from the king's council, London's sheriff hastily sets up a gibbet for the rebels. Lincoln is the first to hang. Speaking from the scaffold, he at first presents himself as a citizen martyr. "I must confess I had no ill intent / But against such as wronged us overmuch," he declares, confessing only to zeal on behalf of English workers (7.53–54). But he soon stages his own conversion from working class hero to moral exemplum. Lincoln continues,

> And now I can perceive it was not fit
> That private men should carve out their redress
> Which way they list. No, learn it now by me:
> Obedience is the best in each degree.
> And, asking mercy meekly of my king,
> I patiently submit me to the law.   (7.55–60)

Lincoln disavows the entire course of the rising, from his call for the commons to pursue their own "redress" to his rallying the rioters as

---

[53] Pettegree, *Foreign Protestant Communities*; Waddell, "Evil May Day"; Scott Oldenburg, *Alien Albion: Literature and Immigration in Early Modern England* (Toronto: University of Toronto Press, 2014), 160–61.

[54] Consitt, *London Weavers' Company*, 316.

132   Libels on the Elizabethan Stage

"rough ministers at law." His "me"/"degree" rhyme neatly sums up the lesson of obedience. Moments like this one seemingly lend support to William B. Long's otherwise implausible suggestion that the play was a piece of government propaganda designed to drive home "the unfortunate consequences of disobedience to the rule of the sovereign" at a time of civil unrest.[55]

But the play is at the very least ambivalent about the citizens' efforts to carve out their own redress. Here, it is instructive to compare Lincoln's speech with its chronicle source. Holinshed's Lincoln likewise insists that he "meant well." Unlike his dramatic counterpart, however, he shows no contrition at all. Instead, he pointedly reminds the nobles that they were the ones who failed to redress the citizens' grievances. "My lords," he admonishes them, "if you knew the mischiefe that is insued in this realme by strangers, you would remedie it, & manie times I haue complained, and then I was called a busie fellow."[56] In *Sir Thomas More*, it is not Lincoln but Cholmley who chides the nobles for failing to remedy the "daily wrongs" committed by the strangers. Giving this complaint to Cholmley – in Holinshed a bit character and "no great freend to the citie" – points in two opposing directions.[57] On the one hand, the change validates the citizens' fateful decision to take their bill public as the only way to make their complaints heard. On the other, it simultaneously lets the playwrights temper the portrait of Lincoln as a citizen martyr with the orthodox lesson of obedience that a critic such as Long wants to take from the play. *Sir Thomas More* recuperates the extralegal method of Lincoln's bill while condemning the "violent intent" at its core (6.208).

This ambivalence runs through the play's depiction of the rising, especially when we read across the patchwork manuscript in which *Sir Thomas More* survives. Probably in response to Tilney's censorship, one of the revisers (usually identified as Heywood) introduced a clown amid the riotous citizens. Another hand, generally taken to be Shakespeare's, showed More quelling the rising with a "noble plea for toleration."[58] Not without reason, scholars largely agree that the revised rebellion scenes

---

[55] William B. Long, "The Occasion of *The Book of Sir Thomas More*," in *Shakespeare and "Sir Thomas More": Essays on the Play and Its Shakespearian Interest*, ed. T. H. Howard-Hill (Cambridge: Cambridge University Press, 1989), 50.
[56] Holinshed, *Third volume*, sig. Llllll6r.   [57] Ibid., sig. Lllll5v.
[58] R. W. Chambers, *Man's Unconquerable Mind: Studies of English Writers, from Bede to A. E. Housman and W. P. Ker* (London: Jonathan Cape, 1939), 249, quoted in E. A. J. Honigmann, "Shakespeare, *Sir Thomas More* and Asylum Seekers," *Shakespeare Survey* 57 (2004): 235.

Libel, Equity, and Law in Sir Thomas More 133

"tend to discredit the actions of the rebels," playing up their crude xenophobia and reducing the citizens to "a clownish mob led by an ignorant demagogue."[59] But there are two problems with this view. First, the original version of the key moment – when More defuses the rebellion – is lost, so we cannot say whether the revised, likely Shakespearean scene departs or develops from the original text. And second, recent scholars have shown that this scene does not necessarily represent an ideological rupture from the original text of the play. Scott Oldenburg notes the appeal to transnational class solidarity in More's moving image of exiled refugees, "the wretched strangers, / Their babies at their backs, with their poor luggage, / Plodding to th' ports and coasts for transportation" (6.85–87).[60] And Nina Levine points out the "common strangeness" in the universalist hypothetical that More deploys to placate the citizens.[61] Perhaps echoing Finch's words in the 1593 parliament, More tells the rebels that, if the king were to banish them, "you must needs be strangers" (6.146).[62] He rebukes the citizens' own "barbarous temper" and "hideous violence," and asks, "What would you think / To be thus used? This is the strangers' case, / And this your mountainish inhumanity" (6.147, 148, 154–56). More's lines sharply rebut the xenophobia of the earlier scenes. But they do so by suggesting that the experience of precarity behind the citizens' grievances is in fact shared by the strangers themselves.

Yet I think it goes too far to argue, as Oldenburg does, that the play "attempts to separate anti-alien sentiment from class antipathy," suggesting that strangers no less than English artisans "are part of the London community that suffers the abuses of the privileged."[63] There are moments in the play that sustain such a cosmopolitan vision of the civic community (and I will return to one such scene at the end of this chapter). Yet separating xenophobia from economic grievance is no easier in *Sir Thomas More* than it was in London in the 1590s. Even on the scaffold, both the penitent Lincoln and the not-so-penitent Doll get in jabs at strangers. As I noted above, Lincoln prefaces his

---

[59] Vittorio Gabrieli and Giorgio Melchiori, introduction to Anthony Munday et al., *Sir Thomas More*, ed. Gabrieli and Melchiori (Manchester: Manchester University Press, 1990), 27. See also Tracey Hill, "'The Cittie is in an uproare': Staging London in *The Booke of Sir Thomas More*," *Early Modern Literary Studies* 11.1 (2005), http://purl.oclc.org/emls/11-1/more.htm.

[60] Oldenburg, *Alien Albion*, 163–64.   [61] Levine, *Practicing*, 71.

[62] On the echo of Finch, see Margaret Tudeau-Clayton, "'This Is the Strangers' Case': The Utopic Dissonance of Shakespeare's Contribution to *Sir Thomas More*," *Shakespeare Survey* 65 (2012): 239–54.

[63] Oldenburg, *Alien Albion*, 161, 166.

134   Libels on the Elizabethan Stage

supposedly meek submission to the law by reminding the onlookers that his only targets were "such as wronged us overmuch." And Doll defiantly recalls those wrongs in the charged idioms of sexual violence and English nationalism:

> Now let me tell the women of this town
> No stranger yet brought Doll to lying down.
> So long as I an Englishman can see,
> Nor French nor Dutch shall get a kiss of me.
> And when that I am dead, for me yet say
> I died in scorn to be a stranger's prey.   (7.126–31)

Casting the stranger once more as the sexual predator thwarted by English resistance surely would have inflamed anew the xenophobia tamped down by More's speech. Indeed, the playwrights went out of their way to make these lines especially inflammatory. Doll's speech changes the aggressor from the Lombard de Barde to the Dutch and the French, the main targets of anti-alien resentment in the 1590s. This authorial choice is difficult to square with any intimation of solidarity between English artisans and strangers.

    If the citizens do not seem to have taken More's message to heart, nor is shared humanity the only argument that he deploys in the revised rebellion scenes. Unsurprisingly, his deeply empathetic lines have long attracted much of the attention devoted to his character and, indeed, to the play itself. But More also makes a rather blunter appeal to divine right: "to the king God hath his office lent / Of dread, of justice, power and command; / Hath bid him rule, and willed you to obey" (6.112–14). Yet More's injunction to obey, as critics have pointed out, is deeply ironic given that his tragic fall is the direct result of him failing to heed his own advice.[64] By declining to sign the unnamed articles from Henry VIII – historically, the Oath of Succession – More "refuse[s] / The duty that the law of God bequeaths / Unto the king," precisely the offense for which he castigates the rebellious citizens (10.105–7). The questions about law and justice raised in the first scenes remain very much unresolved. From its inauspicious beginnings in popular xenophobia, the play soon stages an array of avenues for redressing the inequities of the law.

---

[64] See, e.g., Alistair Fox, "The Paradoxical Design of *The Book of Sir Thomas More*," *Renaissance and Reformation / Renaissance et Réforme* 5.3 (1981): 163–64; Honigmann, "Shakespeare," 231; Susannah Brietz Monta, *Martyrdom and Literature in Early Modern England* (Cambridge: Cambridge University Press, 2005), 168; and Woods, "Strange Discourse," 12.

Libel, Equity, and Law in Sir Thomas More   135

The Court of Conscience

I have already discussed in detail the citizens' recourse. Lincoln and his comrades take their grievances public, and the result is riot (although we should note that, beyond one "little knock" on the head [5.2], the violence lands on property rather than people). Thomas More embodies a very different solution, one described by the interrelated concepts of equity, mercy, and conscience. More himself invokes the latter two terms at key moments in the play (6.164, 10.73). "Equity" appears only in an earlier draft of a passage, when More labels himself "a man of [Righte and] equetie / equallie to deuide true Righte his [h]owne."[65] But the revised version is even more telling. While the initial draft has More somewhat redundantly characterize himself as a man of equity who deals equitably, the revision makes clear that More's equitable dealings follow directly from his recent ascension to the chancellorship. He calls himself not a man of equity but "a man by office truly ordained / Equally to divide true right his own" (9.343–44). At least in theory, this was indeed the office of the Lord Chancellor: to judge "according to equitie and reason" in the Court of Chancery, England's highest court of equity.[66]

But administering equity was not so simple a matter. Recent scholarship has shown that equity was a "contested concept" in the sixteenth and early seventeenth centuries.[67] Aristotelian, canon law and civil law, and theological traditions variously defined equity and its relationship to the common law. The early moderns themselves recognized the challenge of theorizing, let alone doling out, equitable judgments. Late sixteenth-century writers observed that equity "is diuersly termed in the Law" and that there is "scarce any thing more obscure and difficult."[68] To get some sense of equity's semantic range, consider a sample of the definitions included in William West's popular 1594 lawbook: "that which is commonly called equall & good," "a mitigation, or moderation of the Lawe

---

[65] Anthony Munday et al., *The Book of Sir Thomas More*, ed. W. W. Greg (Oxford: Malone Society, 1911), Addition VI, ll. 29–30. The brackets denote deletions.

[66] Thomas Smith, *De Republica Anglorum*, ed. Mary Dewar (Cambridge: Cambridge University Press, 1982), 93.

[67] Mark Fortier, *The Culture of Equity in Early Modern England* (Aldershot, UK: Ashgate, 2005), 22. See also Dennis R. Klinck, *Conscience, Equity and the Court of Chancery in Early Modern England* (Farnham, UK: Ashgate, 2010); and D. Ibbetson, "A House Built on Sand: Equity in Early Modern English Law," in *Law & Equity: Approaches in Roman Law and Common Law*, ed. E. Koops and W. J. Zwalve (Leiden: Martinus Nijhoff, 2014), 55–77.

[68] William West, *Treatise of Equitie*, in *Three Treatises, Of the second part of Symbolaeographie* (London, 1594), sig. A2v; Cambridge University Library MS Gg 2.31, fols. 12–17, quoted in Ibbetson, "House," 68.

136 Libels on the Elizabethan Stage

written," "a ruled kind of Iustice, allaied with the sweetnes of mercie," "plain dealing," "natural Iustice, or the Law of Nature," and, finally, "the correction or amendement of a good Law, which is defectiue in some part, by reason of the generality of it."[69] As a moral principle, equity means apportioning things fairly – in the words of the fictional Thomas More, "Equally to divide true right his own." As a legal principle, it mitigates, tempers, or otherwise corrects the law. Chancery steps in when the common law fails to provide an adequate remedy.

This is what More repeatedly does in the first half of the play. He makes his first appearance introducing the cutpurse Lifter to the mayor's court at Guildhall. Not yet Lord Chancellor but merely "Master Sheriff More," he already emerges as a figure of equity (2.3). He tells Lifter that he has often "saved ye from this place" – that is, the Guildhall sessions – and promises to "procure thy pardon" in return for a "jest": stealing the purse of the sanctimonious Justice Suresby (2.52, 60). Despite his office of sheriff, More has evidently devoted his energies to mitigating the harsh justice of the law. He does the same for the rebellious citizens, tempering "the law's debt / Which hangs upon their lives" with the promise of "mercy" (5.43–44, 6.164). The pattern continues in his encounter with the "ruffian" Falconer (8.57). In one of his first acts as Lord Chancellor, More offers to rescind Falconer's sentence of three years in Newgate if the youth should cut his very long hair. The original (although not the revised) version of this scene has More appeal to Falconer's "conscience" (OT2b.19), the guiding principle (as I will shortly discuss) of equity in Chancery. Falconer ultimately complies, and More immediately sets him free. These scenes present More, both before and after his elevation to Chancellor, as the avatar of equity.

More's equitable judgments suggest that equity may have been the answer for the rebels too, if only they had taken their bill to the Lord Chancellor. In contrast with the common law system, pleadings in Chancery (as in Star Chamber) began with a bill of complaint submitted by the plaintiff. William Lambarde spells out the ideal form of the proceedings: the Chancellor "relieveth those that complaine (by *English Bill*) either for that the *Common Law* oppresseth them with rigour, or else for that it hath not fit medicine for their diseases and griefe."[70] This is precisely the predicament of *Sir Thomas More*'s citizens. "Bridled by law"

---

[69] West, *Treatise*, sigs. A2r–v. See Fortier, *Culture*, 67–68. Ibbetson points out that West is drawing from the civil law dictionary of Simon Schardius ("House," 66–67).

[70] William Lambarde, *Archeion, or, A Discourse upon the High Courts of Justice in England* (London, 1635), sig. E1r.

Libel, Equity, and Law in Sir Thomas More 137

and bound to "strict obedience," they are indeed oppressed by the rigor of the law. Chancery's equity jurisdiction might have offered a legitimate venue for seeking redress, albeit one only fully realized once More ascends to the chancellorship.

Yet the play also sustains a far more cynical view of More's equity. If from one angle his proceedings seem to mitigate the rigor of the law, from another they appear shockingly arbitrary or even unjust. More dangles a pardon before Lifter in exchange for participating in a practical joke, and the scene ends after a guilty verdict is returned with no mention of the thief's fate. In Falconer's case, More doesn't even want to hear the accused's "trivial noise" and summarily commands that he be committed to Newgate (8.74). When Falconer insists on a hearing, it is More himself who sentences him to three years in prison unless he should comply with the new Lord Chancellor's latest arbitrary condition and cut his hair. The most explicit interrogation of More's supposed justice comes in his treatment of the rebels. He makes a similar assurance to them as he had to Lifter, convincing them to submit on the condition that he "procure [their] pardon" (6.160). Yet that pardon, as I noted above, comes only after Lincoln has been hanged. "[H]ad't not been for his persuasion, / John Lincoln had not hung here as he does," Doll bitterly remarks (7.92–93). She soon joins in the unanimous praise for More when the pardon does arrive, but she has already complicated the portrait of More's equity with a deeply cynical couplet: "Men are but men, and so / Words are but words, and pays not what men owe" (7.104–5). Doll blames More for the arbitrary execution of justice.

Similar complaints about arbitrary judgment swirled around Chancery in the sixteenth and seventeenth centuries.[71] The main issue was not equity per se but another slippery concept that lay behind it: conscience. In his influential account of the Elizabethan polity, Thomas Smith notes that the Court of Chancery is popularly known as "the court of conscience, because that the chauncellor is not strained by rigour or forme of wordes of lawe to judge but *ex aequo* and *bono*, and according to conscience."[72] But judging according to conscience was easier said than done. The word itself was

---

[71] Fortier, *Culture*, 59–81; M. Macnair, "Arbitrary Chancellors and the Problem of Predictability," in *Law & Equity*, ed. Koops and Zwalve, 79–104.

[72] Smith, *De Republica*, 93–94. See also West, *Treatise*, sig. B1r. "Ex aequo et bono," literally "according to what is equitable and good," was the legal term for judging by equity; see Lorenzo Maniscalco, "*Interpretatio ex aequo et bono*: The Emergence of Equitable Interpretation in European Legal Scholarship," in *Networks and Connections in Legal History*, ed. Michael Lobban and Ian Williams (Cambridge: Cambridge University Press, 2020), 233–61.

138 Libels on the Elizabethan Stage

highly multivalent. There was the juridical conscience, a term of art for the
fact-finding procedures peculiar to equity jurisdictions.[73] There was
the medieval conscience of applied moral knowledge. And then there was
the emerging modern conscience of personal conviction. These meanings
could hardly be separated, especially in the wake of the Reformation.[74] As
early as the 1520s and 1530s, critics of Chancery argued that "conscience is
a thinge of great uncerteyntie . . . And so divers men, divers conscience."[75]
This concern persisted. A century later, John Selden archly compared the
Chancellor's conscience to the "uncertain measure" of the Chancellor's
foot: "One Chancellor has a long Foot, another a short Foot, a Third an
indifferent Foot: 'Tis the same thing in the Chancellors Conscience."[76]

As the authors of *Sir Thomas More* surely knew, controversies around
equity, law, and conscience ran through the historical More's career.[77]
A common lawyer by training, More's rise to Chancellor in 1529 put him in
charge of Chancery at a moment when the court's jurisdiction was increasingly contested. He wrote several polemical tracts centrally concerned with
England's competing legal systems. And he famously insisted that his
conscience prevented him from taking the Oath of Succession.[78]
Questions of law and conscience accordingly recur throughout Nicholas
Harpsfield's mid-sixteenth-century *Life and Death of Sir Thomas More*, the
primary source for the play's second half.[79] In a now widely cited anecdote,
Harpsfield recounts how More tried to resolve the clash between equity
and law. When some common law judges complained about More's
Chancery injunctions, he offered to stop issuing the orders if the judges
should "by their owne discretions (as they were, as he thought, in conscience bounden) mittigate and reforme the rigo*ur* of the lawe

---

[73] Mike Macnair, "Equity and Conscience," *Oxford Journal of Legal Studies* 27.4 (2007): 659–81.

[74] Klinck, *Conscience*.

[75] *The Replication of a Serjeant at the Laws of England*, in J. A. Guy, *Christopher St German on Chancery and Statute* (London: Selden Society, 1985), 101. See also "Thomas Audley's Reading on Uses (1526)," in John Baker, *Baker and Milsom Sources of English Legal History: Private Law to 1750*, 2nd ed. (Oxford: Oxford University Press, 2010), 118.

[76] John Selden, *Table-Talk: being the Discourses of John Selden Esq* (London, 1689), sig. C3v.

[77] Discussions of these controversies include J. A. Guy, "Thomas More and Christopher St. German: The Battle of the Books," *Moreana* 21 (1984): 5–25; Timothy A. O. Endicott, "The Conscience of the King: Christopher St. German and Thomas More and the Development of English Equity," *University of Toronto Faculty of Law Review* 47.2 (1989): 549–70; Bradin Cormack, *A Power to Do Justice: Jurisdiction, English Literature, and the Rise of Common Law, 1509–1625* (Chicago: University of Chicago Press, 2007), 85–129; and Brian Cummings, "Conscience and the Law in Thomas More," *Renaissance Studies* 23.4 (2009): 463–85.

[78] The word "conscience" appears more than a hundred times in his final letters, including forty-three occurrences in one letter alone (Cummings, "Conscience," 483).

[79] Jowett, introduction to *Sir Thomas More*, 53–58.

Libel, Equity, and Law in Sir Thomas More   139

themselues."[80] But the judges refused. Evidently, they did not feel bound in conscience to temper their judgments with equity. Yet More continued trying to negotiate the faultlines between conscience and law up to the very end. During his confinement in the Tower, he maintained that "a man is not by the lawe of one Realme so bounde in [his] conscience where there is [a] lawe of the whole corps [of christendome to the contrarie in matter touching beleife]."[81] More tellingly frames "conscience" not merely as a matter of private belief but as a question of competing jurisdictions: English law versus Christian consensus.

These juridical tensions lie behind the climactic moment of *Sir Thomas More*, when Sir Thomas Palmer brings in the king's unnamed articles "first to be viewed, / And then to be subscribed to" (10.69–70). In response, More distills the essence of his dilemma into an understated yet powerful couplet: "Subscribe these articles? Stay, let us pause. / Our conscience first shall parley with our laws" (10.72–73). Before this scene, the word "conscience" has occurred only twice (once in the revised text), both times referring to the conscience of the defendant (Lifter and then Falconer) (2.97, OT2b.19). Now More finds himself on the other side of the law. Still, he attempts to apply the same judicial procedure as he had before and as the historical More did many times in Chancery: testing the letter of the law against the dictates of conscience. The difference is that More no longer has an authorized forum for dispensing equity. He is judge and defendant alike in the court of conscience of his own soul.[82]

It is perhaps fitting, then, that More should find no more justice from conscience than did the supposed beneficiaries of his equitable decisions. This is not to say that the play endorses the rigor of the law. Rather, it shows that the alternatives – libel, riot, equity and conscience – are all in their own ways imperfect. My account of More's conscience thus qualifies the prevailing view of him as a "martyred subject" caught between "private

---

[80] Nicholas Harpsfield, *The Life and Death of Sr Thomas Moore, Knight, Sometymes Lord High Chancellor of England*, ed. Elsie Vaughan Hitchcock and R. W. Chambers, Early English Text Society (London: Oxford University Press, 1932), 55.

[81] Ibid., 177. The phrases enclosed in brackets are not found in the copy of Harpsfield's biography that Munday may well have used for the play (see Jowett, introduction to *Sir Thomas More*, 10). But they are included in a letter printed in More's 1557 English works, and the friction between law and conscience is clear either way (*The workes of Sir Thomas More Knyght* [London, 1557], sig. ZZ3v).

[82] The "court of conscience" was not just a popular name for Chancery but also a common metaphor, used by Protestants and Catholics alike, for the Christian's inward self-examination before God. In *A Watch-woord to Englande* (London, 1584), Anthony Munday himself claimed to have written a piece of anti-Catholic polemic under the title *The Court of Conscience* (sig. N2v).

140   Libels on the Elizabethan Stage

conscience" and "state religion."[83] *Sir Thomas More* does track the court of conscience as it moves from external sites of judgment to the inward tribunal of the soul. But More's conscience is never solely a private matter. It is instead the juridico-theological conscience of the historical Thomas More, an uncertain medley of legal principle, Christian consensus, and private conviction. This multivalence produces a fractured portrait of More, at once hagiographical and sharply critical – at least when it comes to his arbitrary applications of equity.

Fellow-Like Feeling

More's court of conscience ultimately takes its place alongside the other extralegal recourses in the play. As several critics have noted, his passive resistance to the law echoes the citizens' own principled (and deeply xenophobic) stand.[84] Among the many parallels is one that has gone largely overlooked: More's own act of publication. Forms of the verb "publish" appear three times in the play: twice in reference to Doctor Beal reading Lincoln's bill from the pulpit and one final time at More's execution. As More ascends the scaffold, the Earl of Shrewsbury urges him to "publish to the world / Your great offence unto his majesty" (17.70–71). Yet More proceeds to publish not his offense but instead its metatheatrical consequence: "I confess his majesty hath been ever good to me, and my offence to his highness makes me, of a state pleader, a stage player – though I am old and have a bad voice – to act this last scene of my tragedy" (17.73–77). Merely confessing – with, I think, more than a hint of sarcasm – the king's goodness rather than his own crime is itself a challenge to the script of the contrite traitor. And More immediately goes on to draw attention to the metamorphosis that his disobedience has wrought, turning him from "state pleader" to "stage player." His conscience has given him a public part to play on the same stage of state – and on the same fatal scaffold – onto which Lincoln and his compatriots had likewise unlawfully intruded.

In a likely source for More's metatheatrical metaphor, the historical More's *History of King Richard III*, the people reflect that such "matters

---

[83] David Womersley, *Divinity and State* (Oxford: Oxford University Press, 2010), 192, 194. See also Stephen Longstaffe, "Puritan Tribulation and the Protestant History Play," in *Literature and Censorship in Renaissance England*, ed. Andrew Hadfield (Basingstoke, UK: Palgrave, 2001), 40–45; and Monta, *Martyrdom*, 160–72.

[84] Levine, *Practicing*, 72–74; Oldenburg, *Alien Albion*, 169; Stephanie Elsky, *Custom, Common Law, and the Constitution of English Renaissance Literature* (Oxford: Oxford University Press, 2020), 171–74.

Libel, Equity, and Law in Sir Thomas More   141

bee Kynges games, as it were stage playes, and for the more part plaied vpon scafoldes. In which pore men be but ye lokers on. And thei y^t wise be, wil medle no farther."[85] Poor men (and at least one woman) make their own doomed foray onto those scaffolds in the play's first movement. By the end, though, the people have returned to being mere onlookers. But two scenes leading up to More's execution show the poor carving out a different role, neither meddling actors nor silent spectators. On his way to the Tower, More is accosted by a "poor woman" with a suit pending in Chancery (14.23). This moment may be another implicit critique of More's equity proceedings: the woman's suit has evidently dragged on for two years, and she fears that she will be "utterly undone" if he does not return "all the evidence" that she has lodged with the court (14.26, 25). But the episode also displays the play's characteristic ambivalence. When More tells her that he can no longer help her, the woman responds by paying tribute to his beneficence: "Farewell, the best friend that the poor e'er had" (14.44). This humble looker-on, at any rate, takes More's side in the king's games.

The next scene elaborates the popular sympathy for More. As their master is on trial, four of More's devoted servants gather to discuss the matter. Ned Butler begins to reiterate the orthodox view that the people ought not to meddle in such lofty affairs – "I have nothing to do with matters above my capacity" – but then turns sharply to offer his own opinion: "but, as God judge me, if I might speak my mind, I think there lives not a more harmless gentleman in the universal world" (15.11–14). His fellows likewise speak their minds, and their praise for More is unanimous. When the news comes that More has been condemned, Giles Porter lauds their erstwhile lord while flouting the state's verdict. "God bless his soul, and a fig then for all worldly condemnation!" he exclaims (15.31–32). The servants' deep affection for More only grows when they learn that he has bequeathed twenty nobles to each of them, "[t]he best and worst together, all alike" (15.51). More's steward Catesby ends the scene by invoking the affective community brought together by More's fall and final act of generosity. "Come and receive your due," he says, "and after go / Fellow-like hence, co-partners of one woe" (15.59–60). "All alike," "fellow-like," "co-partners": such is the egalitarian community of woe conjured in sympathy for More and, as Giles Porter's exclamation attests, in defiance of the law.

---

[85] Thomas More, *The History of King Richard III*, ed. Richard S. Sylvester, in *The Complete Works of St. Thomas More*, vol. 2 (New Haven: Yale University Press, 1963), 81.

142   Libels on the Elizabethan Stage

Catesby's language speaks not just to the band of sympathizers gathered on the stage but also to the experience of playgoing itself. Eliciting collective feeling was, as Musa Gurnis puts it, "the basic, declared goal of early modern stagecraft."[86] "Co-partners of woe" might equally describe the "ten thousand spectators at least" whom Thomas Nashe famously describes "newe embalm[ing]" Shakespeare's brave Talbot with their tears.[87] What Catesby reminds us too is that this communal feeling did not evaporate at the playhouse door. Playgoers come and receive their due, and afterward part affected in some way by what they have undergone. "[T]heir affective and cognitive experiences would have accompanied them home or to the tavern," Steven Mullaney imagines, "where they would continue to grow and develop, sometimes in face-to-face conversation or debate, sometimes in a virtual sense, as memories often do."[88] In this way the audience begins to form a public. From the confines of the playhouse to a fuzzy network of physical and virtual spaces, playgoers continue to feel themselves involved in a shared affective experience.

Sir Thomas More sustains this vision of affective community through the final scenes, making room even for strangers themselves. No sooner have More's servants trudged "fellow-like" from the stage than their lord himself appears. Talking with the lieutenant of the Tower, More comments on the "strange commodities" that he has purchased with his takings from Chancery (16.51). Strange – and estranged – commodities were one of the central grievances of the anti-immigrant libels and petitions of the 1590s. As the Dutch Church libel puts it, the strangers allegedly "transport goods, & bring vs gawds good store," that is, export English commodities and import foreign (strange) ones. But More's strange commodities are of a different nature: "Crutches, . . . and bare cloaks, / For halting soldiers and poor needy scholars" (16.55–56). More refigures foreign imports as domestic charity, redeeming the economic populism of the play's first scenes from the vicious xenophobia that accompanied it. If only elliptically, his language gestures toward the "common strangeness" (to borrow Levine's phrase) experienced by strangers and citizens alike.

---

[86] Musa Gurnis, *Mixed Faith and Shared Feeling: Theater in Post-Reformation London* (Philadelphia: University of Pennsylvania Press, 2018), 51. See also Jeremy Lopez, *Theatrical Convention and Audience Response in Early Modern Drama* (Cambridge: Cambridge University Press, 2003); and Matthew Steggle, *Laughing and Weeping in Early Modern Theatres* (Aldershot, UK: Ashgate, 2007).
[87] Thomas Nashe, *Pierce Penilesse His Supplication to the Diuell* (London, 1592), sig. F3r.
[88] Steven Mullaney, *The Reformation of Emotions in the Age of Shakespeare* (Chicago: University of Chicago Press, 2015), 172.

Libel, Equity, and Law in Sir Thomas More   143

Yet the surge of sympathy unleashed by More's fall is not the only instance of collective feeling in the play. There is also the "tide of rage" against the strangers, given voice and direction by Lincoln's libel (3.62). Both Lincoln's libel and More's martyrdom elicit intense emotions from their citizen audiences, and those emotions in turn instill a sense of solidarity – a "fellow-like" feeling, in Catesby's words. Both are "publish[ed] to the world," as Shrewsbury puts it, or at least to the citizens of London (17.70). And both threaten to touch an audience beyond the play's Henrician world, as we see from Tilney's censorship of the rising and from the play's final metatheatrical turn. *Sir Thomas More* begins and ends with glimpses of how shared affect might organize citizen publics, from the violently xenophobic to the movingly utopian.

In the next chapter, I will have more to say about collective emotion and its place in the public sphere.[89] At least in *Sir Thomas More*, though, the community of co-partners in woe remains a fleeting vision. The play grants no more staying power to this fellowship than it does to the rebellious "commons knit and united to one part" invoked by Lincoln's bill. Neither the shared sympathy for More nor his strangely charitable commodities erase the xenophobic edge of the opening scenes. Rather, the play follows the politics of public feeling from sedition to sympathy. Thomas More's equity, offered to all alike, might seem to bridge the two extremes. But, as I have argued above, that equity is riven with its own internal contradictions. In this, *Sir Thomas More* does justice to the messy reality of late Elizabethan popular politics. The play's citizens cope with the inequities of the law in all sorts of ways, some uglier than others. If *Sir Thomas More* ever made it to the stage, it would have been up to the audience to chart their own courses through the competing visions of communal affect and action – in More's terms, to parley with the law themselves.

---

[89] The place of passion (or affect or emotion) in the early modern public sphere has attracted much attention of late: see, among others, John Staines, "Compassion in the Public Sphere of Milton and King Charles," in *Reading the Early Modern Passions: Essays in the Cultural History of Emotion*, ed. Gail Kern Paster, Katherine Rowe, and Mary Floyd-Wilson (Philadelphia: University of Pennsylvania Press, 2004), 89–110; Paul Yachnin, "Performing Publicity," *Shakespeare Bulletin* 28.2 (2010): 201–19; Mullaney, *Reformation*; Gurnis, *Mixed Faith*; Jacqueline Vanhoutte, *Age in Love: Shakespeare and the Elizabethan Court* (Lincoln: University of Nebraska Press, 2019); and Patricia Fumerton, *The Broadside Ballad in Early Modern England: Moving Media, Tactical Publics* (Philadelphia: University of Pennsylvania Press, 2020).

CHAPTER 5

Jane Shore's Public: Pity and Politics in Heywood's Edward IV

The long literary history of Jane Shore begins in the pages of Thomas More's *History of King Richard III* (*c.*1514–18). More worries that "some shal think this woman to sleight a thing, to be written of & set amonge the remembraunces of great matters," yet set her among great matters he does.[1] So too did the authors of the second edition of the *Mirror for Magistrates* (1563), who included her among the cast of history-making rulers and rebels who speak from the grave. In the 1590s, a spate of first-person verse complaints kept her story in circulation. All versions follow roughly the same outline. Still lacking a first name, the figure known only as Shore's wife or Mistress Shore rises to power as Edward IV's favorite mistress and then falls precipitously once his brother, Richard III, seizes the throne. This could well be a cautionary tale, as indeed it often was. But the two-part history play *Edward IV* (1599), generally attributed to Thomas Heywood, tells a very different story. Heywood gives Mistress Shore not only the name Jane but also a central role in the political and affective life of late medieval England. While the play's kings are variously incompetent and tyrannical, Jane Shore steadfastly stands up for the poor and oppressed. Richard tries to counter her popularity with a vigorous propaganda campaign, but he completely fails to dislodge her from the people's hearts. The citizens of London make clear whose side they are on through collective displays of emotion and, we will see, through libeling.

Jane Shore's popularity in the play's medieval London was matched by her enthusiastic reception in Heywood's England. *Edward IV* was printed in both its parts six times between 1599 and 1626, and its heroine continued

---

[1] Thomas More, *The History of King Richard III*, ed. Richard S. Sylvester, in *The Complete Works of St. Thomas More*, vol. 2 (New Haven: Yale University Press, 1963), 56. On the early literary history of Jane Shore, see Richard Danson Brown, "'A Talkatiue Wench (Whose Words a World Hath Delighted in)': Mistress Shore and Elizabethan Complaint," *Review of English Studies* 49 (1998): 395–415; and Richard Helgerson, *Adulterous Alliances: Home, State, and History in Early Modern European Drama and Painting* (Chicago: University of Chicago Press, 2000), 33–56.

144

Pity and Politics in Heywood's Edward IV

to hold the stage well into the seventeenth century. Perhaps the most detailed report of her theatrical sway comes in Christopher Brooke's narrative poem *The Ghost of Richard the Third* (1614). Brooke's spectral tyrant gleefully recalls the hypocritical *"Iustice"* he inflicted on "Mistresse *Shore*," "when (with a fained hate / To vnchast *Life*) I forced her to goe / Bare-foote, on penance, with deiected *State*." But this punishment apparently backfired. Moving from medieval England to seventeenth-century London, Richard bitterly complains,

> But now her Fame by a vild Play doth grow;
> Whose Fate, the Women so commisserate,
>   That who (to see my Iustice on that Sinner)
>   Drinks not her Teares; & makes her Fast, their dinner?[2]

This account parallels the scenes of sympathetic citizens dramatized in *Edward IV* itself. In the theater too Jane Shore's fate evidently elicited outpourings of pity, especially (Brooke's Richard claims) from women playgoers.

I begin with Brooke's report because it so powerfully evokes Jane Shore's public: the collectivity of strangers joined across time and space in a shared affective-political experience. "Commisserat[ing]" her fate brings audiences together in defiance of Ricardian tyranny. As the final rhetorical question suggests, this community is decidedly open-ended: there is scarcely anyone who does not participate in the public pity for Jane Shore. The "Fame" that grows around her is akin to what we now call celebrity, a phenomenon recently traced back as far as the early modern era. Celebrity inheres not just in the public figure (real or fictional) but in the way she is represented and talked about. It is necessarily mediated – in print, on the stage, or, today, on the screen – yet relies on the feeling of immediate, even somatic contact.[3] Brooke describes a similar triangulation of public figure, media, and audience. From her humble late medieval origins, Jane Shore posthumously wins a mass following on the early modern stage. The "vild Play" feeds her fame, and her tears and fast in turn nourish an avid public of playgoers and readers. This is the sort of deeply felt yet commodified relation that we today attribute to celebrities

---

[2] Christopher Brooke, *The Ghost of Richard the Third* (London, 1614), sig. F1r.
[3] My understanding of celebrity draws especially from Joseph A. Boone and Nancy J. Vickers, "Introduction: Celebrity Rites," *PMLA* 126.4 (2011): 900–11; Graeme Turner, *Understanding Celebrity*, 2nd ed. (Los Angeles: Sage, 2014); Sharon Marcus, *The Drama of Celebrity* (Princeton: Princeton University Press, 2019); and Allison K. Deutermann, Matthew Hunter, and Musa Gurnis, eds., *Publicity and the Early Modern Stage: People Made Public* (Cham: Palgrave Macmillan, 2021).

146   Libels on the Elizabethan Stage

and their fans. Even as her audiences share vicariously in Jane Shore's suffering, they eagerly pay to consume it in the theater or in print. Their communal commiseration brings them into affective contact not just with her but also with each other.

As Brooke's 1614 report indicates, Jane Shore's public extended well beyond the premier of Heywood's play in 1599. Like all publics, it had "an ongoing life" sustained by continued circulation and representation (in this case, of the Jane Shore persona).[4] The public's prehistory saw Shore's wife travel from chronicle histories to verse complaints to a brief cameo in the drama of the late 1580s or early 1590s. In 1599, its life proper began with the crowd of playgoers who gathered at the Boar's Head to see the Earl of Derby's Men put on a new play advertising not only the history of King Edward IV but also "Mistress Shore, her great promotion, fall, and misery."[5] From there Heywood's story of Jane Shore took off across acting companies, venues, and media, from its revision (tellingly called "the Booke of Shoare") for the Earl of Worcester's Men at the Rose in 1603, to its move with the company (now named Queen Anne's Men) to the Red Bull a few years later, to its many printings and the ballads it inspired.[6] In the final section of this chapter, I follow Jane Shore's itinerary across some two decades of performance history.

Yet this fragmentary reception history can tell us only so much. If the glimpses of Jane Shore's commiserating, clamoring fans point to the existence of a public, they render in only the broadest terms its social, political, and affective texture. Whatever further we can learn about Jane Shore's public must come from the document at its center: *Edward IV* itself. To be sure, a playscript alone does not reveal how audiences responded to it, let alone to a particular character. But it is not without reason that Musa Gurnis calls scripts "the richest and most extensive records of early modern English playhouse experiences."[7] As recent scholarship has shown, plays encoded their own cues for affective response.[8] Particularly relevant to this chapter is Matthew Steggle's argument that

---

[4] Michael Warner, *Publics and Counterpublics* (New York: Zone Books, 2002), 97.
[5] Thomas Heywood, *The First and Second Parts of King Edward IV*, ed. Richard Rowland (Manchester: Manchester University Press, 2005), 79; hereafter cited parenthetically in the text.
[6] For the play's theater history, see Rowland, introduction to *Edward IV*, 3–6.
[7] Musa Gurnis, *Mixed Faith and Shared Feeling: Theater in Post-Reformation London* (Philadelphia: University of Pennsylvania Press, 2018), 51.
[8] See Jeremy Lopez, *Theatrical Convention and Audience Response in Early Modern Drama* (Cambridge: Cambridge University Press, 2003); Matthew Steggle, *Laughing and Weeping in Early Modern Theatres* (Aldershot, UK: Ashgate, 2007); Allison P. Hobgood, *Passionate Playgoing in Early Modern England* (Cambridge: Cambridge University Press, 2014); and Gurnis, *Mixed Faith*.

Pity and Politics in Heywood's Edward IV

staged displays of emotion were "a powerful index to the reaction playwrights expected from their early audience."[9] This does not mean that such cues were always followed.[10] But at least in the case of *Edward IV*, the records of its reception strongly suggest that they were. Early modern accounts of Jane Shore's pathos-laden proto-celebrity reprise the plot of the play itself. Together with this external evidence, *Edward IV* maps the affective communities that came together around Jane Shore in the playhouse and beyond.

To See and Be Seen: Politics, Playgoing, and Mistress Shore

In his *Apology for Actors* (1612), Heywood himself suggests that the English theater had long been a platform for popularity. He reports that "one of our best *English* Chroniclers [John Stow] records, that when *Edward* the fourth would shew himselfe in publicke state to the view of the people, hee repaired to his Palace at S. *Iohnes*, where he accustomed to see the Citty Actors."[11] This apocryphal anecdote is not actually in Stow and may well be Heywood's invention.[12] While affiliating the theater with England's royal past, the story also has Edward IV perform for the people: he attends plays not just to see but to be seen. And in this he was far from alone. Not least of all in the playhouse, late sixteenth-century Londoners of all stripes came out to show themselves in public to the view of strangers.[13] The middling and lower sorts increasingly got a taste of the theatrical experience formerly reserved (in Queen Elizabeth's words) for "princes ... set on stages in the sight and view of all the world."[14] Among the humble figures who entered the public sphere in these years was Mistress Shore herself. In the 1587 edition of the *Mirror for Magistrates* – just one year after Elizabeth's comment about princes "set on stages" – the spirit of Shore's wife declared,

---

[9] Steggle, *Laughing*, 4.

[10] See Lopez, *Theatrical Convention*; and Richard Preiss, *Clowning and Authorship in Early Modern Theatre* (Cambridge: Cambridge University Press, 2014).

[11] Thomas Heywood, *An Apology for Actors* (London, 1612), sig. E1v.

[12] Anita Gilman Sherman, "Forms of Oblivion: Losing the Revels Office at St. John's," *Shakespeare Quarterly* 62.1 (2011): 83.

[13] Paul Yachnin, "The Reformation of Space in Shakespeare's Playhouse," in *Making Space Public in Early Modern Europe: Performance, Geography, Privacy*, ed. Angela Vanhaelen and Joseph P. Ward (New York: Routledge, 2013), 262–80; Matthew Hunter, *The Pursuit of Style in Early Modern Drama: Forms of Talk on the London Stage* (Cambridge: Cambridge University Press, 2022).

[14] *Elizabeth I: Collected Works*, ed. Leah S. Marcus, Janel Mueller, and Mary Beth Rose (Chicago: University of Chicago Press, 2000), 194. For a detailed survey of Tudor publicity tactics, see Kevin Sharpe, *Selling the Tudor Monarchy: Authority and Image in Sixteenth-Century England* (New Haven: Yale University Press, 2009).

148   Libels on the Elizabethan Stage

"and so step I on the stage."[15] This section tracks the politics of public affect in the playhouse, setting the scene for the entrance of Heywood's Jane Shore in 1599.

Perhaps the best-known comment on audience affect comes from Francis Bacon. To explain the peculiar power of theater, Bacon avers "that the minds of men are more open to impressions and affections [*affectibus et impressionibus*] when many are gathered together than when they are alone."[16] Scholars have taken this dictum to illustrate the early modern view that emotion – named "passion" or "affection" – was primarily an embodied social experience.[17] And as Bacon suggests, nowhere was this truer than in the playhouse. Theater takes an assembly of strangers and joins them in collective feeling. To describe this social, physiological dimension, early modernists have increasingly turned to the language of affect theory.[18] Passion or affection is not quite what modern theorists mean by affect.[19] Glossing Gilles Deleuze and Félix Guattari's riff on Spinoza, Brian Massumi influentially defines affect as the "ability to affect and be affected."[20] Massumi distinguishes affect from emotion, limiting the latter to feelings as they are perceived by the subject experiencing them.[21] But other writers – I think more convincingly – see the difference as a matter of degree rather than kind. Following Sianne Ngai, I use the terms "more or less interchangeably," with affect generally located toward the hazier end of the spectrum of feeling.[22] Whatever we call it, though, the

---

[15] Lily B. Campbell, ed., *The Mirror for Magistrates* (1938; New York: Barnes & Noble, 1960), 372.

[16] Francis Bacon, *Of the Dignity and Advancement of Learning*, trans. Francis Headlam, in *The Works of Francis Bacon*, ed. James Spedding, Robert Leslie Ellis, and Douglas Denon Heath, 7 vols. (London, 1857–59), 4:316. For the Latin, see Bacon, *De Augmentis Scientiarum*, in *Works*, 1:519. Bacon's claim stands as the epigraph to Andrew Gurr's influential *Playgoing in Shakespeare's London*, 3rd ed. (Cambridge: Cambridge University Press, 2004).

[17] Steggle, *Laughing*, 7; Hobgood, *Passionate Playgoing*, 188–89.

[18] See, e.g., Hobgood, *Passionate Playgoing*; Katharine A. Craik and Tanya Pollard, eds., *Shakespearean Sensations: Experiencing Literature in Early Modern England* (Cambridge: Cambridge University Press, 2013); Steven Mullaney, *The Reformation of Emotions in the Age of Shakespeare* (Chicago: University of Chicago Press, 2015); Ronda Arab, Michelle M. Dowd, and Adam Zucker, eds., *Historical Affects and the Early Modern Theater* (New York: Routledge, 2015); and Amanda Bailey and Mario DiGangi, eds., *Affect Theory and Early Modern Texts: Politics, Ecologies, and Form* (New York: Palgrave Macmillan, 2017).

[19] See Benedict S. Robinson, "Feeling Feelings in Early Modern England," in *Affect and Literature*, ed. Alex Houen (Cambridge: Cambridge University Press, 2020), 213–28.

[20] Gilles Deleuze and Félix Guattari, *A Thousand Plateaus: Capitalism and Schizophrenia*, trans. Brian Massumi (Minneapolis: University of Minnesota Press, 1987), xvi.

[21] Brian Massumi, *Parables for the Virtual: Movement, Affect, Sensation* (Durham, NC: Duke University Press, 2002).

[22] Sianne Ngai, *Ugly Feelings* (Cambridge, MA: Harvard University Press, 2005), 27.

Pity and Politics in Heywood's Edward IV 149

notion of affecting and being affected well describes the reciprocal circulation of "impressions and affections" in the early modern theater.[23]

Yet what has been largely overlooked in the affect-oriented discussions of Bacon's claim is that his analysis of collective emotion serves a clear political end.[24] His argument is that, while "modern states" relegate theater to the realm of entertainment and play, the ancients properly understood it to be a powerful instrument for inculcating virtue.[25] This is where audience affect comes in. It is because crowds are especially susceptible to emotion that the state ought to take an interest in theater and theatricality. In other words, Bacon implicates theater and its cultivation of collective affect in what the early moderns had taken to calling "popularity": the arts of public address and political performance.

In the 1590s, the meanings of "popularity" followed the career of one figure above all: Robert Devereux, the second Earl of Essex. I will discuss Essex's final years at some length in the next chapter. For now, though, I want to note his reputation for political performance in and out of the theater. The earl was known for his "impromptu street performances."[26] According to his secretary Henry Wotton, Essex "committ[ed] himself in his recreations and shooting matches to the publique view of so many thousand Citizens which usually flocked to see him."[27] He reportedly brought the same flair to the playhouses, frequenting English histories and "with great applause geving countenance and lyking to the same."[28] These reports portray Essex as a savvy playgoer and performer.

Perhaps taking their cue from their leader, a band of Essex's followers went to the Globe themselves on February 7, 1601, the eve of his ill-fated rising. The play they commissioned and came to see told the story "of Kyng Harry the iiiith and of the kyllyng of Kyng Richard the Second" – likely Shakespeare's *Richard II*.[29] Paul Hammer suggests that these malcontents

---

[23] Hobgood develops this insight at length in *Passionate Playing*.
[24] The one exception is Katrin Beushausen, *Theatre and the English Public from Reformation to Revolution* (Cambridge: Cambridge University Press, 2018), 30.
[25] Bacon, *Advancement of Learning*, 316.
[26] Jeffrey S. Doty, *Shakespeare, Popularity and the Public Sphere* (Cambridge: Cambridge University Press, 2017), 16. On Essex and early modern popularity, see also Paul Hammer, "The Smiling Crocodile: The Earl of Essex and Late Elizabethan 'Popularity,'" in *The Politics of the Public Sphere in Early Modern England*, ed. Peter Lake and Steven Pincus (Manchester: Manchester University Press, 2007), 95–115; and Alexandra Gajda, *The Earl of Essex and Late Elizabethan Political Culture* (Oxford: Oxford University Press, 2012).
[27] Henry Wotton, *Reliquiae Wottonianae* (London, 1651), sig. B12v.
[28] TNA, SP 12/275, fol. 56r. See Paul E. J. Hammer, "Shakespeare's *Richard II*, the Play of 7 February 1601, and the Essex Rising," *Shakespeare Quarterly* 59.1 (2008): 21–22.
[29] TNA, SP 12/278, fol. 130r, quoted in Hammer, "Shakespeare's *Richard II*," 1.

150   Libels on the Elizabethan Stage

"wanted a public audience for their own self-staging as watchers of this particular play." For Essex and his supporters, he argues, Shakespeare's Bolingbroke offered both "models of behavior worthy of emulation" and, in the final two acts, a "*negative* example."[30] While Bolingbroke (soon to be Henry IV) forcibly usurps the throne, Essex claimed that he and his followers had planned to go to the queen and "*pro*stratinge our selues at hir Ma*jesti*es feete to haue put *ou*rselues vnto hir mercy."[31] But the Londoners watching these gentlemen watching *Richard II* may well have come away with a very different message.[32] At least to some in the audience, Bolingbroke's deposition of Richard II could have signaled that a seditious plot was brewing among Essex and his men.

Especially in the theater, historical allegory was liable to misfire. Aristocrats might put playgoing to their own ends, but they could not control how audiences would respond. So it went in early August 1628, when the Duke of Buckingham arranged and attended a performance of Shakespeare and Fletcher's *Henry VIII* at the Globe.[33] By then Buckingham, the notorious favorite of James and Charles, faced relentless criticism from both parliament and people. Angry MPs denounced him as "the cause of all our miseries"; libelers tarred him with all sorts of scandalous accusations.[34] Like Essex's followers, Buckingham evidently commissioned the performance in an effort to tell his own story: namely, to align himself with the play's Duke of Buckingham, a virtuous peer persecuted by the evil counselor Cardinal Wolsey. At the moment of the stage duke's fall, the real-life Buckingham and his entourage abruptly got up and left the theater.[35] This performance did not end well for Buckingham, however. Not only did he fail to recast himself as his Henrician namesake, but some people instead took him to be a corrupt counselor in the mold of Wolsey. Unconvinced by his dramatic exit, these observers reportedly remarked that "he should rather have seen ye fall of Cardinall Woolsey, who was a more lively type of himself."[36] The duke failed

---

[30] Hammer, "Shakespeare's *Richard II*," 26, 34.   [31] TNA, SP 12/278, fol. 175r.

[32] As Gajda remarks, "Hammer's interpretation rests on a particular reading of Shakespeare's *Richard II*," a reading that fails to account for the opacity of Bolingbroke's motives in the play (*Earl of Essex*, 50).

[33] See Thomas Cogswell and Peter Lake, "Buckingham Does the Globe: *Henry VIII* and the Politics of Popularity in the 1620s," *Shakespeare Quarterly* 60.3 (2009): 253–78.

[34] Mary Frear Keeler, Maija Jansson Cole, and William B. Bidwell, eds., *Commons Debates 1628*, vol. 4 (New Haven: Yale University Press, 1978), 115; Alastair Bellany and Thomas Cogswell, *The Murder of King James I* (New Haven: Yale University Press, 2015).

[35] Cogswell and Lake, "Buckingham," 269–72.

[36] BL, Harley MS 383, fol. 65r, quoted in Shakespeare and John Fletcher, *King Henry VIII (All Is True)*, ed. Gordon McMullan (London: Arden Shakespeare, 2000), 15–16.

Pity and Politics in Heywood's Edward IV

to rehabilitate his reputation, and before the month was out he fell to the dagger of a disgruntled lieutenant.[37]

Essex and his followers likewise failed to find a sympathetic audience when it mattered most. No rapturous crowd came out to greet them when they rode into London on the day after the performance of *Richard II*, and the Essex Rising came to an ignominious end with the earl's swift arrest and execution.[38] Such were the perils of popularity. Through their forays to the Globe in 1601 and 1628, Essex's followers and Buckingham staked their political theater on the uncertain judgment of the playgoing public.

If for rather different reasons, commoners too saw that playgoing might give them a moment in the limelight. We find such a figure in Heywood's own *Apology for Actors*. In a prefatory poem, the actor Richard Perkins anticipates Heywood's apocryphal story of Edward IV's playgoing. Of course, Perkins is no prince or politician. He merely wants to vindicate his "recreation" and "modest mirth" from those who uncharitably "raile at me for seeing a play." Yet king and commoner share a proclivity for publicity. "Still when I come to playes," Perkins proudly declares,

> I loue to sit,
> That all may see me in a publike place:
> Euen in the stages front, and not to git
> Into a nooke, and hood-winke there my face.[39]

Perkins was far from alone in his love for sitting front and center. In the words of Ben Jonson's Fitzdottrel, to "[s]it i'the view" of the audience is the playgoer's "special end."[40] One of the main draws of the theater was the chance to be not just a spectator but also a spectacle oneself.

Critics of the stage were especially troubled that women should have access to this kind of publicity.[41] They imagine the playhouse to conceal a minefield of lusting sightlines, "where the woman is desired with so many eyes, where so many faces looke vpon hir, and againe she vppon so

---

[37] Thomas Cogswell, "John Felton, Popular Political Culture, and the Assassination of the Duke of Buckingham," *Historical Journal* 49.2 (2006): 357–85.

[38] Hammer, "Shakespeare's *Richard II*," 3–4. [39] Heywood, *Apology*, sigs. a2v, a3r.

[40] Ben Jonson, *The Devil Is an Ass*, ed. Anthony Parr, in *CWBJ*, 4:1.6.32, 35.

[41] On women's attendance and influence at the theater, see Richard Levin, "Women in the Renaissance Theatre Audience," *Shakespeare Quarterly* 40.2 (1989): 165–74; Andrew Gurr, *Playgoing in Shakespeare's London*, 3rd ed. (Cambridge: Cambridge University Press, 2004), 65–76; Pamela Allen Brown and Peter Parolin, eds., *Women Players in England, 1500–1660: Beyond the All-Male Stage* (Aldershot, UK: Ashgate, 2005); Andrew Gurr and Karoline Szatek, "Women and Crowds at the Theater," *Medieval and Renaissance Drama in England* 21 (2008): 157–69; and Clare McManus and Lucy Munro, eds., "Renaissance Women's Performance and the Dramatic Canon: Theater History, Evidence, and Narratives," special issue, *Shakespeare Bulletin* 33.1 (2015).

152   Libels on the Elizabethan Stage

manye."[42] This reciprocal gazing quickly became a central trope of antitheatrical polemic.[43] "Looking eyes, haue lyking hartes, liking harts may burne in lust," Stephen Gosson admonishes the "Gentlewomen Citizens of London."[44] Beyond their stark misogyny, these views reflect the widely held belief in what scholars have aptly termed "affective contagion": the promiscuous spread of passions through the playhouse.[45]

Antitheatricalists and defenders of the stage alike pinned this contagion not just on the activity of playgoers but, especially, on the plays themselves. For Gosson and his ilk, theatrical shows all too easily penetrate the hearts and minds of their audiences. "The diuel is not ignorant," he warns, "how mightely these outward spectacles effeminate, & soften the hearts of men, ... & those impressions of mind are secretly conueyed ouer to the gazers, which the plaiers do counterfeit on the stage."[46] In his *Apology for Actors*, Heywood takes issue not with this scene of affective transformation but only with its allegedly "effeminate" outcome. Like Philip Sidney before him, he argues that the theater induces not vice but virtue, not moral disorder but social cohesion.[47] He singles out "our domesticke hystories" for their "liuely and well spirited action, that ... hath power to new mold the harts of the spectators and fashion them to the shape of any noble and notable attempt."[48] At stake for both Heywood and Gosson are the hearts of the spectators, whether softened or fortified by the spectacles on the stage.

For Heywood, female playgoers are especially affected by these moving spectacles. Near the end of the *Apology*, he sets out to prove that plays "haue beene the discouerers of many notorious murders, long concealed from the eyes of the world." He gives just two examples, both of women who killed their husbands. Several years ago at King's Lynn in Norfolk, a "townes-woman" supposedly attended a play about "a woman, who

[42] John Northbrooke, *A Treatise wherein Dicing, Dauncing, Vaine playes or Enterluds ... are reproued* (London, 1577), sig. I4r.
[43] See Jean E. Howard, *The Stage and Social Struggle in Early Modern England* (London: Routledge, 1994), 74–93.
[44] Stephen Gosson, *The Schoole of Abuse* (London, 1579), sigs. F2r–v, F1v.
[45] See Katherine Rowe, "Humoral Knowledge and Liberal Cognition in Davenant's *Macbeth*," in *Reading the Early Modern Passions: Essays in the Cultural History of Emotion*, ed. Gail Kern Paster, Rowe, and Mary Floyd-Wilson (Philadelphia: University of Pennsylvania Press, 2004), 176; Hobgood, *Passionate Playgoing*; and Evelyn Tribble, "Affective Contagion on the Early Modern Stage," in *Affect Theory*, ed. Bailey and DiGangi, 195–212.
[46] Stephen Gosson, *Playes Confuted in fiue Actions* (London, 1582), sig. G4r.
[47] See Philip Sidney, *A Defence of Poetry*, in *Miscellaneous Prose of Sir Philip Sidney*, ed. Katherine Duncan-Jones and Jan van Dorsten (Oxford: Clarendon Press, 1973), 95–97.
[48] Heywood, *Apology*, sig. B4r.

Pity and Politics in Heywood's Edward IV 153

insatiately doting on a yong gentleman, had ... mischieuously and seceretly murdered her husband, whose ghost haunted her, ... in most horrid and fearefull shapes." In the middle of the performance, Heywood recounts, the townswoman cried out, "Oh my husband, my husband! I see the ghost of my husband fiercely threatning and menacing me." Her fellow playgoers "inquired the reason of her clamour," and the woman promptly confessed that she had poisoned her own husband, "whose fearefull image personated it selfe in the shape of that ghost" on the stage.[49] Art imitates life imitates art: the players unwittingly reprise the Norfolk widow's crime, and she in turn acts out the haunting portrayed on the stage. Driving this scene is the transmission of fear, as Allison P. Hobgood points out.[50] At least one member of the Norfolk audience found herself playing her own part in the "fearefull" experience of the play.

That part was soon to end, however. No sooner had the Norfolk townswoman confessed than she was arrested, examined, and condemned. For a moment, her outcry in the theater had made her the involuntary star of her own domestic tragedy. In fact, an earlier version of the anecdote has the woman explicitly identify herself as the inspiration for the tragedy she is watching play out on the stage. At the sight of the ghost, the story goes in *A Warning for Fair Women*, "she cryed out, the Play was made by her."[51] Hers is the crime that scripted the drama, that it was "made by" (patterned after). Yet the end – and her end – is never really in doubt. Ellen MacKay identifies "the expostulating widow" as a "forensic cliché," her guilt practically predetermined from the moment she cries out.[52] At least for Heywood, the widow must immediately confess her guilt "vn-urged" for her fearful exclamation to serve his defense of the theater's affective currents.[53]

But there were other scripts of female confession in early modern England. On the scaffold, Frances E. Dolan has shown, the condemned woman could be "presented as using her execution to challenge the church or courts that judge her and to show up the very men who are supposed to govern her."[54] Take one of Dolan's examples, the case of Elizabeth Caldwell. Convicted of inadvertently poisoning a child in an attempt on her husband's life, Caldwell reportedly offered herself as "a warning and

---

[49] Ibid., sig. GIV. [50] Hobgood, *Passionate Playgoing*, 55–57.
[51] Charles Dale Cannon, ed., *A Warning for Fair Women: A Critical Edition* (The Hague: Mouton, 1975), l. 2047.
[52] Ellen MacKay, *Persecution, Plague, and Fire: Fugitive Histories of the Stage in Early Modern England* (Chicago: University of Chicago Press, 2011), 63.
[53] Heywood, *Apology*, sig. GIV.
[54] Frances E. Dolan, "'Gentlemen, I have one thing more to say': Women on Scaffolds in England, 1563–1680," *Modern Philology* 92.2 (1994): 177–78.

154   Libels on the Elizabethan Stage

example vnto all there present" at her execution. Yet in a letter to her husband printed in the same contemporary pamphlet, Caldwell pointedly reminds him that there is plenty of blame to go around: "remember in what a case you haue liued, howe poore you haue many times left me, how long you haue beene absent from mee."[55] Caldwell's case draws out the latent tensions running through the tale of the Norfolk townswoman. If the official narrative assimilates these guilty women to the moralizing cliché, the affective energies swirling around them may point in a very different direction.

This was the case too for Mistress Shore. In the sixteenth century, her adultery and fall could offer a clear moral lesson. Heywood himself lists "Mistresse *Shore*" among those stage characters through whom "the vnchaste are ... shewed their errors."[56] Yet from her earliest appearances in prose and verse, hers was a far more complicated story. More himself remarks on the "pit[y]" her fall elicited even from those "good folke" who were "glad ... to se sin corrected."[57] In Thomas Churchyard's "Shore's Wife," printed in the second edition of the *Mirror for Magistrates*, she even casts doubt on her culpability for that supposed sin. Like Elizabeth Caldwell, she reserves much of the "blame" for her male relatives, for those "friends" who "my youth ... did abuse." "I was enticed by trains and trapped by trust," Shore's wife laments, "[b]esieged" by a king and fatally misled by kinsmen who married her off too young.[58]

Churchyard's heroine still does present herself as a warning to "both maid and wife." She concludes her complaint, "Defy this world and all his wanton ways; / Beware by me that spent so ill her days."[59] But she does not seem to have spent her days so ill at all. In his *History of King Richard III*, More describes in detail how the royal mistress used her power for good. "For many that had highly offended," he recalls, "shee obtained pardon. Of great forfetures she gate men remission. And finally in many weighty sutes, she stode many men in gret stede."[60] Expanding this account, Churchyard imagines her as the protector of the commonwealth:

> To purchase praise and win the people's zeal,
> Yea, rather bent of kind to do some good,
> I ever did uphold the commonweal;

---

[55] Gilbert Dugdale, *A True Discourse of the practises of Elizabeth Caldwell* (London, 1604), sigs. D1v, C1v. See Dolan, "Gentlemen," 170–71.

[56] Heywood, *Apology*, sig. G1v.   [57] More, *History*, 55.

[58] "Shore's Wife," in *A Mirror for Magistrates: A Modernized and Annotated Edition*, ed. Scott C. Lucas (Cambridge: Cambridge University Press, 2019), ll. 106, 107, 135, 153.

[59] Ibid., ll. 388, 391–92.   [60] More, *History*, 56.

Pity and Politics in Heywood's Edward IV

> I had delight to save the guiltless blood.
> Each suitor's cause, when that I understood,
> I did prefer as it had been mine own
> And helped them up that might have been o'erthrown.
>
> My power was prest to right the poor man's wrong;
> My hands were free to give where need required.[61]

Whether she aims to win the people's love or simply to "do some good," Shore's wife stoutly defends the poor and oppressed.

So too does Heywood's Jane Shore. Poets and playwrights – including Heywood himself – often cited Mistress Shore as "an example for all wicked women," to quote the title page of *The True Tragedie of Richard the Third*.[62] But in the verse complaints of the later sixteenth century, Shore's wife also came to tell her own story. That story grew more varied still: hers was a tale of beauty dishonored, of sin punished, of ingratitude suffered – or even of populism and popularity.[63] Heywood's heroine is more folk hero than patriarchal cliché, more champion of the commons than wicked woman.[64] Across the play's two parts, she attains a degree of political celebrity matched in the late 1590s only (if we exclude the monarch) by the Earl of Essex himself. Yet early modern publicity was not the sole property of politicians such as Essex. From Richard Perkins to Gosson's "gentlewomen citizens" to Heywood's Norfolk widow, ordinary playgoers hazarded the affective perils of the playhouse to stake out their own places in public life. Elements of the Jane Shore experience would have resonated especially with urban playgoers, not least of all with gentlewomen citizens targeted for their visibility and with any Londoner skeptical of monarchical meddling in civic affairs.[65] In the rest of this chapter, I follow the affective-political currents put into play by the story of Jane Shore.

---

[61] "Shore's Wife," ll. 197–205.   [62] *The True Tragedie of Richard the Third* (London, 1594), sig. A2r.

[63] See Anthony Chute, *Beawtie dishonoured written under the Title of Shores Wife* (London, 1593); Thomas Deloney, *The Garland of Good Will*, in *The Works of Thomas Deloney*, ed. Francis Oscar Mann (Oxford: Clarendon Press, 1912), 302–4; Thomas Churchyard, *Churchyards Challenge* (London, 1593), sigs. T1r–X1v; Michael Drayton, *Englands Heroicall Epistles* (London, 1597), sigs. I1v–I4r; *True Tragedie*, sigs. E1r–E3v.

[64] Compare the arguments of Nora L. Corrigan, "The Merry Tanner, the Mayor's Feast, and the King's Mistress: Thomas Heywood's *1 Edward IV* and the Ballad Tradition," *Medieval and Renaissance Drama in England* 22 (2009): 39–40; and Christina M. Squitieri, "Jane Shore's Political Identity in Thomas Heywood's *Edward IV*," *Studies in English Literature 1500–1900* 60.2 (2020): 299–322.

[65] For studies of the play along the axes of gender and civic culture, see Wendy Wall, "Forgetting and Keeping: Jane Shore and the English Domestication of History," *Renaissance Drama* 27 (1996): 123–56; Jesse M. Lander, "'Faith in Me vnto this Commonwealth': *Edward IV* and the Civic Nation," *Renaissance Drama* 27 (1996): 47–78; and Helgerson, *Adulterous Alliances*, 33–56.

156 Libels on the Elizabethan Stage

Jane Shore and the Politics of Popularity

The first part of *Edward IV* initially seems to validate the antitheatricalist anxieties about women being seen in public. Matthew Shore all-too-predictably laments that his wife, pursued by King Edward, has become what one moralist derisively calls "an obiect to al mens eies."[66] "Keep we our treasure secret," Matthew asks, "yet so fond / As set so rich a beauty as this is / In the wide view of every gazer's eye?" (17.149–51). And just as Gosson feared, "looking eyes, haue lyking hartes, liking harts may burne in lust." Edward's "[p]roud, saucy, roving eye," as he himself terms it, quickly fixates on Jane (16.120). Liking then turns to lust: the king resolves that his "greedy eyes" must "find rest, where heart's desire doth bide" (17.37–38).

But the play soon undermines this antitheatricalist lesson. Lena Cowen Orlin rightly points out that Heywood locates "agency for immorality in men" rather than in women.[67] To go further still, I would argue that he makes Jane Shore's publicity as good for England as the king's roving eyes are bad for it. The play's first part begins in the aftermath of an earlier act of royal lust. Apparently on a whim, Edward has just married the widow Elizabeth Woodville even though he already sent Warwick, "[t]hat like a column propped the house of York," to broker a marriage with the daughter of the King of France (1.30). Edward's mother, the Duchess of York, is horrified: "Son, I tell ye, you have done – you know not what!" the play begins (1.1). While the king is busy cracking bawdy jokes, his mother (prophetically, for anyone who knew their English history) demands, "Is't possible your rash, unlawful act / Should not breed mortal hate betwixt the realms?" (1.22–23). "Rash" and "unlawful," Edward's lust is not just unwise but tyrannical.

The same is true when the king's eyes alight on their latest victim. Edward finds little success when he tries to seduce Jane Shore: his loyal subject offers her king everything save for "mine honour, which I cannot grant" (17.98). "I may not wander," she later reiterates (19.94). So Edward turns from seduction to command, from the conditional mood and future tense – "that thou *mightst* our affection know," "straight the gladsome morning *will* appear" (19.86, 93; italics mine) – to the imperative. "Thou

---

[66] Salvian [and Anthony Munday], *A second and third blast of retrait from plaies and Theaters* (London, 1580), sig. G3r.

[67] Lena Cowen Orlin, "Making Public the Private," in *Forms of Association: Making Publics in Early Modern Europe*, ed. Paul Yachnin and Marlene Eberhart (Amherst: University of Massachusetts Press, 2015), 99.

Pity and Politics in Heywood's Edward IV

must, sweet Jane, repair unto the court," he decrees (19.103). The king invokes his royal authority to preclude choice altogether:

> His tongue entreats, controls the greatest peer;
> His hand plights love, a royal sceptre holds;
> And in his heart he hath confirmed thy good;
> Which may not, must not, shall not be withstood. (19.104–7)

As "may" becomes "must" becomes "shall," Edward brings his power to bear not on "the greatest peer" but on an ordinary subject.

"If you enforce me," Jane responds, "I have nought to say" (19.108). Yet she has plenty to say when she next takes the stage. As her husband prepares to embark on his self-imposed exile, Jane Shore enters, "*ladylike attired, with diverse supplications in her hand; she unpinning her mask, and attended on by many suitors*" (22.2 sd). Matthew, who has not yet recognized his wife, learns that this lady "of no mean countenance" is "Mistress Shore, the King's beloved: / A special friend to suitors at the court" (22.4, 8–9). Following More's history and Churchyard's poem, Heywood's Jane Shore has already earned a name for helping the helpless. Matthew, however, thinks only of the reputation his wife has lost. He bitterly recalls, "When she with me was wont to walk the streets, / The people then, as she did pass along, / Would say 'There goes fair, modest, Mistress Shore'" (22.13–15). Matthew's nostalgia reveals the impossible demands of his bourgeois ideology: he wants to show off his "fair" and "modest" wife in the streets, yet he earlier blamed her adultery on that same display "in the wide view of every gazer's eye."

Yet Jane has her own agenda. Surrounded by petitioners, she appears in public not as an object of desire or exemplar of chastity but as the prime agent of mercy and justice. She quickly secures a pardon for the son of Thomas Aire; she vows to restore the lands of Palmer and Jockie, seized wrongfully by royal officers and by a neighbor, respectively. The suitors let loose a chorus of praise: "God's blessing light on that gudely fair face!"; "God bless the care you have of doing good"; "Pity she should miscarry in her life, / That bears so sweet a mind in doing good" (22.54, 56, 57–58). What so moves these commoners is the good she has done, not yet her rise or fall. Heywood's audiences evidently had a similar reaction, as I discuss at greater length below. "Thy good deeds done doth spread thy fame," an early seventeenth-century ballad informs Jane Shore, and "thousands thanke thee for thy paine."[68] So too did "many thousand Citizens" gather to see the Earl of Essex just a few

---

[68] *A most sorrowfull Song, setting forth the miserable end of Banister*, Pepys Ballads 1.64–65, EBBA 20265 (registered 1600; this version *c.*1630); dating in Hyder Edward Rollins, ed., *The Pepys Ballads*, 8 vols. (Cambridge, MA: Harvard University Press, 1929–32), 2:128–29.

158   Libels on the Elizabethan Stage

years earlier. Indeed, Essex himself was known for coming to the aid of
petitioners. Francis Bacon lists among the earl's "points of popularitie" his
habit of giving "audience to suters," and Heywood' own play *The Fair Maid
of the West* depicts Essex in dumb show meeting "[p]etitioners ... with
papers" and handing them "bags of money."[69] On the stage and in verse,
Jane Shore's charity likewise wins her the people's love.

But it is her decisive rejection of the final petition that confirms her role as
the protector of the people. Prompted by the merchant Rufford, Jane turns to
his suit "for a licence to transport corn / From this land, and lead to foreign
realms" (22.62–63). This request would have been deeply unpopular, to say
the least, for Heywood's early audiences. From 1594 to 1597, a series of poor
harvests sparked what historians have called the "crisis of the 1590s": years of
scarcity, skyrocketing prices, and periodic unrest.[70] At least nineteen food riots
broke out between 1594 and 1598; libels circulated widely in London and
beyond.[71] In 1597, a rumor accusing the mayor of hoarding grain spread
through the capital, and in 1600, "lewd libels" attacked the Lord Treasurer for
granting grain export licenses.[72] Stow reports that "common opinion" blamed
greedy merchants for the dearth. "[B]y meanes of the late transporting of
graine into forraine countries," he adds, "the same was here growen to an
excessiue price."[73]

The export of lead and of other metals used in the manufacture of
ordnance was hardly more popular. Posted in May 1593, the Dutch Church
libel complained that foreigners and their "Machiavellian Marchant" were
exporting "[o]ur Leade, our Vittaile, our Ordenance" and importing only
"gawds good store."[74] The previous year, a royal proclamation restricting

---

[69] Francis Bacon, *A Declaration of the Practises & Treasons attempted and committed by Robert late Earle
of Essex and his Complices* (London, 1601), sig. B1r; Thomas Heywood, *The Fair Maid of the West,
Parts I and II*, ed. Robert K. Turner, Jr. (Lincoln: University of Nebraska Press, 1967), pt. 1, 1.4 sd.
See Gajda, *Earl of Essex*, 168; and Doty, *Shakespeare*, 36–43.

[70] M. J. Power, "London and the Control of the 'Crisis' of the 1590s," *History* 70 (1985): 371–85; Ian
W. Archer, *The Pursuit of Stability: Social Relations in Elizabethan London* (Cambridge: Cambridge
University Press, 1991), 9–14.

[71] John Bohstedt, *The Politics of Provisions: Food Riots, Moral Economy, and Market Transition in
England, c. 1550–1850* (Farnham, UK: Ashgate, 2010), 30–31; Buchanan Sharp, "Shakespeare's
Coriolanus and the Crisis of the 1590s," in *Law and Authority in Early Modern England: Essays
Presented to Thomas Garden Barnes*, ed. Sharp and Mark Charles Fissel (Newark: University of
Delaware Press, 2007), 48–50.

[72] *TRP*, 3:182–83, 216. See Sharp, "Shakespeare's *Coriolanus*," 49.

[73] John Stow, *The Annales of England* (London, 1600), sig. Pppp1r. See John Walter, "'A Foolish
Commotion of Youth'? Crowds and the 'Crisis of the 1590s' in London," *London Journal* 44.1
(2019): 20.

[74] Dutch Church Libel, ll. 5, 18, 17, transcribed in Arthur Freeman, "Marlowe, Kyd, and the Dutch
Church Libel," *English Literary Renaissance* 3.1 (1973): 50–51.

the export of ordnance noted that "it is most evidently seen by daily experience that by such unlawful transportations her majesty's enemies are either directly or indirectly furnished for the most part with such ordnance."[75] And when a bill to the same effect was introduced in the parliament of 1601, one MP maintained that if the queen "would but fforbid the transportacion of ordynance but ffor vij^{en} yeares yt would breed suche a scarsitye in the Spanyard that we might have him where we would."[76]

Rufford's petition, then, would have called to mind the policies and practices that many blamed for the social and economic strain of the 1590s. Imbued with the righteous anger of the commons, Jane tells Rufford that she has ripped his bill to pieces and threatens him with the same treatment:

> I had your bill, but I have torn your bill;
> And 'twere no shame I think to tear your ears,
> That care not how you wound the commonwealth.
> The poor must starve for food to fill your purse,
> And the enemy bandy bullets of our lead?
> No, Master Rufford, I'll not speak for you –
> Except it be to have you punished.   (22.64–70)

Jane tellingly speaks not of the kingdom or realm but of the "commonwealth," a word that here denotes both the common good and, especially, the good of the commons.[77] It is "the poor" who suffer most from the profiteering of corrupt merchants such as Rufford – a claim that surely would have fallen on sympathetic ears during the grain scarcities of the late 1590s. Heywood's Jane Shore is not just a medieval benefactor but also a populist heroine for the late Elizabethan age.

As Jane's popularity grows, her king only squeezes more from his poorest subjects. Hobs the tanner speaks for the commons when he remarks (to Edward himself in disguise), "we fear we shall be troubled to lend [the king] money, for we doubt he's but needy" (13.32–34). Hobs proves all too

---

[75] *TRP*, 3:107.

[76] T. E. Hartley, ed., *Proceedings in the Parliaments of Elizabeth I*, 3 vols. (London: Leicester University Press, 1981–95), 3:443. On anxiety about England's arms trade, see Matthew Dimmock, "Guns and Gawds: Elizabethan England's Infidel Trade," in *A Companion to the Global Renaissance: English Literature and Culture in the Era of Expansion*, ed. Jyotsna G. Singh (Chichester: Wiley-Blackwell, 2009), 215–18.

[77] On the meanings of "commonwealth," see William H. Sherman, "Anatomizing the Commonwealth: Language, Politics, and the Elizabethan Social Order," in *The Project of Prose in Early Modern Europe and the New World*, ed. Elizabeth Fowler and Roland Greene (Cambridge: Cambridge University Press, 1997), 104–21; and Phil Withington, *Society in Early Modern England: The Vernacular Origins of Some Powerful Ideas* (Cambridge: Polity, 2010), 134–68.

160   Libels on the Elizabethan Stage

prescient. To fund his invasion of France, the king sends officers to extract money from the people. Because Edward's "coffers are unfurnished," they inform the commons, "He prays his faithful loving subjects' help / To further this, his just, great enterprise" (18.10, 13–14). Hobs comically translates the officers' "long purgation" into a blunt demand: "the King wants money, and would have some of his commenty [commonality]" (18.16, 17–18). Still, the king's collectors insist that although Edward "[m]ight have exacted or imposed a tax, / Or borrowed greater sums than we can spare," he merely "doth entreat / Our kind benevolence" – not a "loan or tribute" but a "gift" (18.22–23, 25–26, 33). Yet when the landless Master Hadland begs them not to "rack my purse," the officers demand a portion of the proceeds from the land he recently had to sell: "Then you have money; let the King have part" (18.40, 42). And when Harry Grudgen reluctantly concedes a mere forty pence, they rail at him and threaten to have him "soundly plagued" (18.99). The king's "benevolence" looks less and less benevolent.

Benevolences – like their close cousin, the forced loan – had long been unpopular in Heywood's England. According to Holinshed, some contributors to Edward's benevolence grumbled that it was in fact a "maleuolence."[78] Several benevolences and loans were levied to finance the Spanish wars during the long 1590s, and in 1599 the crown solicited a benevolence to fund Essex's disastrous expedition to Ireland.[79] As Michael J. Braddick points out, although benevolences in theory "rested on consent, that consent could not be withheld without denying the necessity for the appeal."[80] Certainly the commoners in *Edward IV* have little choice but to comply. "Here's old polling, subsidy, fifteen, soldiers, and to the poor," Grudgen complains, comparing the benevolence to "other forms of compulsory taxation" that fell heavily on the needy (18.73–74).[81]

If Edward's benevolence is just a tax by another name, Jane offers a true benevolence to the poor and oppressed. The second part of *Edward IV* begins with the war in France, but before long we are back in England – and we immediately witness Jane Shore's latest act of charity. Hers are the first lines spoken on English soil. "Have you bestowed our small benevolence / On the poor prisoners in the common gaol?" she asks Jockie, now her

---

[78] Raphael Holinshed, *The Third volume of Chronicles* (London, 1587), sig. Tttᵥ.
[79] Michael J. Braddick, *The Nerves of State: Taxation and the Financing of the English State, 1558–1714* (Manchester: Manchester University Press, 1996), 84–87; Braddick, *State Formation in Early Modern England, c. 1550–1700* (Cambridge: Cambridge University Press, 2000), 244–45; Charles W. Crupi, "Ideological Contradiction in Part I of Heywood's *Edward IV*: 'Our Musicke Runs . . . Much upon Discords,'" *Medieval and Renaissance Drama in England* 7 (1995): 224–26.
[80] Braddick, *State Formation*, 245.   [81] Heywood, *Edward IV*, 18.73–74n.

Pity and Politics in Heywood's Edward IV

devoted servant (9.1–2). Unlike Edward's, Jane's benevolence really is a gift – and one given to, not taken from, the poor. This charity, Sir Robert Brackenbury notes, has earned her a reputation as a "comforting, minist'ring, kind physician, / That once a week, in her own person, visits / The prisoners and the poor in hospitals" (9.25–27). Jane grows only more popular as the play's second part continues. Brackenbury seeks a pardon for a sea captain and his crew, and Jane, of course, gets him one. Once again the praise flows. "God save the King, and God bless Mistress Shore," the prisoners cry in unison (12.126). "Mistress Shore" challenges the king himself for pride of place in the hearts of the English people.

At least in Heywood's telling, however, it isn't much of a competition. While Edward is off frolicking with the tanner of Tamworth and fighting wars at his subjects' expense in France, Jane has labored tirelessly on behalf of the commons. Moreover, her charitable efforts repeatedly tend toward the theatrical. She herself brings the pardon for the sailors, and just in the nick of time: her husband (disguised among the prisoners) has already ascended the gallows when Jane enters "*in haste, in her riding cloak and save-guard, with a pardon in her hand*" (12.119 sd). Public pardons were among the most gripping spectacles of power deployed by the Tudor monarchs.[82] Recounting the king's mass pardoning of the rioters in the aftermath of the 1517 May Day rising, the secretary to the Venetian ambassador wrote, "It was a very fine spectacle and well arranged, and the crowd of people present was innumerable."[83] Heywood displaces the king and instead, against the admonitions of the antitheatricalists, puts a gentlewoman citizen at the center of these spectacles.[84] Jane Shore's newfound celebrity gives her the power to defend the commonwealth and, as Heywood would write in the *Apology for Actors*, "to new mold the harts of the spectators."

Richard, Jane, and the Politics of Pity

For all their differences, Jane Shore and Richard III share a proclivity for publicity. Jane proves to be an affecting political performer, whether answering petitions, delivering pardons, or visiting the impoverished and

---

[82] K. J. Kesselring, *Mercy and Authority in the Tudor State* (Cambridge: Cambridge University Press, 2003), 136–62.

[83] *Four Years at the Court of Henry VIII: Selection of Despatches Written by the Venetian Ambassador, Sebastian Giustinian*, trans. Rawdon Brown, 2 vols. (London, 1854), 2:75. See Kesselring, *Mercy*, 159–60.

[84] See Squitieri, "Jane Shore's Political Identity."

162 Libels on the Elizabethan Stage

imprisoned. In the play's second part, Richard too tries his hand at the politics of popularity. To secure his usurped throne, the infamous tyrant publishes a proclamation against Jane and then tries "[t]o prove the lawful issue of [Edward], / Got out of wedlock, illegitimate" through a sermon "at Paul's Cross," one of the prime platforms for public address in early modern London (19.5–6, 4).[85] The upshot of these public pitches is to make ordinary Londoners the arbiters of political legitimacy. Or, as Peter Lake and Steven Pincus put it, it is to conjure "an adjudicating public or publics."[86] What *Edward IV* makes clear, though, is that political judgment was an affective-critical process. Thought and feeling, reason and passion worked in tandem. Thus it is the circulation of pity for Jane Shore that turns the play's citizens against their king.

Ironically, the catalyst for this affective community is precisely the instrument designed to stamp it out: Richard's proclamation. Several years before the premiere of Heywood's play, in the anonymous *True Tragedie of Richard the Third*, the king's proclamation had been a complete success. This Richard imposes "open penance" on Shore's wife (as she is called) and issues a proclamation "that none shall releeue her nor pittie her ... for as her beginning was most famous aboue all, so will I haue her end most infamous aboue all." In the next scene, Shore's wife begs for alms but finds no charity. The same men whose suits she had furthered now shrink in fear of Richard's "straight proclamation" and brand her "the dishonour to the King," "the shame to her husband, the discredit to the Citie," "my Kings enemy."[87] No one relieves her or even pities her; her fame has become infamy.

By contrast, Richard's proclamation in *2 Edward IV* not only fails to prevent but even incites outpourings of pity. Brackenbury, now Jane's loyal friend, tells her of the tyrant's proclamation and the emotion that it has elicited:

> the King in every street
> Of London, and in every borough town,
> Throughout this land hath publicly proclaimed,
> On pain of death, that none shall harbour you,
> Or give you food, or clothes to keep you warm;
> But, having first done shameful penance here,

---

[85] Mary Morrissey, *Politics and the Paul's Cross Sermons, 1558–1642* (Oxford: Oxford University Press, 2011).

[86] Peter Lake and Steven Pincus, "Rethinking the Public Sphere in Early Modern England," in *Politics of the Public Sphere*, ed. Lake and Pincus, 6.

[87] *True Tragedie*, sigs. E1r, E2r, E2v, E3r.

Pity and Politics in Heywood's Edward IV

> You shall be then thrust forth the city gates,
> Into the naked, cold, forsaken field.
> I fable not; I would to God I did.
> See, here's the manner of it, put in print;
> 'Tis to be sold in every stationer's shop,
> Besides a number of them clapped on posts;
> Where people crowding, as they read your fall
> Some murmur, and some sigh, but most of them
> Have their relenting eyes e'en big with tears. (18.99–113)

Brackenbury's report conjures a recognizably Elizabethan media landscape.[88] Like so many early modern political actors, Richard has published his message as widely as possible: from the streets of London to provincial towns, from oral declamation ("publicly proclaimed") to printing ("put in print"). This appearance of print may be anachronistic. No printed proclamation survives before the reign of Henry VII. Nor were early modern proclamations typically sold in stationers' shops, as Richard has decreed.[89] Yet Heywood nonetheless invites us to imagine the proclamation circulating through a vibrant media marketplace – the same marketplace through which competing representations of Jane Shore circulated in the 1590s.

In the final lines of his report, Brackenbury points to the agency of audiences – including Heywood's own – in parsing those representations. People crowd to read (and presumably to hear read) the official story of Jane's fall. Their responses are not identical: "some murmur, and some sigh." "But," Brackenbury continues, most share in the physiological expression of pity, "their relenting eyes e'en big with tears." Richard has inadvertently unleashed a tide of popular feeling. Moved by his cruel sentence, clusters of tearful readers and listeners have gathered across England to express their emotion. Together they make up a virtual, nationwide community joined in pity for Jane's plight.

This community is joined too, as we soon see, in defiance of Richard's decree. Banished from the city, Jane welcomes "lack of meat, and lack of friends" and complains to herself, "All things that breathe, in their

---

[88] On the circulation of early modern proclamations, see Chris R. Kyle, "Monarch and Marketplace: Proclamations as News in Early Modern England," *Huntington Library Quarterly* 78.4 (2015): 771–87.

[89] Joad Raymond, *Pamphlets and Pamphleteering in Early Modern Britain* (Cambridge: Cambridge University Press, 2003), 102; Alan B. Farmer and Zachary Lesser, "What Is Print Popularity? A Map of the Elizabethan Book Trade," in *The Elizabethan Top Ten: Defining Print Popularity in Early Modern England*, ed. Andy Kesson and Emma Smith (Farnham, UK: Ashgate, 2013), 26.

164 Libels on the Elizabethan Stage

extremity / Have some recourse of succour; thou hast none" (20.37, 40–41). But she is soon proved wrong. A procession of friends comes with succor: Brackenbury with a prayer book and food; Master Aire with a purse; Matthew Shore (still in disguise) with food and wine; Jockie and Jeffrey with bread, cheese, and ale (20.56–278). If anything, Jane has only become more popular in the wake of Richard's proclamation. Even her estranged husband feels a renewed surge of "pity" (18.235). Tellingly described in theatrical terms, her "woeful spectacle" or "pageant" of suffering moves its onlookers not only to compassion but also to brazen disobedience (20.133, 18.228). I think the metatheatrical language marks this as the kind of politically oriented feeling that the play itself seeks from its audiences. This is not to say that Heywood set out to demystify the cult of Elizabeth. But, at the end of a difficult decade, he does show how popular feeling might lead at least some subjects to cast a critical eye on the propaganda put out by the crown.[90]

In any case, Richard's public relations campaign is a total failure. His proclamation only intensifies Jane Shore's affective sway. Defiant to the last, her sympathizers gladly pay the price for their compassion. The corrupt merchant Rufford, now tasked with enforcing the king's proclamation, catches Jockie giving Jane bread and cheese, and sends him to be whipped. When Aire and Matthew Shore come to her aid, Rufford apprehends them too. Jane's husband sarcastically appeals to Richard's mercy: "God save the King, a true heart means no ill. / I trust he hath reclaimed his sharp edict, / And will not that his poorest subject perish" (20.292–94). Richard, of course, means all sorts of ill. The king actually does repeal his "heavy sentence 'gainst Shore's wife," but only after her death – "else I ne'er had spoke such words," he sneers in an aside (23.58, 62). As Matthew suggests, the people's civil disobedience is an indictment of Richard's tyranny.

Among the wave of oppositional responses unleashed by Richard's proclamation are not only murmuring, sighing, crying, and empathetic defiance but also libeling. In a curious scene toward the end of the play, Matthew Shore seemingly invents a libel out of thin air. When Rufford hauls him before the king for relieving Jane, he has a counteraccusation ready. Matthew tells Richard,

---

[90] On the turmoil of the 1590s, see John Guy, ed., *The Reign of Elizabeth I: Court and Culture in the Last Decade* (Cambridge: Cambridge University Press, 1995); on fractures in the cult of Elizabeth, see Julia M. Walker, ed., *Dissing Elizabeth: Negative Representations of Gloriana* (Durham, NC: Duke University Press, 1998).

Pity and Politics in Heywood's Edward IV   165

> I do know the man
> Which doth abet that traitorous libeller,
> Who did compose and spread that slanderous rhyme
> Which scandals you, and doth abuse the time.   (21.52–55)

This is a puzzling claim. Matthew knows that Rufford is guilty, but not of libel: he has just witnessed the merchant procuring counterfeit letters patent for the export of corn and hides (20.214 sd). The mention of "that traitorous libeller," however, immediately seizes Richard's attention. "What libeller? Another Collingbourne?" the king anxiously asks, "That wrote: *The Cat, the Rat, and Lovell, our Dog, / Do rule all England, under a Hog?*" (21.56–58). The chronicles relate that one William Collingbourne was "abbreuiated shorter by the head" for composing this mocking rhyme against Richard (the hog) and his minions, Catesby the cat, Ratcliffe the rat, and Lovell the dog.[91]

Collingbourne's couplet enjoyed a long afterlife in early modern England. Despite its relative antiquity, it was among the most popular verse libels of the age.[92] Most readers seem to have taken Collingbourne's fate as yet another sign of Richard's tyranny. This was the view, at any rate, articulated by the spirit of the man himself through several editions of the *Mirror for Magistrates*. The *Mirror*'s Collingbourne is a free-speaking poet martyred for mocking Ricardian tyranny. He warns others to learn from his miserable end that tyrants' "vicious acts may not be touched in verse," that "the poet's ancient liberties" have been extinguished by "newfound tyrannies." Yet he also defends his verse at length. "The rhyme I made, though rude, was sound in sense," he protests, "For they therein whom I so fondly named / So ruled all that they were foul defamed."[93] Collingbourne maintains that Richard and his cronies earned their animalistic epithets through their cruel rule. He reframes defamation not as false accusation but as well-deserved reputation.

But at least one influential lawyer had a very different view of Collingbourne's offense. In his 1605 prosecution of Lewis Pickering for libel, Edward Coke (then Attorney General) cited the rhyme and Collingbourne's punishment as evidence that it was "[a] blessed time for lawe & euen examples." The issue for Coke is not truth or falsity but the threat to "ye state & gouernmente." He maintains that "allthoughe the

---

[91] Holinshed, *Third volume*, sig. Ccc5v.
[92] Steven W. May and Alan Bryson, eds., *Verse Libel in Renaissance England and Scotland* (Oxford: Oxford University Press, 2016), 7 n21.
[93] "Collingbourne," in *Mirror*, ed. Lucas, ll. 5, 197, 199, 243–45.

166   Libels on the Elizabethan Stage

libelle be true & ye person infamous, yet it is a greate offence."[94] The popular tradition of Collingbourne as poet-martyr stood in direct opposition to the crime of libel. For Coke and for the judges who sentenced Pickering, Collingbourne was a proto-libeler who suffered an exemplary punishment for undermining the government.

Heywood's Richard unsurprisingly takes Coke's line. Yet his rush to identify this new libeler gives Matthew Shore the chance to recite a sequel to Collingbourne's infamous couplet. When the king asks Matthew to repeat the poem, he is eager to oblige:

> The crook-backed Boar the way hath found
> To root our Roses from our ground.
> Both flower and bud will he confound,
> Till king of beasts the swine be crowned.
> And then the Dog, the Cat, and Rat,
> Shall in his trough feed and be fat.
> "Finis," quoth Master Fogge, chief secretary
> and counsellor to Master Rufford.

(21.62–68)

This libel appears to be Heywood's own invention, recited by Matthew Shore who in turn attributes it to Master Fogge. As was so often the case, authorship remains elusive: the poem could equally be the work of Fogge (aided and abetted by Rufford), of Matthew Shore, or of some anonymous critic of Richard's rule. Whatever its origins, its message is clear. While Richard repeatedly tries to convince the people that he is the "lawful prince by true succession," the libel makes him the swinish star of a beast fable (23.11). The "crook-backed Boar" who digs up "our Roses" – the Houses of Lancaster and York, contenders for the throne in the Wars of the Roses – is an illegitimate ruler, crowned "king of beasts" only after he has laid waste to the kingdom. Spoken by a commoner in front of the king himself, the libel counters Richard's public performances of power with mocking satire. It takes the movement coalescing around Jane Shore in a starkly anti-tyrannical direction.

Soon after reading the libel aloud, Matthew suggests how it might spread nearly as widely as Richard's own proclamation. He knows that Rufford is concealing only counterfeit letters patent, yet he nonetheless claims that Rufford's doublet is "stuffed with trait'rous libels" – bursting with scraps of verse ready to be scattered throughout the city or even the realm (21.82). This false accusation taps into deep anxieties about the

---

[94] John Hawarde, *Les Reportes del Cases in Camera Stellata, 1593 to 1609*, ed. William Paley Baildon (London, 1894), 225.

Pity and Politics in Heywood's Edward IV 167

circulation of libels. Stuck to doors and posts, walls and crosses, libels spoke to the same audiences addressed by royal proclamations (like the one that Richard has "clapped on posts").[95] Collingbourne himself reportedly posted his verse on the doors of St. Paul's Cathedral or, according to a different account, on Cheapside Cross and elsewhere throughout London.[96] Civic hubs such as St. Paul's and Cheapside regularly hosted official displays, from proclamations and preaching to public punishments.[97] But that was also what made them so appealing to libelers like Collingbourne and his early modern successors. This seems to have been the case, at any rate, for a band of Wiltshire troublemakers in 1611. For these men, the perfect spot for their libel was not just the local market cross but the precise post upon which proclamations were displayed. One of their number allegedly decided that the verse was not "sett up publiquely enough" until he had learned "uppon which poste of the crosse [the king's] proclamacons used to be sett" and posted it there, "in open viewe of the towne."[98] This libeler sought maximum publicity by turning the site of royal authority into a defamatory display.

When Richard has Rufford searched, only the forged letters patent turn up. Yet the libel's mockery continues to resonate. For the crime of "counterfeit[ing] my hand and seal," the king sentences Rufford to death (21.88). He orders his lackeys, "Lovell and Catesby, go: / Command the sheriffs of London presently / To see [Rufford] drawn, and hanged, and quartered" (21.98–100). If Richard wants to forget about the libel, Heywood's audience surely would not have forgotten: Catesby the cat and Lovell the dog are among its prime targets, second only to Richard "the crook-backed Boar" himself. Against the proclamation pinned on posts, Heywood's play shows the people taking Jane Shore's side through pity, material aid, and, finally, libelous verse.

By the end of the play, the surge of popular affection for Matthew and Jane transforms the topography of London itself. The penultimate scene sees the Shores finally reunited in death. "O, dying marriage! O, sweet married death!" Jane exclaims, expiring in a ditch with a kiss from her husband (22.102). As Matthew follows her to their humble grave, he distills

---

[95] Andrew Gordon, "The Act of Libel: Conscripting Civic Space in Early Modern England," *Journal of Medieval and Early Modern Studies* 32.2 (2002): 387.

[96] Holinshed, *Third volume*, sig. Ccccsv; A. H. Thomas and I. D. Thornley, eds., *The Great Chronicle of London* (London: George W. Jones, 1938), 236.

[97] Vanessa Harding, "Cheapside: Commerce and Commemoration," *Huntington Library Quarterly* 71.1 (2008): 77–96; Morrissey, *Politics*.

[98] TNA, STAC 8/240/26, quoted in Adam Fox, *Oral and Literate Culture in England, 1500–1700* (Oxford: Clarendon Press, 2000), 316.

168 Libels on the Elizabethan Stage

their dissident message, crying, "Now, tyrant Richard, do the worst thou canst: / She doth defy thee!" (22.108–9). So too have the people of England defied their king. In a final act of resistance, they memorialize Jane and Matthew Shore by inscribing their name on London's civic landscape. As Catesby relates,

> The people, for the love they bear to her
> And her kind husband, pitying his wrongs,
> For ever after mean to call the ditch
> Shores' Ditch, as in the memory of them.   (23.71–74)

The district of Shoreditch, located in the northern suburbs, housed two of the city's earliest public playhouses, the Theatre and the Curtain.[99] In a compelling reading of this scene, Wendy Wall contends that "Heywood identifies the audience with the play's citizenry and thus enjoins them to reflect on the potential power of everyday practices" – including play-going – "for challenging official proclamations and acts."[100] The people gathered in Heywood's theater witness the people of Ricardian England challenge their king and leave their mark on the city. Like the story of Collingbourne's libel, Heywood's apocryphal etymology binds the medieval past to the early modern present. The name Shoreditch endured, a testament to the Shores' affective sway – and to the political power of the people's love.

Yet it is only through her suffering and death that Jane attains this peak of popularity. While she spent her days protecting the people, she herself repeatedly falls victim to Heywood's tyrannical kings. She ultimately becomes a Lucretia figure, subjected to a peculiarly English version of the "republican rape topos."[101] Seized by Edward and martyred by Richard, Jane sparks anti-tyrannical and perhaps even anti-monarchical feeling at the cost of her life. Heywood himself dramatizes the archetype of this trope in his play *The Rape of Lucrece*. His Lucrece insists that suicide alone can expiate "[m]y blot, my scandall and my shame." She gathers her kinsmen and commands, "Sweare youle reuenge poore Lucrece on her foe." As soon as these Roman lords have vowed to prosecute "the iust reuenge / Of this chaste rauisht Lady," Lucrece kills herself.[102] Her life ends with the birth of a republican community of men united in pursuit of revenge.

---

[99] Helgerson, *Adulterous Alliances*, 49; Wall, "Forgetting," 140.   [100] Wall, "Forgetting," 146.
[101] Oliver Arnold, *The Third Citizen: Shakespeare's Theater and the Early Modern House of Commons* (Baltimore: Johns Hopkins University Press, 2007), 102. See Stephanie H. Jed, *Chaste Thinking: The Rape of Lucretia and the Birth of Humanism* (Bloomington: Indiana University Press, 1989).
[102] Thomas Heywood, *The Rape of Lucrece* (London, 1608), sigs. H1v, H2r, H3r.

Pity and Politics in Heywood's Edward IV 169

But things go rather differently in late medieval England. To be sure, Jane and Matthew (like Heywood's Lucrece) fret about "this badge of obloquy," "thy dishonoured life," "the scandal of my name" (*1 Edward IV*, 20.89, 22.84; *2 Edward IV*, 9.35). Jane even anticipates the Lucretian trajectory early on, telling her husband, "These hands shall make this body a dead corse / Ere force or flattery shall mine honour stain" (*1 Edward IV*, 8.30–31). Yet she nevertheless lives on, staking out her own place in the public sphere. And the affective energies she unleashes, I have argued, have more to do with her hard-earned popularity than with the bare fact of her suffering. She galvanizes not merely "an emerging bourgeois cult" (Richard Helgerson) or "a discourse of resistance" (Orlin) but a new kind of political celebrity.[103] Or, rather, elements of both civic fantasy and dissident discourse go into the affective-political matrix that takes shape around her. Far from a republican revenge cult, the result is an English public joined in the shared experience of pity.

Jane Shore's Public

As I explained at the beginning of this chapter, I call this collectivity a "public" based not just on the way *Edward IV* imagines strangers coming together but also on the evidence of the play's reception over the course of its long career on the stage and in print. We don't know much about how the play fared with Derby's Men at the Boar's Head, where it likely originated in 1599. But it was evidently popular enough to move with Worcester's Men to the Rose and then, perhaps in revised form, with Queen Anne's Men to the Red Bull. This third playhouse was a fitting venue in which to achieve lasting popularity. Situated in the northwest suburb of Clerkenwell – not so far from Shoreditch – the Red Bull was known for its citizen audiences and crowd-pleasing fare.[104]

By the early seventeenth century, Jane Shore's stage life had become linked to a certain class of playgoer. One of the first allusions to *Edward IV* (or to its later revision) appears in the prologue to Francis Beaumont's *Knight of the Burning Pestle* (1607). The play has just begun when a citizen

---

[103] Helgerson, *Adulterous Alliances*, 50; Orlin, "Making Public," 112.
[104] For recent reevaluations of the Red Bull, its repertory, and its audiences, see Lucy Munro, Anne Lancashire, John Astington, and Marta Straznicky, "Issues in Review: Popular Theatre and the Red Bull," *Early Theatre* 9.2 (2006): 99–156; Mark Bayer, *Theatre, Community, and Civic Engagement in Jacobean London* (Iowa City: University of Iowa Press, 2011); and Eva Griffith, *A Jacobean Company and Its Playhouse: The Queen's Servants at the Red Bull Theatre* (c. 1605–1619) (Cambridge: Cambridge University Press, 2013).

Libels on the Elizabethan Stage

interjects and climbs onto the stage. He demands a play "in honour of the commons of the city" starring "a citizen ... of my own trade": a grocer. Not to be left out, his wife joins him onstage, and the two are seated in view of the audience. "I was ne'er at one of these plays, as they say, before," his wife admits, "but I should have seen *Jane Shore* once."[105] Beaumont's satire turns on the perceived opposition between the more rarefied audiences of the Blackfriars, where the *Knight* premiered, and the artisan playgoers who flocked to open-air playhouses such as the Red Bull.[106] His mockery is aimed squarely at the latter, sending up their class pretensions and theatrical tastes. In the process, however, Beaumont also offers a partial snapshot of Jane Shore's public. His unruly citizens stand for a larger civic body, "the commons of the city," coming together to see themselves onstage. This collective is marked not only by class but also by gender: the citizen's wife is the one who wishes she'd had the chance to see Jane Shore, quite possibly at the Red Bull.

Yet this is not the only account of Jane Shore's audiences. Two years later, an anonymous writer suggested that her popularity cut across class lines. This observer expressed amazement

> to see a Crowd
> Of *Ciuill Throats* stretchd out so lowd:
> (As at a *New-play*) all the Roomes
> Did swarme with *Gentiles* mix'd with *Groomes*.
> So that I truly thought, all *These*
> Came to see *Shore*, or *Pericles*.[107]

At least according to this writer, *Edward IV* or its revision remained as popular as a new play even at the end of the first decade of the seventeenth century. And that popularity captivates gentles and grooms alike, all mixed indiscriminately in the "swarme" of bodies. Here, attachment to Jane Shore does not distinguish the citizen class but instead brings all Londoners together in noisy acclamation.

I have already discussed two other notable allusions to Jane Shore's celebrity: the report in a seventeenth-century ballad that "thousands thanke thee for thy paine," and Brooke's 1614 account of women commiserating her fate in a "vild Play." These scattered pieces of evidence do not

---

[105] Francis Beaumont, *The Knight of the Burning Pestle*, ed. Sheldon P. Zitner (Manchester: Manchester University Press, 1984), Induction, 25–26, 29–30, 50–52.

[106] Gurr, *Playgoing*, 86–87, 121–24. But Beaumont's play flopped, quite possibly because audiences were not as stratified by class as he thought (or hoped) they were (ibid., 87).

[107] *Pimlyco. Or, Runne Red-Cap* (London, 1609), sig. C1r.

Pity and Politics in Heywood's Edward IV

fully align. For Beaumont, class is the defining characteristic of the play's audiences, followed by gender. For the anonymous observer, Jane's popularity brings people together across class lines. And for Brooke's ghost of Richard III, it is women in particular who pity her tale. Taken together, though, these reports trace the contours of Jane Shore's public. This was a public expansive enough to include gentles and grooms yet organized by citizen interests, united in collective emotion and oriented against royal tyranny. Perhaps women were especially prominent in it, although Beaumont's and Brooke's accounts may have as much to do with misogynistic tropes as with actual playgoing practices. In any case, I think it is no coincidence how closely these reports reflect the action of *Edward IV*. Through several decades if not longer, Heywood's heroine cultivated a highly visible strain of civic feeling in the playhouse and beyond.

CHAPTER 6

Turning Plays into Libels: Satire and Sedition in Jonson's Poetaster

Ben Jonson never tired of railing against those who would apply his supposedly innocent satire to particular persons. In the second prologue to *Epicene* (1609–10), he warns his audiences,

> If any yet will, with particular sleight
> Of application, wrest what he doth write,
> And that he meant or him or her will say,
> They make a libel which he made a play. (11–14)[1]

"Application," Jonson insists, turns his plays into libels by discerning personal caricatures where none are intended. Unlike "lewd verses such as libels be," his satires "spare men's persons and but tax their crimes" (*Poetaster*, 3.5.130, 134). Anyone who finds otherwise only has themselves to blame. This is a familiar refrain in the Jonsonian corpus, appearing in the paratexts, prologues, and metadramatic scenes of *Every Man Out of His Humour* (1599), *Poetaster* (1601), *Sejanus* (1603), *Volpone* (1606), *The Alchemist* (1610), *Bartholomew Fair* (1614), and *The Magnetic Lady* (1632).[2] From these complaints emerges a lexicon of libel-making. The playwright's alleged misinterpreters are "narrow-eyed decipherers" and "invading interpreters" (*Every Man Out*, 2.3.348–49; *Volpone*, Epistle, 51); they "pervert and poison" with their "contagious comments" and their "malice of misapplying" (*Every Man Out*, 2.3.353–54; *Magnetic Lady*, Chorus 2, 33). As early as its induction, *Poetaster* signals that it will be about precisely this problem. The personification of Envy enumerates the varieties of malicious misinterpretation: "wrestings, comments, applica- tions, / Spy-like suggestions, privy whisperings, / And thousand such

---

[1] All quotations of Jonson's works in this chapter come from *CWBJ* and are cited parenthetically in the text.
[2] *Every Man Out*, 2.3.326–54; *Sejanus*, 3.226–29; *Volpone*, Epistle, 49–53; *Alchemist*, Prologue, 19–24; *Bartholomew Fair*, Induction, 101–8; *Magnetic Lady*, Chorus 2, 20–36.

172

Satire and Sedition in Jonson's Poetaster

promoting sleights as these" (24–26). And so "they make a libel which he made a play."

The stakes of application were especially high in 1601, the year *Poetaster* was written and first performed. From 1599 to 1601, the Earl of Essex's declining fortunes unleashed torrents of verse satires and seditious libels, which in turn were met with unusually harsh reactions from Elizabeth and her ministers. Satires were banned and burned; actors were interrogated; and at least one libeler (a lawyer's clerk named Waterhouse) was hanged. Just months after the Essex Rising of February 1601, John Weever published *The Whipping of the Satyre*, a verse pamphlet branding Jonson and two other satirists "Seminaries of seditious strife."[3] Yet Jonson was not at all cowed. In *Poetaster* – set in an Augustan Rome that clearly stands for England – the playwright sharply criticizes the crackdown on satire and libel through the figure of Lupus, the corrupt and ignorant tribune. Over two decades ago, Tom Cain proposed that Jonson's play is "an oblique satirical commentary on the atmosphere, events, and policies leading up to the rebellion and arraignment of the Earl of Essex in February 1601."[4] His account of the play is convincing yet, I believe, does not go far enough. Building on Cain's work, I show that the play subjects the government's paranoid pursuit of libel and sedition to withering – and not particularly oblique – critique.

Yet Jonson's attack on the "wrestings" of spies, informers, and corrupt magistrates belies the libelous topicality of his own play. In fact, the central irony of *Poetaster* – and of Jonson's playwriting career – is that he undeniably did lampoon specific individuals, not to mention the host of more ambiguous topical analogies that scholars have found in his plays.[5] *Poetaster* itself was a clear salvo in "that terrible *Poetomachia*," the dramatists' exchange of personal abuse circa 1599–1601 now known as the War of the

---

[3] John Weever, *The Whipping of the Satyre*, in *The Whipper Pamphlets (1601)*, ed. A. Davenport, vol. 1 (Liverpool: University Press of Liverpool, 1951), l. 734. Hereafter cited parenthetically by line number in the text.

[4] Tom Cain, "'Satyres, That Girde and Fart at the Time': *Poetaster* and the Essex Rebellion," in *Refashioning Ben Jonson: Gender, Politics and the Jonsonian Canon*, ed. Julie Sanders, Kate Chedgzoy, and Susan Wiseman (Basingstoke, UK: Macmillan, 1998), 51–52.

[5] See, for instance, B. N. De Luna, *Jonson's Romish Plot: A Study of "Catiline" and its Historical Context* (Oxford: Clarendon Press, 1967); Richard Dutton, *Ben Jonson: To The First Folio* (Cambridge: Cambridge University Press, 1983), 134–55; Dutton, *Mastering the Revels: The Regulation and Censorship of English Renaissance Drama* (Basingstoke, UK: Macmillan, 1991); Dutton, *Ben Jonson, "Volpone" and the Gunpowder Plot* (Cambridge: Cambridge University Press, 2008); Matthew Steggle, *Wars of the Theatres: The Poetics of Personation in the Age of Jonson* (Victoria: English Literary Studies, 1998); and Janet Clare, *'Art made tongue-tied by authority': Elizabethan and Jacobean Dramatic Censorship*, 2nd ed. (Manchester: Manchester University Press, 1999).

174 Libels on the Elizabethan Stage

Theaters or the Poets' War.[6] The riskiest allusions, though, were those that glanced at the state. For his plays Jonson was imprisoned (twice), brought before the Privy Council (at least once), and accused of libel, sedition, and even, on one occasion, treason.[7] *Poetaster* likewise got him in trouble, this time with "the greatest justice of this kingdom": presumably Sir John Popham, Lord Chief Justice of England (*Poetaster*, "To ... Richard Martin," 5–6). In the play, Jonson at once decries and practices the art of libel. For some critics, this contradiction makes *Poetaster*'s satire self-defeating. M. Lindsay Kaplan, for example, contends that "Jonson's attacks against slanderers redound to his own discredit, and the distinction between satire and slander dissolves."[8]

But the equation of satire with libel is less a sign of artistic failure or self-contradiction than it is the seemingly inevitable fate of the satirical dramatist in 1601. Even an older history play such as Shakespeare's *Richard II* could acquire renewed (and treasonous) topicality during the furor around Essex. I think Jonson was far more sensitive to his own complicity in the culture of libelous "application" than he has generally been given credit for. In this I concur with R. Malcolm Smuts, who has recently called *Poetaster* "a coy and clever play about how to violate government decrees against defamatory and politically provocative writing while pretending not to do so."[9] The collapse of satire into libel does not undermine but rather animates Jonson's poetic and political project. For most of the play, this generative paradox – the paradox of the satirist who veers toward libel while at the same time decrying it – remains largely submerged. But Jonson brings it to the fore in the play's final scene. Horace, the virtuous satirist and authorial stand-in, is accused of seditious libel for composing an enigmatic emblem. Through the emblem – and through a hitherto unnoticed etymological pun – Jonson mocks the judgment of malign interpreters even as he appeals to the judgment of his audiences.

---

[6] Thomas Dekker, *Satiromastix*, in *The Dramatic Works of Thomas Dekker*, ed. Fredson Bowers, vol. 1 (Cambridge: Cambridge University Press, 1953), "To the World," 7. For varying appraisals of the exchange, see Steggle, *Wars*; James P. Bednarz, *Shakespeare and the Poets' War* (New York: Columbia University Press, 2001); and Roslyn Lander Knutson, *Playing Companies and Commerce in Shakespeare's Time* (Cambridge: Cambridge University Press, 2001).

[7] See Jonson, *Discoveries*, 952–53n.

[8] M. Lindsay Kaplan, *The Culture of Slander in Early Modern England* (Cambridge: Cambridge University Press, 1997), 90. For similar views, see, more recently, James Loxley and Mark Robson, *Shakespeare, Jonson, and the Claims of the Performative* (New York: Routledge, 2013), 63; and Bill Angus, *Metadrama and the Informer in Shakespeare and Jonson* (Edinburgh: Edinburgh University Press, 2016), 128–29.

[9] R. Malcolm Smuts, "Jonson's *Poetaster* and the Politics of Defamation," *English Literary Renaissance* 49.2 (2019): 245.

I am by no means the first to suggest that Jonson was deeply concerned with his audiences' judgment. For most scholars, however, his complaints about topical application are part of his long-running and quixotic campaign to police audience interpretation. Matthew Steggle claims that "Jonson fears the idea that the spectator is an active constructor of the drama they are watching," and Eric D. Vivier contends that "Ben Jonson really did not think anyone other than Ben Jonson should judge the work of Ben Jonson."[10] Not without reason, the playwright's antagonistic relationship with his audiences – or at least with the popular element among them – has become a critical commonplace.[11] Yet this view obscures who was actually turning his plays into libels. Sir James Murray, a Scottish courtier, complained about the anti-Scottish satire in *Eastward Ho!*; Lady Arabella Stuart, King James's first cousin, took offense at an allusion to her in *Epicene*; Henry Howard, Earl of Northampton, found "popery and treason" in *Sejanus*; and *Poetaster*, as noted above, apparently attracted unwanted attention from Lord Chief Justice Popham.[12] In *Discoveries*, his posthumously published commonplace book, Jonson himself notes that he has "been accused to the lords, to the king, and by great ones" (952–53). The (mis)interpretations that threaten the playwright (and, for that matter, the state) are not those concocted by theater audiences but those invented by "great ones" and their hangers-on.

So what is the satirist to do when accused, quite plausibly, of libel by ministers of the state? Jonson's complaints about those who "make a libel which he made a play" suggest an answer: insist on the interpretive agency of the audience. At least in *Poetaster*, Jonson relies on his audiences to draw precisely those topical applications that he stridently denies. Passing the blame to the playgoers is, of course, an exculpatory strategy for the playwright accused of libel. But it also points to the collusive uptake that

---

[10] Steggle, *Wars*, 55; Eric D. Vivier, "Judging Jonson: Ben Jonson's Satirical Self-Defense in *Poetaster*," *Ben Jonson Journal* 24.1 (2017): 1. For the contrary view, see Michelle O'Callaghan, *The English Wits: Literature and Sociability in Early Modern England* (Cambridge: Cambridge University Press, 2007), 44.

[11] See, e.g., George E. Rowe, Jr., "Ben Jonson's Quarrel with Audience and its Renaissance Context," *Studies in Philology* 81.4 (1984): 438–60; John Gordon Sweeney III, *Jonson and the Psychology of Public Theater: To Coin the Spirit, Spend the Soul* (Princeton: Princeton University Press, 1985); Rebecca Yearling, *Ben Jonson, John Marston and Early Modern Drama: Satire and the Audience* (Basingstoke, UK: Palgrave Macmillan, 2016); and Victor Lenthe, "Ben Jonson's Antagonistic Style, Public Opinion, and *Sejanus*," *Studies in English Literature 1500–1900* 57.2 (2017): 349–68.

[12] See, respectively, Jonson, *Informations to William Drummond of Hawthornden*, 207–10; Rawdon Brown et al., eds., *Calendar of State Papers and Manuscripts, Relating to English Affairs, Existing in the Archives and Collections of Venice*, 38 vols. (London, 1864–1947), 11:427; and Jonson, *Informations*, 252.

176 Libels on the Elizabethan Stage

made the early modern libel so difficult to police. If we doubt Jonson's protestations of innocence – and he gives us every reason to do so – then his complaints do not so much exonerate the playwright as implicate his audiences in the act of libel. So it goes in *Poetaster*. Jonson entangles the audience in his libelous criticism of the surveillance state. If they make his play a libel, it is because he has turned playgoers into libel-makers.

Satire, Sedition, and the Earl of Essex

More clearly than any contemporary satirist, John Weever articulates the stakes of writing satire in the aftermath of the Essex Rising. I thus begin by examining Weever's *The Whipping of the Satyre* (1601) and its literary-political context. Many of the central accusations that he levels against satirists reappear in one form or another in *Poetaster*. Weever charges them with libel, sedition, and treason; he contends that they usurp judicial and political authority, and even foment rebellion. For Weever – and, I'll argue, for Jonson – all these allegations are bound up with a figure never named by either writer but everywhere present: Robert Devereux, the second Earl of Essex.

From the very first sentence of the prefatory epistle, Weever sketches his paradoxical project: to satirize the satirists. His primary targets are John Marston (the "Satyrist"), Everard Guilpin (the "Epigrammatist"), and Ben Jonson (the "Humorist"), each named for his distinctive brand of satire ("To the Vayne-Glorious"). Weever mocks all three for their pretensions to moral, even quasi-judicial authority. Punning on the title of justice of the peace and quorum, he calls the satirists "iust Asses of Coram" who "had sate of a commission, *ad Inquirendum de moribus*" (5, 6–7). Justices of the peace (JPs) were appointed by the crown "to looke vnto the good gouerne-ment of hir subiects"; justices of the quorum (colloquially rendered "coram"), supposedly the most learned among the JPs, were invested with special judicial powers.[13] Just as these magistrates were commissioned "*ad inquirendum &c.*" – "to enquire of al *Felonies*, and *Trespasses*" – so Weever's "iust Asses" claim a commission "*ad Inquirendum de moribus*," to investigate and chastise England's mores.[14]

---

[13] William Harrison, *An Historicall description of the Iland of Britaine*, in Raphael Holinshed, *The First and second volumes of Chronicles* (London, 1587), sig. O5v. See also William Lambarde, *Eirenarcha: or of The Office of the Iustices of Peace* (London, 1581), sigs. E4r–v. At the beginning of Shakespeare's *Merry Wives of Windsor*, we learn that Justice Shallow is "Justice of Peace and Coram" (*The Merry Wives of Windsor*, ed. Giorgio Melchiori [Walton-on-Thames: Thomas Nelson, 2000], 1.1.4–5).
[14] Lambarde, *Eirenarcha*, sigs. E1r, E3v.

Satire and Sedition in Jonson's Poetaster

Like Jonson, however, Weever implicates himself in the abuse that he condemns. "I thought good to sollicite a *Melius inquirendum*," he informs the three satirists, "because yours, after some examination being found false, and forged, was . . . put downe in the house of office" (10–13).[15] Even as he rejects the satirists' commission as spurious, Weever appeals to his own mock writ: a "*Melius inquirendum*," defined in Cowell's law dictionary as "a writ that lyeth for a second inquiry . . . where partiall dealing is suspected."[16] Weever takes up the mantle of the judicial inquisitor while lampooning the satirists for doing the same.

The Whipping of the Satyre exemplifies this satirical strategy. The poem itself begins with an allegorical encounter in which England's "sacred Church and Common wealth" charge the poet "[t]o take vp *Satyre*, and take downe his [i.e., Satyre's] pride" (135, 150). Fulfilling this commission to use satire against satire, Weever devotes nearly 900 lines to his assault on Marston, Guilpin, and Jonson. His catalogue of their crimes is extensive, but especially egregious is the usurpation of state power. "Well looke the rowles, no office ouerskippe," he admonishes the "Satyrist" (Marston),

> And see if you can finde the Satyrshippe.
> If not, dare you vsurpe an office then,
> Without the licence of her Maiestie,
> To punish all her Subiects with the pen,
> Against the Law of all Ciuilitie? (581–86)

As Debora Shuger comments, Weever "denies that private persons can play the magistrate by lashing, even verbally, those whom they judge faulty."[17] Yet Weever himself does just that. Allegedly at the behest of church and state, he conducts his own inquiry into the three satirists' crimes. And those crimes turn out to be serious indeed. "I haue him vp, t'is pettie treason all," he gloats, "And therefore feare to breake his necke this fall" (587–88). "This fall" is both the satirist's fall to the ground in an allegorical wrestling match and his fatal fall from the gallows. Weever arraigns the satirist for "vsurp[ing] an office," in his view a form of "pettie treason" – a capital crime.[18]

---

[15] The joke here seems to be scatological – a "house of office" is a privy ("house, n.1 and int.," *OED Online* [Oxford University Press, 2022]) – and may also allude to the Bishops' Ban of 1599 (see below).

[16] John Cowell, *The Interpreter* (Cambridge, 1607), sig. Vv4v.

[17] Debora Shuger, *Censorship and Cultural Sensibility: The Regulation of Language in Tudor-Stuart England* (Philadelphia: University of Pennsylvania Press, 2006), 149.

[18] On high and petty treason, see Michael Dalton, *The Countrey Iustice* (London, 1618), sigs. S3v–T1v.

178   Libels on the Elizabethan Stage

For Weever, then, satire no less than libel is a hanging offense. "Was not one hang'd of late for libelling?" he asks, and he does not hesitate to answer:

> Yes questionlesse. And you deserue the same:
> For you before whole volumes foorth did bring,
> And whome you pleas'd, did liberally defame.
> For shall we his by right a Libell call,
> That toutcht but some? not yours, that aym'd at all?   (331–36)

Weever rejects the traditional distinction between libel and satire. While the former attacks clearly identifiable individuals, satirists such as Marston insisted that the "nature of a Satyre ... is vnder fained priuate names, to note generall vices."[19] In *Poetaster*, Jonson's Horace likewise distinguishes libels from those "sharp yet modest rhymes / That spare men's persons and but tax their crimes" (3.5.133–34). But Weever takes issue precisely with that diffuse, prolific mockery. An explicitly topical poem touches "but some" whereas a satire that reproves "generall vices" (Marston's phrase) takes aim "at all." In this view, satire is merely a scattershot form of libel.

As Jonson's own legal troubles suggest, Weever was certainly not the only one to accuse satirists of libel. Yet Weever's eagerness to see the satirist-turned-libeler hanged is extreme even by the standards of the age. For all their overheated rhetoric, the governors of Elizabethan and Jacobean England rarely executed anyone just for libel.[20] As Weever warns, however, someone indeed was "hang'd of late for libelling." *The Whipping of the Satyre* was entered in the Stationers' Register in August 1601, so Weever evidently has in mind a hanging that took place earlier that year.[21] In late February – just weeks after the Essex Rising – one Waterhouse, a lawyer's clerk, was reportedly hanged in Smithfield "for makinge of lybelles."[22] Weever suggests that the same fate awaits the

---

[19] John Marston, *The Scourge of Villanie*, in *The Poems of John Marston*, ed. Arnold Davenport (Liverpool: Liverpool University Press, 1961), 176. See also John Davies, *Epigrammes*, in *The Poems of Sir John Davies*, ed. Robert Krueger (Oxford: Clarendon Press, 1975), 1.9–14.

[20] Capital punishment for seditious and slanderous writings was usually reserved for religious dissidents (see Chapter 3 for some examples).

[21] Edward Arber, ed., *A Transcript of the Registers of the Company of Stationers of London; 1554–1640 A.D.*, 5 vols. (London and Birmingham, 1875–94), 3:190.

[22] TNA, SP 12/281, fol. 125r. This manuscript, described as "Chronological contemporary notes relating to the Earl of Essex's rebellion" in Mary Anne Everett Green, ed., *Calendar of State Papers, Domestic Series, of the Reign of Elizabeth, 1601–1603* (London, 1870), names him "Waterhowse" and dates the hanging to "[a] littell after" February 16 (88). The historian John Stow dates the execution to "[t]he last of February," calls the clerk "a young man named Woodhouse," and offers a fuller account of his offense, discussed below (*The Annales of England* [London, 1605], sig. Rrrr4v). See Richard A. McCabe, "Elizabethan Satire and the Bishops' Ban of 1599," *Yearbook of English Studies* 11 (1981): 193; and *TRP*, 3:233n1.

Satire and Sedition in Jonson's Poetaster

satirists if they do not "change [their] mis-employed course, / And weane [their] wit from sucking still of shame" (961–62).

Waterhouse's hanging points to the exceptionally paranoid and repressive climate that prevailed at the turn of the century. For Weever, the execution represents the proper administration of justice. But not all satirists would have agreed. Despite their public protestations to the contrary, many if not most were intimately involved in the culture of libel.[23] At the universities and, especially, at the Inns of Court, a vogue for neoclassical verse satire took hold in the late 1590s. At least seven books of satirical verse were published between 1597 and 1599, some in multiple editions; other satires, most notably John Donne's, circulated in manuscript.[24] At the same time, members of these elite socioliterary circles were also composing, copying, and circulating libels. In fact, one of the most popular libels of the early seventeenth century, "The Censure of the Parliament Fart," was likely written by a group of lawyers and MPs trained at the Inns of Court.[25] Michelle O'Callaghan has shown that the Inns – and the theaters – were "caught up in the libellous politics" of the late 1590s.[26] All sorts of mocking verses proliferated in manuscript, print, and performance.

At the center of this libelous vortex was the Earl of Essex. In the previous chapter, I commented on his notorious popularity. The earl's fortunes were already on the decline when, in March 1599, he set out to Ireland at the head of an English army.[27] Sent to quell the Earl of Tyrone's rebellion, Essex instead forged a truce with Tyrone after an expensive and largely unsuccessful campaign. Essex rushed back to England to explain himself to the queen, but he was soon arrested, stripped of his offices, and barred from court. Politically and financially ruined, Essex finally launched what the government would call an "open action of rebellion": the Essex Rising of February 8, 1601.[28] The earl and his followers marched into London, aiming (they claimed) to rally the people to his defense and beg the queen to save him from the nefarious plots of his enemies at court. This

---

[23] See Andrew McRae, *Literature, Satire and the Early Stuart State* (Cambridge: Cambridge University Press, 2004); O'Callaghan, *English Wits*, 31–34; and Vivier, "Judging Jonson," 16–17.

[24] McCabe, "Elizabethan Satire," 191.   [25] O'Callaghan, *English Wits*, 86, 93.   [26] Ibid., 11.

[27] The following account of Essex's late career draws from Paul E. J. Hammer, "Devereux, Robert, second earl of Essex (1565–1601)," *Oxford Dictionary of National Biography* (*ODNB*), online ed. (Oxford University Press, 2008); and Hammer, "Shakespeare's *Richard II*, the Play of 7 February 1601, and the Essex Rising," *Shakespeare Quarterly* 59.1 (2008): 1–35. See also Alexandra Gajda, *The Earl of Essex and Late Elizabethan Political Culture* (Oxford: Oxford University Press, 2012).

[28] *TRP*, 3:231.

180   Libels on the Elizabethan Stage

"rebellion" quickly fizzled out. Essex and his supporters were proclaimed traitors and arrested that night; a few weeks later, the earl was beheaded.

By the time of his death in 1601, Essex had been involved in the culture of libel for at least a decade. His political rivalries in the 1590s generated barrages of largely anonymous verse libels, some of which were attributed to Essex himself. The pace and scope of the libeling escalated drastically in 1599, around the time of the earl's failed Irish expedition and final fall from grace.[29] By November, some malcontents were reportedly scattering libels against the queen's ministers "in many partes of the Cittie of London, yea and in her Maiesties Court it self."[30] The libeling continued even after the earl's execution. Fearing further unrest, Elizabeth issued a proclamation in April 1601 against "divers traitorous and slanderous libels ... dispersed in divers parts of our city of London and places near thereunto adjoining ... tending to the slander of our royal person and state, and stirring up of rebellion and sedition within this our realm." The queen offered a reward of £100 for information leading to the apprehension of "the authors, writers, or dispersers of any of the said libels."[31]

The surviving verse libels leave little doubt why the government was so anxious to suppress them. They viciously mock Essex's enemies, reserving special animus for Robert Cecil, Secretary of State and (at least in Essex's view) the principal architect of his downfall. One especially vituperative poem brands Cecil a "Proude and ambitious wretch," a "Dissemblinge smothfac'd dwarfe," and a "Crookebacke spider."[32] While their origins remain uncertain, the libels were taken as evidence of widespread sympathy for the disgraced earl.[33] Too late did Essex see the danger of this "popularity," as the early moderns disapprovingly called it. In a May 1600 letter to the Privy Council, he complained of "practising libellers who since my committment haue shadowed ther intended mischeefe to me vnder

---

[29] Steven W. May and Alan Bryson, eds., *Verse Libel in Renaissance England and Scotland* (Oxford: Oxford University Press, 2016), 35–38; "Essex, Ralegh and Late-Elizabethan Politics (c. 1590–1603)," in *Early Stuart Libels: An Edition of Poetry from Manuscript Sources*, ed. Alastair Bellany and Andrew McRae, Early Modern Literary Studies Text Series 1 (2005), http://purl.oclc.org/emls/texts/libels/.

[30] TNA, SP 12/273, fol. 61r.   [31] *TRP*, 3:233, 234.

[32] "Proude and ambitious wretch that feedest on naught but faction," in *Early Stuart Libels*, ed. Bellany and McRae, A9, ll. 1, 6, 9. On the pro-Essex (and anti-Cecil) libels, see Gajda, *Earl of Essex*, 206–11.

[33] Steven W. May and Alan Bryson argue that the libels were part of an "all-out blitz of scribal propaganda launched by the Essex camp" (*Verse Libel*, 37), while Gajda notes that they could just as well be "genuine products of the earl's popular appeal" (*Earl of Essex*, 174). And Fulke Greville, Essex's friend and former follower, made an altogether different claim: that the libels were made and published by Essex's "enemies" to tarnish his name and "to bring his innocent friends in question" (*A Dedication to Sir Philip Sidney*, in *The Prose Works of Fulke Greville, Lord Brooke*, ed. John Gouws [Oxford: Clarendon Press, 1986], 94).

Satire and Sedition in Jonson's Poetaster

pretended greefe or passion for me."[34] Neither Elizabeth and her ministers nor Essex and his followers could control the feverish discourse of the early modern public sphere.

It was at this moment of intense political anxiety that libel became a hanging offense. In November 1599, shortly after Essex's return from Ireland, the Privy Council went after the libelers in a series of Star Chamber speeches. "I call them Traytors," Lord Keeper Thomas Egerton declared, "because the auncient Lawes of England accompt them so."[35] Lord Treasurer Buckhurst concurred. "These viperous and secrete Libellors doe much more in my opinion deserue death, then those which Committ open rebellion agaynst the State," he said.[36] For a time, the government seems to have held off on such draconian measures. But Essex's rebellion and the subsequent outpouring of seditious speech realized the authorities' worst fears about the danger of libeling. A week after the failed rising, the queen imposed martial law on the "great multitude of base and loose people ... listening after news and stirs, and spreading rumors and tales."[37] Before the end of the month, Waterhouse was hanged for libeling. The historian John Stow later filled in the details of the clerk's crime: "speaking and Libelling against the Queenes Proclamation, and apprehending of the Earle of Essex."[38] Waterhouse's fate is yet another sign of the regime's acute sensitivity to satire and libel in 1601. Within the space of just a few days, the Earl of Essex lost his head and this young sympathizer died on the gallows.

As Weever's allusion to the hanging suggests, printed verse satire as well as scurrilous scribal poetry tracked the final years of Essex's career. In January 1599, the earl's friend Lord Willoughby revealingly wrote to Essex, "tho Ireland calls you, satirs can heare that England cries out for you."[39] Satirists did indeed hear the popular clamor for Essex – and they were not much taken with it. In his anonymously published *Skialetheia, or A Shadowe of Truth, in Certaine Epigrams and Satyres* (1598), Everard Guilpin comments acerbically on what Francis Bacon would call the earl's "points of popularitie."[40] Guilpin (an Inns of Court satirist and

---

[34] CP 80/2.

[35] TNA, SP 12/273, fol. 60v. According to a different account of his speech, Egerton explicitly acknowledged that the state had hitherto been more lenient: "I call them Traytors, for the lawe Condemnes [them] as Traytors, but our state doe not so seuerely punishe yt, and yet they are traytors" (Folger Shakespeare Library, MS V.b.142, fol. 49r).

[36] TNA, SP 12/273, fol. 64r.   [37] *TRP*, 3:232.   [38] Stow, *Annales*, sig. Rrrr4v.

[39] CP 59/10. See Cyndia Susan Clegg, *Press Censorship in Elizabethan England* (Cambridge: Cambridge University Press, 1997), 207.

[40] Francis Bacon, *A Declaration of the Practises & Treasons attempted and committed by Robert late Earle of Essex and his Complices* (London, 1601), sig. B1r.

182 Libels on the Elizabethan Stage

one of Weever's three primary targets) caricatures Essex as "great *Foelix*," who "passing through the street, / Vayleth his cap to each one he doth meet." But beneath this show of courtesy lurks "yeastie ambition." "*Signior Machiauell* / Taught him this mumming trick," Guilpin continues, "with curtesie / T'entrench himselfe in popularitie."[41] Or, as Bacon put it in the aftermath of the rising, the earl's "affable gestures" and other demagogic performances were "the forerunners of treasons following."[42] At least some satirists were just as suspicious of the earl's popularity. In Guilpin's poem, a single syllable is all that stands between *Felix* and *Essex* – between authorized (if anonymous) satire and seditious libel.

Less than a year after *Skialetheia* was published, the gap between satire and libel threatened to vanish altogether. On June 1, 1599, Archbishop Whitgift and Bishop Bancroft ordered the Stationers' Company to cease any further printing of nine specific books, most of them satires, and to consign all copies that could be found to the fire. The Bishops' Ban also restricted the printing of English histories and plays, but it was the satire (as well as the closely related genre, the epigram) that was prohibited without qualification: "That noe Satyres or Epigramms be printed hereafter."[43] Three days after the bishops' order, *Skialetheia* – along with six other books – was burned in Stationers' Hall.[44] The motives of the ban remain the subject of debate. However, Cyndia Susan Clegg has convincingly argued that this act of censorship was not merely a general crackdown on satire but rather a specific reaction to the libelous politics of the late 1590s – and in particular, to the spate of thinly veiled commentary on Essex's controversial career.[45] Clegg identifies allusions to Essex – or at least passages that Whitgift and Bancroft may very well have taken as such – not only in Guilpin's *Skialetheia, or A Shadowe of Truth* but also in satires by Thomas Middleton, Tailboys Dymoke, and Thomas Nashe.[46] If Felix could safely stand for Essex when *Skialetheia* was licensed and published in 1598, by June 1599 at least some members of

---

[41] Everard Guilpin, *Skialetheia, or A Shadowe of Truth, in Certaine Epigrams and Satyres*, ed. D. Allen Carroll (Chapel Hill: University of North Carolina Press, 1974), Satire 1, ll. 63–64, 72–74.

[42] Bacon, *Declaration*, sig. B1r.   [43] Quoted in McCabe, "Elizabethan Satire," 188.

[44] Arber, *Transcript*, 3:678.

[45] Clegg, *Press Censorship*, 198–217. For other explanations of the ban, see McCabe, "Elizabethan Satire"; Lynda E. Boose, "The 1599 Bishops' Ban, Elizabethan Pornography, and the Sexualization of the Jacobean Stage," in *Enclosure Acts: Sexuality, Property, and Culture in Early Modern England*, ed. Richard Burt and John Michael Archer (Ithaca: Cornell University Press, 1994), 185–200; and William R. Jones, "The Bishops' Ban of 1599 and the Ideology of English Satire," *Literature Compass* 7.5 (2010): 332–46.

[46] Clegg, *Press Censorship*, 211–15.

the Elizabethan regime found there to be too much truth in such satirical "Shadowe[s] of Truth."[47]

Yet Essex continued to haunt satire on the stage and on the page – not least of all in Weever's *Whipping of the Satyre*. Not only does Weever enthusiastically endorse the government's repressive measures, but he even casts the satirists as coconspirators in the earl's rising. He not-so-subtly rehearses this allegation near the beginning of the prefatory epistle. After recounting how the satirists' commission was "put downe in the house of office" – perhaps alluding to the Bishops' Ban – Weever describes what would have happened if they had been allowed to proceed unchecked (12–13). He writes to the satirists, "had ye gone forward with approbation, as ye began with presumption, ye would shortly haue proued as mischieuous to the Inhabitants of England, as Tyrone hath bene to the Frontiers of Ireland" (13–16). In 1601, it would have been impossible to read these lines without thinking of Essex's alleged treason. As I mentioned above, Essex was sent to Ireland in March 1599 to put down the Earl of Tyrone's revolt but instead forged what Egerton branded "a private and secrete Composicion" with the Irish rebel.[48] This ill-advised truce was central to the propaganda churned out in the weeks following the rising. The very first of the "divers treasonable actions" that the government publicly attributed to Essex and his accomplices was that they "had laid plots with the traitor Tyrone."[49] By describing the satirists as English Tyrones, Weever implicates them in Essex's "treasonable actions" against the Elizabethan state.

Weever's allusions to the Essex Rising and its libelous fallout reveal just how thoroughly the figure of the earl had permeated the literary scene by 1601. This was true not only of printed and scribal verse but also of the London theater. Any regular playgoer in late Elizabethan and early Jacobean London would have encountered references to Essex's late career, some veiled and others decidedly less so. Such allusions appear in plays by

---

[47] For the licensing of *Skialetheia*, see Arber, *Transcript*, 3:126.   [48] TNA, SP 12/273, fol. 62v.

[49] *TRP*, 3:230, 231. This became the official refrain: Robert Cecil declared in Star Chamber that Essex and Tyrone had planned to "Ioyne their forces" and depose the Queen, and preachers were instructed to allege that Essex had been "plottinge with [Tyrone] all his traitorous intentions" (TNA, SP 12/278, fols. 91r, 108r). The regime's public relations campaign may not have been particularly successful, however. The day before Essex's execution, the prolific letter-writer John Chamberlain reported, "I must needes say that one thing sticks much in many mens mindes, that whereas divers preachers were commaunded the Sunday before to deliver to the people among his other treasons that he had complotted with Tirone . . . there was no such matter once mentioned at [Essex's] arraignment, and yet there was time enough for yt" (*The Letters of John Chamberlain*, ed. Norman Egbert McClure, 2 vols. [Philadelphia: American Philosophical Society, 1939], 1:120). See Gajda, *Earl of Essex*, 36.

184   Libels on the Elizabethan Stage

Jonson, Shakespeare, Heywood, Thomas Dekker, George Chapman, Samuel Daniel, and Gervase Markham.[50] "On the public stages," Jeffrey S. Doty argues, "Essex was a by-word for heroism and generosity to the commons" – at least before his fortunes sharply declined.[51] Essex himself eventually realized that he had lost all control of his public persona. In a May 1600 letter to the queen, he lamented (perhaps a little disingenuously) that he was now the hot topic of popular discourse: "The prating tavern-ha[u]nter speaks of me what he list: the frantick libeller writes of me what he list; alredy they print me, & make speake to *th*e world; and shortlye they will play me in what formes they list vpon *th*e stage."[52] This carefully constructed sentence moves from tavern talk to manuscript libel to printed polemic to theatrical performance – roughly the trajectory that I traced in my first chapter. This is not to say that libels always emerged from popular gossip and reached their apotheosis in performance. Yet Essex's mind moves in the direction of increasing publicity, and that movement takes him to the stage.

Up to the very end, Essex's supporters tried to exploit the publicity of the theater. We don't know exactly why a group of the earl's followers commissioned the Lord Chamberlain's Men to perform *Richard II* at the Globe on the eve of the Essex Rising.[53] But scholars have long taken Shakespeare's account of Bolingbroke's "courtship to the common people" to allude to Essex's popularity.[54] This allusion may have been oblique in 1595, the likely date of the play's composition, but it would have been unmistakable in 1601.

Certainly the parallel between Essex and Bolingbroke deeply concerned the authorities. Within weeks of the rising, the actor Augustine Phillips – like Shakespeare, a principal member of the Chamberlain's Men and a shareholder in the Globe – was interrogated by Popham and two other

---

[50] Grace Ioppolo, "Robert Devereux, 2nd Earl of Essex, and the Practice of Theatre," in *Essex: The Cultural Impact of an Elizabethan Courtier*, ed. Annaliese Connolly and Lisa Hopkins (Manchester: Manchester University Press, 2013), 73–74. Ioppolo downplays the significance of the evidence that she gathers, arguing (to my mind unconvincingly) that the host of what she calls "minor" references do not mean that "dramatists wrote plays with embedded clues, explicit references or consistent patterns of references to Essex" (73, 74).

[51] Jeffrey S. Doty, *Shakespeare, Popularity and the Public Sphere* (Cambridge: Cambridge University Press, 2017), 38.

[52] TNA, SP 12/274, fol. 232r.

[53] See Hammer, "Shakespeare's *Richard II*"; Gajda, *Earl of Essex*, 50–51, 244–51; and my discussion in Chapter 5 above.

[54] Shakespeare, *King Richard II*, ed. Charles R. Forker (London: Arden Shakespeare, 2002), 1.4.24. See Doty, *Shakespeare*, 45–46. These lines were probably the source for Guilpin's satirical sketch of "great *Foelix*" (*Skialetheia*, 157–59).

Satire and Sedition in Jonson's Poetaster

judges.[55] While the actors apparently suffered no penalty, their performance gave the government a useful piece of propaganda. Attorney General Edward Coke cited it as evidence of the defendants' treasonous intent at the trial of Essex's followers, and Francis Bacon disseminated that claim in his printed justification of the regime's proceedings. Essex's steward, Sir Gelly Meyrick, shouldered most of the blame. "So earnest hee was to satisfie his eyes with the sight of that Tragedie," Bacon writes of Meyrick, "which hee thought soone after his Lord should bring from the Stage to the State."[56] This was probably not the most accurate assessment of Meyrick's motives.[57] Regardless of its veracity, however, Bacon's claim articulates two crucial facts of the late Elizabethan public sphere. First, what Bacon a decade before had called "the stile of the stage" continued – in both a comic and a tragic vein – to shape political culture.[58] And second, when poems or plays veered too close to matters of state between 1599 and 1601, the Earl of Essex was more often than not the subject or the cause.

"Rebellion Now": The Theater of Treason

Essex's prophecy – "shortlye they will play me in what formes they list vpon *the* stage" – was soon fulfilled by Jonson himself. *Cynthia's Revels*, first performed at the Blackfriars in late 1600 or early 1601, does not bring Essex in person onstage. But Jonson does allude to the earl's recent tribulations in another form: through the mythological figure Actaeon, turned into a stag by Diana and torn to pieces by his own hounds for stumbling upon the goddess bathing.[59] Indeed, the play's central conceit, the revels of the goddess Cynthia (also known as Diana), is motivated by a wave of defamatory criticism not unlike the one that Elizabeth faced from 1599 to 1601. In the first scene, Cupid reports that "Diana, in regard of some black and envious slanders hourly breathed against her for her divine justice on Actaeon, as she pretends, hath here in the vale of Gargaphie proclaimed

[55] TNA, SP 12/278, fol. 139r. For a transcription, see E. K. Chambers, *William Shakespeare: A Study of Facts and Problems*, 2 vols. (Oxford: Clarendon Press, 1930), 2:325. On Phillips, see Peter Thomson, "Phillips, Augustine (*d.* 1605)," *ODNB*, online ed. (Oxford University Press, 2006).

[56] Bacon, *Declaration*, sig. K3r. See Chambers, *William Shakespeare*, 2:325–26.

[57] Hammer, "Shakespeare's *Richard II*," 19–20; Jonathan Bate, "Was Shakespeare an Essex Man?" *Proceedings of the British Academy* 162 (2009): 4–9.

[58] Bacon, *An advertisement touching the controuersyes of the Church of England*, in *The Oxford Francis Bacon*, vol. 1, ed. Alan Stewart with Harriet Knight (Oxford: Clarendon Press, 2012), 163.

[59] See Dutton, *Mastering*, 132–33; Janet Clare, "Jonson's 'Comical Satires' and the Art of Courtly Compliment," in *Refashioning Ben Jonson*, ed. Sanders, Chedgzoy, and Wiseman, 36–37; and, especially, Hester Lees-Jeffries, *England's Helicon: Fountains in Early Modern Literature and Culture* (Oxford: Oxford University Press, 2007), 255–78.

186 Libels on the Elizabethan Stage

a solemn revels" (1.1.68–70). So too were the queen's proceedings against Essex, both before and after his death, dogged by what the regime considered "black and envious slanders." More than a hint of skepticism about Cynthia's – and Elizabeth's – so-called "justice" seems to lurk in the qualifying phrase "as she pretends."[60] When Cynthia herself comes onstage to justify Actaeon's fate, she imperiously warns, "Let suffice / That we take notice and can take revenge / Of these calumnious and lewd blasphemies" (5.5.117–19). The revels have apparently failed to counter the tide of defamation, and "justice" gives way to "revenge."

In *Poetaster* – his next play – Jonson develops this ambivalent allegory into a scathing satire of the regime's crackdown on illicit speech. The play fittingly begins by reviving one of the poems proscribed by the Bishops' Ban two years before. Among the works prohibited were two collections of poetry printed together (likely under a false imprint) in the mid-late 1590s: "Davyes Epigrams, with marlowes Elegyes."[61] *Poetaster*'s opening lines come from Marlowe's *Elegies*, a posthumously published translation of Ovid's *Amores*. Ovid himself takes the stage, reciting Jonson's revision of Marlowe's translation of an Ovidian elegy: "Then, when this body falls in funeral fire, / My name shall live, and my best part aspire" (1.1.1–2). Defying the bishops' "funeral fire" (book burning) of 1599, Jonson smuggles Marlovian verse into Augustan Rome.[62]

Soon after this implicit criticism of state censorship, Jonson introduces Rome's prime censor: the tribune Asinius Lupus. Ovid's father bursts in with Captain Tucca and Lupus in tow. Railing against his son's career choice, Ovid senior laments, "Verses? Poetry? Ovid, whom I thought to see the pleader, become Ovid the play-maker?" (1.2.6–7). Lupus seconds the attack on the theater:

> Indeed, Marcus Ovid, these players are an idle generation and do much harm in a state, corrupt young gentry very much; I know it; I have not been a tribune thus long and observed nothing. Besides, they will rob us, us that are magistrates, of our respect, bring us upon their stages and make us ridiculous to the plebeians; they will play you, or me, the wisest men they

---

[60] See Lees-Jeffries, *England's Helicon*, 269.

[61] Quoted in McCabe, "Elizabethan Satire," 188. On the book's complicated textual history, see Roma Gill and Robert Krueger, "The Early Editions of Marlowe's Elegies and Davies's Epigrams: Sequence and Authority," *The Library*, 5th ser., 26.3 (1971): 242–49; and Fredson Bowers, "The Early Editions of Marlowe's *Ovid's Elegies*," *Studies in Bibliography* 25 (1972): 149–72.

[62] See Howard Erskine-Hill, *The Augustan Idea in English Literature* (London: Edward Arnold, 1983), 111–12; Tom Cain, introduction to Jonson, *Poetaster*, ed. Cain (Manchester: Manchester University Press, 1995), 19; and Jane Rickard, "'To Strike the Ear of Time': Ben Jonson's *Poetaster* and the Temporality of Art," *Renaissance Drama* 48.1 (2020): 64–65.

Satire and Sedition in Jonson's Poetaster 187

can come by, still – me! – only to bring us in contempt with the vulgar and make us cheap. (1.2.28–34)

These are the first words spoken by the first (and, for much of the play, the only) representative of the Roman government to appear onstage. At least for the moment, Lupus seems to articulate the official stance of the Augustan regime. And that stance could hardly be clearer: players "do much harm in a state."

As he expounds the subversive threat of the theater, this Roman magistrate sounds very much like his early modern counterparts. Just as some libelers (in the words of William Hudson) mock their victim "by the personating him, thereby to make him ridiculous," so Lupus complains that the players "bring us upon their stages and make us ridiculous to the plebeians."[63] In Chapter 2, I traced the politics of personation across England. Around 1600 it would not have been unusual to see living people, including magistrates, impersonated on the London stage – not least of all at the height of the War of the Theaters in 1601. Jonson himself brings his rival playwrights John Marston and Thomas Dekker onstage in the guise of the titular poetasters (hack-poets), Crispinus and Demetrius. Demetrius in turn is hired "to abuse Horace and bring him in in a play with all his gallants," an allusion to Dekker's forthcoming return salvo, *Satiromastix* (1601) (3.4.262–63). *Poetaster* dizzyingly stages the Poetomachia (to use Dekker's term) in which it participates.

But it was not the Poets' War that had the authorities so on edge at the turn of the century. Like Lupus, they were principally concerned with the personation of those whom Jonson called "great ones": gentlemen, nobles, and magistrates. In May 1601, just months before *Poetaster*'s first performance, the Privy Council ordered Middlesex's JPs to investigate reports that players at the Curtain "do represent upon the stage in their interludes the persons of some gentlemen of good desert and quallity that are yet alive under obscure manner, but yet in such sorte as all the hearers may take notice both of the matter and the persons that are meant thereby."[64] Lupus makes the same complaint. "They will play you, or me, the wisest men they can come by," he grumbles. In a reputation-driven society like Jonson's Rome or Elizabethan England, defamatory personation threatens the authority of the good and the great.

---

[63] William Hudson, *A Treatise of the Court of Star Chamber*, in *Collectanea Juridica*, ed. Francis Hargrave, vol. 2 (London, 1792), 100.

[64] *APC*, 31:346, reproduced in E. K. Chambers, *The Elizabethan Stage*, 4 vols. (Oxford: Clarendon Press, 1923), 4:332.

188   Libels on the Elizabethan Stage

The threat was especially acute for public figures. To cite a complaint
nearly contemporary with *Poetaster*, the Earl of Lincoln alleged in
November 1601 that his nephew Tailboys Dymoke – the same Tailboys
Dymoke whose pseudonymous *Caltha Poetarum* was proscribed by the
Bishops' Ban – contrived "The Death of the Lord of Kyme" "to scandalize
and dishonor your said Subiect and to bring him into the scorne and
Contempte of the vulgar people."[65] Lupus makes a similar claim: that the
players intend "to bring us in contempt with the vulgar and make us
cheap." Amid the surge of libeling in 1599, the queen's privy councilors
used the same language to describe the danger of libels. Lord Chief Justice
Popham, for example, claimed that "the purpose of these Libellors is . . . by
defaming and disgracing these in authoritie, so to bring them in Contempt
not to be obeyed though they ruled."[66] This fear of viral disobedience
underlies Lupus' claim that the players "will rob us, us that are magistrates,
of our respect . . . and make us ridiculous to the plebeians." And as Popham
explains, the upshot of popular contempt for authority is dire indeed: "to
sett sedicion betwixt the Prince and the Subiectes, which is the kindling of
all rebellions."[67]

Of course, we are not meant to sympathize with Lupus in the least. He is
a "turbulent informer," one of those "officious spies" or "moths and scarabs
of a state" (5.3.13, 4.7.54, 40); he is (as his name Asinius Lupus indicates) an
"ass" and a "wolf" (5.3.80, 4.7.51). Indeed, his methods are precisely those
prescribed by Envy in *Poetaster*'s induction. "For I am risse here with
a covetous hope," Envy gloats,

> To blast your pleasures and destroy your sports
> With wrestings, comments, applications,
> Spy-like suggestions, privy whisperings,
> And thousand such promoting sleights as these.   (22–26)

As critics have pointed out, Envy here invokes the early modern "culture of
informing."[68] Informers, spies, and magistrates relentlessly sought out the
nefarious plots supposedly concocted by seditious subjects, many of them
(like Jonson in 1601) Catholics. Several years later, Barnabe Barnes would

---

[65] James Stokes, ed., *REED: Lincolnshire*, 2 vols. (Toronto: University of Toronto Press, 2009), 1:269.
[66] TNA, SP 12/273, fol. 73r.   [67] Ibid.
[68] Angus, *Metadrama*, 118. See also Norbert H. Platz, "Ben Jonson's *Ars Poetica*: An Interpretation of
Poetaster in Its Historical Context," *Salzburg Studies in English Literature* 12 (1973): 14–15;
John Michael Archer, *Sovereignty and Intelligence: Spying and Court Culture in the English
Renaissance* (Stanford: Stanford University Press, 1993), 98–100; Alan Sinfield, "*Poetaster*, the
Author, and the Perils of Cultural Production," *Renaissance Drama* 27 (1996): 7; and Smuts,
"Jonson's *Poetaster*."

Satire and Sedition in Jonson's Poetaster

condemn the insidious reach of state surveillance in similar terms. He lists among the signs of tyranny "[t]he dispersing through all places of the Commonwealth priuie whisperers & informers, for the secret groping and mining into the peopels hearts."[69] For Jonson as for Barnes, these spies are the corrupt instruments of a tyrannical state.

The explosion of libeling around Essex only intensified the atmosphere of suspicion and paranoia. In their November 1599 Star Chamber speeches, Elizabeth's chief ministers not only condemned the libelers but also admonished the queen's subjects to report any libelous or seditious talk to the authorities. Egerton took pains to correct the evident misconception "that to be hearers or present at such sedicious discourses, or to knowe of the making and contriving of such Libells, is a small offence or none at all." He instead argues that the audiences are at least as culpable as the authors – a claim that Jonson, given his repeated complaints about people turning his plays into libels, evidently would have endorsed. "But lett none be deceaued," Egerton warned, "for whosoeu*er* doth but praebere aures [listen], and doe conceale and not discou*er* such Talkers and discoursers, and such sedicious Libellors, ... cannot be deemed, but as maynteyners and favourers of the same, and to be punished as severely, as the principall Actors."[70] Where Egerton threatened, Popham appealed to patriotic duty. "Therefore lett noe man heare of this," the Lord Chief Justice concluded, "as yf he weare not concerned in it, yf he wish well vnto his Country, but lett eu*erie* man thinck him self interessed in this cause, and give his dilligence to the fynding out of these Vipers in the Com*m*on Wealth."[71] Egerton and Popham want to see a nation of spies and informers, a country in which "eu*erie* man" does his part to root out libelers.

So too does Lupus. Based on intelligence from player-informers, the tribune charges two of Rome's leading poets with grave crimes against the state: Ovid with treason and Horace with seditious libel. Ovid is the first to suffer the magistrate's "wrestings, comments, applications," as Envy calls them. Behind closed doors, the actor Histrio tips Lupus off to an alleged "conspiracy": Ovid and his fellow poets have borrowed props from the player's company in order to stage a banquet of the gods (4.4.12). Cain convincingly argues that Lupus' questioning of Histrio "allude[s] in a very straightforward way" to Popham's examination of Augustine Phillips in the wake of the Essex Rising: both the Elizabethan

[69] Barnabe Barnes, *Foure Bookes of Offices* (London, 1606), sig. R2v.
[70] TNA, SP 12/273, fol. 61r.   [71] Ibid., fol. 73r.

190 Libels on the Elizabethan Stage

judge and the Roman tribune interrogate an actor "in search of conspiracy and rebellion."[72] Lupus takes only a moment to reflect on the props before reaching the same conclusion as did the Elizabethan regime. "A crown and a sceptre? This is good! Rebellion now?" he muses (4.4.18). Like Bacon, Lupus imagines the theater of treason migrating "from the Stage to the State."

Ironically, Lupus – who railed against players in the first act – wants to play a self-aggrandizing part of his own in that political theater. The tribune calls for his "buskins," the boots of the Greek tragedian, and blusters, "I'll act a tragedy, i'faith" (4.4.13, 14). Swelling with self-importance, he struts off the stage crying, "Treason! Treason!" (4.4.38). But this incipient tragedy quickly becomes (at least for Lupus) a "Comicall Satyre," as Jonson labeled *Poetaster* in the 1616 folio.[73] Enraged by the poets' "impious" personation of the gods – not to mention his own daughter Julia's starring role in the "pageant" – Augustus confines Julia and banishes Ovid on pain of death (4.6.8, 15). Lupus, however, comes away empty-handed. Horace and Maecenas ridicule the tribune's venal motives:

HORACE Nay, why pursue you not the emperor
  For your reward now, Lupus?

MAECENAS   Stay, Asinius,
  You and your stager and your band of lictors.
  I hope your service merits more respect
  Than thus, without a thanks, to be sent hence! (4.7.26–30)

Instead of acting a tragedy, Lupus finds himself the object of the satirist's scorn.

As Lupus stands silently by, Horace launches into a tirade against corrupt magistrates and informers like him. "Such as thou," the satirist bitterly remarks,

> They are the moths and scarabs of a state,
> The bane of empires, and the dregs of courts;
> Who, to endear themselves to any employment,
> Care not whose fame they blast, whose life they endanger;
> And under a disguised and cobweb mask
> Of love unto their sovereign, vomit forth
> Their own prodigious malice.   (4.7.39–46)

---

[72] Cain, "Satyres," 63, 64.   [73] Jonson, *Poetaster*, ed. Gabriele Bernhard Jackson, in *CWBJ*, 2:19.

Maecenas completes the scathing portrait by implicating the emperor himself in the paranoid political climate that prevails when informers and spies get the ear of the prince:

> Princes that will but hear or give access
> To such officious spies can ne'er be safe:
> They take in poison with an open ear,
> And, free from danger, become slaves to fear. (4.7.53–56)

Horace and Maecenas sharply contrast the poets' "innocent mirth" with the malignant machinations of Lupus and his ilk (4.7.37). Such spies lurk about the court, indiscriminately "blast[ing]" reputations and "endanger-[ing]" lives; they mask their "prodigious malice" under a show of "love unto their sovereign." And given that the emperor himself has just "hear[d]" and "give[n] access" to Lupus, Maecenas' closing lines clearly blame the prince – Augustus and, in a Rome that closely resembles Jonson's London, perhaps even Elizabeth.[74] Jonson himself echoes Maecenas' lines in *Discoveries*, remarking that "the merciful prince is safe in love, not in fear. He needs no emissaries, spies, intelligencers, to entrap true subjects. He fears no libels, no treasons" (852–53). At this point in the play, we have seen much scheming by "emissaries, spies, intelligencers, to entrap true subjects" and no evidence of Augustus' mercy. Horace and Maecenas suggest that the real threat to the state is not the satirist nor even the libeler but instead the malicious plots of corrupt informers.

Jonson himself already had firsthand experience with officious spies when he wrote *Poetaster* in 1601. In 1597, an impoverished informant brought a "sedyceoos [seditious] play *Cawlled The Ile of doggs*" to the attention of the infamous interrogator Richard Topcliffe.[75] Several players were soon arrested, including one who "was not only an actor but a maker of parte of the said plaie": Ben Jonson.[76] Even in prison Jonson was not safe from spies and informers. Years later, he would tell William Drummond that the authorities "placed two damned villains to catch advantage of him, with him, but he was advertised by his keeper" (*Informations*, 193–97).[77] Having narrowly escaped the spies in 1597, Jonson dramatizes Envy's

---

[74] See Lynn S. Meskill, *Ben Jonson and Envy* (Cambridge: Cambridge University Press, 2009), 102–3.

[75] CP 54/20, quoted in Misha Teramura, "Richard Topcliffe's Informant: New Light on *The Isle of Dogs*," *Review of English Studies* 68 (2017): 48. Teramura convincingly identifies the informant as William Udall. In his biography of Jonson, Ian Donaldson speculates that the play (which has not survived) may have been "a political satire . . . generally friendly to Essex, and tactlessly critical of the Cecils" (*Ben Jonson: A Life* [Oxford: Oxford University Press, 2011], 122).

[76] *APC*, 27:338, reproduced in Chambers, *Elizabethan Stage*, 4:323.

[77] See Mark Eccles, "Jonson and the Spies," *Review of English Studies* 13 (1937): 385–97.

192   Libels on the Elizabethan Stage

efforts to catch him once more in *Poetaster*'s induction.[78] "Help me to
damn the author," Envy urges the audience, casting about "snakes" and
"vipers" "to forge, and then declaim, / Traduce, corrupt, apply, inform,
suggest" (46, 44, 49, 53–54). For Jonson, the real "vipers" are not (as
Popham and the other privy councilors claimed) seditious libelers but
rather the envious informers who accuse him of libel.[79]

No one takes up Envy's call, however. As she sinks despondently back
down to hell, an armed Prologue strides onstage and triumphantly plants
his foot on her head. The Prologue then explains his armor:

> 'tis a dangerous age,
> Wherein who writes had need present his scenes
> Forty-fold proof against the conjuring means
> Of base detractors and illiterate apes.   (67–70)

It was "a dangerous age" indeed for the likes of Jonson – and it would have
been more dangerous still if Weever had his way and satirists were hanged
for libel. But Jonson remained defiant. London and its playhouses may
have teemed with informers and detractors, but the playwright stridently
insisted on his play's "innocence" ("To ... Richard Martin," 4). His
protestations, however, are no more convincing than were those of the
verse satirists of the late 1590s.[80] Indeed, *Poetaster*'s induction cues the
audience to look for the very topical analogies that it denounces.
The allegorical encounter between the Prologue and Envy – between the
play and its critics – only underscores Jonson's imbrication in the "dangerous age" of 1601.

In *Poetaster*, then, Jonson skewers the regime's reaction to the
supposedly seditious literature caught up in Essex's fall. The echoes
of Popham's proceedings against both libelers and players are particularly suggestive. In a dedicatory letter printed in the 1616 folio, Jonson
indicates (as I noted above) that the play landed him in trouble with
Popham himself. He thanks "My Worthy Friend, Master Richard
Martin" for saving the play, "for whose innocence, as for the author's,
you were once a noble and timely undertaker to the greatest justice of
this kingdom" (4–6). Although no records of any legal or political
repercussions survive, scholars agree that "the greatest justice of this

---

[78] John Michael Archer goes so far as to argue that *Poetaster* is "a satirical fantasia upon its author's
recent experiences with *The Isle of Dogs* and the accusations and counteraccusations of the 'war of the
theaters'" (*Sovereignty and Intelligence*, 98).
[79] For a similar argument, see Smuts, "Jonson's *Poetaster*," 243.
[80] See Vivier, "Judging Jonson," 16–17.

kingdom" is Popham, Lord Chief Justice of England until his death in 1607.[81] The Chief Justice is unlikely to have missed the satirical commentary on his recent activities. Whatever the nature of Martin's intervention, however, it was apparently enough to exonerate Jonson.[82]

Jonson does not say exactly what (or who) brought the play to Popham's attention. But the remainder of his prefatory letter links *Poetaster*'s contentious history to the prevalence of malign interpreting in the play's Rome and in Jonson's England. According to Jonson, it was the "ignorance and malice of the times" that "conspired to have [the play] suppressed" (8–9). This is precisely the language that Jonson's Virgil and Horace use to excoriate informers and venal magistrates. Horace lambasts the "prodigious malice" of Lupus and his ilk; Virgil condemns "the sinister application / Of the malicious, ignorant, and base / Interpreter" (4.7.46, 5.3.120–22). If not for Martin, Jonson suggests, he would have fallen victim to the same sort of malicious interpreters who had ensnared him for his part in *The Isle of Dogs*.

The irony, of course, is that Jonson decries informing and interpreting in a play filled with topical, and even libelous, allusions.[83] Anyone who wanted to turn the play into a libel would have found no shortage of parallels to the present. To vindicate his satire from accusations of libel, Jonson would have to deny his own topical commentary. And so he does in *Poetaster*'s induction – and so Horace does in the play's last scene, the subject of my final section. Horace quite literally assumes the office of the "Satyrshippe," to borrow Weever's coinage, in order to accuse and punish his envious detractors. Yet Horace's satire, like Jonson's, hinges on its proximity to the libeling that he supposedly detests. The playwright and his metadramatic persona play the same dangerous game. Under the shadow of Augustan (and Elizabethan) censorship, I will now argue, Horace shows how author and audience might together turn a play into a libel.

---

[81] See, e.g., David Riggs, *Ben Jonson: A Life* (Cambridge, MA: Harvard University Press, 1989), 80; Dutton, *Mastering*, 139; Cain, "Satyres," 49; and Donaldson, *Ben Jonson*, 170–71.

[82] Martin, like the Chief Justice some forty years his elder, was a Middle Templar. The two men evidently enjoyed some sort of personal relationship around the time of *Poetaster*'s first performance. In July 1601, Chamberlain related that Popham and Cecil "have taken great paines to compound the quarrell twixt Martin and [John] Davies" (*Letters*, 1:126). See Douglas Walthew Rice, *The Life and Achievements of Sir John Popham, 1531–1607* (Madison, NJ: Fairleigh Dickinson University Press, 2005), 161.

[83] Many critics have pointed this out: see, e.g., Kaplan, *Culture*, 85–91; O'Callaghan, *English Wits*, 42–44; Angus, *Metadrama*, 115–33; and Smuts, "Jonson's *Poetaster*," 244–45.

194 Libels on the Elizabethan Stage

A Libel in Greek

For the play's characters and for modern scholars alike, the interpretive crux of *Poetaster*'s climactic scene is an image that Jonson's audience may never get to see. Lupus bursts into the emperor's palace, interrupting Virgil's reading from his "famous *Aeneids*" (5.2.6). At first, Augustus dismisses this "turbulent informer" and his "officious tongue" (5.3.13, 15). But when Lupus claims that his "business ... may concern the life of Caesar," the emperor immediately changes his mind (5.3.19–20). "The life of Caesar? Let him enter," Augustus commands (5.3.21). The emperor's self-absorbed response confirms Maecenas' diagnosis of those paranoid princes who "will but hear or give access / To such officious spies": "They take in poison with an open ear, / And, free from danger, become slaves to fear."[84] Envy's vipers poison the prince once more.

Granted access to the emperor, Lupus arrests Horace and Maecenas, and produces the evidence of their crime: a so-called "libel" (5.3.35). But while Lupus offers the paper as a clear sign of their guilt, its meaning is not at all transparent to Augustus. The emperor asks, "What is this, Asinius Lupus? I understand it not" (5.3.34). Lupus responds incredulously, "Not understand it? A libel, Caesar. A dangerous, seditious libel! A libel in picture" (5.3.35–36). Several years later, Attorney General Coke would note that a libel "may be ... *Picturis* [in pictures], as to paint the party in any shameful and ignominious manner."[85] This is Horace and Maecenas' alleged offense. "I challenge the penalty of the laws against 'em!" the tribune exclaims (5.3.38–39). Arrogating interpretive authority from both poet and sovereign, Lupus conscripts the law of libel into the service of his inquisition against the poets.

In Jonson's England, things might very well have ended badly for the satirist accused of libel. From the Bishops' Ban in 1599 to Waterhouse's execution in 1601, Elizabeth and her ministers moved vigorously to suppress satire and libeling. As discussed above, Jonson himself ended up in prison for his part in *The Isle of Dogs* – allegedly a "lewd plaie ... contanynge very seditious and sclanderous matter" – and in 1605 he was again imprisoned for cowriting an offensive play, *Eastward Ho!*[86] The problem of misinterpretation was as urgent for the playwright as it is for his Horace.

---

[84] See Victoria Moul, *Jonson, Horace and the Classical Tradition* (Cambridge: Cambridge University Press, 2010), 157–58.

[85] *De libellis famosis* (1605), 5 Co. Rep. 125b, adapting William West, *Three Treatises, Of the second part of Symbolaeographie* (London, 1594), sigs. I1v–I2r.

[86] *APC*, 27:338, reproduced in Chambers, *Elizabethan Stage*, 4:323.

Satire and Sedition in Jonson's Poetaster

In a remarkable series of letters written during his 1605 confinement, Jonson suggests just how perilous the satirist's pursuit could be. "It hath ever been my destiny to be misreported and condemned on the first tale," he laments to Thomas Howard, Earl of Suffolk ("Letters from Prison" 2, 16–17). We might take this to be hyperbole were it not for his earlier run-ins with the authorities over *The Isle of Dogs* and *Poetaster*. Indeed, the prison letters underscore *Poetaster*'s biographical relevance. Recalling the malicious wresting, applying, and interpreting dramatized in (and subsequently directed at) his earlier play, Jonson condemns those who "utter sometimes their own malicious meanings under our words" and complains that he has been imprisoned "without examining, without hearing, or without any proof, but malicious rumour" ("Letters from Prison" 3, 20; 5, 11–12). Such seems to be the fate of Horace and Maecenas, who are apprehended even before Lupus has leveled his accusation of libel against them. And the tribune is identified with "malicious rumour" from the moment he rushes onto the stage and interrupts Virgil's anatomy of the monster *Fama* – "Fame" or "rumour" (5.2.75, 69).[87]

Unlike in England, however, the satirist in Jonson's Rome receives a full hearing. Horace rebukes the "foolish tribune" and defies the entire apparatus of the surveillance state: "the malice of traducing tongues, / The open vastness of a tyrant's ear, / The senseless rigour of the wrested laws," "the red eyes of strained authority" (5.3.49, 50–52, 53).[88] Against these malign forces of misinterpretation, he defends his work as "the imperfect body of an emblem" that he began for Maecenas (5.3.45). Renaissance emblems joined image and text in all sorts of ways, but their typical form consisted of a picture preceded by a brief motto and followed by an explanatory epigram.[89] The picture was known as the "body" and the words as the "soul."[90] Horace's "imperfect body" is an image without the poetic exegesis.

Ever the malicious interpreter, Lupus accepts Horace's claim but plunges ahead nonetheless. "An emblem? Right. That's Greek for a libel," he declares, betraying his own ignorance (5.3.47). He seizes the paper and identifies its image as an eagle that (he claims) clearly represents

---

[87] See Erskine-Hill, *Augustan Idea*, 120; and Moul, *Jonson*, 158.   [88] See Sinfield, "*Poetaster*," 9–10.

[89] Peter M. Daly, "Emblems: An Introduction," in *Companion to Emblem Studies*, ed. Daly (New York: AMS Press, 2008), 1–3. On the varieties of the emblem, see also Michael Bath, *Speaking Pictures: English Emblem Books and Renaissance Culture* (London: Longman, 1994); and John Manning, *The Emblem* (London: Reaktion Books, 2002).

[90] Jonson was well versed in this terminology: see D. J. Gordon, "Poet and Architect: The Intellectual Setting of the Quarrel between Ben Jonson and Inigo Jones," *Journal of the Warburg and Courtauld Institutes* 12 (1949): 154–56.

Caesar (5.3.56–58). But Horace once more has an answer ready. He asserts that the true meaning – "[t]he soul to my device" – lies in a couplet that he has not yet written down: "Thus, oft the base and ravenous multitude / Survive to share the spoils of fortitude" (5.3.65, 66–67). The bird, he says, is not an eagle but a vulture, depicted (alongside a wolf) "[p]reying upon the carcass of an ass" (5.3.79). As Maecenas explains, the ass "figure[s] . . . / Patience, frugality, and fortitude" (5.3.85–86). Horace and Maecenas construct an allegory of the long-suffering poet at the mercy of the multitude. But Lupus remains undaunted, modifying his interpretation to keep up with the evolving imagery. As Horace narrates the picture, he interjects, "A wolf? Good. That's I; I am the wolf. My name's Lupus; I am meant by the wolf" and "An ass? Good still: that's I, too. I am the ass. You mean me by the ass" (5.3.77–78, 80). Jonson stages an encounter between the authoritative (and authorial) interpreter and the "ridiculous commenter," as Horace calls the tribune (5.3.64).

This time, the poet comes out on top. Augustus unquestioningly accepts Horace's interpretation of the emblem and metes out poetic justice: whipping for the player who informed Lupus of the alleged libel and a pair of ass's ears for the tribune as a public sign of his "fierce credulity" (5.3.109). Countering Weever's *Whipping of the Satyre*, Jonson whips not the satirist but the informer who went after Horace. And, as Weever complained, the satirist's vindication paves the way for his elevation to the office of the "Satyrshippe." Rome's leading poets preside over a mock trial of the poetasters Crispinus and Demetrius (caricatures of Marston and Dekker, respectively). Horace himself "arrests them on the statute of calumny," and they are soon found guilty and duly punished (5.3.149). Although the official charge is that they have "gone about to deprave and calumniate the person and writings of Quintus Horatius Flaccus," Horace also aligns them with the surveillance state (5.3.188–90). "[S]uch speckled creatures as thyself," the satirist says, "Will carry tales, do basest offices, / . . . / . . . will reveal / Each secret that's committed to their trust" (5.3.284, 291, 293–94). Even when Jonson finally arraigns the poetasters for personal calumny, their covert political activities seem at least as egregious – and are certainly more damaging to the state, as Horace, Maecenas, and Virgil have already emphasized. Horace's allegations pull the personal abuse of the Poets' War into the play's derisive allegory of the Elizabethan spy system.

In light of this sustained satire of government surveillance, Lupus' interpretation of the emblem may not be as ridiculous as Horace claims. Whatever the satirist's intent, the ravenous wolf is a fitting figure for the predatory magistrate. And Horace and Maecenas do nothing to disabuse

Satire and Sedition in Jonson's Poetaster

Lupus of his claim to be the ass.[91] "Pray thee, leave braying then," Maecenas mocks; "If you will needs take it, I cannot with modesty give it from you," Horace jabs (5.3.81, 82–83). But Horace's emblem may be more seditious still; it may, as Lupus initially alleges, even strike at Caesar. Predatory birds commonly stood for oppressive rulers in early modern culture, and the tyrant in particular was often figured as a ravening wolf.[92] "It is entirely plausible," Alan Sinfield contends, "that [Horace] designed a satire on imperial exploitation, and saves himself with a quick-witted reinterpretation."[93] If there was any truth to the allegations behind his imprisonment for *The Isle of Dogs*, Jonson had to squirm out of a similar situation several years earlier. And that was in 1597, before the maelstrom of libel, satire, and censorship that erupted around the Earl of Essex. Lupus might misinterpret a satirical emblem as a seditious libel, but it's just as likely that Horace turns a libel into an emblem to save his own skin.

There is even an Essexian precedent for such a libelous emblem – and one produced in circles that Jonson himself may well have frequented. In November 1595, the Catholic priest and Essex follower Thomas Wright composed a series of satirical emblem verses directed against the earl's rivals at court. Most are animal allegories in the same vein as Horace's, including one featuring an "ould Asse" (representing William Cecil, Lord Burghley) and another with an eagle.[94] The emblems' precise purpose remains unclear, but their anti-Cecilian message is unmistakable. Jonson knew Wright. Not only did the playwright write a commendatory sonnet for Wright's 1604 edition of his treatise on the passions, but Wright was probably the priest who converted Jonson to Catholicism in prison in 1598. Scholars have likewise located Jonson in or at least adjacent to the Essex circle in the late 1590s.[95] Given his place in this Catholic and Essexian literary milieu, Jonson could easily have seen Wright's emblems for himself. But he would not have needed firsthand knowledge to understand how an emblem might bend toward factional libel in 1595, let alone in 1601.

In fact, Jonson himself slyly gestures toward the vanishingly fine line between satirical emblem and seditious libel. He does this through an etymological pun that, to my knowledge, has gone unnoticed by scholars

---

[91] See Cain, "Satyres," 63; Angus, *Metadrama*, 130; and Loxley and Robson, *Shakespeare*, 63.

[92] See, e.g., Robert Persons, *A Conference about the Next Succession to the Crowne of Ingland* ([Antwerp], 1594/5), sig. V4r; Barnes, *Foure Bookes*, sigs. I4v–K1r; Daniel Price, *Sauls Prohibition Staide* (London, 1609), sig. B4r; and Thomas Wilson, *A Christian Dictionarie* (London, 1612), sig. Mm6v.

[93] Sinfield, "*Poetaster*," 14.

[94] "Thomas Wright's Emblem Verses," in *Verse Libel*, ed. May and Bryson, 126, 128. On the politics of Wright's emblems, see Gajda, *Earl of Essex*, 131–38.

[95] Donaldson, *Ben Jonson*, 120–22, 138–44; Cain, "Satyres," 52–53.

198 Libels on the Elizabethan Stage

of *Poetaster*. When Lupus says that "emblem" is "Greek for a libel," he is revealing himself to be a "ridiculous commenter" (Horace's term) and an "ignorant ... / Interpreter" (Virgil's phrase). "Emblem," of course, is not Greek for "libel." Once more, however, the tribune is not as far off the mark as it at first seems. The Greek origins of the word "emblem" were well known. As Geffrey Whitney writes in his *Choice of Emblemes*, "this worde Embleme ... be borrowed of others, & not proper in the Englishe tonge, ... which worde being in Greeke ἐμβάλλεσθαι [*emballesthai*], vel ἐπεμβλῆσθαι [*epemblēsthai*] is as muche to saye in Englishe as *To set in, or to put in*."[96] This is not Greek for libel, but it is closer than it may appear to modern eyes. Libel or slander in Greek is διαβολή (*diabolē*), from διαβάλλειν (*diaballein*), meaning to throw across or to put through but also to accuse or to slander.[97] Emblem and *diabolē* thus derive from the same Greek root: βάλλειν (*ballein*), to throw or to put. Given (as we vividly see in *Titus*) that early modern libels were often themselves projectiles, it is fitting that the root should be a verb of forcible movement. In the words of one seventeenth-century preacher, "Slander hath its Name in Greek from thrusting thorough."[98] It is only the prefix – em- ("in") for emblem and dia- ("through") for *diabolē* – that separates an emblem from a libel.

The joke is not as abstruse as it might seem. Emblem books were enormously popular: thousands of editions were printed across Renaissance Europe in Latin and in the vernacular languages.[99] At least some of these, like Whitney's, traced the etymology of the word "emblem" for a broad readership.[100] The meaning of *diabolē* was likewise well known, largely through its English cognate, "devil." Preachers, theologians, and polemicists all derived the word "devil" from its Greek roots. "In Greeke his name is διάβολος [*diabolos*], a deuill, that is, a slanderer, because he falsly accuseth," reads an abridged translation of Jean Calvin's *Institutes*.[101]

---

[96] Geffrey Whitney, *A Choice of Emblemes, and Other Devises* (Leiden, 1586), sig. **4r.
[97] Henry George Liddell and Robert Scott, *A Greek-English Lexicon*, rev. Henry Stuart Jones with Roderick McKenzie (Oxford: Clarendon Press, 1940), s.v. "διαβάλλω."
[98] Thomas Willes, *A Word in Season, for a Warning to England* (London, 1659), sig. D1v.
[99] Peter M. Daly, *Literature in the Light of the Emblem: Structural Parallels between the Emblem and Literature in the Sixteenth and Seventeenth Centuries*, 2nd ed. (Toronto: University of Toronto Press, 1998), 211 n12.
[100] See, e.g., Joannes Sambucus, *Emblemata* (Antwerp, 1564), sig. A2r; and Andrea Alciato, *Emblemata / Les Emblemes* (Paris, 1584), sig. a7v.
[101] Johannes Piscator, *Aphorismes of Christian Religion: Or, A Verie Compendious abridgement of M. I. Calvins Institutions*, trans. Henry Holland (London, 1596), sig. C1v. For other examples, see George Gifford, *Certaine Sermons, upon Divers Textes of Holie Scripture* (London, 1597), sig. C4v; Hugh Broughton, *A Revelation of the Holy Apocalyps* ([Middleburg], 1610), sig. V1r; and George Webbe, *The Araignement of an vnruly Tongue* (London, 1619), sigs. G1or–G11v.

Satire and Sedition in Jonson's Poetaster

This etymology furnished the government and its allies with a powerful rhetorical device for stigmatizing alleged libelers. Matthew Sutcliffe, dean of Exeter, reminded his readers that the devil "is a raylour, and slaunderour, and so are all libellers, and reuellers, the right disciples of Sathan."[102] Invoking the Greek origins of "devil," Robert Cecil made the same point in his November 1599 speech in Star Chamber. Cecil, addressing the "false & wicked libles agaynst her Maiesties late proceedings," declared that "all vntrue speakers are naturall Children of the Devill (whoe for denomination of the word Diabolos is intituled the ffather of lyes)."[103] By leveling a supposedly false accusation against Horace, Lupus is doing the devil's work.

The etymological pun in Lupus' "That's Greek for a libel" could thus be taken in two ways. By unwittingly calling to mind *diabolē*, the actual Greek word for libel, Lupus reveals himself to be the *diabolos* – the slanderer, the false accuser, the devil. Jonson once more turns the regime's own rhetoric against it. The real "Children of the Devill," he implies, are not those poets who satirize the state but instead the malign inquisitors who seek them out. Yet the Greek etymology also suggests that an emblem and a libel are not so far apart. After all, the difference between an emblematic image and "a libel in picture," as Lupus calls it, lies in the eye of the beholder – and presumably Jonson's playgoers (and certainly his readers) do not see the emblem for themselves. The audience must instead assess the characters' competing interpretations and come to their own conclusions about its meaning, libelous or otherwise.

It is no accident that Jonson uses an emblem to dramatize the challenges and the perils of interpretation. The Renaissance emblem tradition, which he knew well, held that the form needed to be parsed carefully by the viewer.[104] Returning to the word's etymology, Joannes Sambucus observes that "'*emballesthai*' in Greek still means 'to insert,' 'present' something obscure that requires explanation and reflection."[105] Whitney similarly

---

[102] Matthew Sutcliffe, *An Answere to a Certaine Libel Supplicatorie, or Rather Diffamatory . . . put forth vnder the name and title of a Petition directed to her Maiestie* (London, 1592), sig. L4r.

[103] TNA, SP 12/273, fols. 69r, 69v.

[104] On Jonson and the emblem, see Alan R. Young, "The Emblematic Art of Ben Jonson," *Emblematica* 6 (1992): 17–36; and Robert C. Evans, "Jonson and the Emblematic Tradition: Ralegh, Brant, the Poems, *The Alchemist*, and *Volpone*," *Comparative Drama* 29.1 (1995): 108–32.

[105] Sambucus, *Emblemata*, sig. A2r, translated in A. S. Q. Visser, *Joannes Sambucus and the Learned Image: The Use of the Emblem in Late-Renaissance Humanism* (Leiden: Brill, 2005), 89, adapting the translation in Ari Wesseling, "Testing Modern Emblem Theory: The Earliest Views of the Genre (1564–1566)," in *The Emblem Tradition and the Low Countries*, ed. John Manning, Karel Porteman, and Marc van Vaeck (Turnhout: Brepols, 1999), 14.

posits that emblems contain "somethinge obscure to be perceiued at the first, whereby, when with further consideration it is vnderstood, it maie the greater delighte the beholder."[106] But how can that "somethinge obscure" be understood without the explanatory poem, the "soul to my device" (as Horace calls it)? Horace himself admits that his composition is "the imperfect body of an emblem," a picture with no poetry. In the absence of the couplet about "the base and ravenous multitude" that the satirist claims he was going to add, Lupus' interpretation is at least as plausible as Horace's.

Turning a play (or an emblem) into a libel, then, is not merely the business of malicious interpreters. Horace's emblem shows how a libel emerges from a dialogic exchange between author and audience. Like other instances of the genre, the obscure image "requires explanation and reflection." Jonson's Greek pun, along with the conflicting interpretations of the emblem that follow, reminds his playgoers and readers that they have their own part to play in the drama of interpretation. This is especially true of *Poetaster*'s initial run at the Blackfriars, an indoor theater frequented by Inns of Court men steeped in the cultures of classical and vernacular satire. Not only were these learned spectators primed to catch the multilingual joke, but they were also deeply involved in the libelous upheaval around Essex in the late 1590s.[107] Horace's emblem thus reproduces in miniature the logic of the satirical drama in which it appears. Apparently, the recipe for making a libel from an emblem or a play is as follows: 1) write a highly topical satire under the guise of a supposedly classical form; 2) deny any hint of libelous or seditious allusion; 3) wittily evoke that topical application at every turn, giving the audience plenty of material for libel-making. This game seems designed for "*Englands* wits," as Guilpin calls Inns of Court satirists like himself.[108] Perhaps Jonson's ideal audience would have been composed solely of people like Richard Martin, the Middle Templar who vouched for *Poetaster*'s innocence despite its obvious topicality.

Yet I think it would be wrong to conclude that the play's meaning was reserved for "Jonson's more sophisticated readers and spectators," as several critics have suggested.[109] Most of the topical analogies that I examined

---

[106] Whitney, *Choice*, sig. **4r.

[107] Christopher Highley, *Blackfriars in Early Modern London: Theater, Church, and Neighborhood* (Oxford: Oxford University Press, 2022), 133–34; O'Callaghan, *English Wits*, 31–34; Cain, "Satyres," 52–53.

[108] Guilpin, *Skialetheia*, Epigram 1, l. 9. O'Callaghan argues that the Inns of Court culture of learned play was an essential influence on Jonson's comedies (*English Wits*, 35–59).

[109] Smuts, "Jonson's *Poetaster*," 245. See also O'Callaghan, *English Wits*, 36–44; and Cain, "Satyres," 52, both of whom argue that the play was (in Cain's words) "clearly aimed at the Inns of Court."

Satire and Sedition in Jonson's Poetaster

above could have been grasped by a strikingly broad audience. Of course, the Greek pun was probably aimed at the kind of spectator or "reader extraordinary" whom Jonson addresses in the 1611 quarto of *Catiline* (although, as I discussed above, the etymologies of "emblem" and "devil" could be found in vernacular sources) ("To the Reader Extraordinary"). But it would not have taken any special learning to notice that the emblem's imagery of predatory animals echoed the populist rhetoric of the pulpit. And few Londoners could have ignored the waves of libels and government propaganda that surged through the city in the wake of the Essex Rising. Jonson's play, like Horace's emblem, demands application – and the playwright gives his audiences ample reason to apply it to the overzealous inquisitors of Elizabethan England.

Far from casting his audiences as his antagonists, Jonson instead makes them his collaborators in producing the kind of drama that Inigo Jones would decades later call a "Libell-play."[110] This symbiotic relationship between author and audience realizes Egerton's fiery warning that those who hear libels "and doe conceale and not discou*er* such Talkers and discoursers, and such sedicious Libellors, . . . cannot be deemed, but as maynteyners and favourers of the same." Jonson invites his audiences to join him in libeling government ministers and their pursuit of libel. And for Jonson as for Horace, the gravest threat to this satirical project comes not from popular playgoers but from well-connected enemies. In a scene printed only in the folio, the lawyer Trebatius warns Horace that "some great man's friend will be thy death" after Horace declares, "I will write satires still, in spite of fear" (3.5.102, 100).[111] Jonson too defies the judgment of the great even as he appeals to the judgment of his audiences – or at least to those complicit playgoers who saw his play and declined to "discou*er*" him to the authorities.

That is also the message of the play's closing song. Turning to the audience, the characters sing, "Here's none that fears / The wagging of an ass's ears, / Although a wolfish case he wears" (5.3.555–57). These verses apply the emblem's imagery to both Rome's and England's surveillance states. Horace's cryptic ass and wolf are now clearly identified with Lupus. The tribune's punishment has him outfitted with "a pair of larger [ass's] ears" befitting his praenomen, Asinius, and he still wears the "wolfish case" of his second name, Lupus (5.3.110). "A just man cannot fear," Horace had

---

[110] Inigo Jones, "To his False Friend mr: Ben Johnson," in *CWBJ Online* (Cambridge University Press, 2014), Literary Record 23, l. 10.

[111] This scene, as a marginal note in the folio points out, translates Horace's *Satires* 2.1.

202 Libels on the Elizabethan Stage

proclaimed as he defied Lupus and the entire regime of surveillance, from "traducing tongues" like the tribune's all the way up to the "tyrant's ear" (5.3.49). Jonson expects (or at least hopes) to find an equally just audience, an audience undaunted by the government's threats to punish anyone who does not turn informer. Like Horace's emblem – and, indeed, like Jonson's play itself – the song counts on the audience to decipher its imagery yet not succumb to the political paranoia of 1601.

Given its hostile reception by "the greatest justice of this kingdom," *Poetaster* apparently met with an audience not entirely free from fear. Yet Jonson continued to write highly topical plays, and "great ones" (as he would write in his commonplace book) continued to accuse him of libel. Despite his frequent complaints about his audiences' judgment, Jonson again and again put his fate in their hands. O'Callaghan thus argues that Jonson, in *Poetaster* and in his other early comical satires, was "turning the theatre into a law court."[112] Jonson establishes the analogy between theater and court at the very beginning of his play. Envy rises and reads the title under which *Poetaster* first appeared on the stage: "Th'Arraignment" (Induction, 3). That title not only evokes the very recent arraignment of Essex and his supporters but also prepares Jonson's audience to render judgment themselves.[113] Just as Stephen Gosson complained, Jonson makes his audiences "the iudges of faultes there painted out."[114]

So too did the other dramatists who took part in the War of the Theaters. In an address "To the World" printed in the 1602 quarto of *Satiromastix*, Dekker takes up Jonson's vision of the theater as law court. He situates his play in "that terrible *Poetomachia*, lately commenc'd betweene *Horace the second*, and a band of leane-witted *Poetasters*." Dekker unsurprisingly thinks he and his fellow poetasters have come out on top. Yet he nonetheless leaves it for the audience to decide: "*Horace* hal'd his *Poetasters* to the Barre, the *Poetasters* vntruss'd *Horace*: how worthily eyther, or how wrongfully, (*World*) leaue it to the Iurie."[115] This defamatory back-and-forth makes the theater precisely what Gosson or, for that matter, Weever feared: a travesty of a trial, prosecuted by poets and decided by a jury of playgoers whose judgment is itself "a kinde of libelling, and defaming."[116]

What Dekker reveals that Gosson and Weever fail to mention, however, is that this kind of libeling had its own commercial logic. In the epilogue to

---

[112] O'Callaghan, *English Wits*, 35.
[113] Dekker likewise refers to the play as Jonson's "Arraignement" in *Satiromastix*, "To the World," 29. On the title's allusion to Essex, see Cain, "Satyres," 54.
[114] Stephen Gosson, *Playes Confuted in fiue Actions* (London, 1582), sig. D1r.
[115] Dekker, *Satiromastix*, "To the World," 7–9, 12–14.   [116] Gosson, *Playes Confuted*, sig. D1r.

Satiromastix, Captain Tucca looks to the audience to keep the War of the Theaters going. If they hiss, he tells them, "you blowe away *Horaces reuenge*: but if you set your hands and Seales to this, *Horace* will write against it, and you may haue more sport: . . . my Poetasters will not laugh at him, but will vntrusse him agen, and agen, and agen."[117] Dekker's self-reflexive appeals to the audience lend support to the revisionist view that the War of the Theaters was at least in part a marketing strategy, drummed up to draw paying playgoers.[118] As Tucca makes clear, it is up to the audience to sustain the libelous sport. Their laughter, their applause, and, most importantly, their continued attendance allow the companies to stage their comical satires "agen, and agen, and agen." Like Jonson, Dekker makes his audiences complicit in the production of defamatory drama – and of the playgoing public that gathered again and again to consume it.

To be sure, Jonson was rather less assured that the jury would find in his favor. Yet that did not stop him from arraigning not only his rival dramatists but also the insidious agents of late Elizabethan surveillance. His methods in *Poetaster* in fact resemble those prescribed by one of the few figures to speak positively of libels: John Donne, his friend and fellow satirist.[119] In his 1612 letter on libels, Donne contends that "one may do his Countrey good service, by libelling" – "this extraordinary accusing" – when the target is "too great . . . to be brought under a judiciary accusation."[120] Jonson may not have been trying to serve his country, but he nonetheless put the great on trial in the theater. And for all his grumbling, the success of his poetico-political project turned on the same incorrigible interpreters whom he claimed to detest. After all, extraordinary accusing demands extraordinary judgment.

---

[117] Dekker, *Satiromastix*, "Epilogus," 19–21, 23–24.

[118] Reavley Gair, *The Children of Paul's: The Story of a Theatre Company, 1553–1608* (Cambridge: Cambridge University Press, 1982), 134; Knutson, *Playing Companies*; David M. Bergeron, "Did a 'War of the Theaters' Occur?" in *Practicing Renaissance Scholarship: Plays and Pageants, Patrons and Politics* (Pittsburgh: Duquesne University Press, 2000), 123–46.

[119] On Jonson and Donne, see Donaldson, *Ben Jonson*, 150–52. Donaldson argues that Jonson's comical satires "are recognizably Donneian both in tone and subject matter" (152).

[120] John Donne, *Letters to Severall Persons of Honour* (London, 1651), sigs. N1v, N2r.

EPILOGUE

Staging Libel in Early Stuart England

Neither defamatory drama nor drama about defamation vanished from the stage in 1603. If anything, both grew more frequent. Samuel Calvert wrote in 1605 of players representing "the whole Course of this present Time, not sparing either King, State or Religion," and in 1620 the Venetian ambassador reported that "the comedians have absolute liberty to say whatever they wish against any one soever."[1] These may be exaggerations, yet they reflect the temper of the times. The vogue for Tacitean dramas of court corruption took off in the early Stuart era. On the stage, libels were a symptom of the darkening political mood. As the two libelers in Barnabe Barnes's *The Devil's Charter* (1607) put it, "wee Poets now with paine, / . . . / Are forc'd of mens impietie to plaine."[2]

This epilogue traces two early Stuart scenes of libeling to their Elizabethan roots. Namely, I consider overlooked echoes of *Edward IV* and *Poetaster* in, respectively, the anonymous *Nobody and Somebody* (*c.*1605) and Philip Massinger's *The Roman Actor* (1626). These examples show that the late Elizabethan scenes of libel continued to inform Stuart representations of censorship, corruption, and popular complaint. To be sure, the two later plays are not uncritical retellings. Each in its own way revises the paradigm of libel formulated by its dramatic predecessor. But together they offer compelling evidence that the theatrical publics I've sketched in previous chapters endured in some form well beyond the horizons of the plays themselves.

[1] Samuel Calvert to Ralph Winwood, March 28, 1605, in *Memorials of Affairs of State in the Reigns of Q. Elizabeth and K. James I*, ed. Edmund Sawyer, 3 vols. (London, 1725), 2:54; Rawdon Brown et al., eds., *Calendar of State Papers and Manuscripts, Relating to English Affairs, Existing in the Archives and Collections of Venice*, 38 vols. (London, 1864–1947), 16:111.
[2] Barnabe Barnes, *The Devil's Charter*, ed. Jim C. Pogue (New York: Garland, 1980), ll. 218, 220.

204

Nobody's Libels

Defamation drives *Nobody and Somebody*'s comic subplot, a farcical affair starring its titular characters. The play itself is a peculiar hybrid of chronicle history, morality play, and city comedy. While the play's British lords jockey for power, Nobody and Somebody reenact in a comic vein Heywood's story of Jane Shore and Richard III. No single allusion proves the play's debt to *Edward IV* beyond a doubt. But taken together, the number of linguistic and substantive parallels makes a convincing case. In fact, Heywood himself may well have contributed to the play. The title page of the 1606 quarto records that it was performed by Queen Anne's Men, the company for which he was churning out plays in the early seventeenth century. Heywood later claimed to "haue had either an entire hand, or at the least a maine finger" in "two hundred and twenty" plays.[3] Whether or not Heywood did have a hand in *Nobody and Somebody* – and I think it likely that he did – the internal evidence strongly suggests that its playwright drew on *Edward IV*.

In *Nobody and Somebody*'s allegorical subplot, Nobody plays the persecuted protector of the people and Somebody the tyrannical antagonist. Like Jane Shore, Nobody is renowned for "virtue, almsdeeds, and for charity" (304).[4] Just as she relieves "the poor prisoners in the common gaol" and "the poor in hospitals," so he frees "poor prisoners" and builds "large hospitals" (541, 323).[5] Somebody sees Nobody's immense popularity – "he's talked of far and near, / Fills all the boundless country with applause" – as a threat to his own position at court (306–7). So, in order to "bring [Nobody's] name in public scandal," he plots to "sow seditious slanders through the land" (350, 355). Somebody sends his minions to "[o]ppress the poor" in ways reminiscent of Heywood's corrupt kings and courtiers – "rack" rents, "extort" tenants, "transport" grain – and pin the blame on Nobody (356, 553). To apprehend his adversary, he even copies Richard III's multimedia push to defame Jane Shore. Just as Heywood's tyrant prints a proclamation against Jane "to be sold in every stationer's shop, / Besides a number of them clapped on posts," so Somebody commands,

> Let [Nobody] be straight imprinted to the life.
> His picture shall be set on every stall,
> And proclamation made that he that takes him,
> Shall have a hundred pounds of Somebody.   (886–89)[6]

---

[3] Thomas Heywood, *The English Traveller* (London, 1633), sig. A3r.
[4] All quotations of the play come from David L. Hay, ed., *Nobody and Somebody: An Introduction and Critical Edition* (New York: Garland, 1980), cited parenthetically by line number in the text.
[5] Thomas Heywood, *2 Edward IV*, in *The First and Second Parts of King Edward IV*, ed. Richard Rowland (Manchester: Manchester University Press, 2005), 9.2, 27.
[6] Ibid., 18.109–10.

206 Epilogue

Somebody's schemes immediately succeed. When Nobody enters the play asking for "some news, some news," he learns that he has acquired "an ill name" (379, 385). "I am slandered through the world," he laments (407). The defamation has ruined Nobody's reputation.

The play culminates in a peculiar scene that revises Matthew Shore's encounter with the corrupt merchant Rufford near the end of *2 Edward IV*. Somebody hauls Nobody before King Elidure and rehearses a litany of false accusations against him: impoverishing the commons in the country, fomenting disorder and vice in the city, and assorted abuses at court. As evidence of the last, the lords produce "dangerous libels 'gainst the state, / And no name to them, therefore Nobody's" and cite the "strange rumors and false buzzing tales / Of mutinous leesings raised by Nobody" (1956–57, 1958–59). But if Nobody's ontological status makes him vulnerable to false charges, it also means that the allegations ultimately slide right off him. Nobody sensibly remarks, "If things were done, they must be done by Somebody, / Else could they have no being" (1884–85). The ultimate proof of Nobody's innocence and Somebody's guilt is, as in *2 Edward IV*, a search of their persons urged by the accused. Just as Rufford's doublet conceals the king's "hand and signet counterfeit," so Somebody's hides "[t]he king's hand counterfeit" (1992).[7] Somebody – whose crimes, like Rufford's, "stain and blemish / . . . the weal public" – suffers the same fate too: "the death of traitors" (2002–3, 2012).

Like the story of Jane Shore, the Nobody and Somebody subplot centers citizen identities and interests. Nobody himself sets out to "get myself a name mongst citizens" through his largesse (543). While "representative display" prevails at court, Samuel Fallon argues, Nobody embodies a new kind of publicity: common, anonymous, "spatially and socially democratized."[8] In Chapter 5, I ascribed a similar kind of civic celebrity to the figure of Jane Shore. I believe this shared vision is no coincidence. By 1606, both *Nobody and Somebody* and *Edward IV* were in the repertory of Queen Anne's Men, Heywood's company. Their plays at the Red Bull, not least of all Heywood's, quickly earned them a name for drawing crowds of citizens and apprentices.[9] Without overestimating the stratification of

---

[7] Ibid., 21.91.
[8] Samuel Fallon, "Nobody's Business," in *Publicity and the Early Modern Stage: People Made Public*, ed. Allison K. Deutermann, Matthew Hunter, and Musa Gurnis (Cham: Palgrave Macmillan, 2021), 234, 237.
[9] Mark Bayer, *Theatre, Community, and Civic Engagement in Jacobean London* (Iowa City: University of Iowa Press, 2011); Eva Griffith, *A Jacobean Company and Its Playhouse: The Queen's Servants at the Red Bull Theatre (c. 1605–1619)* (Cambridge: Cambridge University Press, 2013), 73–79.

Staging Libel in Early Stuart England 207

theater audiences, we might locate both plays within the discursive ambit of a citizen-centric playgoing public.

The two plays likewise share an anti-monarchical (or at least anti-tyrannical) thrust. When Nobody tells the king of the many good deeds done by "Nobody / . . . in these days" (1942–43), the sarcasm is practically palpable: under Elidure, nobody at all is looking out for the common people. In Fallon's reading, however, Nobody's ultimate vindication requires that he be "absorbed into the representative apparatus of the state," changed from a figure for ordinary, anonymous talk to a symbol of royal authority.[10] It is King Elidure who gets the final word. Having condemned Somebody, he ends the play with a return to the ritual pomp of kingship: "Now forward, lords, long may our glories stand, / Three sundry times crowned king of this fair land" (2048–49). Yet oddly enough, this final couplet is immediately preceded by an epilogue directed by Nobody to the audience. And the very first thing he says is a not-so-veiled criticism of the king. "Here if you wonder why the king, Elidurus, bestows nothing on me for all my good services in his land," Nobody begins, "if the multitude should say he hath preferred Nobody, Somebody or other would say it were not well done, for in doing good to Nobody he should but get himself an ill name" (2030–35). Nobody's defense of Elidure ironically implicates the king in Somebody's abuses. It is because Elidure is so concerned with those Somebodies who might give him an "ill name" that he has failed to reward the "good services" of Nobody, his faithful subject.

Up to the very end, Nobody's self-exculpatory wordplay affiliates him with the same seditious, slanderous talk of which he is falsely accused. This is perhaps most evident in his response to the charge of libel. When the courtiers try to pin the anonymous libels and tales on Nobody, he turns to the well-worn but legally unsound defense that (in William Hudson's words) "it is no libel if the party put his hand unto it."[11] He responds,

> Are libels cast? If Nobody did make them,
> And Nobody's name to them, they are no libels,
> For he that sets his name to any slander,
> Makes it by that no libel. (1968–71)

Whether or not this defense would have held up in court, it dissolves his dramatic character into the anonymous collective – "the undifferentiated

---

[10] Fallon, "Nobody's Business," 240.
[11] William Hudson, *A Treatise of the Court of Star Chamber*, in *Collectanea Juridica*, ed. Francis Hargrave, vol. 2 (London, 1792), 102.

208 Epilogue

mass of nobodies" – that he represents.[12] Nobody is Anonymous, the ubiquitous yet ever elusive author of the early modern libel. No sooner has he made this admission than he revokes it, turning instead to blame Somebody for "forg[ing] those slanderous writs to scandal me" (1972). Yet Nobody's logic makes him Somebody's invisible collaborator, the persona put on by demagogues and dissidents alike. He is, paradoxically, at once the victim and the author of the libels against the state.

It is fitting that Nobody should be the figure for libel in a play that survives only in an anonymous quarto sold in a stationer's shop at the sign of Nobody.[13] *Nobody and Somebody* sharpens the satirical edge of the Heywoodian script by making Nobody the locus of popularity. In the play's mythical Britain, Nobody (or nobody) is renowned for charity, Nobody (or nobody) defends the poor. This is social satire far too blunt to have escaped notice.[14] And especially in the theater, the line between satire and libel was tenuous at best. All that it took to turn a play into a libel was a measure of what Jonson called "application." Given that *Nobody and Somebody*'s Britain is very clearly early modern England, at least some members of the audience surely would have applied Somebody's all-too-familiar abuses to their own experience of economic precarity. Nobody's libels belong to us too.

Turning Plays into Libels, Again

My second case study, *The Roman Actor*, signals its Jonsonian genealogy from the start. Scholars have long noted Massinger's extensive borrowings from Jonson's *Sejanus*.[15] Yet the echoes of *Poetaster* have gone overlooked, and a near verbatim quotation from the second prologue to *Epicene* has received virtually no comment. Clustered in the metatheatrical opening scenes, these allusions set up a critical reappraisal of Jonson's satirical method.

Set in the reign of the emperor Domitian, Massinger's Tacitean Rome closely resembles the imperial courts of *Poetaster* and, especially, *Sejanus*. Informers and spies lurk at every turn; corruption and flattery prevail at

---

[12] Fallon, "Nobody's Business," 239. [13] *Nobody and Somebody*, p. 73.

[14] See Anthony Archdeacon, "The Publication of *No-body and Some-body*: Humanism, History and Economics in the Early Jacobean Public Theatre," *Early Modern Literary Studies* 16.1 (2012), http://purl.org/emls/16-1/archnobo.htm.

[15] William Dinsmore Briggs, "The Influence of Jonson's Tragedy in the Seventeenth Century," *Anglia* 35 (1912): 316–18, 320; C. A. Gibson, "Massinger's Use of His Sources for 'The Roman Actor,'" *Journal of the Australasian Universities Language and Literature Association* 15 (1961): 65–66.

Staging Libel in Early Stuart England

court. Like *Poetaster*, Massinger's play is centrally concerned with the literary and performing arts. It opens with three actors lamenting that their trade has fallen on hard times. The problem is not just Romans' degenerate tastes but also that the players have crossed powerful foes. As Aesopus the player reminds his colleagues,

> We have enemies,
> And great ones too, I fear. 'Tis given out lately
> The consul Aretinus (Caesar's spy)
> Said at his table, ere a month expired
> (For being galled in our last comedy)
> He would silence us for ever. $\qquad$ (1.1.33–38)[16]

This is likewise the predicament of Jonson's free-speaking Romans put on trial for their art (Horace in *Poetaster* and the historian Cremutius Cordus in *Sejanus*).[17] And it was the predicament of Jonson himself too. As he recorded in his commonplace book, he had again and again "been accused to the lords, to the king, and by great ones."[18] Massinger's vision of "great ones" galled by comic satire echoes Jonson's life and art alike.

The allusions to Jonson draw near to direct quotation when Paris the tragedian faces his accuser in the play's third scene. Aretinus hauls Paris before the senate and charges him with the same crimes imputed to Jonson's Horace and Cordus:

> In thee, as being the chief of thy profession,
> I do accuse the quality of treason,
> As libellers against the state and Caesar.
> . . .
> $\qquad$ You are they
> That search into the secrets of the time,
> And under feigned names on the stage present
> Actions not to be touched at, and traduce
> Persons of rank and quality of both sexes,
> And with satirical and bitter jests
> Make even the senators ridiculous
> To the plebeians. $\qquad$ (1.3.32–34, 36–43)

Aretinus synthesizes and extends the anti-satirical arguments made by Lupus in *Poetaster*. His complaint joins Lupus' climactic accusation of

---

[16] All quotations of the play come from Philip Massinger, *The Roman Actor: A Tragedy*, ed. Martin White (Manchester: Manchester University Press, 2007), cited parenthetically in the text.

[17] For Jonson's Horace, see Chapter 6 above; for Cordus, see Jonson, *Sejanus His Fall*, ed. Tom Cain, in *CWBJ*, 2:3.370–469.

[18] Ben Jonson, *Discoveries*, ed. Lorna Hutson, in *CWBJ*, 7:545, ll. 952–53.

210 Epilogue

libel with the tribune's early diatribe against the players: "they will rob us, us that are magistrates, of our respect, bring us upon their stages and make us ridiculous to the plebeians."[19] Just so do the players in *The Roman Actor* probe the secrets of state and mock "persons of rank and quality" on the stage, making them "ridiculous / To the plebeians." These echoes of *Poetaster* point to Aretinus' Jonsonian lineage. He is the corrupt informer and magistrate, the malign misinterpreter who turns plays into libels.

In characteristically Jonsonian fashion, Massinger has his Roman actor publicly vindicate himself from the supposedly false allegations. Paris answers Aretinus with a lengthy defense of his craft. Rehearsing arguments from Sidney's *Defence of Poetry*, Heywood's *Apology for Actors*, and several of Jonson's plays, Paris maintains that the theater's anatomies of vice and virtue instruct audiences just as well as do the "golden principles" of the philosophers (1.3.64).[20] He insists that if any see themselves in the assorted evildoers represented onstage, "we cannot help it" (1.3.114). In an especially brazen move, he turns to the senators and makes the same argument about Aretinus himself:

> If any in this reverend assembly –
> Nay, e'en yourself, my lord, that are the image
> Of absent Caesar – feel something in your bosom
> That puts you in remembrance of things past
> Or things intended, 'tis not in us to help it. (1.3.136–40)

Given that it was indeed Aretinus who was "galled in our last comedy," Paris' remark is bluntly ironic. It is as much a threat as a defense: to complain of the stage's satire is to implicate oneself in the abuses it mocks. In fact, Paris begins his speech by making this point in Jonsonian terms. Repeating nearly verbatim Jonson's disclaimer in the prologue to *Epicene* ("They make a libel which he made a play"), Paris sets out to prove that "they make that a libel which the poet / Writ for a comedy" (1.3.46–47).[21] For Paris as for Jonson, it is the malicious members of the audience – corrupt magistrates above all – who turn plays into libels.

Yet Jonson's dramatic satire did often take a turn for the libelous, not least of all in *Poetaster*. Massinger's Jonsonian allusions thus threaten to undermine Paris' own argument. We might take this as a quixotic defense

---

[19] Jonson, *Poetaster*, ed. Gabriele Bernhard Jackson, in *CWBJ*, 2:1.2.30–32.
[20] See Jonas Barish, "Three Caroline 'Defenses' of the Stage," in *Comedy from Shakespeare to Sheridan: Change and Continuity in the English and European Dramatic Tradition*, ed. A. R. Braunmuller and J. C. Bulman (Newark: University of Delaware Press, 1986), 196.
[21] Jonson, *Epicene*, ed. David Bevington, in *CWBJ*, 3:second prologue, 14.

Staging Libel in Early Stuart England 211

of his predecessor's stance. After all, the allusions put Paris in the tradition of Jonson's Horace and Cordus, intrepid authorial figures fighting for their creative liberty in a world of malign misinterpreters. But I think it is more likely that Massinger is instead ironizing the conventional apologies for the theater. The action of Massinger's play bears this view out. Paris puts on a series of performances that, as critics have pointed out, not only fail to reform but even further corrupt their spectators. It is for this reason that Martin Butler labels *The Roman Actor* "the most anti-theatrical play of the English Renaissance."[22] The plays within the play utterly belie Paris' initial defense. In the previous chapter, I argued that *Poetaster* redeems the satirist even as Jonson slyly invites his audiences to make the very applications that he decries. But this stance hardly seems tenable in *The Roman Actor*. The echoes of Jonson do more to incriminate than to exculpate Paris, and when the play's various spectators do apply Paris' performances to their present state, the result is vice and bloodshed. Massinger lays bare the unresolved ironies at the heart of Jonson's satirical project.

***

There is further evidence from the early Stuart period that Heywood's and Jonson's visions of libel proved especially enduring. Like *Edward IV*, the anonymous, likely Jacobean history play *Thomas of Woodstock* invents a verse libel against the favorites of a tyrannical English king.[23] And William Davenant's *The Cruel Brother* (1627) includes among its corrupt court a "satirical Courtier," Castruchio, whose envious "rail[ing]" and villainous informing are reminiscent of the activities of Jonson's poetasters.[24] Heywood's and Jonson's respective influence is perhaps unsurprising given the enormous popularity of *Edward IV* and Jonson's unmatched cultural

[22] Martin Butler, "Romans in Britain: *The Roman Actor* and the Early Stuart Classical Play," in *Philip Massinger: A Critical Reassessment*, ed. Douglas Howard (Cambridge: Cambridge University Press, 1985), 160. See also Barish, "Three Caroline 'Defenses,'" 195–201.

[23] Peter Corbin and Douglas Sedge, eds., *Thomas of Woodstock, or Richard the Second, Part One* (Manchester: Manchester University Press, 2002), 3.3.162–204. Traditionally assigned to the early 1590s, *Woodstock* has more recently been dated to the first decade of James's reign: see D. J. Lake, "Three Seventeenth-Century Revisions: *Thomas of Woodstock*, *The Jew of Malta*, and *Faustus B*," *Notes and Queries* 30.2 (1983): 135–38; MacDonald P. Jackson, "Shakespeare's *Richard II* and the Anonymous *Thomas of Woodstock*," *Medieval and Renaissance Drama in England* 14 (2001): 17–65; and Martin Wiggins with Catherine Richardson, *British Drama 1533–1642: A Catalogue*, 10 vols. (Oxford: Oxford University Press, 2012–), 6:171.

[24] William Davenant, *The Cruel Brother*, in *The Dramatic Works of Sir William D'Avenant*, ed. James Maidment and W. H. Logan, vol. 1 (Edinburgh, 1872), 118, 125; see also 141–42, 151–52, 162–63. Castruchio has long been identified as a caricature of the satirist George Wither, who exchanged abuse with Jonson himself in the 1620s (111–12).

212 Epilogue

sway among seventeenth-century dramatists.[25] Of course, this does not mean that the other Elizabethan scenes of libel faded altogether. *Sir Thomas More* may never have been printed or (perhaps) performed, but *Titus Andronicus* remained popular with playgoers for decades.[26] The story of libel on the Stuart stage remains to be told.

In any case, the plays I have discussed show that the Elizabethan scenes of libel remained legible to Jacobean and Caroline audiences. They suggest too what I have argued in this book: that the long 1590s were the pivotal years in the dramatic history of the early modern libel. This is something of a reversal of the standard narrative. Until recently, scholars have suggested that the libel flourished primarily in the first decades of the seventeenth century. Elizabethan libels have largely remained confined to the genealogical background of their early Stuart successors. Even Steven W. May and Alan Bryson, in their exemplary 2016 edition of Elizabethan verse libels, contrast their objects of study with Stuart libels: "native" as opposed to "neo-classical," "apolitical" as opposed to intensely "engaged with political figures."[27] At least from the perspective of theater history, however, the received narratives do not hold. Late Elizabethan dramatists staged innovative scenes of libel, providing a cultural vocabulary that playwrights would remix over the following decades. And that vocabulary was as much neoclassical as native. *Titus* and *Poetaster* assimilate classical scripts to Elizabethan controversy, while *Sir Thomas More* and *Edward IV* are filled with native strains of seditious speech. These visions of libel put defamatory discourse at the center of England's burgeoning media ecosystem.

Taken together, the plays chart a late Elizabethan public sphere animated by forces that remain uncannily familiar: economic populism and popular xenophobia, state violence and sectarian strife, proto-celebrity and political demagoguery. There are many – too many – threads that might be traced up to our own post-truth social media age. Instead, I want to return in closing to the constitutive tension from which this book began. Francis

---

[25] One (very imperfect) measure of Jonson's influence is the number of surviving allusions to his works: from 1600–1640, roughly 519 for Jonson compared to 305 for Shakespeare (Gerald Eades Bentley, *Shakespeare and Jonson: Their Reputations in the Seventeenth Century Compared*, 2 vols. [Chicago: University of Chicago Press, 1945], 1:38–45). With the grant of a royal pension in 1616, Jonson became England's unofficial poet laureate (David Riggs, *Ben Jonson: A Life* [Cambridge, MA: Harvard University Press, 1989], 220–21).

[26] Ben Jonson, *Bartholomew Fair*, ed. John Creaser, in *CWBJ*, 4:Induction, 79–82; Jonathan Bate, introduction to Shakespeare, *Titus Andronicus*, ed. Bate (London: Routledge, 1995), 71.

[27] Steven W. May and Alan Bryson, eds., *Verse Libel in Renaissance England and Scotland* (Oxford: Oxford University Press, 2016), 68, 33.

Staging Libel in Early Stuart England

Bacon puts it as well as anyone when he calls libels "the Gustes of Libertie of speech restrained, and the females of Sedition."[28] Poised between protest and threat, the early modern libel shows just how fine the line between free speech and false news could be. Anyone who picked up a screed against the Earl of Leicester or watched local landlords go to hell could join in a public political conversation. But that conversation was just as likely to end in derision or violence as in measured judgment. Onstage and off, the scenes of libel circulated a particularly volatile recipe for making publics, one that threatened to explode the very discursive conditions that made public formation possible. Or, to put it in early modern terms, the gusts of free speech were precisely the seeds of sedition.

---

[28] Francis Bacon, *The Historie of the Raigne of King Henry the Seventh*, ed. Michael Kiernan, in *The Oxford Francis Bacon*, vol. 8 (Oxford: Clarendon Press, 2012), 97. Against the usual gloss of "females" as "mothers," Martin Dzelzainis suggests that Bacon's gendering instead comes from the Virgilian genealogy of *Fama*, in which – according to Bacon's own allegory – "*Seditious Tumults*, and *Seditious Fames*, differ no more, but as Brother and Sister, Masculine and Feminine" (*The Essayes or Counsels, Civill and Morall*, ed. Michael Kiernan, in *Oxford Francis Bacon*, vol. 15 [Oxford: Clarendon Press, 2000], 43). See Dzelzainis, "'The Feminine part of every Rebellion': Francis Bacon on Sedition and Libel, and the Beginning of Ideology," *Huntington Library Quarterly* 69.1 (2006): 147–48 n26.

Bibliography

Primary Sources

Manuscript

British Library, London
Harley MS 6849.
Lansdowne MSS 13, 33, 39, 54, 66, 71, 77, 81, 87.

Folger Shakespeare Library, Washington, D.C.
V.b.142.
X.d.634.

Hatfield House, Hertfordshire
CP 37/3, 54/20, 59/10, 76/97, 77/25, 80/2, 128/78, 140/119, 140/121, 141/173, 180/21, 181/127, 185/129.

The National Archives of the UK
SP 1/48, 12/81, 12/150, 12/176, 12/179, 12/273, 12/274, 12/275, 12/278, 12/279, 12/281, 14/203.
STAC 8/34/4.

Printed

Addison, Joseph. *Spectator* 239. December 4, 1711. In *The Spectator*, ed. Donald F. Bond, vol. 2, 428–32. Oxford: Clarendon Press, 1965.
Alciato, Andrea. *Emblemata / Les Emblemes*. Paris, 1584.
Allen, William. *A True Sincere and Modest Defence of English Catholiques*. [Rouen, 1584].
Andrewes, Lancelot. *Lancelot Andrewes: Selected Sermons and Lectures*. Ed. Peter McCullough. Oxford: Oxford University Press, 2005.

Bibliography

215

Arber, Edward, ed. *A Transcript of the Registers of the Company of Stationers of London; 1554–1640 A.D.* 5 vols. London and Birmingham, 1875–94.

Bacon, Francis. *An aduertisement touching seditious writing.* Ed. Alan Stewart with Harriet Knight. In *Oxford Francis Bacon*, vol. 1.

An advertisement touching the controuersyes of the Church of England. Ed. Alan Stewart with Harriet Knight. In *Oxford Francis Bacon*, vol. 1.

De Augmentis Scientiarum. In Bacon, *Works*, vol. 1.

Certaine obseruations vppon a libell. Ed. Alan Stewart with Harriet Knight. In *Oxford Francis Bacon*, vol. 1.

A Declaration of the Practises & Treasons attempted and committed by Robert late Earle of Essex and his Complices. London, 1601.

Of the Dignity and Advancement of Learning. Trans. Francis Headlam. In Bacon, *Works*, vols. 4–5.

The Essayes or Counsels, Civill and Morall. Ed. Michael Kiernan. In *Oxford Francis Bacon*, vol. 15.

The Historie of the Raigne of King Henry the Seventh. Ed. Michael Kiernan. In *Oxford Francis Bacon*, vol. 8.

The Letters and the Life of Francis Bacon. Ed. James Spedding. 7 vols. London, 1861–74.

The Oxford Francis Bacon. Ed. Graham Rees et al. 16 vols. Oxford: Oxford University Press, 1996-.

The Works of Francis Bacon. Ed. James Spedding, Robert Leslie Ellis, and Douglas Denon Heath. 7 vols. London, 1857–59.

Baker, John. *Baker and Milsom Sources of English Legal History: Private Law to 1750.* 2nd ed. Oxford: Oxford University Press, 2010.

Bancroft, Richard. *Daungerous Positions and Proceedings, published and practised within this Iland of Brytaine, vnder pretence of Reformation, and for the Presbiteriall Discipline.* London, 1593.

Barnes, Barnabe. *The Devil's Charter.* Ed. Jim C. Pogue. New York: Garland, 1980.

Foure Bookes of Offices. London, 1606.

Beaumont, Francis. *The Knight of the Burning Pestle.* Ed. Sheldon P. Zitner. Manchester: Manchester University Press, 1984.

Bellany, Alastair, and Andrew McRae, eds. *Early Stuart Libels: An Edition of Poetry from Manuscript Sources.* Early Modern Literary Studies Text Series 1. 2005. http://purl.oclc.org/emls/texts/libels/.

The Bible and Holy Scriptures Conteined in the Olde and Newe Testament. London, 1576.

Birch, Thomas, comp. *The Court and Times of James the First.* Ed. Robert Folkestone Williams. 2 vols. London, 1848.

Brooke, Christopher. *The Ghost of Richard the Third.* London, 1614.

Broughton, Hugh. *A Revelation of the Holy Apocalyps.* [Middleburg], 1610.

Brown, Rawdon, et al., eds. *Calendar of State Papers and Manuscripts, Relating to English Affairs, Existing in the Archives and Collections of Venice.* 38 vols. London, 1864–1947.

Bullokar, John. *An English Expositor.* London, 1616.

Bibliography

Calthorpe, Charles. *The Relation betweene the Lord of a Mannor and the Coppyholder His Tenant.* London, 1635.

Campbell, Lily B., ed. *The Mirror for Magistrates.* 1938; New York: Barnes & Noble, 1960.

Cannon, Charles Dale, ed. *A Warning for Fair Women: A Critical Edition.* The Hague: Mouton, 1975.

Carroll, Robert, and Stephen Prickett, eds. *The Bible: Authorized King James Version.* Oxford: Oxford University Press, 1997.

Cecil, William. *The Execution of Iustice in England for maintenaunce of publique and Christian peace.* London, 1583.

Chamberlain, John. *The Letters of John Chamberlain.* Ed. Norman Egbert McClure. 2 vols. Philadelphia: American Philosophical Society, 1939.

Chambers, E. K. *The Elizabethan Stage.* 4 vols. Oxford: Clarendon Press, 1923.

Charnock, Robert. *A Reply to a notorious Libell Intituled A Briefe Apologie or defence of the Ecclesiastical Hierarchie.* [London], 1603.

Christopherson, John. *An exhortation to all menne to take hede and beware of rebellion.* London, 1554.

Churchyard, Thomas. *Churchyards Challenge.* London, 1593.

Chute, Anthony. *Beawtie dishonoured written under the Title of Shores Wife.* London, 1593.

Cicero. *De Oratore.* Trans. E. W. Sutton and H. Rackham. 2 vols. Cambridge, MA: Harvard University Press, 1948.

    De Re Publica. In *De Re Publica, De Legibus,* trans. Clinton Walker Keyes. Cambridge, MA: Harvard University Press, 1928.

Coke, Edward. *The Compleate Copy-holder.* London, 1641.

    Quinta Pars Relationum / The Fift Part of the Reports. London, 1605.

    The Reports of Sir Edward Coke, Knt. In Thirteen Parts. Ed. John Henry Thomas and John Farquhar Fraser. 6 vols. London, 1826.

Cooper, Charles Henry. *Annals of Cambridge.* 5 vols. Cambridge, 1842–1908.

Corbin, Peter, and Douglas Sedge, eds. *Thomas of Woodstock, or Richard the Second, Part One.* Manchester: Manchester University Press, 2002.

Cosin, Richard. *Conspiracie, for Pretended Reformation: viz. Presbyteriall Discipline.* London, 1592.

Cowell, John. *The Interpreter.* Cambridge, 1607.

Croke, George. *The First Part of the Reports of Sr George Croke.* London, 1661.

D'Ewes, Simonds. *The Diary of Sir Simonds D'Ewes (1622–1624).* Ed. Elisabeth Bourcier. Paris: Didier, 1974.

Dalton, Michael. *The Countrey Iustice.* London, 1618.

Dasent, John Roche, et al., eds. *Acts of the Privy Council of England.* 46 vols. London, 1890–1964.

Davenant, William. *The Cruel Brother.* In The *Dramatic Works of Sir William D'Avenant,* ed. James Maidment and W. H. Logan, vol. 1. Edinburgh, 1872.

Davies, John. *Epigrammes.* In *The Poems of Sir John Davies,* ed. Robert Krueger. Oxford: Clarendon Press, 1975.

Le primer report des cases & matters en ley resolues & adiudges en les courts del Roy en Ireland. Dublin, 1615.

Dekker, Thomas. *The Guls Horne-booke*. London, 1609.

  Satiromastix. In *The Dramatic Works of Thomas Dekker*, ed. Fredson Bowers, vol. 1. Cambridge: Cambridge University Press, 1953.

Deloney, Thomas. *The Garland of Good Will*. In *The Works of Thomas Deloney*, ed. Francis Oscar Mann. Oxford: Clarendon Press, 1912.

Donne, John. *Letters to Severall Persons of Honour*. London, 1651.

Douglas, Audrey, and Peter Greenfield, eds. *REED: Cumberland, Westmorland, Gloucestershire*. Toronto: University of Toronto Press, 1986.

Drayton, Michael. *Englands Heroicall Epistles*. London, 1597.

Dugdale, Gilbert. *A True Discourse of the practises of Elizabeth Caldwell*. London, 1604.

Earle, John. *Micro-cosmographie. Or, A Peece of the World Discovered*. London, 1628.

Elizabeth I. *Elizabeth I: Collected Works*. Ed. Leah S. Marcus, Janel Mueller, and Mary Beth Rose. Chicago: University of Chicago Press, 2000.

Elyot, Thomas. *The boke named the Gouernour*. London, 1531.

Erler, Mary C., ed. *REED: Ecclesiastical London*. Toronto: University of Toronto Press, 2008.

Foxe, John. *The First Volume of the Ecclesiasticall history contaynyng the Actes and Monumentes of thynges passed*. London, 1570.

Fuller, Thomas. *The History of the University of Cambridge*. Printed with *The Church-History of Britain*. London, 1655.

Gardiner, Samuel Rawson, ed. *Reports of Cases in the Courts of Star Chamber and High Commission*. London, 1886.

Gayangos, Pascual de, ed. *Calendar of Letters, Despatches, and State Papers, Relating to the Negotiations between England and Spain, Preserved in the Archives at Simancas and Elsewhere*. Vol. 4, pt. 2. London, 1882.

Gibson, James M., ed. *REED: Kent: Diocese of Canterbury*. 3 vols. Toronto: University of Toronto Press, 2002.

Gifford, George. *Certaine Sermons, upon Divers Textes of Holie Scripture*. London, 1597.

Giustinian, Sebastian. *Four Years at the Court of Henry VIII: Selection of Despatches Written by the Venetian Ambassador, Sebastian Giustinian*. Trans. Rawdon Brown. 2 vols. London, 1854.

Gosson, Stephen. *Playes Confuted in fiue Actions*. London, 1582.

  The Schoole of Abuse. London, 1579.

Green, Mary Anne Everett, ed. *Calendar of State Papers, Domestic Series, of the Reign of Elizabeth, 1601–1603*. London, 1870.

Greenwood, John, and Henry Barrow. *The Writings of John Greenwood and Henry Barrow, 1591–1593*. Ed. Leland H. Carlson. Elizabethan Nonconformist Texts 6. London: George Allen and Unwin, 1970.

Greville, Fulke. *A Dedication to Sir Philip Sidney. In The Prose Works of Fulke Greville, Lord Brooke*, ed. John Gouws. Oxford: Clarendon Press, 1986.

218   *Bibliography*

Guilpin, Everard. *Skialetheia, or A Shadowe of Truth, in Certaine Epigrams and Satyres*. Ed. D. Allen Carroll. Chapel Hill: University of North Carolina Press, 1974.

Harding, Thomas. *A Confutation of a Booke Intituled An Apologie of the Church of England*. Antwerp, 1565.

  A Detection of Sundrie Foule Errours, Lies, Sclaunders, Corruptions, and Other false dealinges . . . vttered and practized by M. Iewel. Louvain, 1568.

Harpsfield, Nicholas. *The Life and Death of Sr Thomas Moore, Knight, Sometymes Lord High Chancellor of England*. Ed. Elsie Vaughan Hitchcock and R. W. Chambers. Early English Text Society. London: Oxford University Press, 1932.

Harrison, William. *An Historicall description of the Iland of Britaine*. In Raphael Holinshed, *The First and second volumes of Chronicles*. London, 1587.

Hartley, T. E., ed. *Proceedings in the Parliaments of Elizabeth I*. 3 vols. London: Leicester University Press, 1981–95.

Hawarde, John. *Les Reportes del Cases in Camera Stellata, 1593 to 1609*. Ed. William Paley Baildon. London, 1894.

Hay, David L., ed. *Nobody and Somebody: An Introduction and Critical Edition*. New York: Garland, 1980.

Hays, Rosalind Conklin, C. E. McGee, Sally L. Joyce, and Evelyn S. Newlyn, eds. *REED: Dorset, Cornwall*. Toronto: University of Toronto Press, 1999.

Helmholz, R. H., ed. *Select Cases on Defamation to 1600*. London: Selden Society, 1985.

Herrick, Robert. *The Complete Poetry of Robert Herrick*. Ed. Tom Cain and Ruth Connolly. 2 vols. Oxford: Oxford University Press, 2013.

Heylyn, Peter. *Examen Historicum: Or A Discovery and Examination of the Mistakes, Falsities, and Defects in some Modern Histories*. London, 1659.

Heywood, Thomas. *An Apology for Actors*. London, 1612.

  The English Traveller. London, 1633.

  The Fair Maid of the West, Parts I and II. Ed. Robert K. Turner, Jr. Lincoln: University of Nebraska Press, 1967.

  The First and Second Parts of King Edward IV. Ed. Richard Rowland. Manchester: Manchester University Press, 2005.

  The Rape of Lucrece. London, 1608.

Historical Manuscripts Commission. *Fourteenth Report, Appendix, Part IV: The Manuscripts of Lord Kenyon*. London, 1894.

  Report on the Manuscripts of Lord de L'Isle and Dudley Preserved at Penshurst Place. Vol. 2. Ed. C. L. Kingsford. London: His Majesty's Stationery Office, 1934.

Holinshed, Raphael. *The Third volume of Chronicles*. London, 1587.

Hooker, Richard. *Of the Laws of Ecclesiastical Polity: A Critical Edition with Modern Spelling*. Ed. Arthur Stephen McGrade. 3 vols. Oxford: Oxford University Press, 2013.

Horace. *Satires*. In *Satires, Epistles, Ars Poetica*, trans. H. Rushton Fairclough. Cambridge, MA: Harvard University Press, 1929.

Bibliography

Hudson, William. *A Treatise of the Court of Star Chamber*. In *Collectanea Juridica*, ed. Francis Hargrave, vol. 2. London, 1792.

Hughes, Paul L., and James F. Larkin, eds. *Tudor Royal Proclamations*. 3 vols. New Haven: Yale University Press, 1964–69.

The humble petition of the communaltie. [1587]; rept. 1588.

James VI and I. *Basilicon Doron*. In *King James VI and I: Political Writings*, ed. Johann P. Sommerville. Cambridge: Cambridge University Press, 1994.

Jewel, John. *A Defence of the Apologie of the Churche of Englande*. London, 1567.

Jones, Inigo. "To his False Friend mr: Ben Johnson." In Jonson, *Cambridge Edition*, online edition (Cambridge University Press, 2014), Literary Record 23.

Jonson, Ben. *The Alchemist*. Ed. Peter Holland and William Sherman. In Jonson, *Cambridge Edition*, vol. 3.

   Bartholomew Fair. Ed. John Creaser. In Jonson, *Cambridge Edition*, vol. 4.

   The Cambridge Edition of the Works of Ben Jonson. Gen. ed. David Bevington, Martin Butler, and Ian Donaldson. 7 vols. Cambridge: Cambridge University Press, 2012.

   Catiline His Conspiracy. Ed. Inga-Stina Ewbank. In Jonson, *Cambridge Edition*, vol. 4.

   Cynthia's Revels. Ed. Eric Rasmussen and Matthew Steggle. In Jonson, *Cambridge Edition*, vol. 1.

   The Devil Is an Ass. Ed. Anthony Parr. In Jonson, *Cambridge Edition*, vol. 4.

   Discoveries. Ed. Lorna Hutson. In Jonson, *Cambridge Edition*, vol. 7.

   Epicene, or The Silent Woman. Ed. David Bevington. In Jonson, *Cambridge Edition*, vol. 3.

   Every Man Out of His Humour. Ed. Randall Martin. In Jonson, *Cambridge Edition*, vol. 1.

   Informations to William Drummond of Hawthornden. Ed. Ian Donaldson. In Jonson, *Cambridge Edition*, vol. 5.

   The Magnetic Lady, or Humours Reconciled. Ed. Helen Ostovich. In Jonson, *Cambridge Edition*, vol. 6.

   Poetaster. Ed. Tom Cain. Manchester: Manchester University Press, 1995.

   Poetaster, or His Arraignment. Ed. Gabriele Bernhard Jackson. In Jonson, *Cambridge Edition*, vol. 2.

   Sejanus His Fall. Ed. Tom Cain. In Jonson, *Cambridge Edition*, vol. 2.

   Volpone, or The Fox. Ed. Richard Dutton. In Jonson, *Cambridge Edition*, vol. 3.

   and George Chapman. "Letters from Prison by Jonson and Chapman." Ed. Ian Donaldson. In Jonson, *Cambridge Edition*, vol. 2.

Journals of the House of Lords. Vol. 2, 1578–1614. London, n.d.

Keeler, Mary Frear, Maija Jansson Cole, and William B. Bidwell, eds. *Commons Debates 1628*. Vol. 4. New Haven: Yale University Press, 1978.

Kesselring, K. J., ed. *Star Chamber Reports: BL Harley MS 2143*. Kew: List and Index Society, 2018.

Bibliography

Kyd, Thomas. *The Spanish Tragedy*. In *English Renaissance Drama: A Norton Anthology*, ed. David Bevington, Lars Engle, Katharine Eisaman Maus, and Eric Rasmussen. New York: W. W. Norton, 2002.

Lambarde, William. *Archeion, or, A Discourse upon the High Courts of Justice in England*. London, 1635.

Eirenarcha: or of The Office of the Iustices of Peace. London, 1581.

A Lamentable Complaint of the Commonalty. [London], 1585.

Larkin, James F., and Paul L. Hughes, eds. *Stuart Royal Proclamations*. 2 vols. Oxford: Clarendon Press, 1973–83.

Laud, William. *The Works of the Most Reverend Father in God, William Laud*. Ed. William Scott and James Bliss. 7 vols. Oxford, 1847–60.

Littleton, Thomas. *Littleton's Tenures*. Ed. Eugene Wambaugh. Washington, D.C.: John Byrne, 1903.

Lucas, Scott C., ed. *A Mirror for Magistrates: A Modernized and Annotated Edition*. Cambridge: Cambridge University Press, 2019.

Lyly, John. *Pappe with an Hatchet*. In *The Complete Works of John Lyly*, ed. R. Warwick Bond, vol. 3. Oxford: Clarendon Press, 1902.

March, John. *Actions for Slaunder*. London, 1647.

Mar-Martine. [London, 1589].

Marprelate, Martin. *The Martin Marprelate Tracts: A Modernized and Annotated Edition*. Ed. Joseph L. Black. Cambridge: Cambridge University Press, 2008.

Marston, John. *The Scourge of Villanie*. In *The Poems of John Marston*, ed. Arnold Davenport. Liverpool: Liverpool University Press, 1961.

Martins Months minde. [London], 1589.

Massinger, Philip. *The Roman Actor: A Tragedy*. Ed. Martin White. Manchester: Manchester University Press, 2007.

May, Steven W., and Alan Bryson, eds. *Verse Libel in Renaissance England and Scotland*. Oxford: Oxford University Press, 2016.

Mead, Joseph. "A Critical Edition of the Letters of the Reverend Joseph Mead, 1626–1627, Contained in British Library Harleian MS 390." Ed. David Anthony John Cockburn. Unpublished PhD thesis, University of Cambridge, 1994.

Melton, John. *A Sixe-folde Politician*. London, 1609.

Mommsen, Theodor, with Paul Krueger, ed. *The Digest of Justinian*. Trans. Alan Watson. Vol. 4. Philadelphia: University of Pennsylvania Press, 1985.

More, Thomas. *The History of King Richard III*. Ed. Richard S. Sylvester. In *The Complete Works of St. Thomas More*, vol. 2. New Haven: Yale University Press, 1963.

The workes of Sir Thomas More Knyght. London, 1557.

A most sorrowfull Song, setting forth the miserable end of Banister. Pepys Ballads 1.64–65, EBBA 20265. Registered 1600; this version *c*.1630.

Munday, Anthony. *A Watch-woord to Englande*. London, 1584.

et al. *The Book of Sir Thomas More*. Ed. W. W. Greg. Oxford: Malone Society, 1911.

Bibliography

Sir Thomas More. Ed. John Jowett. Arden Shakespeare Third Series. London: Arden Shakespeare, 2011.

Sir Thomas More. Ed. Vittorio Gabrieli and Giorgio Melchiori. Manchester: Manchester University Press, 1990.

Nashe, Thomas. *Pierce Penilesse His Supplication to the Diuell*. London, 1592.

Nelson, Alan H., ed. *REED: Cambridge*. 2 vols. Toronto: University of Toronto Press, 1989.

Nicolson, Joseph, and Richard Burn. *The History and Antiquities of the Counties of Westmorland and Cumberland*. 2 vols. London, 1777.

Northbrooke, John. *A Treatise wherein Dicing, Dauncing, Vaine playes or Enterluds ... are reproued*. London, 1577.

Ovid. *Metamorphoses*. Trans. Frank Justus Miller. Rev. G. P. Goold. 2 vols. Cambridge, MA: Harvard University Press, 1977–84.

Parker, Matthew. *Articles for to be inquired of, in the Metropolitical visitation of the moste Reuerende father in God Matthew ... Archebyshop of Canterbury*. London, 1560.

Peacham, Henry. *The Garden of Eloquence*. London, 1593.

Peck, D. C., ed. *Leicester's Commonwealth: The Copy of a Letter Written by a Master of Art of Cambridge (1584) and Related Documents*. Athens: Ohio University Press, 1985.

"'The Letter of Estate': An Elizabethan Libel." *Notes and Queries* 28.1 (1981): 21–35.

"'News from Heaven and Hell': A Defamatory Narrative of the Earl of Leicester." *English Literary Renaissance* 8.2 (1978): 141–58.

Penry, John. *A Treatise Containing the Aequity of an Humble Supplication*. Oxford, 1587.

A viewe of some part of such publike wants & disorders as are in the seruice of God. [Coventry, 1589].

Persons, Robert. *A Conference about the Next Succession to the Crowne of Ingland*. [Antwerp], 1594/5.

A petition directed to her most excellent Maiestie. [1591].

Pimlyco. Or, Runne Red-Cap. London, 1609.

Piscator, Johannes. *Aphorismes of Christian Religion: Or, A Verie Compendious abridgement of M. I. Calvins Institutions*. Trans. Henry Holland. London, 1596.

Price, Daniel. *Sauls Prohibition Staide*. London, 1609.

Pulton, Ferdinando. *An abstract of all the penall Statutes which be generall, in force and vse*. London, 1577.

De Pace Regis et Regni. London, 1609.

The Replication of a Serjeant at the Laws of England. In J. A. Guy, *Christopher St German on Chancery and Statute*. London: Selden Society, 1985.

Rogers, Thomas. *Leicester's Ghost*. Ed. Franklin B. Williams, Jr. Chicago: University of Chicago Press, 1972.

Rollins, Hyder Edward, ed. *The Pepys Ballads*. 8 vols. Cambridge, MA: Harvard University Press, 1929–32.

Bibliography

Salvian [and Anthony Munday]. *A second and third blast of retrait from plaies and Theaters*. London, 1580.

Sambucus, Joannes. *Emblemata*. Antwerp, 1564.

Sanderson, Robert. *Ten Sermons Preached*. London, 1627.

Sawyer, Edmund, ed. *Memorials of Affairs of State in the Reigns of Q. Elizabeth and K. James I*. 3 vols. London, 1725.

Selden, John. *Table-Talk: being the Discourses of John Selden Esq*. London, 1689.

Shakespeare, William. *Julius Caesar*. Ed. David Daniell. Arden Shakespeare Third Series. Walton-on-Thames: Thomas Nelson, 1998.

King Richard II. Ed. Charles R. Forker. Arden Shakespeare Third Series. London: Arden Shakespeare, 2002.

The Merry Wives of Windsor. Ed. Giorgio Melchiori. Arden Shakespeare Third Series. Walton-on-Thames: Thomas Nelson, 2000.

The Rape of Lucrece. In *Shakespeare's Poems*, ed. Katherine Duncan-Jones and H. R. Woudhuysen. Arden Shakespeare Third Series. London: Arden Shakespeare, 2007.

Titus Andronicus. Ed. Eugene M. Waith. Oxford: Clarendon Press, 1984.

Titus Andronicus. Ed. Jonathan Bate. Arden Shakespeare Third Series. London: Routledge, 1995.

Titus Andronicus. In *The New Oxford Shakespeare: The Complete Works: Critical Reference Edition*, gen. ed. Gary Taylor, John Jowett, Terri Bourus, and Gabriel Egan, vol. 1. Oxford: Oxford University Press, 2017.

Twelfth Night. Ed. Keir Elam. Arden Shakespeare Third Series. London: Arden Shakespeare, 2008.

and John Fletcher. *King Henry VIII (All Is True)*. Ed. Gordon McMullan. Arden Shakespeare Third Series. London: Arden Shakespeare, 2000.

Sidney, Philip. *A Defence of Poetry*. In *Miscellaneous Prose of Sir Philip Sidney*, ed. Katherine Duncan-Jones and Jan van Dorsten. Oxford: Clarendon Press, 1973.

Smith, G. C. Moore, ed. *Club Law: A Comedy Acted in Clare Hall, Cambridge, about 1599–1600*. Cambridge: Cambridge University Press, 1907.

Smith, Henry. *The Sermons of Master Henrie Smith, gathered into one volume*. London, 1592.

Smith, Thomas. *De Republica Anglorum*. Ed. Mary Dewar. Cambridge: Cambridge University Press, 1982.

Somerset, J. Alan B., ed. *REED: Shropshire*. 2 vols. Toronto: University of Toronto Press, 1994.

REED: Staffordshire. REED Online. Accessed 27 Mar. 2019. https://ereed.libra ry.utoronto.ca/collections/staff/.

Southwell, Robert. *An Humble Supplication to Her Maiestie*. Ed. R. C. Bald. Cambridge: Cambridge University Press, 1953.

Spenser, Edmund. *The Faerie Queene*. Ed. A. C. Hamilton. Text ed. Hiroshi Yamashita and Toshiyuki Suzuki. Rev. 2nd ed. Harlow, UK: Pearson Longman, 2007.

The Statutes of the Realm. 11 vols. London, 1810–28; repr. 1963.

Bibliography

Stokes, James, ed. *REED: Lincolnshire*. 2 vols. Toronto: University of Toronto Press, 2009.

and Robert J. Alexander, eds. *REED: Somerset, including Bath*. 2 vols. Toronto: University of Toronto Press, 1996.

Stow, John. *The Annales of England*. London, 1600.

The Annales of England. London, 1605.

Strype, John. *Annals of the Reformation and Establishment of Religion . . . during Queen Elizabeth's Happy Reign*. 4 vols. Oxford, 1824.

Stubbes, Phillip. *The Anatomie of Abuses*. London, 1583.

Sutcliffe, Matthew. *An Answere to a Certaine Libel Supplicatorie, or Rather Diffamatory . . . put forth vnder the name and title of a Petition directed to her Maiestie*. London, 1592.

The Supplication of Certaine Masse-Priests falsely called Catholikes. Directed to the Kings most excellent Maiestie, now this time of Parliament, but scattered in corners, to mooue mal-contents to mutinie. Published with a Marginall glosse, and an answer to the Libellers reasons. London, 1604.

Tacitus. *Dialogus de Oratoribus*. Trans. W. Peterson. Rev. M. Winterbottom. In *Agricola, Germania, Dialogus*. Cambridge, MA: Harvard University Press, 1970.

The Ende of Nero and Beginning of Galba. Fower Bookes of the Histories of Cornelius Tacitus. The Life of Agricola. Trans. Henry Savile. Oxford, 1591.

Talpin, Jean. *A forme of Christian pollicie*. Trans. Geoffrey Fenton. London, 1574.

Thomas, A. H., and I. D. Thornley, eds. *The Great Chronicle of London*. London: George W. Jones, 1938.

The True Narration of the Entertainment of his Royall Maiestie. London, 1603.

The True Tragedie of Richard the Third. London, 1594.

Verstegan, Richard. *A Declaration of the True Causes of the Great Troubles, Presupposed to be Intended against the realme of England*. [Antwerp], 1592.

The Letters and Despatches of Richard Verstegan (c. 1550–1640). Ed. Anthony G. Petti. Catholic Record Society 52. London, 1959.

Vives, Juan Luis. *De disciplinis libri XX*. Antwerp, 1531.

"From *On the Causes of the Corruption of the Arts*." In *Renaissance Debates on Rhetoric*, ed. and trans. Wayne A. Rebhorn, 82–96. Ithaca: Cornell University Press, 2000.

Webbe, George. *The Araignement of an vnruly Tongue*. London, 1619.

Webster, John. *The Duchess of Malfi*. Ed. Brian Gibbons. 5th ed. London: Methuen Drama, 2014.

Weever, John. *The Whipping of the Satyre*. In *The Whipper Pamphlets (1601)*, ed. A. Davenport, vol. 1. Liverpool: University Press of Liverpool, 1951.

West, William. *Three Treatises, Of the second part of Symbolaeographie*. London, 1594.

Whitgift, John. *The Defense of the Aunswere to the Admonition, against the Replie of T.C.* London, 1574.

Whitney, Geffrey. *A Choice of Emblemes, and Other Devises*. Leiden, 1586.

224   *Bibliography*

Willes, Thomas. *A Word in Season, for a Warning to England*. London, 1659.
Wilson, Thomas. *A Christian Dictionarie*. London, 1612.
Wotton, Henry. *Reliquiae Wottonianae*. London, 1651.

Secondary Sources

Adams, Simon. *Leicester and the Court: Essays on Elizabethan Politics*. Manchester:
    Manchester University Press, 2002.
Angus, Bill. *Metadrama and the Informer in Shakespeare and Jonson*. Edinburgh:
    Edinburgh University Press, 2016.
Appleby, Andrew B. *Famine in Tudor and Stuart England*. Stanford: Stanford
    University Press, 1978.
Arab, Ronda, Michelle M. Dowd, and Adam Zucker, eds. *Historical Affects and the
    Early Modern Theater*. New York: Routledge, 2015.
Archdeacon, Anthony. "The Publication of *No-body and Some-body*: Humanism,
    History and Economics in the Early Jacobean Public Theatre." *Early Modern
    Literary Studies* 16.1 (2012), http://purl.org/emls/16-1/archnobo.htm.
Archer, Ian W. *The Pursuit of Stability: Social Relations in Elizabethan London*.
    Cambridge: Cambridge University Press, 1991.
Archer, John Michael. *Sovereignty and Intelligence: Spying and Court Culture in the
    English Renaissance*. Stanford: Stanford University Press, 1993.
Arendt, Hannah. *The Human Condition*. 2nd ed. Chicago: University of Chicago
    Press, 1998.
Arnold, Oliver. *The Third Citizen: Shakespeare's Theater and the Early
    Modern House of Commons*. Baltimore: Johns Hopkins University
    Press, 2007.
Bahr, Stephanie M. "*Titus Andronicus* and the Interpretive Violence of the
    Reformation." *Shakespeare Quarterly* 68.3 (2017): 241–70.
Bailey, Amanda, and Mario DiGangi, eds. *Affect Theory and Early Modern Texts:
    Politics, Ecologies, and Form*. New York: Palgrave Macmillan, 2017.
Baker, John. *An Introduction to English Legal History*. 5th ed. Oxford: Oxford
    University Press, 2019.
Barber, C. L. *Shakespeare's Festive Comedy: A Study of Dramatic Form and its
    Relation to Social Custom*. Princeton: Princeton University Press, 1959.
Barish, Jonas. "Three Caroline 'Defenses' of the Stage." In *Comedy from
    Shakespeare to Sheridan: Change and Continuity in the English and European
    Dramatic Tradition*, ed. A. R. Braunmuller and J. C. Bulman, 194–212.
    Newark: University of Delaware Press, 1986.
Bate, Jonathan. "Was Shakespeare an Essex Man?" *Proceedings of the British
    Academy* 162 (2009): 1–28.
Bath, Michael. *Speaking Pictures: English Emblem Books and Renaissance Culture*.
    London: Longman, 1994.
Bayer, Mark. *Theatre, Community, and Civic Engagement in Jacobean London*.
    Iowa City: University of Iowa Press, 2011.

Bibliography

Beal, Peter. *Catalogue of English Literary Manuscripts 1450–1700*. www.celm-ms.org.uk.

Bednarz, James P. *Shakespeare and the Poets' War*. New York: Columbia University Press, 2001.

Bellany, Alastair. "The Embarrassment of Libels: Perceptions and Representations of Verse Libelling in Early Stuart England." In *Politics of the Public Sphere*, ed. Lake and Pincus, 144–67.

"A Poem on the Archbishop's Hearse: Puritanism, Libel, and Sedition after the Hampton Court Conference." *Journal of British Studies* 34.2 (1995): 137–64.

The Politics of Court Scandal in Early Modern England: News Culture and the Overbury Affair, 1603–1660. Cambridge: Cambridge University Press, 2002.

"Railing Rhymes Revisited: Libels, Scandals, and Early Stuart Politics." *History Compass* 5.4 (2007): 1136–79.

"Singing Libel in Early Stuart England: The Case of the Staines Fiddlers, 1627." *Huntington Library Quarterly* 69.1 (2006): 177–93.

and Thomas Cogswell. *The Murder of King James I*. New Haven: Yale University Press, 2015.

Bentley, Gerald Eades. *Shakespeare and Jonson: Their Reputations in the Seventeenth Century Compared*. 2 vols. Chicago: University of Chicago Press, 1945.

Bergeron, David M. "Did a 'War of the Theaters' Occur?" In *Practicing Renaissance Scholarship: Plays and Pageants, Patrons and Politics*, 123–46. Pittsburgh: Duquesne University Press, 2000.

Berry, Edward. *Shakespeare's Comic Rites*. Cambridge: Cambridge University Press, 1984.

Beushausen, Katrin. *Theatre and the English Public from Reformation to Revolution*. Cambridge: Cambridge University Press, 2018.

Black, Joseph. "The Rhetoric of Reaction: The Martin Marprelate Tracts (1588–89), Anti-Martinism, and the Uses of Print in Early Modern England." *Sixteenth Century Journal* 28.3 (1997): 707–25.

Bohstedt, John. *The Politics of Provisions: Food Riots, Moral Economy, and Market Transition in England, c. 1550–1850*. Farnham, UK: Ashgate, 2010.

Boone, Joseph A., and Nancy J. Vickers. "Introduction: Celebrity Rites." *PMLA* 126.4 (2011): 900–911.

Boose, Lynda E. "The 1599 Bishops' Ban, Elizabethan Pornography, and the Sexualization of the Jacobean Stage." In *Enclosure Acts: Sexuality, Property, and Culture in Early Modern England*, ed. Richard Burt and John Michael Archer, 185–200. Ithaca: Cornell University Press, 1994.

Bowers, Fredson Thayer. "The Early Editions of Marlowe's *Ovid's Elegies*." *Studies in Bibliography* 25 (1972): 149–72.

Elizabethan Revenge Tragedy, 1587–1642. Princeton: Princeton University Press, 1940.

Braddick, Michael J. *The Nerves of State: Taxation and the Financing of the English State, 1558–1714*. Manchester: Manchester University Press, 1996.

State Formation in Early Modern England, c. 1550–1700. Cambridge: Cambridge University Press, 2000.

Bibliography

Briggs, William Dinsmore. "The Influence of Jonson's Tragedy in the Seventeenth Century." *Anglia* 35 (1912): 277–337.

Bristol, Michael D. *Carnival and Theater: Plebeian Culture and the Structure of Authority in Renaissance England.* New York: Methuen, 1985.

Brown, Pamela Allen, and Peter Parolin, eds. *Women Players in England, 1500–1660: Beyond the All-Male Stage.* Aldershot, UK: Ashgate, 2005.

Brown, Richard Danson. "'A Talkatiue Wench (Whose Words a World Hath Delighted in)': Mistress Shore and Elizabethan Complaint." *Review of English Studies* 49 (1998): 395–415.

Butler, Martin. "Romans in Britain: *The Roman Actor* and the Early Stuart Classical Play." In *Philip Massinger: A Critical Reassessment*, ed. Douglas Howard, 139–70. Cambridge: Cambridge University Press, 1985.

Cain, Tom. "'Satyres, That Girde and Fart at the Time': *Poetaster* and the Essex Rebellion." In *Refashioning Ben Jonson*, ed. Sanders, Chedgzoy, and Wiseman, 48–70.

Calhoun, Craig. "Imagining Solidarity: Cosmopolitanism, Constitutional Patriotism, and the Public Sphere." *Public Culture* 14.1 (2002): 147–71.

Campbell, Mildred. *The English Yeoman Under Elizabeth and the Early Stuarts.* New Haven: Yale University Press, 1942.

Cavanagh, Dermot, and Tim Kirk, eds. *Subversion and Scurrility: Popular Discourse in Europe from 1500 to the Present.* Aldershot, UK: Ashgate, 2000.

Chambers, E. K. *William Shakespeare: A Study of Facts and Problems.* 2 vols. Oxford: Clarendon Press, 1930.

Cheney, Patrick. *Shakespeare's Literary Authorship.* Cambridge: Cambridge University Press, 2008.

Chernaik, Warren. *The Myth of Rome in Shakespeare and His Contemporaries.* Cambridge: Cambridge University Press, 2011.

Clare, Janet. *'Art made tongue-tied by authority': Elizabethan and Jacobean Dramatic Censorship.* 2nd ed. Manchester: Manchester University Press, 1999.

———. "Jonson's 'Comical Satires' and the Art of Courtly Compliment." In *Refashioning Ben Jonson*, ed. Sanders, Chedgzoy, and Wiseman, 28–47.

Clegg, Cyndia Susan. *Press Censorship in Elizabethan England.* Cambridge: Cambridge University Press, 1997.

———. *Press Censorship in Jacobean England.* Cambridge: Cambridge University Press, 2001.

———. "Truth, Lies, and the Law of Slander in *Much Ado About Nothing.*" In *The Law in Shakespeare*, ed. Constance Jordan and Karen Cunningham, 167–88. Basingstoke, UK: Palgrave Macmillan, 2007.

Coast, David. "Speaking for the People in Early Modern England." *Past and Present* 244 (2019): 51–88.

Coffey, John. *Persecution and Toleration in Protestant England, 1558–1689.* Harlow, UK: Longman, 2000.

Cogswell, Thomas. *The Blessed Revolution: English Politics and the Coming of War, 1621–1624.* Cambridge: Cambridge University Press, 1989.

Bibliography

"John Felton, Popular Political Culture, and the Assassination of the Duke of Buckingham." *Historical Journal* 49.2 (2006): 357–85.

"Underground Verse and the Transformation of Early Stuart Political Culture." In *Political Culture and Cultural Politics in Early Modern England: Essays Presented to David Underdown*, ed. Susan D. Amussen and Mark A. Kishlansky, 277–300. Manchester: Manchester University Press, 1995.

and Peter Lake. "Buckingham Does the Globe: *Henry VIII* and the Politics of Popularity in the 1620s." *Shakespeare Quarterly* 60.3 (2009): 253–78.

Colclough, David. *Freedom of Speech in Early Stuart England*. Cambridge: Cambridge University Press, 2005.

"Talking to the Animals: Persuasion, Counsel and their Discontents in *Julius Caesar*." In *Shakespeare and Early Modern Political Thought*, ed. David Armitage, Conal Condren, and Andrew Fitzmaurice, 217–33. Cambridge: Cambridge University Press, 2009.

"Verse Libels and the Epideictic Tradition in Early Stuart England." *Huntington Library Quarterly* 69.1 (2006): 15–30.

Collinson, Patrick. "Ecclesiastical Vitriol: Religious Satire in the 1590s and the Invention of Puritanism." In *Reign of Elizabeth I*, ed. Guy, 150–70.

The Elizabethan Puritan Movement. Berkeley: University of California Press, 1967.

Consitt, Frances. *The London Weavers' Company*. Vol. 1. Oxford: Clarendon Press, 1933.

Cormack, Bradin. *A Power to Do Justice: Jurisdiction, English Literature, and the Rise of Common Law, 1509–1625*. Chicago: University of Chicago Press, 2007.

Corrigan, Nora L. "The Merry Tanner, the Mayor's Feast, and the King's Mistress: Thomas Heywood's *1 Edward IV* and the Ballad Tradition." *Medieval and Renaissance Drama in England* 22 (2009): 27–41.

Craig, Hugh. "The Date of *Sir Thomas More*." *Shakespeare Survey* 66 (2013): 38–54.

Craik, Katharine A., and Tanya Pollard, eds. *Shakespearean Sensations: Experiencing Literature in Early Modern England*. Cambridge: Cambridge University Press, 2013.

Cressy, David. *Dangerous Talk: Scandalous, Seditious, and Treasonable Speech in Pre-Modern England*. Oxford: Oxford University Press, 2010.

Croft, Pauline. "Libels, Popular Literacy and Public Opinion in Early Modern England." *Historical Research* 68 (1995): 266–85.

"The Reputation of Robert Cecil: Libels, Political Opinion and Popular Awareness in the Early Seventeenth Century." *Transactions of the Royal Historical Society* 1 (1991): 43–69.

Croft, Ryan J. "Embodying the Catholic *Ruines of Rome* in *Titus Andronicus*: du Bellay, Spenser, Peele, and Shakespeare." *Spenser Studies* 31/32 (2018): 319–48.

Crupi, Charles W. "Ideological Contradiction in Part I of Heywood's *Edward IV*: 'Our Musicke Runs . . . Much upon Discords.'" *Medieval and Renaissance Drama in England* 7 (1995): 224–56.

Cummings, Brian. "Conscience and the Law in Thomas More." *Renaissance Studies* 23.4 (2009): 463–85.

228   Bibliography

Cust, Richard. "News and Politics in Early Seventeenth-Century England." *Past and Present* 112 (1986): 60–90.

Daly, Peter M. "Emblems: An Introduction." In *Companion to Emblem Studies*, ed. Daly, 1–24. New York: AMS Press, 2008.

Literature in the Light of the Emblem: Structural Parallels between the Emblem and Literature in the Sixteenth and Seventeenth Centuries. 2nd ed. Toronto: University of Toronto Press, 1998.

Dawson, Anthony B. "The Arithmetic of Memory: Shakespeare's Theatre and the National Past." *Shakespeare Survey* 52 (1999): 54–67.

Daybell, James. "The Scribal Circulation of Early Modern Letters." *Huntington Library Quarterly* 79.3 (2016): 365–85.

De Luna, B. N. *Jonson's Romish Plot: A Study of "Catiline" and its Historical Context.* Oxford: Clarendon Press, 1967.

Deleuze, Gilles, and Félix Guattari. *A Thousand Plateaus: Capitalism and Schizophrenia.* Trans. Brian Massumi. Minneapolis: University of Minnesota Press, 1987.

Deutermann, Allison K., Matthew Hunter, and Musa Gurnis, eds. *Publicity and the Early Modern Stage: People Made Public.* Cham: Palgrave Macmillan, 2021.

Dickson, Vernon Guy. "'A pattern, precedent, and lively warrant': Emulation, Rhetoric, and Cruel Propriety in *Titus Andronicus.*" *Renaissance Quarterly* 62.2 (2009): 376–409.

Dimmock, Matthew. "Guns and Gawds: Elizabethan England's Infidel Trade." In *A Companion to the Global Renaissance: English Literature and Culture in the Era of Expansion*, ed. Jyotsna G. Singh, 207–22. Chichester: Wiley-Blackwell, 2009.

"Tamburlaine's Curse: An Answer to a Great Marlowe Mystery." *Times Literary Supplement*, November 19, 2010, 16–17.

Doelman, James. *The Epigram in England, 1590–1640.* Manchester: Manchester University Press, 2016.

Dolan, Frances E. "'Gentlemen, I have one thing more to say': Women on Scaffolds in England, 1563–1680." *Modern Philology* 92.2 (1994): 157–78.

Dollimore, Jonathan. *Radical Tragedy: Religion, Ideology and Power in the Drama of Shakespeare and His Contemporaries.* 2nd ed. New York: Harvester Wheatsheaf, 1989.

Donaldson, Ian. *Ben Jonson: A Life.* Oxford: Oxford University Press, 2011.

"'Misconstruing Everything': *Julius Caesar* and *Sejanus.*" In *Shakespeare Performed: Essays in Honor of R. A. Foakes*, ed. Grace Ioppolo, 88–107. Newark: University of Delaware Press, 2000.

Doty, Jeffrey S. *Shakespeare, Popularity and the Public Sphere.* Cambridge: Cambridge University Press, 2017.

Duncan, Helga L. "'Sumptuously Re-edified': The Reformation of Sacred Space in *Titus Andronicus.*" *Comparative Drama* 43.4 (2009): 425–53.

Dutton, Richard. *Ben Jonson: To The First Folio.* Cambridge: Cambridge University Press, 1983.

Bibliography

Ben Jonson, "Volpone" and the Gunpowder Plot. Cambridge: Cambridge University Press, 2008.

Licensing, Censorship and Authorship in Early Modern England: Buggeswords. Basingstoke, UK: Palgrave, 2000.

Mastering the Revels: The Regulation and Censorship of English Renaissance Drama. Basingstoke, UK: Macmillan, 1991.

ed. *The Oxford Handbook of Early Modern Theatre.* Oxford: Oxford University Press, 2009.

Shakespeare, Court Dramatist. Oxford: Oxford University Press, 2016.

Dzelzainis, Martin. "'The Feminine part of every Rebellion': Francis Bacon on Sedition and Libel, and the Beginning of Ideology." *Huntington Library Quarterly* 69.1 (2006): 139–52.

Eccles, Mark. "Jonson and the Spies." *Review of English Studies* 13 (1937): 385–97.

Eckhardt, Joshua. *Manuscript Verse Collectors and the Politics of Anti-Courtly Love Poetry.* Oxford: Oxford University Press, 2009.

Egan, Clare. "Jacobean Star Chamber Records and the Performance of Provincial Libel." In *Star Chamber Matters: An Early Modern Court and Its Records*, ed. K. J. Kesselring and Natalie Mears, 135–53. London: University of London Press, 2021.

"'Now fearing neither friend nor foe, to the worldes viewe these verses goe': Mapping Libel Performance in Early-Modern Devon." *Medieval English Theatre* 36 (2014): 70–103.

"Performing Early Modern Libel: Expanding the Boundaries of Performance." *Early Theatre* 23.2 (2020): 155–68.

"Reading *Mankind* in a Culture of Defamation." *Medieval English Theatre* 40 (2018): 122–54.

Elsky, Stephanie. *Custom, Common Law, and the Constitution of English Renaissance Literature.* Oxford: Oxford University Press, 2020.

Endicott, Timothy A. O. "The Conscience of the King: Christopher St. German and Thomas More and the Development of English Equity." *University of Toronto Faculty of Law Review* 47.2 (1989): 549–70.

Erne, Lukas. "'Popish Tricks' and 'a Ruinous Monastery': *Titus Andronicus* and the Question of Shakespeare's Catholicism." *SPELL: Swiss Papers in English Language and Literature* 13 (2000): 135–55.

Erskine-Hill, Howard. *The Augustan Idea in English Literature.* London: Edward Arnold, 1983.

Evans, Robert C. "Jonson and the Emblematic Tradition: Ralegh, Brant, the Poems, *The Alchemist*, and *Volpone.*" *Comparative Drama* 29.1 (1995): 108–32.

Fallon, Samuel. "Nobody's Business." In *Publicity and the Early Modern Stage*, ed. Deutermann, Hunter, and Gurnis, 217–43.

Farmer, Alan B., and Zachary Lesser. "What Is Print Popularity? A Map of the Elizabethan Book Trade." In *The Elizabethan Top Ten: Defining Print Popularity in Early Modern England*, ed. Andy Kesson and Emma Smith, 19–54. Farnham, UK: Ashgate, 2013.

Bibliography

Fawcett, Mary Laughlin. "Arms/Words/Tears: Language and the Body in *Titus Andronicus*." *ELH* 50.2 (1983): 261–77.

Feingold, Mordechai. "Scholarship and Politics: Henry Savile's Tacitus and the Essex Connection." *Review of English Studies* 67 (2016): 855–74.

Finkelpearl, Philip J. "'The Comedians' Liberty': Censorship of the Jacobean Stage Reconsidered." *English Literary Renaissance* 16.1 (1986): 123–38.

Fitter, Chris. *Radical Shakespeare: Politics and Stagecraft in the Early Career*. New York: Routledge, 2012.

Fletcher, A. J. "Honour, Reputation and Local Officeholding in Elizabethan and Stuart England." In *Order and Disorder in Early Modern England*, ed. Fletcher and John Stevenson, 92–115. Cambridge: Cambridge University Press, 1985.

Fortier, Mark. *The Culture of Equity in Early Modern England*. Aldershot, UK: Ashgate, 2005.

Fox, Adam. *Oral and Literate Culture in England, 1500–1700*. Oxford: Clarendon Press, 2000.

    "Rumour, News and Popular Political Opinion in Elizabethan and Early Stuart England." *Historical Journal* 40.3 (1997): 597–620.

Fox, Alistair. "The Paradoxical Design of *The Book of Sir Thomas More*." *Renaissance and Reformation / Renaissance et Réforme* 5.3 (1981): 162–73.

Fraser, Nancy. "Rethinking the Public Sphere: A Contribution to the Critique of Actually Existing Democracy." In *Habermas and the Public Sphere*, ed. Craig Calhoun, 109–42. Cambridge, MA: MIT Press, 1992.

Freeman, Arthur. "Marlowe, Kyd, and the Dutch Church Libel." *English Literary Renaissance* 3.1 (1973): 44–52.

    Thomas Kyd: Facts and Problems. Oxford: Clarendon Press, 1967.

Fumerton, Patricia. *The Broadside Ballad in Early Modern England: Moving Media, Tactical Publics*. Philadelphia: University of Pennsylvania Press, 2020.

Gair, Reavley. *The Children of Paul's: The Story of a Theatre Company, 1553–1608*. Cambridge: Cambridge University Press, 1982.

Gajda, Alexandra. *The Earl of Essex and Late Elizabethan Political Culture*. Oxford: Oxford University Press, 2012.

Gibson, C. A. "Massinger's Use of His Sources for 'The Roman Actor.'" *Journal of the Australasian Universities Language and Literature Association* 15 (1961): 60–72.

Gill, Roma, and Robert Krueger. "The Early Editions of Marlowe's Elegies and Davies's Epigrams: Sequence and Authority." *The Library*, 5th ser., 26.3 (1971): 242–49.

Goldie, Mark. "The Unacknowledged Republic: Officeholding in Early Modern England." In *Politics of the Excluded*, ed. Harris, 153–94.

Goose, Nigel. "'Xenophobia' in Elizabethan and Early Stuart England: An Epithet Too Far?" In *Immigrants in Tudor and Early Stuart England*, ed. Goose and Lien Luu, 110–35. Brighton, UK: Sussex Academic Press, 2005.

Gordon, Andrew. "The Act of Libel: Conscripting Civic Space in Early Modern England." *Journal of Medieval and Early Modern Studies* 32.2 (2002): 375–97.

Bibliography

Gordon, D. J. "Poet and Architect: The Intellectual Setting of the Quarrel between Ben Jonson and Inigo Jones." *Journal of the Warburg and Courtauld Institutes* 12 (1949): 152–78.

Gowing, Laura. "Women, Status and the Popular Culture of Dishonour." *Transactions of the Royal Historical Society* 6 (1996): 225–34.

Greenblatt, Stephen. *Shakespearean Negotiations: The Circulation of Social Energy in Renaissance England*. Berkeley: University of California Press, 1988.

Greg, W. W. Review of *Club Law*, ed. G. C. Moore Smith. *Modern Language Review* 4.2 (1909): 268–69.

Griffin, Eric. "Shakespeare, Marlowe, and the Stranger Crisis of the Early 1590s." In *Shakespeare and Immigration*, ed. Ruben Espinosa and David Ruiter, 13–36. Farnham, UK: Ashgate, 2014.

Griffith, Eva. *A Jacobean Company and Its Playhouse: The Queen's Servants at the Red Bull Theatre (c. 1605–1619)*. Cambridge: Cambridge University Press, 2013.

Griffiths, Paul. *Youth and Authority: Formative Experiences in England, 1560–1640*. Oxford: Clarendon Press, 1996.

Gross, Kenneth. *Shakespeare's Noise*. Chicago: University of Chicago Press, 2001.

Gurnis, Musa. *Mixed Faith and Shared Feeling: Theater in Post-Reformation London*. Philadelphia: University of Pennsylvania Press, 2018.

Gurr, Andrew. *Playgoing in Shakespeare's London*. 3rd ed. Cambridge: Cambridge University Press, 2004.

"Professional Playing in London and Superior Cambridge Responses." *Shakespeare Studies* 37 (2009): 43–53.

The Shakespearean Stage, 1574–1642. 4th ed. Cambridge: Cambridge University Press, 2009.

The Shakespearian Playing Companies. Oxford: Clarendon Press, 1996.

and Karoline Szatek. "Women and Crowds at the Theater." *Medieval and Renaissance Drama in England* 21 (2008): 157–69.

Guy, John, ed. *The Reign of Elizabeth I: Court and Culture in the Last Decade*. Cambridge: Cambridge University Press, 1995.

"Thomas More and Christopher St. German: The Battle of the Books." *Moreana* 21 (1984): 5–25.

Habermann, Ina. *Staging Slander and Gender in Early Modern England*. Aldershot, UK: Ashgate, 2003.

Habermas, Jürgen. *The Structural Transformation of the Public Sphere: An Inquiry into a Category of Bourgeois Society*. Trans. Thomas Burger with Frederick Lawrence. Cambridge, MA: MIT Press, 1989.

Hadfield, Andrew. *Shakespeare and Republicanism*. Cambridge: Cambridge University Press, 2005.

Hammer, Paul E. J. "Shakespeare's *Richard II*, the Play of 7 February 1601, and the Essex Rising." *Shakespeare Quarterly* 59.1 (2008): 1–35.

"The Smiling Crocodile: The Earl of Essex and Late Elizabethan 'Popularity.'" In *Politics of the Public Sphere*, ed. Lake and Pincus, 95–115.

Harding, Vanessa. "Cheapside: Commerce and Commemoration." *Huntington Library Quarterly* 71.1 (2008): 77–96.

Bibliography

Harris, Jonathan Gil. *Sick Economies: Drama, Mercantilism, and Disease in Shakespeare's England*. Philadelphia: University of Pennsylvania Press, 2004.

Harris, Tim, ed. *The Politics of the Excluded, c. 1500–1850*. Basingstoke, UK: Palgrave, 2001.

Helgerson, Richard. *Adulterous Alliances: Home, State, and History in Early Modern European Drama and Painting*. Chicago: University of Chicago Press, 2000.

Helmholz, R. H. *The Oxford History of the Laws of England*. Vol. 1, *The Canon Law and Ecclesiastical Jurisdiction from 597 to the 1640s*. Oxford: Oxford University Press, 2004.

Higgins, Siobhán. "'Let us Not Grieve the Soul of the Stranger': Images and Imaginings of the Dutch and Flemish in Late Elizabethan London." *Dutch Crossing* 37.1 (2013): 20–40.

Highley, Christopher. *Blackfriars in Early Modern London: Theater, Church, and Neighborhood*. Oxford: Oxford University Press, 2022.

Hill, Tracey. "'The Cittie is in an uproare': Staging London in *The Booke of Sir Thomas More*." *Early Modern Literary Studies* 11.1 (2005), http://purl.oclc.org/emls/11-1/more.htm.

Hobbs, Mary. *Early Seventeenth-Century Verse Miscellany Manuscripts*. Aldershot, UK: Scolar Press, 1992.

Hobgood, Allison P. *Passionate Playgoing in Early Modern England*. Cambridge: Cambridge University Press, 2014.

Holdsworth, W. S. *A History of English Law*. 17 vols. London: Methuen, 1903–72.

Holmes, Peter. "The Authorship of 'Leicester's Commonwealth.'" *Journal of Ecclesiastical History* 33.3 (1982): 424–30.

Honigmann, E. A. J. "Shakespeare, *Sir Thomas More* and Asylum Seekers." *Shakespeare Survey* 57 (2004): 225–35.

Hopkins, Lisa. *The Cultural Uses of the Caesars on the English Renaissance Stage*. Aldershot, UK: Ashgate, 2008.

Hornback, Robert. *The English Clown Tradition from the Middle Ages to Shakespeare*. Cambridge: D. S. Brewer, 2009.

Hotson, Leslie. "Marigold of the Poets." *Essays by Divers Hands: Being the Transactions of the Royal Society of Literature of the United Kingdom*, n.s., 17 (1938): 47–68.

Houliston, Victor. "Persons' Displeasure: Collaboration and Design in *Leicester's Commonwealth*." In *Publishing Subversive Texts in Elizabethan England and the Polish-Lithuanian Commonwealth*, ed. Teresa Bela, Clarinda Calma, and Jolanta Rzegocka, 155–66. Leiden: Brill, 2016.

Howard, Jean E. *The Stage and Social Struggle in Early Modern England*. London: Routledge, 1994.

Hoyle, R. W. "Lords, Tenants, and Tenant Right in the Sixteenth Century: Four Studies." *Northern History* 20 (1984): 38–63.

"Petitioning as Popular Politics in Early Sixteenth-Century England." *Historical Research* 75 (2002): 365–89.

Hunt, Arnold. *The Art of Hearing: English Preachers and Their Audiences, 1590–1640*. Cambridge: Cambridge University Press, 2010.

Bibliography

Hunter, Matthew. *The Pursuit of Style in Early Modern Drama: Forms of Talk on the London Stage*. Cambridge: Cambridge University Press, 2022.

Hutson, Lorna. *The Invention of Suspicion: Law and Mimesis in Shakespeare and Renaissance Drama*. Oxford: Oxford University Press, 2007.

Hutton, Ronald. *The Stations of the Sun: A History of the Ritual Year in Britain*. Oxford: Oxford University Press, 1996.

Ibbetson, David. "Edward Coke, Roman Law, and the Law of Libel." In *The Oxford Handbook of English Law and Literature, 1500–1700*, ed. Lorna Hutson, 487–506. Oxford: Oxford University Press, 2017.

"A House Built on Sand: Equity in Early Modern English Law." In *Law & Equity*, ed. Koops and Zwalve, 55–77.

Ingram, Martin. "Ridings, Rough Music and Mocking Rhymes in Early Modern England." In *Popular Culture in Seventeenth-Century England*, ed. Barry Reay, 166–97. London: Croom Helm, 1985.

"Ridings, Rough Music and the 'Reform of Popular Culture' in Early Modern England." *Past and Present* 105 (1984): 79–113.

Ioppolo, Grace. "Robert Devereux, 2nd Earl of Essex, and the Practice of Theatre." In *Essex: The Cultural Impact of an Elizabethan Courtier*, ed. Annaliese Connolly and Lisa Hopkins, 63–80. Manchester: Manchester University Press, 2013.

Jackson, MacDonald P. "Deciphering a Date and Determining a Date: Anthony Munday's *John a Kent and John a Cumber* and the Original Version of *Sir Thomas More*." *Early Modern Literary Studies* 15.3 (2011), http://purl.org/emls/15-3/jackdate.htm.

"Shakespeare's *Richard II* and the Anonymous *Thomas of Woodstock*." *Medieval and Renaissance Drama in England* 14 (2001): 17–65.

Jed, Stephanie H. *Chaste Thinking: The Rape of Lucretia and the Birth of Humanism*. Bloomington: Indiana University Press, 1989.

Jones, William R. "The Bishops' Ban of 1599 and the Ideology of English Satire." *Literature Compass* 7.5 (2010): 332–46.

Kaplan, M. Lindsay. *The Culture of Slander in Early Modern England*. Cambridge: Cambridge University Press, 1997.

Kastan, David Scott. "Proud Majesty Made a Subject: Shakespeare and the Spectacle of Rule." *Shakespeare Quarterly* 37.4 (1986): 459–75.

Kendall, Gillian Murray. "'Lend me thy hand': Metaphor and Mayhem in *Titus Andronicus*." *Shakespeare Quarterly* 40.3 (1989): 299–316.

Kermode, Lloyd Edward. *Aliens and Englishness in Elizabethan Drama*. Cambridge: Cambridge University Press, 2009.

Kesselring, K. J. *Mercy and Authority in the Tudor State*. Cambridge: Cambridge University Press, 2003.

Kewes, Paulina. "Henry Savile's Tacitus and the Politics of Roman History in Late Elizabethan England." *Huntington Library Quarterly* 74.4 (2011): 515–51.

"'I Ask Your Voices and Your Suffrages': The Bogus Rome of Peele and Shakespeare's *Titus Andronicus*." *Review of Politics* 78.4 (2016): 551–70.

Bibliography

Kiséry, András. *Hamlet's Moment: Drama and Political Knowledge in Early Modern England*. Oxford: Oxford University Press, 2016.

Klause, John. *Shakespeare, the Earl, and the Jesuit*. Madison, NJ: Fairleigh Dickinson University Press, 2008.

Klinck, Dennis R. *Conscience, Equity and the Court of Chancery in Early Modern England*. Farnham, UK: Ashgate, 2010.

Knowles, James. *Politics and Political Culture in the Court Masque*. Basingstoke, UK: Palgrave Macmillan, 2015.

"To 'scourge the arse / Jove's marrow so had wasted': Scurrility and the Subversion of Sodomy." In *Subversion and Scurrility*, ed. Cavanagh and Kirk, 74–92.

Knowles, Ronald. *Shakespeare's Arguments with History*. Basingstoke, UK: Palgrave, 2002.

Knutson, Roslyn Lander. *Playing Companies and Commerce in Shakespeare's Time*. Cambridge: Cambridge University Press, 2001.

Koops, E., and W. J. Zwalve, eds. *Law & Equity: Approaches in Roman Law and Common Law*. Leiden: Martinus Nijhoff, 2014.

Korda, Natasha. *Shakespeare's Domestic Economies: Gender and Property in Early Modern England*. Philadelphia: University of Pennsylvania Press, 2002.

Kuriyama, Constance Brown. *Christopher Marlowe: A Renaissance Life*. Ithaca: Cornell University Press, 2002.

Kyle, Chris R. "Monarch and Marketplace: Proclamations as News in Early Modern England." *Huntington Library Quarterly* 78.4 (2015): 771–87.

Ladd, Roger A. "Thomas Deloney and the London Weavers' Company." *Sixteenth Century Journal* 32.4 (2001): 981–1001.

Lake, D. J. "Three Seventeenth-Century Revisions: *Thomas of Woodstock*, *The Jew of Malta*, and *Faustus B*." *Notes and Queries* 30.2 (1983): 133–43.

Lake, Peter. *Bad Queen Bess? Libels, Secret Histories, and the Politics of Publicity in the Reign of Queen Elizabeth I*. Oxford: Oxford University Press, 2016.

Hamlet's Choice: Religion and Resistance in Shakespeare's Revenge Tragedies. New Haven: Yale University Press, 2020.

How Shakespeare Put Politics on the Stage: Power and Succession in the History Plays. New Haven: Yale University Press, 2016.

and Steven Pincus, eds. *The Politics of the Public Sphere in Early Modern England*. Manchester: Manchester University Press, 2007.

and Steven Pincus. "Rethinking the Public Sphere in Early Modern England." In *Politics of the Public Sphere*, ed. Lake and Pincus, 1–30.

and Michael Questier. *All Hail to the Archpriest: Confessional Conflict, Toleration, and the Politics of Publicity in Post-Reformation England*. Oxford: Oxford University Press, 2019.

Lander, Jesse M. "'Faith in Me vnto this Commonwealth': *Edward IV* and the Civic Nation." *Renaissance Drama* 27 (1996): 47–78.

Inventing Polemic: Religion, Print, and Literary Culture in Early Modern England. Cambridge: Cambridge University Press, 2006.

Bibliography

Laroque, François. *Shakespeare's Festive World: Elizabethan Seasonal Entertainment and the Professional Stage*. Trans. Janet Lloyd. Cambridge: Cambridge University Press, 1991.

Lees-Jeffries, Hester. *England's Helicon: Fountains in Early Modern Literature and Culture*. Oxford: Oxford University Press, 2007.

Lenthe, Victor. "Ben Jonson's Antagonistic Style, Public Opinion, and *Sejanus*." *Studies in English Literature 1500–1900* 57.2 (2017): 349–68.

Levin, Richard. "Women in the Renaissance Theatre Audience." *Shakespeare Quarterly* 40.2 (1989): 165–74.

Levine, Nina. *Practicing the City: Early Modern London on Stage*. New York: Fordham University Press, 2016.

Levy, Fritz. "The Decorum of News." In *News, Newspapers, and Society in Early Modern Britain*, ed. Joad Raymond, 12–38. London: Frank Cass, 1999.

Liddell, Henry George, and Robert Scott. *A Greek-English Lexicon*. Rev. Henry Stuart Jones with Roderick McKenzie. Oxford: Clarendon Press, 1940.

Liebler, Naomi Conn. *Shakespeare's Festive Tragedy: The Ritual Foundations of Genre*. London: Routledge, 1995.

Lin, Erika T. "Festive Friars: Embodied Performance and Audience Affect." *Journal of Medieval and Early Modern Studies* 51.3 (2021): 487–95.

"Festivity." In *Early Modern Theatricality*, ed. Henry S. Turner, 212–29. Oxford: Oxford University Press, 2013.

Long, William B. "The Occasion of *The Book of Sir Thomas More*." In *Shakespeare and "Sir Thomas More": Essays on the Play and Its Shakespearian Interest*, ed. T. H. Howard-Hill, 45–56. Cambridge: Cambridge University Press, 1989.

Longstaffe, Stephen. "Puritan Tribulation and the Protestant History Play." In *Literature and Censorship in Renaissance England*, ed. Andrew Hadfield, 31–49. Basingstoke, UK: Palgrave, 2001.

Lopez, Jeremy. *Theatrical Convention and Audience Response in Early Modern Drama*. Cambridge: Cambridge University Press, 2003.

Love, Harold. *Scribal Publication in Seventeenth-Century England*. Oxford: Clarendon Press, 1993.

Loxley, James. "On Exegetical Duty: Historical Pragmatics and the Grammar of the Libel." *Huntington Library Quarterly* 69.1 (2006): 83–103.

and Mark Robson. *Shakespeare, Jonson, and the Claims of the Performative*. New York: Routledge, 2013.

Lublin, Robert I. *Costuming the Shakespearean Stage: Visual Codes of Representation in Early Modern Theatre and Culture*. Burlington, VT: Ashgate, 2011.

Luu, Lien Bich. *Immigrants and the Industries of London, 1500–1700*. Aldershot, UK: Ashgate, 2005.

"Migration and Change: Religious Refugees and the London Economy, 1550–1600." *Critical Survey* 8.1 (1996): 93–102.

"'Taking the Bread Out of Our Mouths': Xenophobia in Early Modern London." *Immigrants and Minorities* 19.2 (2000): 1–22.

Mack, Peter. *Elizabethan Rhetoric: Theory and Practice*. Cambridge: Cambridge University Press, 2002.

Bibliography

MacKay, Ellen. *Persecution, Plague, and Fire: Fugitive Histories of the Stage in Early Modern England*. Chicago: University of Chicago Press, 2011.

Macnair, Mike. "Arbitrary Chancellors and the Problem of Predictability." In *Law & Equity*, ed. Koops and Zwalve, 79–104.

"Equity and Conscience." *Oxford Journal of Legal Studies* 27.4 (2007): 659–81.

Maniscalco, Lorenzo. "*Interpretatio ex aequo et bono*: The Emergence of Equitable Interpretation in European Legal Scholarship." In *Networks and Connections in Legal History*, ed. Michael Lobban and Ian Williams, 233–61. Cambridge: Cambridge University Press, 2020.

Manley, Lawrence, and Sally-Beth MacLean. *Lord Strange's Men and Their Plays*. New Haven: Yale University Press, 2014.

Manning, John. *The Emblem*. London: Reaktion Books, 2002.

Manning, Roger B. "The Origins of the Doctrine of Sedition." *Albion* 12.2 (1980): 99–121.

"Richard Shelley of Warminghurst and the English Catholic Petition for Toleration of 1585." *Recusant History* 6.6 (1961–62): 265–74.

Mansky, Joseph. "The Case of Eleazar Edgar: *Leicester's Commonwealth* and the Book Trade in 1604." *Papers of the Bibliographical Society of America* 115.2 (2021): 233–41.

"Edward Coke, William West, and the Law of Libel." *Journal of Legal History* 42.3 (2021): 328–32.

Marcus, Sharon. *The Drama of Celebrity*. Princeton: Princeton University Press, 2019.

Marlow, Christopher. *Performing Masculinity in English University Drama, 1598–1636*. Farnham, UK: Ashgate, 2013.

Marotti, Arthur F. *Manuscript, Print, and the English Renaissance Lyric*. Ithaca: Cornell University Press, 1995.

Martin, Randall. "Elizabethan Civic Pageantry in *Henry VI*." *University of Toronto Quarterly* 60.2 (1990–91): 244–64.

Massumi, Brian. *Parables for the Virtual: Movement, Affect, Sensation*. Durham, NC: Duke University Press, 2002.

McCabe, Richard A. "Elizabethan Satire and the Bishops' Ban of 1599." *Yearbook of English Studies* 11 (1981): 188–93.

McManus, Clare, and Lucy Munro, eds. "Renaissance Women's Performance and the Dramatic Canon: Theater History, Evidence, and Narratives." Special issue. *Shakespeare Bulletin* 33.1 (2015).

McMillin, Scott. *The Elizabethan Theatre and "The Book of Sir Thomas More."* Ithaca: Cornell University Press, 1987.

and Sally-Beth MacLean. *The Queen's Men and their Plays*. Cambridge: Cambridge University Press, 1998.

McRae, Andrew. *Literature, Satire and the Early Stuart State*. Cambridge: Cambridge University Press, 2004.

ed. "'Railing Rhymes': Politics and Poetry in Early Stuart England." Special issue. *Huntington Library Quarterly* 69.1 (2006).

Bibliography

"The Verse Libel: Popular Satire in Early Modern England." In *Subversion and Scurrility*, ed. Cavanagh and Kirk, 58–73.

Mears, Natalie. "Counsel, Public Debate, and Queenship: John Stubbs's *The Discoverie of a Gaping Gulf*, 1579." *Historical Journal* 44.3 (2001): 629–50.

Meskill, Lynn S. *Ben Jonson and Envy*. Cambridge: Cambridge University Press, 2009.

Millstone, Noah. *Manuscript Circulation and the Invention of Politics in Early Stuart England*. Cambridge: Cambridge University Press, 2016.

Milsom, S. F. C. *Historical Foundations of the Common Law*. 2nd ed. Toronto: Butterworths, 1981.

Milward, Peter. "The Jewel-Harding Controversy." *Albion* 6.4 (1974): 320–41.

Monta, Susannah Brietz. *Martyrdom and Literature in Early Modern England*. Cambridge: Cambridge University Press, 2005.

Montrose, Louis. *The Purpose of Playing: Shakespeare and the Cultural Politics of the Elizabethan Theatre*. Chicago: University of Chicago Press, 1996.

Morgan, Victor, with Christopher Brooke. *A History of the University of Cambridge*. Vol. 2, *1546–1750*. Cambridge: Cambridge University Press, 2004.

Morrissey, Mary. *Politics and the Paul's Cross Sermons, 1558–1642*. Oxford: Oxford University Press, 2011.

Moschovakis, Nicholas R. "'Irreligious Piety' and Christian History: Persecution as Pagan Anachronism in *Titus Andronicus*." *Shakespeare Quarterly* 53.4 (2002): 460–86.

"Topicality and Conceptual Blending: *Titus Andronicus* and the Case of William Hacket." *College Literature* 33.1 (2006): 127–50.

Moul, Victoria. *Jonson, Horace and the Classical Tradition*. Cambridge: Cambridge University Press, 2010.

Mullaney, Steven. *The Reformation of Emotions in the Age of Shakespeare*. Chicago: University of Chicago Press, 2015.

Munro, Lucy, Anne Lancashire, John Astington, and Marta Straznicky. "Issues in Review: Popular Theatre and the Red Bull." *Early Theatre* 9.2 (2006): 99–156.

Ngai, Sianne. *Ugly Feelings*. Cambridge, MA: Harvard University Press, 2005.

Nicholl, Charles. *The Reckoning: The Murder of Christopher Marlowe*. New York: Harcourt Brace, 1992.

North, Marcy L. *The Anonymous Renaissance: Cultures of Discretion in Tudor-Stuart England*. Chicago: University of Chicago Press, 2003.

Nuttall, Geoffrey F. "The English Martyrs 1535–1680: A Statistical Review." *Journal of Ecclesiastical History* 22.3 (1971): 191–97.

Oakley-Brown, Liz. "*Titus Andronicus* and the Cultural Politics of Translation in Early Modern England." *Renaissance Studies* 19.3 (2005): 325–47.

O'Callaghan, Michelle. *The English Wits: Literature and Sociability in Early Modern England*. Cambridge: Cambridge University Press, 2007.

"Performing Politics: The Circulation of the 'Parliament Fart.'" *Huntington Library Quarterly* 69.1 (2006): 121–38.

Bibliography

O'Conor, Norreys Jephson. *Godes Peace and the Queenes: Vicissitudes of a House, 1539–1615*. Cambridge, MA: Harvard University Press, 1934.

Oldenburg, Scott. *Alien Albion: Literature and Immigration in Early Modern England*. Toronto: University of Toronto Press, 2014.

Orlin, Lena Cowen. "Making Public the Private." In *Forms of Association*, ed. Yachnin and Eberhart, 93–114.

Packard, Bethany. "Lavinia as Coauthor of Shakespeare's *Titus Andronicus*." *Studies in English Literature 1500–1900* 50.2 (2010): 281–300.

Parker, Barbara L. *Plato's "Republic" and Shakespeare's Rome: A Political Study of the Roman Works*. Newark: University of Delaware Press, 2004.

Paster, Gail Kern, Katherine Rowe, and Mary Floyd-Wilson, eds. *Reading the Early Modern Passions: Essays in the Cultural History of Emotion*. Philadelphia: University of Pennsylvania Press, 2004.

Patterson, Annabel. *Censorship and Interpretation: The Conditions of Writing and Reading in Early Modern England*. Madison: University of Wisconsin Press, 1984.

    "A Petitioning Society." In *Reading between the Lines*, 57–79. Madison: University of Wisconsin Press, 1993.

Patterson, W. B. *Thomas Fuller: Discovering England's Religious Past*. Oxford: Oxford University Press, 2018.

Peltonen, Markku. *Rhetoric, Politics and Popularity in Pre-Revolutionary England*. Cambridge: Cambridge University Press, 2013.

Perry, Curtis. "'If Proclamations Will Not Serve': The Late Manuscript Poetry of James I and the Culture of Libel." In *Royal Subjects: Essays on the Writings of James VI and I*, ed. Daniel Fischlin and Mark Fortier, 205–32. Detroit: Wayne State University Press, 2002.

    Literature and Favoritism in Early Modern England. Cambridge: Cambridge University Press, 2006.

Pettegree, Andrew. *Foreign Protestant Communities in Sixteenth-Century London*. Oxford: Clarendon Press, 1986.

    "'Thirty years on': Progress Towards Integration amongst the Immigrant Population of Elizabethan London." In *English Rural Society, 1500–1800: Essays in Honour of Joan Thirsk*, ed. John Chartres and David Hey, 297–312. Cambridge: Cambridge University Press, 1990.

Phillips, C. B. "Town and Country: Economic Change in Kendal, *c.* 1550–1700." In *The Transformation of English Provincial Towns 1600–1800*, ed. Peter Clark, 99–132. London: Hutchinson, 1984.

Pierce, William. *John Penry: His Life, Times and Writings*. London: Hodder and Stoughton, 1923.

Platz, Norbert H. "Ben Jonson's *Ars Poetica*: An Interpretation of *Poetaster* in Its Historical Context." *Salzburg Studies in English Literature* 12 (1973): 1–42.

Pocock, J. G. A. *The Ancient Constitution and the Feudal Law: A Study of English Historical Thought in the Seventeenth Century*. 2nd ed. Cambridge: Cambridge University Press, 1987.

Politi, Jina. "'The Gibbet-Maker.'" *Notes and Queries* 38.1 (1991): 54–55.

Bibliography

Pollard, Alfred W., ed. *Shakespeare's Hand in the Play of Sir Thomas More.* Cambridge: Cambridge University Press, 1923.

Pollitt, Ronald. "'Refuge of the distressed Nations': Perceptions of Aliens in Elizabethan England." *Journal of Modern History* 52.1, on demand supplement (1980): D1001–19.

Power, M. J. "London and the Control of the 'Crisis' of the 1590s." *History* 70 (1985): 371–85.

Preiss, Richard. *Clowning and Authorship in Early Modern Theatre.* Cambridge: Cambridge University Press, 2014.

Rabb, Theodore K. *Jacobean Gentleman: Sir Edwin Sandys, 1561–1629.* Princeton: Princeton University Press, 1998.

Rackin, Phyllis. *Stages of History: Shakespeare's English Chronicles.* Ithaca: Cornell University Press, 1990.

Raymond, Joad. *Pamphlets and Pamphleteering in Early Modern Britain.* Cambridge: Cambridge University Press, 2003.

Rebhorn, Wayne A. *The Emperor of Men's Minds: Literature and the Renaissance Discourse of Rhetoric.* Ithaca: Cornell University Press, 1995.

Rice, Douglas Walthew. *The Life and Achievements of Sir John Popham, 1531–1607.* Madison, NJ: Fairleigh Dickinson University Press, 2005.

Rickard, Jane. "'To Strike the Ear of Time': Ben Jonson's *Poetaster* and the Temporality of Art." *Renaissance Drama* 48.1 (2020): 57–81.

   Writing the Monarch in Jacobean England: Jonson, Donne, Shakespeare and the Works of King James. Cambridge: Cambridge University Press, 2015.

Riggs, David. *Ben Jonson: A Life.* Cambridge, MA: Harvard University Press, 1989.

   The World of Christopher Marlowe. New York: Henry Holt, 2004.

Robinson, Benedict S. "Feeling Feelings in Early Modern England." In *Affect and Literature*, ed. Alex Houen, 213–28. Cambridge: Cambridge University Press, 2020.

Rosenberg, Eleanor. *Leicester, Patron of Letters.* New York: Columbia University Press, 1955.

Rowe, George E., Jr., "Ben Jonson's Quarrel with Audience and its Renaissance Context." *Studies in Philology* 81.4 (1984): 438–60.

Rowe, Katherine. "Humoral Knowledge and Liberal Cognition in Davenant's *Macbeth.*" In *Reading the Early Modern Passions*, ed. Paster, Rowe, and Floyd-Wilson, 169–91.

Rust, Jennifer R. *The Body in Mystery: The Political Theology of the Corpus Mysticum in the Literature of Reformation England.* Evanston: Northwestern University Press, 2014.

Sanders, Julie, Kate Chedgzoy, and Susan Wiseman, eds. *Refashioning Ben Jonson: Gender, Politics and the Jonsonian Canon.* Basingstoke, UK: Macmillan, 1998.

Schneider, Gary. "Libelous Letters in Elizabethan and Early Stuart England." *Modern Philology* 105.3 (2008): 475–509.

Scott, Joe. "The Kendal Tenant Right Dispute 1619–26." *Transactions of the Cumberland and Westmorland Antiquarian and Archaeological Society* 98 (1998): 169–82.

240

Bibliography

Scouloudi, Irene. *Returns of Strangers in the Metropolis 1593, 1627, 1635, 1639: A Study of an Active Minority*. London: Huguenot Society of London, 1985.

Seaton, Ethel. "Marlowe, Robert Poley, and the Tippings." *Review of English Studies* 5 (1929): 273–87.

Selwood, Jacob. *Diversity and Difference in Early Modern London*. Farnham, UK: Ashgate, 2010.

Shapiro, Barbara J. *Political Communication and Political Culture in England, 1558–1688*. Stanford: Stanford University Press, 2012.

Sharp, Buchanan. "Shakespeare's *Coriolanus* and the Crisis of the 1590s." In *Law and Authority in Early Modern England: Essays Presented to Thomas Garden Barnes*, ed. Sharp and Mark Charles Fissel, 27–63. Newark: University of Delaware Press, 2007.

Sharpe, Kevin. "The King's Writ: Royal Authors and Royal Authority in Early Modern England." In *Culture and Politics in Early Stuart England*, ed. Sharpe and Peter Lake, 117–38. Stanford: Stanford University Press, 1993.

Selling the Tudor Monarchy: Authority and Image in Sixteenth-Century England. New Haven: Yale University Press, 2009.

Shepard, Alexandra. "Contesting Communities? 'Town' and 'Gown' in Cambridge, *c.* 1560–1640." In *Communities in Early Modern England: Networks, Place, Rhetoric*, ed. Shepard and Phil Withington, 216–34. Manchester: Manchester University Press, 2000.

Meanings of Manhood in Early Modern England. Oxford: Oxford University Press, 2003.

Sherman, Anita Gilman. "Forms of Oblivion: Losing the Revels Office at St. John's." *Shakespeare Quarterly* 62.1 (2011): 75–105.

Sherman, William H. "Anatomizing the Commonwealth: Language, Politics, and the Elizabethan Social Order." In *The Project of Prose in Early Modern Europe and the New World*, ed. Elizabeth Fowler and Roland Greene, 104–21. Cambridge: Cambridge University Press, 1997.

Shuger, Debora. *Censorship and Cultural Sensibility: The Regulation of Language in Tudor-Stuart England*. Philadelphia: University of Pennsylvania Press, 2006.

Simmons, J. L. "The Tongue and Its Office in *The Revenger's Tragedy*." *PMLA* 92.1 (1977): 56–68.

Sinfield, Alan. "*Poetaster*, the Author, and the Perils of Cultural Production." *Renaissance Drama* 27 (1996): 3–18.

Sisson, C. J. *Lost Plays of Shakespeare's Age*. Cambridge: Cambridge University Press, 1936.

Slack, Paul. *The Impact of Plague in Tudor and Stuart England*. Oxford: Clarendon Press, 1990.

Smuts, R. Malcolm. "Jonson's *Poetaster* and the Politics of Defamation." *English Literary Renaissance* 49.2 (2019): 224–47.

"Varieties of Tacitism." *Huntington Library Quarterly* 83.3 (2020): 441–65.

Squitieri, Christina M. "Jane Shore's Political Identity in Thomas Heywood's *Edward IV*." *Studies in English Literature 1500–1900* 60.2 (2020): 299–322.

Bibliography

Staines, John. "Compassion in the Public Sphere of Milton and King Charles." In *Reading the Early Modern Passions*, ed. Paster, Rowe, and Floyd-Wilson, 89–110.

Steggle, Matthew. *Laughing and Weeping in Early Modern Theatres*. Aldershot, UK: Ashgate, 2007.

  Wars of the Theatres: The Poetics of Personation in the Age of Jonson. Victoria: English Literary Studies, 1998.

Sterrett, Joseph. *The Unheard Prayer: Religious Toleration in Shakespeare's Drama*. Leiden: Brill, 2012.

Stewart, Alan. *Shakespeare's Letters*. Oxford: Oxford University Press, 2008.

Stirling, Brents. "Shakespeare's Mob Scenes: A Reinterpretation." *Huntington Library Quarterly* 8.3 (1945): 213–40.

Stokes, James. "The Wells Shows of 1607." In *Festive Drama*, ed. Meg Twycross, 145–56. Cambridge: D. S. Brewer, 1996.

Streitberger, W. R. "Adult Playing Companies to 1583." In *Oxford Handbook of Early Modern Theatre*, ed. Dutton, 19–38.

  The Masters of the Revels and Elizabeth I's Court Theatre. Oxford: Oxford University Press, 2016.

Suman, Sonia. "'A Most Notable Spectacle': Early Modern Easter Spital Sermons." In *Spoken Word and Social Practice: Orality in Europe (1400–1700)*, ed. Thomas V. Cohen and Lesley K. Twomey, 228–50. Leiden: Brill, 2015.

Sweeney, John Gordon, III. *Jonson and the Psychology of Public Theater: To Coin the Spirit, Spend the Soul*. Princeton: Princeton University Press, 1985.

Taylor, Gary, and Rory Loughnane. "The Canon and Chronology of Shakespeare's Works." In *The New Oxford Shakespeare: Authorship Companion*, ed. Taylor and Gabriel Egan, 417–602. Oxford: Oxford University Press, 2017.

Teague, Frances. "The Phoenix and the Cockpit-in-Court Playhouses." In *Oxford Handbook of Early Modern Theatre*, ed. Dutton, 240–59.

Teramura, Misha. "Richard Topcliffe's Informant: New Light on *The Isle of Dogs*." *Review of English Studies* 68 (2017): 44–59.

Tribble, Evelyn. "Affective Contagion on the Early Modern Stage." In *Affect Theory and Early Modern Texts*, ed. Bailey and DiGangi, 195–212.

Tudeau-Clayton, Margaret. "Shakespeare and Immigration." *SPELL: Swiss Papers in English Language and Literature* 27 (2012): 81–97.

  "'This Is the Strangers' Case': The Utopic Dissonance of Shakespeare's Contribution to *Sir Thomas More*." *Shakespeare Survey* 65 (2012): 239–54.

Turner, Graeme. *Understanding Celebrity*. 2nd ed. Los Angeles: Sage, 2014.

Underdown, David. "'But the Shows of Their Street': Civic Pageantry and Charivari in a Somerset Town, 1607." *Journal of British Studies* 50.1 (2011): 4–23.

  Fire from Heaven: Life in an English Town in the Seventeenth Century. New Haven: Yale University Press, 1992.

Bibliography

Vanhaelen, Angela, and Joseph P. Ward, eds. *Making Space Public in Early Modern Europe: Performance, Geography, Privacy*. New York: Routledge, 2013.

Vanhoutte, Jacqueline. *Age in Love: Shakespeare and the Elizabethan Court*. Lincoln: University of Nebraska Press, 2019.

Veeder, Van Vechten. "The History of the Law of Defamation." In *Select Essays in Anglo-American Legal History*, vol. 3, 446–73. Boston: Little, Brown, 1909.

Vickers, Brian. *Shakespeare, Co-Author: A Historical Study of Five Collaborative Plays*. Oxford: Oxford University Press, 2002.

Visser, A. S. Q. *Joannes Sambucus and the Learned Image: The Use of the Emblem in Late-Renaissance Humanism*. Leiden: Brill, 2005.

Vivier, Eric D. "Judging Jonson: Ben Jonson's Satirical Self-Defense in *Poetaster*." *Ben Jonson Journal* 24.1 (2017): 1–21.

Waddell, Brodie. "Economic Immorality and Social Reformation in English Popular Preaching, 1585–1625." *Cultural and Social History* 5.2 (2008): 165–82.

"The Evil May Day Riot of 1517 and the Popular Politics of Anti-Immigrant Hostility in Early Modern London." *Historical Research* 94 (2021): 716–35.

Walker, Greg. *Plays of Persuasion: Drama and Politics at the Court of Henry VIII*. Cambridge: Cambridge University Press, 1991.

Walker, Julia M., ed. *Dissing Elizabeth: Negative Representations of Gloriana*. Durham, NC: Duke University Press, 1998.

Wall, Wendy. "Forgetting and Keeping: Jane Shore and the English Domestication of History." *Renaissance Drama* 27 (1996): 123–56.

Walsham, Alexandra. "'Frantick Hacket': Prophecy, Sorcery, Insanity, and the Elizabethan Puritan Movement." *Historical Journal* 41.1 (1998): 27–66.

Walter, John. *Crowds and Popular Politics in Early Modern England*. Manchester: Manchester University Press, 2006.

"'A Foolish Commotion of Youth'? Crowds and the 'Crisis of the 1590s' in London." *London Journal* 44.1 (2019): 17–36.

"'The Pooremans Joy and the Gentlemans Plague': A Lincolnshire Libel and the Politics of Sedition in Early Modern England." *Past and Present* 203 (2009): 29–67.

"Public Transcripts, Popular Agency and the Politics of Subsistence in Early Modern England." In *Negotiating Power in Early Modern Society: Order, Hierarchy and Subordination in Britain and Ireland*, ed. Michael J. Braddick and Walter, 123–48. Cambridge: Cambridge University Press, 2001.

Warner, Michael. *Publics and Counterpublics*. New York: Zone Books, 2002.

Watts, S. J. "Tenant-Right in Early Seventeenth-Century Northumberland." *Northern History* 6 (1971): 64–87.

Weimann, Robert. *Shakespeare and the Popular Tradition in the Theater: Studies in the Social Dimension of Dramatic Form and Function*. Ed. Robert Schwartz. Baltimore: Johns Hopkins University Press, 1978.

Wesseling, Ari. "Testing Modern Emblem Theory: The Earliest Views of the Genre (1564–1566)." In *The Emblem Tradition and the Low Countries*, ed. John Manning, Karel Porteman, and Marc van Vaeck, 3–22. Turnhout: Brepols, 1999.

Bibliography

White, Paul Whitfield. *Drama and Religion in English Provincial Society, 1485–1660.* Cambridge: Cambridge University Press, 2008.

Theatre and Reformation: Protestantism, Patronage, and Playing in Tudor England. Cambridge: Cambridge University Press, 1993.

Whitney, Charles. *Early Responses to Renaissance Drama.* Cambridge: Cambridge University Press, 2006.

Wickham, Glynne. *Early English Stages, 1300 to 1660.* Vol. 2, *1576 to 1660,* pt. 2. London: Routledge and Kegan Paul, 1972.

Wiggins, Martin, with Catherine Richardson. *British Drama 1533–1642: A Catalogue.* 10 vols. Oxford: Oxford University Press 2012–.

Wiles, David. *Shakespeare's Clown: Actor and Text in the Elizabethan Playhouse.* Cambridge: Cambridge University Press, 1987.

Wilson, Bronwen, and Paul Yachnin, eds. *Making Publics in Early Modern Europe: People, Things, Forms of Knowledge.* New York: Routledge, 2010.

Winship, Michael P. "Puritans, Politics, and Lunacy: The Copinger-Hacket Conspiracy as the Apotheosis of Elizabethan Presbyterianism." *Sixteenth Century Journal* 38.2 (2007): 345–69.

Withington, Phil. *Society in Early Modern England: The Vernacular Origins of Some Powerful Ideas.* Cambridge: Polity, 2010.

Wittek, Stephen. *The Media Players: Shakespeare, Middleton, Jonson, and the Idea of News.* Ann Arbor: University of Michigan Press, 2015.

Womersley, David. *Divinity and State.* Oxford: Oxford University Press, 2010.

"Sir Henry Savile's Translation of Tacitus and the Political Interpretation of Elizabethan Texts." *Review of English Studies* 42 (1991): 313–42.

Wood, Andy. *The Memory of the People: Custom and Popular Senses of the Past in Early Modern England.* Cambridge: Cambridge University Press, 2013.

"'Poore men woll speke one daye': Plebeian Languages of Deference and Defiance in England, c. 1520–1640." In *Politics of the Excluded,* ed. Harris, 67–98.

Woodbridge, Linda. *English Revenge Drama: Money, Resistance, Equality.* Cambridge: Cambridge University Press, 2010.

Woods, Gillian. "'Strange Discourse': The Controversial Subject of *Sir Thomas More.*" *Renaissance Drama* 39 (2011): 3–35.

Woudhuysen, H. R. *Sir Philip Sidney and the Circulation of Manuscripts, 1558–1640.* Oxford: Clarendon Press, 1996.

Yachnin, Paul. "Performing Publicity." *Shakespeare Bulletin* 28.2 (2010): 201–19.

"The Reformation of Space in Shakespeare's Playhouse." In *Making Space Public,* ed. Vanhaelen and Ward, 262–80.

and Marlene Eberhart, eds. *Forms of Association: Making Publics in Early Modern Europe.* Amherst: University of Massachusetts Press, 2015.

Yates, Frances A. *Astraea: The Imperial Theme in the Sixteenth Century.* London: Routledge and Kegan Paul, 1975.

Yearling, Rebecca. *Ben Jonson, John Marston and Early Modern Drama: Satire and the Audience.* Basingstoke, UK: Palgrave Macmillan, 2016.

Bibliography

Young, Alan R. "The Emblematic Art of Ben Jonson." *Emblematica* 6 (1992): 17–36.

Yungblut, Laura Hunt. *Strangers Settled Here Amongst Us: Policies, Perceptions and the Presence of Aliens in Elizabethan England.* London: Routledge, 1996.

Zaret, David. *Origins of Democratic Culture: Printing, Petitions, and the Public Sphere in Early-Modern England.* Princeton: Princeton University Press, 2000.

Index

Addison, Joseph, 80
Admiral's Men, 33
affect, 93, 162
    collective, 73–74, 84
    Jane Shore and, 144–47, 155, 161–62, 163–64,
        169, 171
    in *Julius Caesar*, 53
    playgoing and, 8, 96, 142, 148–49, 152–54, 155
    politics of, 143, 145, 149, 167–68, 169
    in *Sir Thomas More*, 141–43
    theories of, 148–49
alehouses, 62, 63, 68
Allen, William, 46–47
Anjou, Duke of, 11
anonymity, 2, 18, 47, 181, 182, 206
    in *Julius Caesar*, 52, 53
    in *Nobody and Somebody*, 206, 207–8
    See also libels, anonymity and
antitheatricalism, 7, 18–19, 21, 23, 152, 156, 161
    in *Poetaster*, 186–87
    in *Roman Actor*, 211
application, 21, 173, 208, 211
    Jonson on, 172–73, 174–76, 195
    in *Poetaster*, 188, 189, 192, 193, 200, 201
apprentices, 122
    playgoing of, 206
    riots of, 118, 125
Archpriest Controversy, 15
Arendt, Hannah, 18
Aristotle, 135
Arthington, Henry, 91, 94, 105, 108–9
artisans, 119, 121
    grievances of, 118, 131
    playgoing of, 170
    in *Sir Thomas More*, 127, 133, 134
    See also citizens
Astraea, 104–5
Attorney General v. *Pickering*. See Coke, Sir
    Edward, *De libellis famosis*
audiences, 4, 7–8, 51, 66, 74, 110, 142, 172
    Caroline, 212

citizen, 143, 169, 206–7
    of *Club Law*, 77, 83
    courtly, 21, 23
    of *Edward IV*, 145–47, 157, 158, 163, 164, 167,
        168, 169–71
    Jacobean, 212
    judgment of, 14–15, 18–19, 22–23, 26, 32, 34,
        35–36, 37–38, 47, 52, 55–56, 57, 89, 96–97,
        150–51, 162, 174–76, 199–203, 213
    of *Julius Caesar*, 56
    of *Leicester's Commonwealth*, 45
    of libels, 6, 23, 60, 62, 63, 65, 66–67, 68–69,
        70, 73–74, 79, 84, 106, 129, 167, 189
    of *Nobody and Somebody*, 207, 208
    of petitions, 88, 92–93, 105
    of *Poetaster*, 192, 194
    of rhetoric, 89, 97, 100, 104, 111
    in *Roman Actor*, 210, 211
    of *Sir Thomas More*, 143
    of *Titus Andronicus*, 95, 98
    See also playgoing

Bacon, Francis, 32, 57, 185, 190
    Aduertisement touching seditious writing,
        34–36, 50
    *Advertisement touching the controuersyes of the
        Church of England*, 34, 37
    on audience affect, 148, 149
    on Essex, 158, 181–82
    on libels, 33–36, 37, 50, 73, 87, 212–13
ballads, 120
    Jane Shore and, 146, 157, 170
    libelous, 12, 62, 68
Bancroft, Richard, 1, 2, 16, 182
Barksted, William
    Insatiate Countess, coauthored with Marston
        and Machin, 23
Barnes, Barnabe, 188–89
    Devil's Charter, 23, 204
    Foure Bookes of Offices, 188–89
Barrow, Henry, 95, 109

245

Index

Bashe, Edward, 107
Bayard, Roger, 65
Beaumont, Francis
  Knight of the Burning Pestle, 169–70, 171
Bellany, Alastair, 2, 31
benevolences, 160–61
Bertie, Peregrine, Lord Willoughby, 181
bills. *See* libels; parliament
bills of complaint, 10–11, 61, 70, 76, 136
  in *Sir Thomas More*, 116–17, 124–30, 132, 140, 143
Bishops' Ban, 182–83, 186, 188, 194
Blackfriars Theater, 170, 185, 200
Boar's Head Theater, 146, 169
Boleyn, Thomas, Earl of Wiltshire, 66
Braddick, Michael J., 160
Broadstreet Ward, London, 115
Brooke, Christopher
  Ghost of Richard the Third, 145–46, 170–71
Bryson, Alan, 41, 212
Buckhurst, Lord Treasurer. *See* Sackville, Thomas, Baron Buckhurst
Buckingham, Duke of. *See* Villiers, George, 1st Duke of Buckingham
Burghley, Lord. *See* Cecil, William, Lord Burghley
Butler, Martin, 211

Cade, Jack, 91
Cain, Tom, 173, 189
Caldwell, Elizabeth, 153–54
Calvert, Samuel, 19, 204
Calvin, Jean, 198
Cambridge, 39, 45
  town–gown relations, 60, 76–84
carnivalesque, the
  libels and, 2
  in *Merry Wives of Windsor*, 64
  in *Sir Thomas More*, 128
  in *Titus Andronicus*, 91
Catholics and Catholicism, 1, 3, 11, 14, 15, 16, 33, 36, 44, 46, 49, 51, 66, 67, 90, 116
  Jonson and, 175, 188, 197
  persecution of, 11, 21, 44, 46, 47, 87–88, 93, 94
  in *Titus Andronicus*, 92, 98, 108
  See also libels, Catholic; petitions, Catholic; polemic, Catholic
Cecil, Robert, 1, 2, 32, 39, 48, 55, 79, 83, 180, 199
Cecil, William, Lord Burghley, 87, 108, 122, 197
  Execution of Justice in England, 46–47
celebrity, 51, 145–46, 212
  Jane Shore's, 147, 155, 161, 169, 170, 206
  See also popularity
censorship, 11, 12, 35, 197
  dramatic, 7, 19–22, 26, 33, 84, 118
  in *Poetaster*, 186, 193

of *Sir Thomas More*, 116, 128, 130, 132, 143
Stuart, 204
in *Titus Andronicus*, 101, 103
See also Bishops' Ban
Chamberlain's Men, 184
Chancery, Court of, 10, 72, 73, 76, 117, 135–39, 141, 142
Chapman, George, 184
  Eastward Ho!, coauthored with Jonson and Marston, 175, 194
  Old Joiner of Aldgate, 20, 60–62, 84
charivari, 64
Charles I, 36, 41, 72, 75, 76, 150
Charnock, Robert, 15, 16
Cheapside Cross, 91, 109, 167
Chesterton, Cambridgeshire, 81, 82
Children of Paul's. *See* Paul's Boys
Christopherson, John, 12–13, 16
Chubb, Matthew, 62
church courts. *See* ecclesiastical law
Churchyard, Thomas, 154–55, 157
Cicero, 89, 97, 101, 106, 113
  in *Julius Caesar*, 54
citizens
  of Cambridge, 60, 77–81, 83–84
  of Chesterton, 82
  in *Club Law*, 80–83
  in *Edward IV*, 144–45, 162, 168
  gentlewomen, 152, 155, 161
  grievances of, 27
  in *Julius Caesar*, 55–56
  of London, 127, 149, 157
  in *Nobody and Somebody*, 206
  playgoing of, 169–71, 206–7
  in *Sir Thomas More*, 116–17, 125–26, 128–30, 131–35, 136, 140, 142–43
  in *Titus Andronicus*, 104, 107–8
  of Wells, 63
civil law. *See* Roman law
civil war, 3
civility, 3, 177
Clare Hall, Cambridge, 77, 78, 79, 83, 84
Claverley, Shropshire, 63
Clegg, Cyndia Susan, 182
Clerkenwell, 169
Clinton, Henry, 2nd Earl of Lincoln, 65–67, 68, 69, 188
clowns, 34, 109–10
  in "Death of the Lord of Kyme", 65
  in Kendal Stage Play, 70–71, 74
  in *Sir Thomas More*, 132
  in *Titus Andronicus*, 91, 104, 109–10
Club Law, 7, 60, 76–84, 129
  manuscript of, 79
cockpit, the, 41–42

Index

247

Coke, Sir Edward, 1, 2, 9, 18, 42, 59, 61, 165–66, 185, 194
De libellis famosis, 15–17, 41, 59, 67
Colclough, David, 41
Collingbourne, William, 165–66, 167, 168
common law, 16
  defamation and, 9, 11
  equity and, 135–37, 138–39
  memory and, 73
commonplace books, 31, 58, 175, 202, 209
commons, the, 1, 2, 123, 184
  in *Edward IV*, 155, 159–60, 161
  of London, 170
  in *Nobody and Somebody*, 206
  in *Sir Thomas More*, 125, 126, 129, 131, 143
  of Westmorland, 74
conscience, 137–39
  in *Sir Thomas More*, 117, 135, 136, 139–40
conspiracy theories, 3
  about Marlowe's murder, 115
contio, 89, 90, 96
Coppinger, Edmund, 91, 94, 105, 108–9
Cosin, Richard, 91
costume, 60, 70, 74, 79
Coventry, Thomas, Attorney General, 75–76
Cowell, John, 10, 177
crisis of the 1590s, 158
cudgel play, 81–82, 83
Curtain Theater, 168, 187
custom. *See* common law; tenant right

D'Ewes, Sir Simonds, 37
Daniel, Samuel, 184
Davenant, William
  Cruel Brother, 24, 211
Davies, John, 72, 186
Day, John
  Isle of Gulls, 24
dearth, 4, 158, 159
"Death of the Lord of Kyme", 65–67, 68, 69, 188
defamation, 4, 5, 9, 18, 19, 21, 50, 90, 165, 202
  in *Cynthia's Revels*, 185–86
  drama and, 9, 26, 204
  law of, 2, 9–10, 11–12, 21–22, 27, 67, 126
  in *Nobody and Somebody*, 205–6
  See also libels; slander
Dekker, Thomas, 96, 184, 187, 196
  Match Me in London, 23
  Noble Spanish Soldier, 24
  Roaring Girl, coauthored with Middleton, 24
  Satiromastix, 24, 187, 202–3
  Whore of Babylon, 24
Deleuze, Gilles, 148
Derby's Men, 25, 146, 169. *See also* Strange's Men

Devereux, Robert, 2nd Earl of Essex, 4, 51, 113, 174, 176, 192, 202
  in Ireland, 160, 179, 180, 181, 183
  libels and, 173, 179, 180–81, 183, 184, 189, 197, 200–1
  playgoing of, 149
  popularity of, 149, 155, 157–58, 179, 180–82, 184
  rising of, 27, 149–50, 151, 173, 176, 178, 179–80, 181, 183, 184, 189, 201
  satire and, 173, 181–83
  theater and, 183–86
devil, the, 62, 65–66, 152
  etymology of, 198–99, 201
Dolan, Frances E., 153
Donne, John, 179
  on libels, 48–49, 203
Dorchester, Dorset, 62
Doty, Jeffrey S., 8, 56, 184
Drummond, William, 191
Dudley, Robert, Earl of Leicester, 43–44, 48–51, 213
Dutch Church Libel, 115, 117, 120–22, 123–24, 131, 142, 158
Dutch Church, London, 115, 120, 123
Dutton, Richard, 20, 21–22
Dymoke, Sir Edward, 65, 66–67, 68, 69
Dymoke, Tailboys, 65, 66–67, 68, 69, 182
  Caltha Poetarum, 188

ecclesiastical law, 9–10, 11, 12, 135
Edward IV, 144, 147, 151. *See also* Heywood, Thomas, *Edward IV*
Egan, Clare, 58, 59, 62
Egerton, Thomas, 95, 181, 183, 189, 201
Elizabeth I, 11, 12, 23, 38, 40, 43, 44, 48, 54, 87, 92, 93, 94, 105, 108, 109, 113, 121, 122, 123, 131, 147, 150, 159, 173, 179, 180, 181, 184, 185–86, 188, 189, 191, 194
  cult of, 164
Elliotts, Humphrey, 63, 64
emblems, 174, 195–202
  etymology of, 197–98, 199, 201
emotion. *See* affect
enclosure, 54, 59, 62, 67, 123
epigrams, 176, 181, 182, 186, 195. *See also* libels, epigrams as
equity, 135–36, 137–39
  in *Sir Thomas More*, 117, 135, 136–37, 139–40, 141, 143
Essex, Earl of. *See* Devereux, Robert, 2nd Earl of Essex
Evil May Day, 118, 119, 161
  in *Sir Thomas More*, 116, 124–34
Ezekiel, Book of, 75

248 — Index

faction, 8, 24, 25, 27, 197
  in *Titus Andronicus*, 90, 91, 92, 97–98, 99, 108, 110, 113
Fallon, Samuel, 206, 207
Falstaff, John, 51
  in *Merry Wives of Windsor*, 64, 83
Fawcett, Mary Laughlin, 102
feeling. *See* affect
Fenton, Geoffrey, 18, 23
festivity, 58–59, 63–65, 67, 68, 80, 81–84
Field, Thomas, 60
Finch, Henry, 119, 133
Finkelpearl, Philip J., 19–20
Flaskett, John, 60–61
Fletcher, John
  Henry VIII, coauthored with Shakespeare, 150
  Thierry and Theodoret, coauthored with Massinger, 24
Folger Shakespeare Library MS X.d.634, 40–43
food riots, 158
football, 81, 82
forced loans, 160
Fox, Adam, 58, 59
freedom of speech, 4, 49, 165, 204, 213
French Church, London, 122
Fuller, Thomas, 76–79, 80, 81, 83–84
Fumerton, Patricia, 5

games. *See* festivity
Garnett, Jasper, 70, 71
Geneva Bible, 75
Globe Theater, 149–51, 184
Gog Magog Hills, 81
gossip, 13, 37, 40, 43, 44, 51, 184. *See also* news; rumor
Gosson, Stephen, 18–19, 23, 152, 155, 156, 202
grain export, 158, 165, 205
grammar school, 89, 102
Greene, Robert
  Looking Glass for London and England, coauthored with Lodge, 24
Greenwood, John, 95, 109
Gross, Kenneth, 7
Guattari, Félix, 148
Guildhall, London, 136
Guilpin, Everard, 176, 177, 200
  Skialetheia, 181–83
Guise family, 40
Gurnis, Musa, 8, 142, 146

Habermas, Jürgen, 4–5, 6, 18, 49
Hacket, William, 88, 90, 91–92, 94, 95, 108–10
Hammer, Paul, 149–50
Harding, Thomas, 14–15, 34
Harpsfield, Nicholas, 138

hate speech, 3
Helgerson, Richard, 169
Helme, Richard, 70–71
Henry III, King of France, 40
Henry VII, 163
Henry VIII, 129, 161. *See also* Shakespeare, William, *Henry VIII*, coauthored with Fletcher; *Sir Thomas More*
Herrick, Robert
  Hesperides, 81
Heywood, Thomas, 184, 206
  Apology for Actors, 69, 147, 151, 152–53, 154, 161, 210
  Edward IV, 4, 23, 25, 26, 27, 84, 144–47, 148, 155–71, 204, 205–7, 208, 211, 212
  Fair Maid of the West, 158
  Rape of Lucrece, 168–69
  Sir Thomas More and, 132
Hobgood, Allison P., 153
Hole, John, 63
holiday. *See* festivity
Holinshed, Raphael, 124, 125–26, 127, 129, 132, 160
Hooker, Richard, 22
Hornback, Robert, 109
Horncastle, Lincolnshire, 66, 69
House of Commons. *See* parliament
House of Lords. *See* parliament
Howard, Henry, Earl of Northampton, 175
Howard, Thomas, Duke of Norfolk, 66
Howard, Thomas, Earl of Suffolk, 195
Howe, Agnes, 60–61
Howe, John, 60, 61
Hudson, William, 9, 13, 17, 54, 68, 84, 90, 187, 207
Humble petition of the communaltie, 109
Hunt, Arnold, 127
Hutson, Lorna, 100

Ill May Day. *See* Evil May Day
immigrants. *See* strangers
informers. *See* spies
Inns of Court, 179, 181, 200
  Middle Temple, 200
insurrection. *See* rebellion
intelligencers. *See* spies
interpretation, 6–7, 23, 31, 32, 56, 65
  charitable, 21–22
  in *Julius Caesar*, 52–56
  in *Poetaster*, 174–76, 193–97, 198, 199–200, 203
  in *Roman Actor*, 210, 211
  See also application; audiences

James VI and I, 1, 2, 19, 32, 39, 41, 75, 150, 175, 204
  Basilikon Doron, 38

Index

on libels, 36–38
on tenant right, 72, 73
Jewel, John, 14–15, 34
Jones, Inigo, 201
Jonson, Ben, 20, 151, 176, 177, 178, 184, 209, 211
  Alchemist, 172
  Bartholomew Fair, 172
  Catiline, 201
  Cynthia's Revels, 185–86
  Discoveries, 175, 191
  Eastward Ho!, coauthored with Chapman and Marston, 175, 194
  Epicene, 172, 175, 208, 210
  Every Man Out of His Humour, 20, 21, 172
  Isle of Dogs, coauthored with Nashe, 19, 20, 21, 25, 191, 193, 194, 195, 197
  letters from prison, 195
  Magnetic Lady, 172
  Poetaster, 4, 7, 20, 23, 26, 27, 84, 172–76, 178, 186–203, 204, 208–11, 212
  Sejanus, 24, 172, 175, 208–9
  Volpone, 172
justices of the peace, 187
  and quorum, 62, 176

Kaplan, M. Lindsay, 21, 174
Kemp, Will, 109, 110
Kendal Castle, 70, 74
Kendal Stage Play, 60, 69–76, 78–79, 83, 84
King James Bible, 75
King's Lynn, Norfolk, 152
Kiséry, András, 8
Klause, John, 109
Korda, Natasha, 64
Kyd, Thomas, 115, 118, 120, 124
  Spanish Tragedy, 50, 100
Kynnersley, Anthony, 62–63

Lake, Peter, 3, 8, 23, 36, 44, 47, 51, 113, 162
Lambarde, William, 136
Lamentable Complaint of the Commonalty, 92–93, 94
landlords, 6, 54, 123, 213
  of Kendal, 60, 70–72, 73–76, 79, 84
Laneham, John, 34
Laud, William, Archbishop of Canterbury, 107
law, 74, 165
  limits of, 48
  martial, 181
  in *Poetaster*, 194, 195
  in *Sir Thomas More*, 117, 127, 128, 129, 131–32, 134–40, 141, 143
  in *Titus Andronicus*, 100, 106, 107
  See also Chancery, Court of; common law;

defamation, law of; ecclesiastical law; libels, law of; Roman law; Star Chamber, Court of
Lees Hill, Staffordshire, 62
Leicester, Earl of. *See* Dudley, Robert, Earl of Leicester
Leicester's Commonwealth, 31, 32, 43–51, 56, 57, 87
  circulation of, 45, 50, 51
  drama and, 50–51
  manuscripts of, 45, 50
Leicester's Men, 24
Lent, 82
letters, 79, 108, 154
  from Essex, 180, 184
  in *Julius Caesar*, 52, 53–55
  Leicester's Commonwealth as, 43, 45, 50
  libelous, 11, 12, 50, 54, 122
  libels and, 40, 45, 48, 203
  seditious, 87, 88, 91, 108
  in *Titus Andronicus*, 89, 91, 101, 104–7, 108, 113–14
Levine, Nina, 133, 142
libellus famosus. See bills of complaint; libels
libels
  anonymity and, 3, 4, 6, 13–15, 16–17, 38–39, 42, 45, 46, 47, 54, 90, 92, 120, 123, 124, 166, 180, 207–8
  bills and, 10–11, 126
  Catholic, 32, 35, 47, 87, 88, 108
  circulation of, 4, 5–6, 7, 13, 14, 17, 26, 31–33, 40, 42–43, 53–54, 62–63, 68, 106–7, 158, 166–67, 179
  in *Club Law*, 80–81
  corners and, 12, 13, 14, 18
  definitions of, 5, 7, 10–11, 13, 14, 15, 17, 26, 48
  in *Edward IV*, 144, 164–65, 166–67
  epigrams as, 10, 17
  etymology of, 6, 9, 10, 12, 18, 47, 126
  in *Julius Caesar*, 52, 53–55, 56, 57
  laughter and, 23, 68, 69, 84
  law of, 7, 9, 10–11, 12, 13, 15–17, 19, 23, 59, 62, 67–68, 181, 194. *See also* defamation, law of
  mobility of, 5–6, 17, 31, 32
  in *Nobody and Somebody*, 206, 207–8
  performance of, 4, 6, 7, 17, 18, 26, 58–59, 60–71, 73–74, 76–79, 84, 184, 187–88
  petitions and, 41, 54, 92, 94–95, 113–14
  pictures as, 17, 67, 194, 199
  in *Poetaster*, 173–76, 189, 194–201
  Protestant, 88
  provincial, 26, 59, 62–84
  Puritan, 16, 87, 88, 109
  reading of, 7, 26, 31–33, 39–40, 42–44, 45–46, 47, 51, 52–57, 62
  representations of, 4, 7, 23–24, 26–27, 32, 204, 211, 212

250   *Index*

libels (cont.)
  rhetoric and, 89
  in *Roman Actor*, 209–10
  satire as, 2, 3, 27, 38, 40, 174, 175–76, 178–79, 193, 200
  satire vs., 172, 178, 182, 197, 208
  sectarian, 12, 27, 87–88, 113–14
  sedition and, 4, 7–8, 12–13, 17, 26, 34–36, 39, 41–42, 47, 53, 54, 57, 59, 73, 75, 117, 126, 180, 182, 189, 192, 197
  in *Sir Thomas More*, 116–17, 126–27, 128, 129, 139, 143
  slander vs., 9, 11, 26–27
  against strangers, 27, 115, 119–24, 125–26, 128, 142
  in *Thomas of Woodstock*, 211
  in *Titus Andronicus*, 88, 90–91, 95, 106–8, 109, 110, 113–14
  truth of, 3, 7, 10, 12, 13, 46, 47, 50, 51, 90, 165–66
  violence and, 3, 8, 59, 76, 117, 123–24, 127, 213
Lin, Erika T., 60
Lincoln, Earl of. *See* Clinton, Henry, 2nd Earl of Lincoln
Lincolnshire, 54, 67, 69, 123
Lodge, Thomas
  Looking Glass for London and England, coauthored with Greene, 24
London, 25, 40, 45, 110, 118–19, 122, 123, 124, 127–28, 145, 151, 162, 179, 191, 201
  aldermen of, 21, 124, 127
  in *Edward IV*, 144, 162, 163, 167–68
  libels in, 42, 53, 87, 105, 107, 108, 115, 120, 127, 128, 158, 167, 180
  mayor of, 21, 33, 107, 120, 127, 158
  playgoers, 147, 150, 152, 155, 170, 183
  sheriff of, 117, 120, 131, 136, 167
  in *Sir Thomas More*, 125, 126, 128, 133, 143
long 1590s, 24, 59, 160, 212
Long, William B., 132
Lucretia, 103, 168, 169
Lyly, John, 33

Machiavelli, Niccolò, 182
  Machiavellianism, 44, 121, 158
Machin, Lewis
  Insatiate Countess, coauthored with Marston and Barksted, 23
MacKay, Ellen, 153
MacLean, Sally-Beth, 25
Mankind, 66
Manley, Lawrence, 25
manuscript, 5, 17, 26, 31, 32, 33, 39–43, 51, 58, 92
  Essex and, 181, 183, 184
  in *Titus Andronicus*, 102

  verse, 9, 38, 68, 179
marginalia, 26, 32, 39, 116
Markham, Gervase, 184
Marlowe, Christopher, 115, 118, 120, 124
  Edward II, 23, 25
  Jew of Malta, 115
  Massacre at Paris, 99, 115
  Ovid's Elegies, 186
  Tamburlaine the Great, 115
Marprelate controversy, 13, 22, 33–34, 87, 109
  plays about, 20, 21, 25, 33, 84
Marston, John, 176, 177, 178, 187, 196
  Eastward Ho!, coauthored with Jonson and Chapman, 175, 194
  Insatiate Countess, coauthored with Barksted and Machin, 23
Martin, Richard, 192–93, 200
martyrdom
  of Collingbourne, 165, 166
  in *Edward IV*, 168
  in *Sir Thomas More*, 116, 131, 132, 139, 143
  in *Titus Andronicus*, 98
  See also violence
Mary I, Queen of England, 12, 13, 119
Mary, Queen of Scots, 44
Massinger, Philip
  Roman Actor, 24, 204, 208–11
  Thierry and Theodoret, coauthored with Fletcher, 24
Massumi, Brian, 148
Master of the Revels, 21. *See also* Tilney, Edmund
May, Steven W., 41, 212
maypole, 65, 68
McRae, Andrew, 69
Mead, Joseph, 39–40, 42, 43, 45
Medici, Catherine de', 40
Melton, John, 18–19
memory, cultural, 72–73, 82, 84, 168
merriment. *See* libels,laughter and
metadrama, 4, 6–7
  in *Club Law*, 80–81, 83
  in *Edward IV*, 164
  in Jonson's plays, 172
  in *Julius Caesar*, 55
  in *Poetaster*, 193
  in *Roman Actor*, 208–11
  in *Sir Thomas More*, 117, 140–41, 143
  in *Titus Andronicus*, 96
Meyrick, Sir Gelly, 185
Middlesex, 187
Middleton, Thomas, 182
  Game at Chess, 84
  Roaring Girl, coauthored with Dekker, 24
Mildmay, Sir Thomas, 121–22, 123
Milward, John, 60, 61

Index

Mirror for Magistrates, 50, 144, 147, 154, 165
miscellanies, 31, 38, 58
misrule. *See* festivity
mitior sensus, 21–22
morality play, 65–66, 205
More, Thomas, 138–39, 140
    History of King Richard III, 140, 144, 154, 157
    See also Sir Thomas More
Morrissey, Mary, 127
Moschovakis, Nicholas R., 91
Mudd, Thomas, 79
Mullaney, Steven, 5, 8, 73, 142
Munday, Anthony, 23, 115. *See also Sir Thomas
    More*
Murray, Sir James, 175

Nashe, Thomas, 33, 142, 182. *See also* Jonson, Ben,
    Isle of Dogs, coauthored with Nashe
new historicism, 8
Newgate Prison, 122
    in *Sir Thomas More*, 136, 137
news, 7, 22, 37, 91, 181
    false, 2, 4, 10, 12, 13, 206, 213
    libels and, 1–3, 4, 31, 40
    in *Nobody and Somebody*, 206
    in *Titus Andronicus*, 91, 109
newsletters, 31, 58, 89
Ngai, Sianne, 148
Nobody and Somebody, 23, 204, 205–8
Northampton, Earl of. *See* Howard, Henry, Earl
    of Northampton

O'Callaghan, Michelle, 179, 202
Oath of Succession, 134, 138
Old Fish Street, London, 42
Oldenburg, Scott, 133
orality, 2, 5, 17, 26, 42
    in *Edward IV*, 163
    in *Titus Andronicus*, 99–101, 102
    See also rhetoric
ordnance export, 121, 158–59
Orlin, Lena Cowen, 156, 169
Ovid
    Amores, 186
    Metamorphoses, 102, 105
    See also Jonson, *Poetaster*

pardons, 154, 161
    in *Edward IV*, 157, 161
    in *Sir Thomas More*, 131, 136, 137
Parker, Matthew, Archbishop of Canterbury, 18
parliament, 39, 40, 74, 89, 92–93, 94, 105, 109, 119,
    120, 133, 150, 159, 179
"Parliament Fart", 31, 179
patronage, 21, 23, 24–25, 44, 90, 93

Paul's Boys, 33, 61
Paul's Cross, 127, 162
Peacham, Henry, 106
Pearce, Edward, 61
Peck, Dwight C., 44
Peele, George, 98. *See also* Shakespeare, William,
    Titus Andronicus, coauthored with Peele
Pembroke Hall, Cambridge, 79
Pembroke's Men, 25, 90
Penry, John, 93, 94, 95, 105, 109
performance, 5, 17, 26, 32, 51, 179
    Essex and, 184
    genres of, 60, 64, 65, 68
    Marprelate controversy and, 33
    political, 147, 149–51, 161, 166, 182
    in *Roman Actor*, 209, 211
    style of, 6, 34, 36, 57, 185
    text and, 68
    See also libels, performance of; theater
Perkins, Richard, 151, 155
Perne, Andrew, Vice-Chancellor of
    Cambridge, 82
persecution
    in *Henry VIII*, 150
    in *Nobody and Somebody*, 205
    religious, 4, 83, 93, 95, 105
    in *Titus Andronicus*, 99, 105–6, 108
    See also Catholics and Catholicism; Puritans
    and Puritanism
Persons, Robert, 15
Petition directed to her most excellent Maiestie,
    92, 94
petitions, 7, 74, 91, 92–95
    Catholic, 88, 92, 93–94, 95, 105
    in *Edward IV*, 157–58, 159, 161
    in *Julius Caesar*, 52, 54
    Puritan, 92–93, 94–95, 105, 109
    against strangers, 118, 121, 122–23, 126, 131, 142
    in *Titus Andronicus*, 88, 89, 92, 105–6, 107, 108,
    109, 110
    See also libels, petitions and
Phillips, Augustine, 184, 189
Pickering, Lewis, 16, 165–66
pillory, 16, 42, 120
Pincus, Steven, 36, 162
pity
    in *Edward IV*, 157, 162–64, 167–68, 169
    for Jane Shore, 145–46, 154, 171
    politics of, 163–64
    in *Titus Andronicus*, 101, 111–13
plague, 115, 118, 119
playgoing, 4, 6, 7–8, 19, 21, 90, 96–97, 110,
    149–53, 155, 183, 207, 212
    Jane Shore and, 169–71
    politics of, 168

252 Index

playgoing (cont.)
women's, 145, 151–54, 170–71
See also affect, playgoing and; audiences
Poets' War. *See* War of the Theaters
polemic, 3, 7, 12, 27, 33, 106, 198
Anglican, 34, 46, 94
antitheatrical, 152
Catholic, 11, 46–47, 49, 87
More's, 138
printed, 9, 26, 184
Protestant, 13
Puritan, 11, 34, 93
religious, 6, 12, 14–15, 16, 33–34, 92–93, 110
Poley, Robert, 95
Popham, Sir John, 87, 174, 175, 184, 188, 189, 192–93
popular politics, 3, 27, 54, 68–69, 143
in *Julius Caesar*, 55
in Kendal, 73–76
rhetoric of, 123–24
in *Titus Andronicus*, 104, 106, 107–8
popularity, 51, 89, 149, 151
in *Edward IV*, 162
Essex and, 149, 158, 179, 180, 181–82, 184
Jane Shore's, 144, 155, 157–59, 161, 163–64, 167–68, 169, 170–71, 211
Nobody's, 205, 208
theater and, 147
in *Titus Andronicus*, 108, 110
See also celebrity
populism, 27, 75, 123, 212
Jane Shore and, 155, 159
in *Julius Caesar*, 56
xenophobia and, 117, 124, 127, 129, 142
preaching. *See* pulpit
Presbyterianism, 33, 87. *See also* Puritans and Puritanism
print, 2, 5, 9, 26, 32, 46–47, 51, 66, 93, 94, 95, 122–23, 179
censorship of, 182
Edward IV and, 144, 145–46, 163, 169
Essex and, 181, 183, 184
Leicester's Commonwealth and, 32, 43, 45, 47
Marprelate controversy and, 33
in *Nobody and Somebody*, 205
publics and, 5, 6
in *Titus Andronicus*, 89, 102–3
privacy, 34, 37, 38–40, 43, 53, 62, 126, 139
in *Julius Caesar*, 52
in *Leicester's Commonwealth*, 43, 45
in *Sir Thomas More*, 139–40
in *Titus Andronicus*, 103–4

Privy Council, 1–2, 12, 19, 20, 21, 23, 33, 77, 78, 82, 109, 115, 118, 119, 120, 122, 126, 129, 131, 174, 180, 181, 187, 188, 192
proclamations, 12, 128
in *Edward IV*, 162–64, 168, 205
against Essex, 180
against libels, 36, 47, 180
libels and, 73, 166–67, 181
in *Nobody and Somebody*, 205
against ordnance exports, 158
against plays, 19, 21, 23
against tenant right, 72–74, 76
propaganda, 2, 24, 47, 127, 164
Anglican, 91, 109
in *Edward IV*, 144
Essex and, 183, 185, 201
Protestant, 24
Sir Thomas More as, 132
props, 60, 63, 66, 68, 77
in *Club Law*, 82
in *Merry Wives of Windsor*, 64
in *Poetaster*, 189–90
protest theater. *See* theater, activist
Protestants and Protestantism, 13, 15, 24, 33, 46, 49, 90, 105, 119
French, 99
in *Titus Andronicus*, 108
Psalms, 106
public shaming, 59, 64, 79, 83, 84, 194
in *Club Law*, 80–81
in *Edward IV*, 162
theater and, 61, 64
public sphere, 2–3, 8, 9, 27, 33, 35, 56, 73, 91, 143, 147, 169, 181, 185, 212
post-Reformation, 36, 127
theories of, 4–5, 14
publics and publicity, 5, 7, 47, 51, 59
anti-Leicestrian, 44, 45, 49, 50, 51
Club Law and, 77, 80
in *Edward IV*, 156, 157, 161–63, 164, 166
Jane Shore's, 145–47, 169, 170–71
in *Julius Caesar*, 53
libelous performance and, 60, 61–63, 67, 68–69, 84
libels and, 2, 3–4, 6–7, 8, 14–15, 17–19, 23, 26, 31–33, 34, 35–36, 37, 43, 45, 48–49, 56, 90, 107, 113, 122–23, 124, 126, 167, 213
in *Nobody and Somebody*, 205–6, 207
petitions and, 92–95
rhetoric and, 89–90, 113
royal, 38, 161
in *Sir Thomas More*, 117, 126, 128, 129, 132, 135, 140, 143

Index

theater and, 5, 6, 8, 18, 19, 22, 23, 25, 26, 52, 56, 73, 84, 96, 142, 147–52, 155, 184, 203, 204, 206–7
  in *Titus Andronicus*, 97, 106–7, 111–12, 113
pulpit, 2, 89, 106, 124, 162, 167, 198
  politics of, 127
  populist, 75, 127, 201
  royal chapel, 42
  in *Sir Thomas More*, 4, 117, 124–25, 126, 129, 140
Puritans and Puritanism, 15, 33, 44, 47, 49, 62, 67, 70, 90
  persecution of, 11, 21, 33, 87–88, 94
  in *Titus Andronicus*, 108–10
  See also libels, Puritan; petitions, Puritan; polemic, Puritan

Queen Anne's Men, 146, 169, 205, 206
Queen's Men, 24, 33, 34

Ralegh, Sir Walter, 119, 120
rationality, 5, 15, 18, 36, 49, 56, 73, 162
  in *Julius Caesar*, 52–53, 55–56
reading. *See* audiences; interpretation; libels, reading of
rebellion, 4, 8, 13, 39, 74, 119, 124, 144, 176, 180, 181, 188
  in *Poetaster*, 190
  in *Sir Thomas More*, 116, 117, 124–27, 128–29, 131, 132–34, 136–37, 139, 143
  in *Titus Andronicus*, 101, 103, 104, 107–8, 113
  See also Devereux, Robert, 2nd Earl of Essex, rising of
Records of Early English Drama, 26, 59
Red Bull Theater, 146, 169, 170, 206
reflexivity, 6–7, 32, 44–45, 47, 56–57, 203. *See also* metadrama
refugees. *See* strangers
republicanism, 168
  decline of, 89
  in Heywood's *Rape of Lucrece*, 168
  in *Julius Caesar*, 55
  in Shakespeare's *Rape of Lucrece*, 103
  in *Titus Andronicus*, 90, 97–98, 99, 103, 112
revenge tragedy, 100
rhetoric
  failures of, 99–101
  history of, 89–90
  republican, 96, 97, 113
  in *Titus Andronicus*, 89, 99–101, 109, 111–12
  violence and, 106, 114, 123–24
Richard III, 144, 145, 165, 171. *See also* Heywood, Thomas, *Edward IV*; More, Thomas, *History of King Richard III*
Richardson, Thomas, 67
Rickard, Jane, 38

Ridge, Elizabeth, 63
Roman law, 10–11, 16
Rome, 89, 96, 113
  in *Julius Caesar*, 53–56
  in *Poetaster*, 173, 186–87, 189, 191, 193, 195, 196, 201
  in *Roman Actor*, 208–9
  in Shakespeare's *Rape of Lucrece*, 103
  in *Titus Andronicus*, 95, 97–98, 100, 104, 106, 107, 108, 110–13
Rose Theater, 146, 169
Rouen, 45
Royal Exchange, 42
rumor, 2, 12, 13, 43, 124, 126, 158, 181
  in *Nobody and Somebody*, 206
  in *Poetaster*, 195
  See also gossip; news

Sackville, Thomas, Baron Buckhurst, 158, 181
Sambucus, Joannes, 199
satire, 2, 7, 19
  censorship of, 182–83, 194–95
  of citizen audiences, 170
  in *Club Law*, 60, 80, 84
  comical, 190, 202, 203, 209
  in *Cruel Brother*, 211
  Donne and, 203
  in *Eastward Ho!*, 175
  in *Edward IV*, 166
  at Inns of Court, 179, 200
  Jonson and, 172–73, 194–95
  in Kendal Stage Play, 70
  law and, 176–77
  Leicester's Commonwealth and, 51
  Marprelate controversy and, 33, 34
  morality play and, 66
  in *Nobody and Somebody*, 208
  Paul's Boys and, 25, 61
  in *Poetaster*, 173–74, 175–76, 178, 186, 190–91, 192–93, 195–97, 199–202
  of Puritans, 109
  in *Roman Actor*, 208–11
  in Spital Sermons, 127
  university drama and, 79
  See also libels; War of the Theaters; Weever, John
scandal. *See* defamation; libels; slander
scandalum magnatum, 10, 12, 13
scarcity. *See* dearth
Scory, John, Bishop of Hereford, 51
Scory, Sylvanus, 51
Scotland, 71, 72, 175
sedition, 27, 43–44, 76, 92, 94–95, 123–24, 143, 188, 212–13
  definitions of, 8

Index

sedition (cont.)
  Essex and, 27, 150, 173, 181, 192
  Jonson and, 19, 174, 191, 194
  laws against, 11, 12, 19
  in *Nobody and Somebody*, 205, 207
  in *Poetaster*, 174, 189, 194, 197, 200
  satire and, 176
  Star Chamber and, 59
  in *Titus Andronicus*, 108–10
  See also libels, sedition and
Selden, John, 138
sermons. *See* pulpit
Shakespeare, William, 4, 8, 26, 51, 109, 142, 184
  2 Henry VI, 91
  Henry IV plays, 20, 21
  Henry VIII, coauthored with Fletcher, 150
  history plays, 23
  Julius Caesar, 4, 23, 24, 32, 52–57
  Merry Wives of Windsor, 64, 83
  Rape of Lucrece, 103
  Richard II, 149–50, 151, 174, 184–85
  Richard III, 23, 25
  Sir Thomas More and, 116, 119, 132–33
  Titus Andronicus, coauthored with Peele, 4, 23, 24, 25, 26, 27, 84, 88–92, 95–114, 198, 212
  Twelfth Night, 22
Shelley, Richard, 94, 95
shopkeepers. *See* artisans; citizens
Shore, Jane. *See* Heywood, *Edward IV*; popularity, Jane Shore's; publics and publicity, Jane Shore's
Shore, scrivener, 120, 124
Shoreditch, 168, 169
Shrove Tuesday, 82
Shuger, Debora, 3, 12, 15, 21–23, 177
Sidney, Philip, 152, 210
Simson, Gabriel, 122
Sinfield, Alan, 197
Sir Thomas More, 4, 20, 23, 24, 25, 26, 27, 84, 115–17, 119, 124–43, 212
  manuscript of, 115–16, 117, 126, 132
Sisson, C. J., 58, 59
skimmington, 64
slander, 4, 10, 11, 12, 22, 26, 56, 106, 174, 198–99
  culture of, 21
  sexual, 9
  See also defamation; libels
Smith, G. C. Moore, 78, 79, 80
Smith, Thomas, 137
Smithfield, 178
Smuts, R. Malcolm, 174
social media, 212
Somerset, 63
South Kyme, Lincolnshire, 65, 83
Southwell, Robert, 94, 105

Humble Supplication to her Maiestie, 92, 93, 95, 109
Spanish Match, 36–37
Spanish wars, 160
spectators. *See* audiences
speech. *See* orality; rhetoric
Spencer, John, Lord Mayor of London, 122–23
Spenser, Edmund
  Faerie Queene, 11
spies, 40, 95, 189, 202
  in *Cruel Brother*, 211
  in *Poetaster*, 4, 172, 173, 176, 188–89, 190–92, 193, 194, 195, 196, 201–2, 203
  in *Roman Actor*, 196, 210
  strangers as, 118, 121–22
Spinoza, Baruch, 148
sport. *See* festivity
St. Bartholomew's Day Massacre, 99
St. Mary's Spital, 124, 125, 126, 127, 128
St. Paul's Cathedral, 1, 3, 42, 167
Stanley, Ferdinando, Lord Strange, 25, 90. *See also* Strange's Men
Star Chamber, Court of, 10, 21, 136, 181, 189, 199
  libel cases, 16, 26, 42, 58, 59, 61–69, 70–76
stationers, 163, 205, 208
  company of, 50, 182
  hall, 182
  register, 178
Staveley Chapel, Westmorland, 74, 75
Steggle, Matthew, 146, 175
Sterrett, Joseph, 88
Stokes, James, 67
Stow, John, 147, 158, 181
Strange's Men, 25, 33, 90
strangers, 117–24
  churches of, 115, 120, 122, 123, 127
  Dutch, 118, 119, 134
  French, 118, 128, 134
  Lombard, 128, 134
  in *Sir Thomas More*, 116, 125–26, 127–34, 142–43
  weavers, 122
Stuart, Lady Arabella, 175
Stubbs, John, 11
Stuteville, Sir Martin, 39–40, 45
succession, royal, 24, 44, 50, 166
  in *Titus Andronicus*, 97–98
Suffolk, Earl of. *See* Howard, Thomas, Earl of Suffolk
sumptuary laws, 70
supplications. *See* libels, petitions and; petitions
surveillance. *See* spies
Sussex's Men, 90
Sutcliffe, Matthew, 94–95, 199
Swarfe, William, 63, 64, 68

Index

table talk. *See* rumor; gossip
Tacitism, 204
  in *Roman Actor*, 208
  in *Titus Andronicus*, 89, 95, 99, 113
Tacitus, 89, 113
  Dialogus de Oratoribus, 89
Tarlton, Richard, 34
taxation. *See* benevolences; forced loans
tenant right, 71–76
tenants, 6, 54, 205
  of Kendal, 60, 70–76, 78, 83, 84
Tenterden, Kent, 14
theater
  activist, 60, 76, 84
  at court, 21
  defenses of, 152, 210–11
  festivity and, 64
  as law court, 18–19, 202
  libels and, 4, 6, 7–8, 18–19, 21, 23, 24–25,
    26–27, 57, 59, 60–61, 63, 68, 78–79, 84, 107,
    115, 179, 204, 208, 211–13
  London, 4, 6, 23, 26, 41, 50, 60, 84, 96, 147, 183,
    187, 192
  news and, 22
  as propaganda, 24–25
  provincial, 6, 23
  religion and, 90
  rhetoric and, 89, 96
  sedition and, 27
  space of, 77
  of state, 37–38, 117, 140–41, 190
  technologies of, 60, 70, 73–74, 84
  visual language of, 62
  See also antitheatricalism; audiences;
    performance; playgoing
Theatre, the, 34, 168
theatricality, 149
  libels and, 6, 58
  sedition and, 8
Thomas of Woodstock, 23, 211
Tilney, Edmund, 116, 124, 128, 130,
  132, 143
Tolbooth, Cambridge, 79
toleration, 113
  religious, 44, 49–50
  of strangers, 117, 132
Topcliffe, Richard, 191
Tower of London, 50, 94, 139,
  141, 142
townsfolk. *See* citizens
traveling players, 63, 69
treason, 46, 47, 48, 176, 191
  Essex and, 174, 180, 182, 183, 185
  Jonson and, 20, 174, 175
  libels and, 47, 165, 166, 180, 181

in *Nobody and Somebody*, 206
petty, 177
in *Poetaster*, 189–90
in *Roman Actor*, 209
in *Sir Thomas More*, 140
in *Titus Andronicus*, 103
True Tragedie of Richard the Third, 155, 162
tyranny, 197
  of corrupt favorites, 49
  of Earl of Lincoln, 69
  in *Edward IV*, 27, 144, 156, 162, 168, 205
  in *Julius Caesar*, 52, 55
  in *Nobody and Somebody*, 205
  in *Poetaster*, 195, 202
  resistance to, 145, 164, 166, 168, 171, 207
  of Richard III, 145, 165
  spies and, 189
  in *Thomas of Woodstock*, 211
  in *Titus Andronicus*, 104
Tyrone, Earl of, 179, 183
Tyxall, William, 62–63, 68

university drama, 7, 59, 60, 78, 79–80, 83. *See also*
  Club Law
uptake. *See* interpretation
Uttoxeter, Staffordshire, 62–63

Villiers, George, 1st Duke of Buckingham, 150–51
violence, 24, 27, 67, 71, 83
  festivity and, 79–80, 81, 82, 83
  religious, 88, 98–99
  in *Sir Thomas More*, 126–27, 129, 132, 133, 134,
    135, 143
  state, 11, 21, 48, 212
  against strangers, 117, 118, 124
  in *Titus Andronicus*, 88, 90, 91, 97, 98–101, 102,
    103–4, 106, 108, 110–11, 112–14
  See also libels, violence and
virality, 4, 6, 91, 188
Vives, Juan Luis, 89, 96
Vivier, Eric D., 175

Waddell, Brodie, 75
Waldegrave, Robert, 33, 94
Walker, Greg, 66
Wall, Wendy, 168
Walter, John, 75, 123
War of the Theaters, 173–74, 187, 196, 202–3
Warner, Michael, 5, 6
Warning for Fair Women, 153
Wars of the Roses, 166
Waterhouse, 173, 178, 179, 181, 194
weavers
  petition of, 122–23, 126, 131
Webbe, George, 106

Index

256

Webster, John
  White Devil, 50
Weever, John
  Whipping of the Satyre, 173, 176–79, 181, 182,
    183, 192, 193, 196, 202
Wells Shows, 63, 64, 67, 68, 83
Wells, Somerset, 62
West, William, 17, 135
Westmorland. *See* Kendal Stage Play
Whitehall Palace, 41
Whitgift, John, 16, 94, 182
Whitney, Geffrey, 198, 199
Wigginton, Giles, 110
Williams, William, 62
Willoughby, Lord. *See* Bertie, Peregrine, Lord
  Willoughby
Wiltshire, 167
Wolsey, Thomas, Cardinal, 66
  in *Henry VIII*, 150
Wood, Andy, 73

Woodford, Thomas, 61
Worcester's Men, 146, 169
Wotton, Henry, 149
Woudhuysen, H. R., 45
Wright, Thomas, 197
writing, 5, 10–11, 17, 21, 58, 67–68
  Hacket conspiracy and, 91–92
  rhetoric and, 89
  in *Sir Thomas More*, 125–26
  in *Titus Andronicus*, 88, 96, 101–8,
    109, 113–14
  See also libels; manuscript; print

xenophobia, 4, 27, 117–24, 130, 212
  in *Sir Thomas More*, 116–17, 127–28, 129,
    133–34, 140, 142–43
  See also libels, against strangers; strangers

Yachnin, Paul, 96
Yarde, Anne, 63